ROBERT SACKVILLE-WEST worked in publishing after studying history at Oxford University. He now chairs Knole Estates, the property and investment company that – in parallel with the National Trust – runs the Sackville family's interests at Knole, the house in Kent where his family have lived for the past 400 years. Robert is the author of the critically acclaimed *Inheritance: The Story of Knole and the Sackvilles* (2010) and *The Disinherited* (2014).

BY THE SPECTATOR

'This carefully researched and beautifully written book reveals the determination of the families of those who have lost loved ones killed in war to find out what happened to them and where their bodies lie. Each year at the Cenotaph, a memorial whose origins are described here in fascinating detail, we see the public manifestation of a private grief that never fades. There may be a commemorative tomb in Westminster Abbey but there is in truth, as Sackville-West explains, no such thing as an Unknown Warrior' David Dimbleby

'Remarkable ... Compelling and often horrifying' John Carey, *Sunday Times*

'Sackville-West handles this grim subject with grace. The excruciatingly personal stories he tells convey perfectly that desperate need for closure that so many grieving relatives felt' Gerard DeGroot, *The Times*

'[Sackville-West documents] all these grim stories with compassion' *Daily Mail*

'A deeply sad but fascinating topic ... Beautifully written' Michael Portillo, *Radio Times*

'[A] poignant account' *Sunday Express*, Christmas Picks

'A fascinating history of the efforts to find and identify the bodies of missing First World War soldiers, both while the conflict raged and today: several dozen are still found each year' *Daily Telegraph*, Books for Christmas

'A scholarly and moving account of those who searched, privately and officially – and still search – for the missing ... Reflects on the meaning of the war's sacrifice and how to commemorate it' *Country Life*

THE
SEARCHERS

The Quest for the Lost of
the First World War

ROBERT SACKVILLE-WEST

BLOOMSBURY PUBLISHING
LONDON · OXFORD · NEW YORK · NEW DELHI · SYDNEY

BLOOMSBURY PUBLISHING
Bloomsbury Publishing Plc
50 Bedford Square, London, WC1B 3DP, UK
29 Earlsfort Terrace, Dublin 2, Ireland

BLOOMSBURY, BLOOMSBURY PUBLISHING and the Diana logo are trademarks of
Bloomsbury Publishing Plc

First published in Great Britain 2021
This edition published 2022

Copyright © Robert Sackville-West, 2021

Robert Sackville-West has asserted his right under the Copyright, Designs and Patents Act, 1988, to
be identified as Author of this work

Bloomsbury Publishing Plc does not have any control over, or responsibility for, any third-party
websites referred to in this book. All internet addresses given in this book were correct at the time
of going to press. The author and publisher regret any inconvenience caused if addresses have
changed or sites have ceased to exist, but can accept no responsibility for any such changes

A catalogue record for this book is available from the British Library

ISBN: HB: 978-1-5266-1315-8; TPB: 978-1-5266-1316-5; PB: 978-1-5266-1314-1;
EBOOK: 978-1-5266-1313-4; EPDF: 978-1-5266-4559-3

2 4 6 8 10 9 7 5 3 1

Typeset by Newgen KnowledgeWorks Pvt. Ltd., Chennai, India
Printed and bound in Great Britain by CPI Group (UK) Ltd, Croydon CRO 4YY

MIX
Paper from
responsible sources
FSC® C171272

To find out more about our authors and books visit www.bloomsbury.com
and sign up for our newsletters

For my mother, Bridget, and in memory of my father,
Hugh Sackville-West M.C.

Contents

Prologue

Under the harsh strip lighting of a mortuary near Arras, four skeletons are laid out on tables. The bones were unearthed during excavation works for a new hospital nearby, and painstakingly pieced together by the exhumations team at the Commonwealth War Graves Commission (CWGC). Three of the skulls are fractured beyond reconstruction, but one is almost perfectly preserved, as it was on site, when a member of the team lifted a rusty steel helmet to reveal it nestling beneath. The nature of the wounds, the trauma, offers some clues to the circumstances of their deaths. One of the bodies has a bullet hole; shards of metal shrapnel are still embedded in the bones of another. And all of the bones, particularly the femurs, are badly damaged, blown apart by the shell blast which buried all four.

No identity discs were found with the men's bodies, but a mass of artefacts was discovered nearby, and is now laid out alongside: a shaving brush, date-stamped boots, a pocket watch, an army service book, and a metal water canteen, swilling half-full with the water its owner never had time to drink. The most revealing items are the regimental shoulder titles, which indicate that the soldiers were from the 5th Battalion, Lincolnshire Regiment, who were in action in the area in the spring of 1917. The new hospital lies very close to the old First World War front line, and occupies the site of two battles, one in 1915 and the other in 1917, from which around 1,500 men are still unaccounted for. One of the soldiers was found beside forty-four grenades, which suggests that the group of four were probably on a bombing raid on a German position when they were killed in no man's land. Soil from the blast then covered their bodies, burying them at a depth of over one and a half metres, which accounts for their state of preservation and the fact that they were not discovered in any of the post-war clearances of the battlefields. Members of the CWGC's recovery unit are hopeful that one of the soldiers, at least, will be identified by name, in which case the other three might follow.

Next door to the room in which the four skeletons are laid out, some 200 sets of human remains await further investigation and analysis, along with the artefacts found with them: pieces of torn kilt belonging to a Scottish soldier, a whistle, leather boots and a knitted tie, preserved in the Flemish soil. One officer of the Northumberland Fusiliers is in the process of being identified by his personalised metal identity disc and an initialled gold signet ring. With any luck, a man who was lost to his nearest and dearest has now been found and will be restored to his descendants, the void in their family history finally filled. When his identity is confirmed, it is hoped that the eight soldiers killed beside him in the trench by a shell blast will also be identified. They will all be buried with full military honours, with members of their families, if they can be traced, in attendance. The families will also be allowed to choose their own personal inscription for a headstone of up to a hundred characters (an increase on the sixty-six characters permitted after the war). The words from John Newton's gospel-inspired hymn, 'Amazing Grace', are incised on many of these headstones: 'I once was lost, but now am found ... and grace will lead me home.'

*

The search to recover, identify and honour those who lost their lives in the First World War is conducted with the same commitment today as it was a century ago. At the time, though, the effort was entirely unprecedented, the newfound respect for the individual very different from the anonymity accorded the British war dead of the past. After the Battle of Waterloo, a hundred years before the

First World War, the dead had been shovelled into mass graves. The most that might have been expected by way of commemoration was a monument to a commanding officer. The common soldier, on the other hand, had generally been regarded as an object of suspicion, an antisocial element almost, for whom death was an occupational hazard. During the First World War, new forms of commemoration were expected for citizen armies composed of volunteers and conscripts.

The first expectation was for a decent burial. Field Marshal Douglas Haig had realised in 1915 that this had a significance for the comrades, relatives and friends of the dead that went beyond the 'purely sentimental'. The nation, he noted, 'will demand an account from the Government as to the steps which have been taken to mark and classify the burial places of the dead'.[1] If it was to depend on the public's continued support for the war, the state needed to accept responsibility, as never before, for identifying, naming and burying those who had died in its service. Yes, the nation wanted to commemorate victory once the war had ended, but even more importantly it had to recognise that individual lives mattered, and that the bereaved needed the time and space to mourn their lost loved ones.

What was so different about the First World War was the sheer scale of the trauma, the sudden deaths of so many. Around three million Britons lost a very close relative – a parent, a child, a sibling, a spouse. But many more, almost the entire population, lost a more distant family member – an uncle or cousin – or simply a friend. The impact of the war still ripples through society. Most people of British descent today have an ancestor who fought in the First World War, most likely on the Western front, and of these many would have been killed.

The profound trauma was acknowledged at the time by Sigmund Freud, the father of modern psychoanalysis, who himself had three sons at the front. In the opening section of his essay 'Thoughts for the Times on War and Death', he recognised the intensity of the war: 'Not only is it more sanguinary and more destructive than any war of other days, because of the enormously increased perfection of weapons of attack and defence; but it is at least as cruel, as embittered, as implacable as any that has preceded it.'[2] He had to find ways of looking at its impact on individuals and society that went beyond the psychosexual models guiding his previous theories. What the war had disturbed, he went on to argue, was 'our attitude towards death'. Whereas there had previously been a tendency to 'eliminate' thoughts of death from life, to deny its existence, this had impoverished our lives by removing 'the highest stake on the game of living', the risk of life itself. The scale of the war, however, was such that 'Death will no longer be denied', and 'Life has, in truth, become interesting again.' Would it not be better, then, to give death the place 'in actuality and in our thoughts' which it deserves, and 'to yield a little more prominence to that unconscious attitude towards death which we have hitherto so carefully suppressed?'[3]

The war also disturbed the order which had seemed natural since the late nineteenth century, as rates of infant mortality began to fall, in which children tended to outlive their parents. Reversing this order, the terrible, disorienting effect of the death of a young son on his parents is charted in the lives of Rudyard Kipling and Sir Oliver Lodge. The individual and collective stories in this book are bound together by a common theme: the search for a body, a grave, a memory, anything that might give meaning to a family's loss. The process itself was grisly, but often therapeutic: the Kiplings' quest for their son's grave, for example, the Lodges' communication with their dead son's spirit, E. M. Forster's conversations with traumatised soldiers in a hospital in Alexandria.

Although the state, as the only institution with sufficient resources, had assumed responsibility for identifying, naming and burying the dead, it was not prepared for the scale of the task. It had not expected the war to go on for so long – over by Christmas 1914, it was hoped – or to be so deadly. The War Office Casualty Branch had to grow rapidly in the first months of the war to cope with the bureaucratic challenge of the slaughter. Even then, its role in tracing the fate of the missing and providing information to the relatives back home had to be supplemented by the volunteer 'searchers' of the Wounded and Missing Enquiry Department, which was run by the Red Cross. The other organisation which had its voluntary origins in the Red Cross was the War Graves Commission, which identified and registered the graves – that 'Empire of the Silent Dead', as it was described.

Of the more than a million soldiers of the British Empire killed in the First World War, the bodies of almost 600,000 had, by 1930, been located and buried in named graves. One of the things that can help the bereaved accept the finality of their loss is actually to see the body. Apart from the relatives of those soldiers who died in hospital back in Blighty, this was not possible for the vast majority whose loved ones had died on or near the battlefield, hundreds or – in the case of the Dominions' armies – thousands of miles from home. In those circumstances, sight, or at least evidence, of a grave could be a second best for the bereaved, providing a physical focus for their grief.

These graves, too, were miles from home, as the British government had banned the repatriation of the bodies of its war dead. It was frequently attacked for this nationalised appropriation and burial of the bodies, over the rights of the families. But the balance between the requirements of the state and the needs of the bereaved for individual spaces in which to grieve was a delicate one. It could be achieved only through what Sir Fabian Ware, the founder of the War Graves Commission, described as 'some form of benevolent autocracy'. He realised that the commission would be dealing with hundreds of thousands of separate claims for 'individualistic treatment of the graves', and that 'chaos must result unless we could lead all these stricken men and women ... to some common form of the expression which monuments and their architects could give to their pride and their grief'.[4]

The commission had to look after the graves of the dead for the sake of the bereaved, while striving to keep alive the ideals for which the soldiers of the Empire had 'laid down their lives ... and to promote a feeling of common citizenship and of loyalty and devotion to [the King] and to the Empire of which they are subjects'.[5] On the Western front at least, it trod this line with great success. The fact that the graves were well cared for reassured the tens of thousands who visited the battlefields every year to pay their last respects. For those who could not go on a pilgrimage, and could only imagine the grave, a photograph might help, or the knowledge that someone else had laid a wreath beside the headstone. Such were the consolations of death at a distance. Pilgrimages fulfilled another function, too. They helped the survivors in their search to make sense of their loss, in their struggle to find a meaning to the war. A narrative arguing that the sacrifice had not been in vain assuaged the feelings of guilt that sometimes accompanied the death of a loved one. As a result, the language of Christian sacrifice was often woven into the pilgrimage literature and into the rhetoric of commemoration: of dying for King and Country, in a just and holy war defending civilisation.

A couple of months after the First World War ended, the whereabouts of more than half a million soldiers of the British Empire were still unknown. The majority had officially been declared dead – or were, for the duration, presumed dead and buried beneath the battlefields of northern France and Flanders. The Armistice had not been the final reckoning that many people thought, the day when a line was drawn between the living and the dead. Of the half a million, around 180,000 were buried in separate graves as unknown British soldiers, known only 'Unto God'. A greater number, though, had never been found: they had simply disappeared, blown to pieces by the blast of a shell, or drowned in the mud of no man's land. All that remained of them were their names inscribed, eventually, on memorials to the missing.

People searched for the disappeared in different ways. Some looked for a grave to prove definitively that they were dead; others sought confirmation, against all hope, that their son, husband, brother, was still alive. It was a time of limbo, when otherwise rational people might turn to spiritualism to contact their dear departed in the afterlife. The Red Cross Wounded and Missing Enquiry Department filled some of the void left by an overstretched War Office, by providing information on missing soldiers. Sifting through the tangled mass of conflicting accounts, it helped the bereaved confront the fact of death, but also helped them construct the all-important story of the victim's last moments.

Many people found it desperately hard to accept the deaths of those closest to them, despite the often overwhelming evidence. The parents of Lieutenant Hugh Williamson were among them. Lieutenant Williamson was killed, aged twenty-one, on the Somme on 15 September 1916, along with twenty-one fellow officers of the Coldstream Guards. There was never any real doubt that Hugh was dead; his name was published in *The Times* in the daily list of officers killed in action, and his parents applied for probate on his estate. But, after the initial shock, their acknowledgement of his death turned to denial. As in so many other cases, eyewitness accounts of his last moments were contradictory, his comrades describing, in the words of his mother, 'a different wound, in a different place and at a different hour'.[6] The poet Robert Graves observed how 'high explosive barrages will make a temporary liar or visionary of anyone';[7] and it was a common feature of the First World War that, in the stress of battle, the minds and memories of the soldiers played tricks on them. Shellshocked and nerve-racked, some of them tried to make sense of those moments of chaos, when time itself seemed to stop still. To restart the clock, and to impose a sense of order and chronology on the action, they constructed a retrospective narrative that might be some way from the truth. False hopes flourished in the hearts of the bereaved whenever there was room for doubt.

Crucially, as in many other cases, Lieutenant Williamson's body was never recovered, and there were no indications as to where he had been buried. His parents were, consequently, unwilling to accept his death. 'I shall never believe,' wrote his mother, 'that my son is dead until his grave is found and it adds greatly to the sorrow of his father and me that we should be left in this awful state of uncertainty.'[8] In a cycle of emotions that became familiar to many families, their denial turned to anger at the War Office for its failure to provide further information, beyond confirmation in 1917 of its original judgement of death.

In 1919, the Williamson parents briefly hoped that their son might be among the prisoners repatriated from German camps at the end of the war. The following year, still distrusting the War Office, they travelled to the Somme to scour the hospitals in case their son was there, suffering from amnesia. Again to no avail. This refusal to countenance their son's death remained with the Williamsons for the rest of their lives. As a result, Hugh's name did not appear on the rolls of honour produced by his school, Eton, or his Oxford college, nor on the Memorial to the Missing at Thiepval when it was inaugurated in 1932. It was only in 2001, almost fifty years after the death of his mother, that Hugh's name was added to an Addenda Panel at Thiepval. The notion that Hugh might simply be lost, languishing in hospital without a memory, in some twilight world of the living dead, was shared by many others: an indication of the lengths to which people would go to believe the incredible.

The missing posed a particular problem for those they left behind: what psychologists today would describe as one of ambiguous, unresolved loss. When a person vanishes, and there is no body to identify, bury or mourn, the loss is not seen to be final. The first reaction of many relatives in the First World War was to hope against hope that their loved one had somehow survived. They had no idea of the destructive brutality of the war, and could not imagine how a body could actually go missing. Added to this was the guilty fear that to accept death as certain would be to abandon and betray the dead. So long as there was the slightest doubt, there were grounds for denial.

As evidence of death mounted, they began to experience some of the other feelings associated with grief, while constantly being interrupted by the belief that their loved ones were still alive: caught indefinitely in a vicious cycle of emotions, they were unable to bring their grief to closure. At the risk of applying contemporary models to the psychology of almost a hundred years ago, they were unable to move on. A study of women whose husbands had disappeared in Bosnia and Herzegovina during the war of 1992–95 has revealed, for example, that the grief of those whose husbands had been confirmed as dead was less long-lived and less traumatising than of those who were still officially classified as 'missing'.[9] The phenomenon of the missing in action was to become a recurring feature of the twentieth century – similar in its impact to the disappearance of individuals in disasters, whether natural – hurricanes, floods, fire – or man-made – the Holocaust, the Gulags, Argentina's Dirty War.

In the absence of bodies that could be brought home to be buried, people needed new ways of laying their dead to rest, to take the place of funerals and other established rituals. The Cenotaph and the Tomb of the Unknown Warrior provided a focus for those mourning the half a million missing, and represented entirely new kinds of shrine. 'It is him,' people cried, pointing towards the surrogate body as they processed past the Tomb of the Unknown Warrior. Similarly, after the terrorist attacks of 9/11, some people chose to believe that the urn containing ash and powdered debris from Ground Zero, that was offered by the city of New York to every bereaved family, actually contained the charred remains of their loved one. Ceremonies, too, assumed a new significance. The rituals at the Cenotaph and the Tomb of the Unknown Warrior on Armistice Day allowed 'communities of the bereaved' to come together in collective acts of mourning, to comfort and support each other in their loss. Any idea that national outpourings of grief are the preserve of more recent decades are belied by contemporary accounts of these events.

The meanings of these memorials and acts of commemoration changed over time. At first, on a personal level, they helped people to mourn, to adjust to their loss. The rhetoric, like that associated with the pilgrimages, justified rather than questioned the sacrifice of those who had died. It offered a deeply consoling story for survivors in their search for sense in the cataclysm; and one that was by its very nature conservative. With time, the monuments and mourning rites acquired different shades of meaning. Celebrating the extraordinary heroism of very ordinary martyrs, they encouraged survivors to follow in the virtuous footsteps of the 'Glorious Dead', to stay true to their memory, and to strive for a similar solidarity. 'Greater love hath no man than this,' read the words from St John's Gospel on many memorials, 'that a man lay down his life for his friends.'

During the 1920s and 1930s, as the horrors of the First World War were remembered, and international tensions mounted, the sacrifice and its commemoration were cast in the cause of international peace. The very names of the dead became a focus for grieving, and were granted an almost sacred status. 'We live in an age of necronominalism,' wrote the cultural historian Thomas W. Laqueur of the twentieth and twenty-first centuries, 'we record and gather the names of the dead in ways, and in places, and in numbers as never before. We demand to know who the dead are. We find unnamed bodies and bodiless names – those of the disappeared – unbearable.'[10] This development began during the First World War, and was responsible for 'a prodigious epigraphic challenge'.[11] Names appeared in unprecedented numbers, in stone on monuments, in wood on honour boards, on paper in memorial registers and books of remembrance. The names of the dead were not to be forgotten, nor the cause for which they had fought.

The state assumed responsibility for the naming of graves and on memorials to the missing. But by far the greatest number of monuments were the local war memorials, erected in their tens of thousands throughout Britain and the Dominions in the 1920s, inspired perhaps by the roadside shrines that had sprung up all over the country during the war. On village greens, and in schools, universities, factories, freemasons' lodges, clubs, town halls, post offices, railway stations and regimental headquarters, 'their name liveth for ever more' – in the case of many soldiers, in multiple places.

It was one of these village war memorials, unveiled like so many others in 1920, which resulted in the recent solving of the mystery of an 'Unknown Captain of the Royal West Kent Regiment'. As well as the First World War bodies which continue to be unearthed and buried with full military honours every year, there are as many instances of the grave of an unknown soldier being identified for the first time, on the basis of new evidence, and rededicated in his name. In 2012, military historian Martin Stoneham began to research the lives and deaths of the soldiers listed on the war

memorial of his village, West Kingsdown in Kent, to commemorate
the centenary of the First World War.[12] The first of the eleven from
the village to die was Private William Payne of 1st Battalion, the
Queen's Own Royal West Kent Regiment, who was killed in action
during the British capture of Hill 60, near Ypres in Flanders, on 18
April 1915. Hill 60 was little more than a mound rising sixty metres
above the surrounding land, made from the spoil created during the
construction of a railway line; but its commanding views of Ypres
gave it a strategic significance and made it the subject of a series
of assaults as it changed hands throughout the war. As Stoneham
pieced together Payne's last moments, he came across a reference in
the regimental war diary to a Captain Tuff lying dead in a crater on
Hill 60 on the morning of 18 April. The hill was 'littered with dead
and dying and the sights witnessed were most distressing'. Captain
Tuff's name lodged in his mind.

The bodies of Private Payne and Captain Tuff, along with
seventy-five others from the Royal West Kent Regiment who were
killed at Hill 60, were never found; they were commemorated by
name on the Menin Gate Memorial to the Missing, while their
bodies were assumed to have been left to lie beneath Hill 60. Several
members of the Royal West Kent Regiment who died that day were
buried, however, in named graves, only a couple of miles away, at
Oosttaverne Wood Cemetery, a Second Lieutenant Walker among
them. On a visit to the cemetery, Stoneham also came across the
graves of unknown soldiers of the Royal West Kent Regiment,
including a headstone marked 'Unknown Captain, Royal West
Kent Regiment'. Could this, he wondered, be the Captain Tuff
mentioned in the war diary?[13]

Seventeen of the Royal West Kent captains killed in action
during the war have no known grave; in a process of elimination,
Stoneham whittled these down to the four who died in the
Ypres area, rather than on the Somme. Of these four, two were
almost certainly buried at Hooge Crater, given the place they
were fighting on the day in October 1917 (rather than April
1915) when they were killed. Tuff, it appeared, was the only Royal
West Kent Regiment captain in action on Hill 60 on 18 April. But

how could anyone be certain that the headstone marked his final resting place? Stoneham's analysis of historic burial returns, held by the Commonwealth War Graves Commission revealed that Tuff, like Lieutenant Walker, had been exhumed from the Hill 60 battlefield in April 1926, identified as a captain by his badges of rank and clothing, and then buried as an 'Unknown Captain' in Oosttaverne Wood Cemetery. The occupant of Plot 6, Row B, Grave 4, he argued, must be Tuff. A report was submitted to the CWGC, which checked Stoneham's conclusions, and passed it on to the Ministry of Defence. After further research by the Joint Casualty and Compassionate Centre and by the National Army Museum, the grave was verified as that of Captain Cecil Thomas Tuff, company commander, D Company, 1st Battalion, Queen's Own Royal West Kent Regiment.

Prunella Scarlett was gardening at home in Kent when a neighbour, who knew her maiden name was Tuff, appeared brandishing a copy of a local newspaper. Martin Stoneham was asking for members of the Tuff family, and in particular relatives of Captain Cecil Tuff, to make contact. In a twist on the typical search of a century ago, this was an appeal to the living to reclaim their dead, rather than an appeal from the living for their dead to be returned to them. On 14 May 2019, Prunella Scarlett and her brother Geoffrey Tuff attended the rededication service at Oosttaverne Wood Cemetery, at which a new, named headstone was provided for their great-uncle. The service was conducted by an army chaplain, with the Royal West Kent Regiment represented by a bugler and officers from its successor regiment. The previous evening Prunella and her brother had attended a Last Post ceremony at the Menin Gate, and seen their great-uncle's name on the Memorial to the Missing (from where it will be removed in due course). After the rededication service, they walked up Hill 60 in the afternoon, and Martin Stoneham pointed out the very spot where Captain Tuff had fallen. The search for Captain Tuff was over. In just twenty-four hours, surviving members of his family had visited the staging posts on a journey of discovery that had taken 104 years to complete: the place where his body had been left behind, like so many others, on the field of battle; the memorial panel where his name was inscribed; the unknown grave, where his body had lain for ninety-three years, and its reincarnation as a rededicated grave with a crisply lettered headstone.

I

In Search of the Missing:
The Enquiry Department

The shots fired at Mons on 22 August 1914 were the first fired by British soldiers in battle on continental Europe for almost a hundred years. Over the coming days, the intensity of the fighting, and the scale of the losses took the War Office by surprise: it was ill-equipped to deal with individual enquiries about soldiers who had been reported wounded or missing in action. With the British Expeditionary Force suffering tens of thousands of casualties in the retreat from Mons and the Battle of the Marne which followed, many families learned of the fate of a loved one through a telegram (in the case of officers) or in a brief letter (for other ranks). They had often read the news first in the Roll of Honour, published by newspapers such as *The Times*, or in a list of the missing men published every day in the London *Evening News* under the title: 'Where are these men?'[1]

For the wealthy and well-connected, it was possible to travel to France to mount freelance enquiries. In September, Lord Kitchener issued a memo declaring that he had 'no objection to parties with Motor Ambulances searching villages that are not in occupation by the Germans for wounded and to obtain particulars of the missing and convey them to hospital';[2] a small fleet of cars converted into ambulances duly left Folkestone for France over the following weeks.

Among those travelling to Dieppe – on 19 September – were Lady Violet Cecil and her brother-in-law Lord Robert 'Bob' Cecil, the Member of Parliament for Hitchin. They were en route for Paris to find out anything they could about Violet's eighteen-year-old son, George, a second lieutenant with the Grenadier Guards, who had been reported missing. According to several accounts, George had last been seen on 1 September leading a bayonet charge, sword in hand, in a forest west of Villers-Cotterêts. Violet was aware that there had been heavy fighting during the retreat from Mons, but for several days in early September she had heard nothing about George. 'We have been in torment,' she wrote, and the War Office had sent hardly any news.[3] 'The state of confusion in the War Office is not to be described – <u>chaos</u>.'[4]

Over the next few weeks, Lady Violet received reports that her son was: wounded and/or missing; shot in the head; blown to pieces by a shell; last seen lying in a ditch; was near Compiègne, or was a German prisoner of war in Aix-la-Chapelle. Their friend the writer Rudyard Kipling, who made enquiries on behalf of the Cecil family that foreshadowed the search for his own son a year later, described Violet's predicament and that of thousands of others: 'And so the horrible see-saw goes on; she dying daily and letters of condolence *and* congratulation crossing each other and harrowing her soul … And that is but one case of many, many hundreds.'[5]

On 23 September, Lord Robert got a lift in a Red Cross ambulance car that was travelling to Villers-Cotterêts to pick up the wounded. He went to the beech wood where the fighting on 1 September had taken place, and reached the nearby village of Vivières, where a woman, who turned out to be the schoolmistress, told him that she had seen 'a very young, very big and fair officer speaking excellent French' being marched off as a prisoner by the Germans. He begged his sister-in-law not to get her hopes up, however, as 'the French people were so kind they would say anything to comfort one, and besides lots of Englishmen speak good French and are fair and big in French eyes'.[6] Lord Robert covered a good deal of ground, but came up with nothing conclusive, regretting in a letter to his wife, Nellie, that his 'visit was purely negative in its results'.[7]

Violet had been planning to join her brother-in-law on the trip, but had been asked at the last moment to give up her seat in the ambulance car to a nurse, and felt that she could not refuse. On Saturday 26th, she succeeded in getting out to Villers-Cotterêts and Vivières, accompanied by Lord Robert. With the help of an old family friend, Georges Clemenceau, who was then between two terms as French prime minister, she had been given permission to visit the battlefield, even though there was still fighting in the vicinity, and had been offered the American ambassador's car for the journey. But she found no trace of her son, beyond his signature on some soldiers' pocket books picked up on the field of battle. 'The villagers would tell us nothing, couldn't answer any questions, everything was despairingly vague,'[8] she reported. Military witnesses were equally vague: the pair were 'given at least three different & inconsistent accounts of poor George's death besides at least three of his being taken prisoner'. As she wrote to her husband on her return to England: 'we had a miserable time turning round and round in a circle'.[9]

Lord Robert had been devoted to his nephew, but his quest for George gradually widened to include enquiries about other soldiers. In this, he joined a handful of British Red Cross volunteers in Paris, who were coordinating the dispatch of the wounded to hospitals around the French capital, the collating of lists of those admitted, and the interviewing of the wounded themselves for information on their missing comrades. He was appointed head of this bureau for tracing the wounded and missing, and he quickly applied his considerable energy, intellect and bureaucratic drive to the task. Too old himself to fight, and with his political career temporarily stalled, Lord Robert was being drawn by personal loss into creating one of the most compassionate, if forgotten, departments of the First World War.

To begin with, Lord Robert and half-a-dozen colleagues occupied two rooms on the top floor of the Hotel d'Iéna, the headquarters in France of the British Red Cross. Compiling lists of people who wanted to know about their relatives and conducting interviews was 'rather a melancholy business', he wrote, 'particularly as in the vast majority of cases nothing comes of it'. This was partly, as he wrote to his brother, because the soldiers themselves are 'hopelessly untrustworthy … sometimes they don't even stick to the same story themselves. At others they reaffirm vehemently what is almost certainly untrue. The stories about George are typical. I've heard every kind of account …'[10]

By November, the French government had ordered the reburial of the war dead for 'sanitary reasons', and on the 16th, Lord Robert was one of several members of a Red Cross party to set off from Paris for Villers-Cotterêts and Vivières to oversee the work from a British perspective. Violet had hoped to go too, because although, as she had written, 'there [was] barely any reasonable hope of George's being alive', she could not 'assume his death until we have certainty'.[11] Lord Robert dissuaded her from accompanying him, but she did leave him with 'one instruction and that was that [George] should be re-buried in the forest near his men'.[12]

About two and a half miles outside the village, in the middle of a wood, they located a grave – or, rather, a burial pit – with a cross over it, bearing an inscription in French to the effect that there were twenty Englishmen buried there. The writing was a bit illegible, however, and according to Lord Killanin, who accompanied the party, as the brother of another missing officer, the number could equally well have read 200. By dusk that evening more than twenty corpses had been disinterred, 'huddled and entangled', wrote Killanin, 'just as thrown in anyhow, one after the other'.[13]

Lord Robert had to return to Paris on the afternoon of the second day for a political engagement. By the morning of the third day, the bodies of eighty soldiers had been exhumed. The six labourers then started to unearth the officers, including Lord Killanin's brother (identified by his wrist watch) – and young George Cecil, identified by the initials 'G.E.C.' on the front of his vest, and by the extraordinary hugeness of his feet.

In total, ninety-eight bodies were found: four officers and ninety-four men. Some could be identified by their identity discs or other personal items, but almost half were not identifiable – their faces and features smashed beyond recognition. The soldiers were laid out in an enlarged mass grave, while the four officers were buried together on 19 November in the village cemetery at Villers-Cotterêts, to the growl of gunfire in the distance. Violet was distraught that, in Lord Robert's absence, her one instruction – that George be buried, as he would have wished, with his men in the 'beautiful forest & not in a crowded French cemetery' – had been ignored.[14]

On Killanin's return to Paris, he gave Lord Robert the three buttons off George's uniform and the initials cut from his vest, 'as a memento for his mother'.[15] However awful the work of exhumation, Killanin wrote, it was to him an abiding consolation 'to know that their remains were rescued from an utterly unknown grave and a most indecorous burial' and laid to rest in such a way that 'everything possible was done to show respect and reverence and affection and honour to their glorious and loved memories'.[16] Lord Robert forwarded Killanin's report to the grief-stricken Violet, with his own words of consolation – although what comfort these gave Violet, who did not share her brother-in-law's (or indeed her husband's) religious beliefs and faith in the afterlife, is unclear: 'somehow the great beauty of the place ... made one see a little that even war with all its horrors was consistent with the Divine government of the world ... It is impossible to grieve for him – a wonderfully perfect life – so affectionate, so upright so true so innocent – followed by a painless and glorious death'.[17] Although the living had lost so much by his death, it was implied, George had gained immeasurably more.

Within weeks the fledgling organisation, of which Lord Robert was in charge, had developed the purpose and working practices that came to define the British Red Cross's 'Wounded and Missing Enquiry Department'. It checked lists of the missing against the casualty lists published in *The Times*; against the lists of the wounded admitted to hospitals in France, and against the lists of prisoners of war provided by the International Red Cross in Geneva. It then forwarded any results to relatives in England – sometimes days before official notification from the War Office. As in the case of George Cecil, the department was also involved, until the work was taken over in March 1915 by the Graves Registration Commission (which itself had grown out of a Red Cross Mobile Ambulance Unit), in locating the graves of those who had been buried in a hurry. At first, its work was limited to tracing officers, but from December its reach extended to other ranks. Over the course of the next four years, the vast majority of its enquiries came from the nearest and dearest of private soldiers and NCOs. It had transcended class barriers.

One particular feature of the work Lord Robert noted in his autobiography, *A Great Experiment*, was the large numbers of letters: 'Those from the more educated writers were bare enquiries. But there were also many from people who found writing laborious but yet expressed themselves with a natural and human pathos which was terribly moving. Altogether my work with the Red Cross made me hate war even more bitterly than I had done before.'[18] The descriptions he heard, in the course of his interviews, of life in the trenches, were 'among the chief causes of my determination to devote the rest of my life to the maintenance of peace'.[19] He was to become one of the founders of the League of Nations after the war, and his work was recognised by the award of the Nobel Peace Prize in 1937.

The Wounded and Missing Enquiry Department had originally been established in Paris, near the French hospitals that served the front at the start of the war. As the focus of the war shifted from the Marne to the Western front, British base hospitals and rest camps were set up around Boulogne for the war of attrition that was developing around Ypres. By the end of October, the centre of gravity had moved there, and the Boulogne office would become, and remain, the department's head office in France until the end of the war. The wounded were arriving in their hundreds by ambulance train every day, for transfer to hospital. The goods shed, behind the Maritime Station, had been converted into a military hospital, as had the Casino, with its gilded cornices and marble pilasters.

The surgeon Sir Frederick Treves described the unloading of an ambulance train in a report from Boulogne for *The Red Cross* journal in February 1915: the men on stretchers lying still, covered with blankets so that it was impossible to see the severity of their wounds; the walking wounded crawling along very slowly. 'They are bowed and listless. They look neither to the right hand nor to the left. They seem dead tired, tired almost to dropping, while more than one man appears to be asleep as he shuffles along … Many of them are literally caked with earth, and one man's greatcoat is so solid with mud that he may have been a figure moulded by a sculptor out of some dull clay. These men left England fine, alert, young soldiers … Now they seem old men, and, above all, they are so silent.'[20] He mentioned a sight that he found sadder still: the green canvas field-service valises containing the kit of dead officers.

Lionel Earle would never forget the scene at Boulogne, where he had gone to interview a wounded fellow officer of his brother in hospital: 'Scores of Indian troops, sitting patiently along the wharf with bandages on their heads, arms, legs, and bodies, some soaked with blood, waiting for some hospital ship to take them away.' Like the Cecils, Lionel was one of those granted special permission to travel to France to search for a loved one: in this case, his younger brother Maxwell, a colonel with the Grenadier Guards – the same regiment as George Cecil – who had been reported wounded and missing in November 1914. The news Lionel received of his brother was no less distressing: the wounded officer had last seen him 'lying on the ground with a bullet through his head and one eye lying on the cheek, but could not say what had happened to him'.[21]

There followed a sequence of conflicting accounts that was typical of so many such searches: a telegram from the British minister in Copenhagen on 23 November, informing Lionel that Maxwell had died of his wounds, and then another one from the same source just over a week later, contradicting the first; followed by a telegram from Amsterdam saying that the officer was alive but severely wounded in a hospital in Brussels. After Maxwell had been missing for several weeks, his wife received a letter directing her to a 'tabernacle' in east London, where a Swiss clergyman handed her a note from her husband, confirming that he was in Brussels in hospital. It would later transpire that after Maxwell had been taken prisoner, he had been moved first to Brussels and then to Frankfurt, where he had undergone eight operations for a bullet that had gone right through his head and another that had wounded him in the leg. When Maxwell was released in 1916 as part of a prisoner exchange, Lionel went to meet his brother in Switzerland, and was 'unspeakably shocked by his appearance'. He had once been 'one of the best looking, best set-up Guards' officers that I ever remember, and now looked like a man who had been many years in a dungeon in the Bastille. We did our outmost to persuade him to shave off his beard, but he had got so accustomed to stroking it in prison that nothing would induce him to discard it.'[22]

*

Towards the end of November 1914, forty-six-year-old Gertrude Bell, adventurer, cartographer and writer, stepped off the steamer from Folkestone to start work in the Red Cross's Wounded and Missing Enquiry Department. She was already familiar with Boulogne from her visits to Europe before the war, but she now found it 'the dirtiest place I have ever been in'.[23] Any familiar sights were completely out of place – such as the London omnibuses used to convey soldiers to the front, under whose coating of mud and grime it was still possible to make out destinations like 'Oxford Street', 'Putney' and 'Kilburn'.

When Gertrude arrived she found the office in 'chaos':[24] piles of paper everywhere, with messengers constantly arriving with more letters and more lists – letters of enquiry from relatives, casualty lists from the newspapers, lists of hospital admissions, prisoner lists, and the reports of the three 'searchers' who went out every day to the hospitals to question the wounded about their missing comrades. Gertrude started to clear away the 'mountain of mistakes' she found on arrival, and to impose a system. 'Nothing was ever verified,' she complained in a letter to her stepmother, 'and we went on, piling error onto error, with no idea of the confusion that was being caused.'[25] She buried herself in ledgers and binders, some bought out of her own pocket, often working through the night, as she corrected the errors, compiled card-indexes on individual soldiers, and created a database of 'the quick and the dead'. 'I think I have an inherited love of office work!' she continued.[26]

Gertrude had been the first woman to be awarded a first in Modern History at the University of Oxford; she was already one of the most daring mountaineers of her day, with an Alpine peak, Gertrudspitze, named after her; as an archaeologist, she had mapped remote sites in Syria and Mesopotamia and ventured 1,800 miles across the deserts of the Arabian peninsula. Yet now, she declared, 'a clerk was what I was meant to be', with an ambition to have one of the best-run offices in France.[27]

For Gertrude, hard work offered a distraction from the hopelessness of the war, and from the anxiety she felt about her younger brother Maurice – who was about to be sent to the front in Flanders – and about 'Dick' Doughty-Wylie, the married man with whom she was in love, and who would die at Gallipoli the following April. Her work, she said, provided a 'little plank across the gulf of wretchedness over which I have walked this long long time': she told her father that she did not want to return home for Christmas, as she feared that if she left, 'it would all fall to pieces again'.[28] 'My work goes on,' she wrote to her friend, the writer Sir Valentine Chirol in January 1915, ' – quite continuous, very absorbing, and so sad that at times I can scarcely bear it. It is as though the intimate dossier of the War passed through my hands.'[29] She was particularly sustained by the importance of the letters and reports she was writing: 'even if one can give these people little news that is good, it comforts them to think that something is being done to find out what has happened to their beloveds'.[30] From time to time, civilians would drop into the office, enquiring about their loved ones. The chances of their being alive were slight. Gertrude was struck by 'the terrible waste of life for such small gains'.[31]

Lord Robert, impressed by Gertrude's work, was contemplating making Boulogne more of a centre, 'the real distributing place of information for which, geographically, it is best fitted'.[32] The greater the responsibility they gave Gertrude, the better she liked it. She was now in charge of responding to all the letters of enquiry from relatives addressed to the Paris office, as well as

those addressed to Boulogne, something she relished, as 'I think
the form in which news is conveyed is one of the most important
points in our work – you can well understand that it should be
when you think of the kind of news we mostly have to convey.
And I know at least that when I do it I spare no pains to make it
less bitter.'[33]

Such was Gertrude's genius for organisation that Lord Robert,
who left Paris in December to take over the Enquiry Department
in London, begged her to return to London to help him run the
office there. It was 'a confounded thing,' she complained to Dick
on 20 March, and 'at first I said no, no, & no; I wouldn't whatever
happened'.[34] But she soon relented. She realised that the London
office had 'been the drag upon us all the time – the work is so
badly done there, & it ought to be the pivot of us all'.[35] Besides,
Gertrude was only too happy to be 'out of the dirt and discomfort
of Boulogne for a time', and she 'loved' Lord Robert: 'He resembles
a very large elf, and elves, as every reader of fairy stories know, are
good colleagues in an uphill job. I have some 20 ladies under me,
4 type-writers (not near enough) and 2 boy scouts who are an
infinite joy.'[36]

Gertrude found the London office as chaotic on arrival as she
had found Boulogne, and the task 'a job for Hercules, no less'.[37]
She could barely find the words, she told Dick, to describe 'the
helpless bewilderment of those who work in it, the mixture of
unsorted, uncomprehended material which spreads itself before
me whichever way I look'. Two things, however, spurred her on.
One was 'the extraordinary deliciousness & personal charm of
Lord Robert – to say nothing of his acute wits'; the other was the
way in which the 'ladies who work for him accept my word &
my bidding. Some understand & some don't, but all, up to their
capacity, obey without a murmur.' Nevertheless, from time to time,
the nonchalance of some of her colleagues made the perfectionist
Gertrude 'rage': 'No one in this country seems to realise that a war
is being fought in France. The miriad [sic] ladies saunter elegantly
in & out, go off to tea parties, dinner parties, without a thought
that they are leaving their work undone.'[38]

By the spring of 1915 the department's London office had moved from 83 Pall Mall to the reception rooms of 20 Arlington Street, a house owned by Lord Robert's older brother, Lord Salisbury. Lord Robert would have attended dinners and dances at No. 20 before the war; and it was here that Violet Cecil had kissed her son George goodbye on the morning of 12 August, the day he left for France. It was now the headquarters and clearing house for all enquiries from the public. As the press baron Lord Northcliffe, whose newspapers had taken a close interest in the fate of the missing since the beginning of the war, wrote: 'Each enquiry is filed separately and becomes soon a dossier … These dossiers are human documents of rare interest which none can read unmoved; they reveal, too, in convincing fashion the extraordinary amount of care and thought which is expended upon the work of tracing and searching for the missing. Indeed in this organisation is to be found the newest and noblest form of detective enterprise, as full of thrills and surprises, of close deductive reasoning and resourceful cleverness as the memoirs of Sherlock Holmes.'[39]

As the volume of work outgrew the premises, the office moved once again, in July, to Norfolk House in St James's Square, which was lent by the Duke of Norfolk; and finally, in November (by which time Gertrude Bell had been offered a post in Cairo), to another aristocratic townhouse, 18 Carlton House Terrace, lent by Lord Astor, where it remained until after the end of the war. Between 1915 and 1918, the office was staffed by typists, paid assistants and 150 voluntary workers, sifting and sorting, card-indexing and cross-referencing. Many of these volunteers would not have felt out of place in Lord Astor's home in its previous incarnation: rustling across the marble hallways in their ankle-length skirts, or sweeping up the double staircase, carrying bundles of files, or sashaying through the ballroom, now the secretarial pool, to the clattering rhythms of typewriters pounding out reports and statistics. The professionalism of this bureaucratic machine, from an organisation that had originally relied on sporadic individual initiatives, owed much to people like Lord Robert and Gertrude Bell.

Over the course of the war, a system like that developed
in Boulogne, was rolled out behind the lines across the war
fronts: Gallipoli (where 1,800 soldiers were still officially 'missing'
more than a year after the landing), the Somme, Messines,
Passchendaele and Villers-Bretonneux. The work followed the
intensity of the fighting and the concentrations of hospitals and
hospital ships: Rouen, Le Tréport, Etaples, Le Havre, Calais,
Marseilles. Offices opened in Malta, where teams of searchers –
or 'watchers' as they were sometimes known – visited the island's
hospitals; in Egypt, where offices were established in Alexandria and
Cairo to answer enquiries about soldiers who had been reported
killed or missing at Gallipoli; in Salonika and Corfu.

In 1915, the Red Cross Wounded and Missing Enquiry
Department (W&MED) was recognised as the sole officially
sanctioned search organisation in the country. The War Office
undertook to pass to the department daily lists of the missing, with
details of the missing man's battalion and company, and the date of
the casualty; and requested the department for any report likely to
throw light on the question, 'before presuming the death of a man
solely on the ground that he has been missing for a certain length
of time'.[40] The names were then classified, indexed and collated at
W&MED headquarters, along with any enquiries that had been
received directly from the relatives – much as they had been in
Paris and Boulogne. Missing names were then checked against
the prisoner-of-war lists received from Germany through the
International Red Cross in Geneva, and any names that featured
on both lists were removed. The names of the missing were then
forwarded to the 'searchers' in the form of a monthly enquiry list,
detailing the dates of their disappearance.

The role of the department's searchers was to make enquiries
among the wounded about soldiers from the same battalion who
had been reported missing. The system focused on the London
hospitals at first, but was soon implemented across the country,
with 'Head Searchers' in each area ensuring that enquiries were
made in all the 'first-line' hospitals that accepted new drafts of
casualties from France.

There were around 1,200 searchers in Britain alone, visiting over a thousand hospitals, with a couple of hundred more searchers in base hospitals and rest camps abroad. In 1921 the Joint War Committee of the British Red Cross Society and the Order of St John published a report on their activities between 1914 and 1919. It found that the only information of any value was obtained by direct questioning, rather than by leaving enquiry lists lying around in the hospitals with an invitation for individuals to volunteer information. The experience of war had left many soldiers reluctant to volunteer for anything, and so it was up to the searchers to identify and follow any positive leads.

The searchers included barristers and solicitors, retired civil servants, clergymen, artists. Many of the Australian Red Cross searchers were lawyers, with investigative skills and an understanding of 'those rules of evidence which obtain in a Court of Law'. As one of them, Frank Pulsford, noted: 'In most cases the witness does not tell his story at all, or gives only a few points of it; the Searcher must usually by skilful cross-examination, exact the real truth in the form in which it is of value as evidence.'[41] An article in the *Continental Daily Mail* described the role of the 'finder' (acknowledging, however, that 'searcher' would be a more accurate term, as people were rarely found): 'He labours in the war's shadows. He explores in human nature's deeps. He is not given a place in the official history of the great conflict, but he has a place in the affections of the mothers and wives of brave men. He can tell heartening stories of soldiers given up for dead who are alive and well. He could tell other stories – stories of long, long trails, ending at wooden crosses ...'[42]

Success depended on the sensitivity and tact of the individual searcher, and their ability to listen to, and win the confidence, of the person they were questioning: quite literally, their bedside manner.[43] A box of cigarettes might come in handy, too, as the report advised. It was particularly important for the searcher to convince the interviewee that he was assisting the families of his missing comrades. Most soldiers remembered how they themselves had dreaded disappearing, and the pain this would have caused their own families. They wished to spare the relatives of others the cruel fate of feeling abandoned in a limbo of the lost.

On the whole, as the report found, former military officers appeared to have had more difficulty doing this than searchers from civilian professions. 'It has certainly occurred that a Searcher has seen and obtained information from a man who has said: "I saw one of your people at ___ but he had been in the Army and I wasn't going to tell him anything."' Ex-officers sometimes struggled to keep the tone of command out of their voices. Furthermore, no witness wanted to arouse the suspicion that an officer, say, was missing because he had lost his nerve, or was a prisoner of war because he had surrendered: it was the duty of an officer to resist capture, and all officers returning from prisoner-of-war camp had to sign a statement describing their capture which, if considered 'inadequate', might lead to disciplinary action.[44]

The interviews were conducted at a patient's bedside in a hospital ward – generally in the afternoon, since in the mornings the medical staff were busy with doctors' rounds and dressings – or over a tea table in the recreation hut of a convalescent camp. The work was monotonous, as Gertrude Bell had found in Boulogne, and to some degree unrewarding – it was estimated that only five interviewees in a hundred yielded information of any value. It could also be heartbreaking.

Practical notes on searching, prepared by an experienced searcher, were published in the Joint War Committee's report. These detailed the preliminary background information required: the place, date and time of the action; the missing soldier's number and platoon; his initials or forename; his appearance, address, previous occupation; a statement of how long the informant had known him; and a summary of where he had trained and how long he had been with the battalion. There were often several soldiers of the same name in a battalion, of a similar height and build; so it was crucial to establish beyond reasonable doubt that the right man was being identified, and that the weight of evidence would satisfy an anxious relative. That is why the physical description and the personal facts – the interests, career, defining traits or characteristics, special musical talent or boxing ability, nicknames, indeed any proof that the eyewitness really did know the missing man – were so important in identifying the name on the list with the man whose last sighting on the battlefield was being described. The greater the detail, the closer the chance of an accurate match. The answers to such questions of identity, and their interpretation, could be decisive in determining whether someone was alive or dead.

The answers also tested the general reliability of the hospital witnesses, most of whom had experienced trauma, and helped the searchers assess the descriptions of the action itself. Here, the level of detail was equally necessary. The 'Notes for Searchers' suggested the following types of information: the distance of the eyewitness from what he was describing, and of the casualty from the British or German line; where in the body the casualty had been hit and by what type of missile; how he fell, and whether he moved or said anything after falling; what was he doing at the time; whether it was light or dark; was the line going forward or retiring; and who held the ground after the attack. This information could be cross-checked against other accounts (up to five accounts per missing person, on average), to provide hard, first-hand, corroborated evidence, rather than rumour or hearsay. Any praise of the missing man was an added crumb of comfort for the family.[45] As the searchers found, accounts could be at best vague and at worst contradictory. After a battle, soldiers generally talked together, concocting and confirming their accounts as they relived the event in a vain attempt to make sense of the chaos, to explain the inexplicable, and provide a collective, authorised, though often inaccurate, version.

Families, too, would go to great lengths to convince themselves of the survival of their loved ones. Roll calls taken after an engagement were often taken in haste, in the dark. It was hard enough to hear the names responding in the noise, let alone to note the voices that remained silent. Similar names or numbers in a battalion might be misheard or confused. Reports from survivors of those who had been seen coming back, and those who had not, were often garbled; and it could take a couple of days for soldiers who had been waiting, disoriented, in a shell hole in no man's land, to feel it was safe to return to the trenches, or to be picked up by a search party. By the time they got back, half the company might have been killed – including the commanding officer – and all the records gone missing. It was easy to make mistakes.

It was also, of course, difficult to identify a body that had been blown to bits by a shell, or left to decompose under a Turkish sun, or buried in a mass grave in a landscape that had itself been obliterated. The bodies of two-thirds of the New Zealand soldiers killed at Gallipoli were never recovered – twice the rate of those who died on the Western front, where bodies were still being turned up in their thousands during the clearance of the battlefields in the decades after the war ended. It was this absence of a body, and this lack of a grave, that allowed people to believe that their loved one had not died.

Until 1916 each British soldier wore only one identity disc, bearing his surname and initials, regiment, number and religious denomination. In the event of his death, this would be removed from the corpse so that his loss, at least, could be accounted for, but would not help a burial party coming along later to identify his body for the grave. Even when double discs were introduced, these were made of a pressed fibre that, like the body, degraded and decomposed over time if left in no man's land – which is why some soldiers chose to wear a metal tag or bracelet of their own device. But what if the soldier had failed to wear a disc at all? Or his body ended up in enemy territory? There were always cases of battlefield scavenging, when distinguishing items, including discs, pay books and personal items, were looted, making the task of identifying the body even harder.

The problems of identification, of locating a grave and of compiling accurate lists of the dead inevitably resulted in the odd administrative error – as happened to the poet Robert Graves. The report of the poet's death in *The Times* in August 1916 turned out to be premature, and the newspaper had to publish a disclaimer from Graves to the effect that he was not dead.[46] The confusion contributed greatly to his recovery from wounds in a hospital in Highgate, as he described in *Goodbye to All That*: 'The people with whom I had been on the worst terms during my life wrote the most enthusiastic condolences: my housemaster, for instance.'[47] Even though such stories were not common, they offered disproportionate hope to other desperate families.

As the notes on searching advised, it was not good enough for a witness to report that 'I heard so-and-so was killed', or 'I believe so-and-so was wounded', or that 'All such and such a platoon were taken prisoner.' Accounts like these should not be taken at face value, the report continued, as soldiers always wanted to believe that their comrades had been taken prisoner and might still be alive. But what if a missing soldier really had been taken prisoner, and his file had disappeared, or his name mislaid on a list? Perhaps the prisoner had been transferred from camp to camp and his name had become lost in the system? Or had been one of the 13,000 estimated to have died as prisoners of war, in the camps, in prison hospitals, in the salt mines in Germany, or on working parties, clearing the battlefields in Belgium. Perhaps he had attempted to escape (this was slightly easier in the First World War, when large areas of Western Europe were 'unoccupied', than in the Second); and if so, had ended up in Holzminden, a secretive, extra-secure camp, with severely proscribed links to the outside world. When it came to these special camps, the Germans, who were generally so meticulous in building the bureaucracy of war – in the making of lists and the keeping of records – sometimes failed to apply their usual high standards. They might fail to communicate the prisoner's name to the Red Cross in Geneva; and there were even rumours that some camp commandants destroyed prisoners' letters to spare themselves the inconvenience of censoring them. There were any number of possibilities that preyed on the minds of the relatives. In this time of shadows and half-truths, of rumours and unconfirmed sightings, how could anyone be completely sure? The relatives of missing men grasped at any information that seemed to give them hope of a loved one's safety, and to find flaws in any evidence of death.

*

The story of the search for Angus Macnaghten is typical of the lengths to which some people would go, in the absence of a grave, to believe that their missing loved ones were still alive; and how vulnerable this made them to conmen and clairvoyants.

In early November 1914, Hazel Macnaghten received a telegram from the War Office announcing that her husband Angus, an officer with the Black Watch, had been reported missing on 29 October, during the First Battle of Ypres. Around the same time, she also received reassuring messages from her husband's fellow officers that he had been captured with, at worst, a slight leg wound. There was no need to worry, they insisted. When she continued to hear no definite news, she made enquiries through contacts in Germany of her friends and family (as did many other wealthy families, exploiting the strong personal and business ties that had linked the two countries before the war); and placed requests for information in the personal columns of newspapers. These yielded similarly reassuring but vague responses. Even the Wounded and Missing Enquiry Department could only suggest that if Lieutenant Macnaghten had been wounded and taken prisoner, it might be some time before she heard from him in a German hospital.

Towards the end of the year, Hazel contacted Edward Page Gaston, an American citizen living in London, who had been featured in the *Daily Graphic*. Gaston claimed that, as a neutral go-between, he could provide 'a comprehensive searching service', with specialist access to camps in Germany which official government or Red Cross channels could not reach. For a fee, he could not only deliver care packages to known prisoners, but also make enquiries about others who might be prisoners. There were 'hundreds, perhaps thousands of officers and men who have been wounded and placed temporarily in peasants' cottages, farmhouses, small hospitals and other places where they are for the time being lost to those at home', he claimed. 'For instance, a man with a bad shrapnel wound in the head might suffer temporary loss of memory and lie for a month or more unknown and unknowing …'[48] His promotional literature boasted the support of the British foreign secretary, Sir Edward Grey, and secretary of state for war, Lord Kitchener, and the American embassy in Berlin.

Hazel entrusted £50 and a photograph of her husband to Gaston so that he could embark on a search, although some of this was returned when Gaston was later discredited. In 1915 the War Office warned that 'the anxiety of relatives is being taken advantage of to get money from people who cannot afford it, with the pretended object of searching for the missing. A hint from the press might save money and disappointment in the case of those who otherwise may be misled by designing persons claiming official recognition which they do not possess.'[49] The American ambassador in Berlin was prompted to disclaim any association with Gaston in a letter to the newspapers.

Warnings about impostors continued throughout the war. In April 1917, the Enquiry Department sent a letter signed by the Earl of Lucan, Lord Robert Cecil's successor as director, in response to an enquiry about Private Albert Barlow of 1st Battalion, Manchester Regiment. 'We have received your letter about the above soldier, but fear there can be no truth in the rumours of his being a prisoner as his name has never come through on any of the list of prisoners in Turkish hands; & it is quite impossible that anyone missing in Mesopotamia should be a "prisoner in Germany". There are several people going about giving false information to the families of missing men. One such was arrested the other day but we must fear there are others still at large. Should we by any unlikely chance learn of his being a prisoner we should inform you but do not encourage his poor wife to hope it.'[50] The earl was to be the grandfather of another Lucan who went missing in very different circumstances half a century later.

Finally, just over a year after her husband's disappearance, Hazel received a letter from the War Office: in view of the lapse of time and the fact that no news had been obtained, the Army Council was regretfully 'constrained to conclude that this Officer died on 29 October 1914 or since that date'. Angus Macnaghten's death was announced in the newspapers in January 1916, although Hazel still clung to the hope that he was alive, stating in the *Morning Post* that 'she wishes her friends to know that, although it was necessary for the name of her husband to appear in the Roll of Honour, neither she nor his sisters have given up hope, as no definite proof of his death has been received'.[51] Their son, also Angus, who was only five months old when his father was reported missing, described in a book published more than fifty years later his mother's quest, and how 'whenever there was a newspaper report of a missing soldier turning up, having suffered from loss of memory, my mother's hopes would be raised'.[52]

To the irritation of the authorities, who always wanted to play down unrealistic expectations and rumours, good-news stories of miraculous returns kept surfacing in the press. These encouraged people, including the Macnaghtens, not to give up – even if they came with complications. In May 1917 a columnist in the *Pall Mall Gazette* reported that 'the son of a well-known peer, who was reported killed at the beginning of the war, has been a prisoner all the time, but has only just been able to write home. Unfortunately, during the period that has elapsed, complications have arisen owing to the fact of his wife having got married again. There is naturally commotion in the families concerned.'[53] There was also the story of a soldier, who had been presumed dead after months of no news – until his bankers informed his mother that he had sent a cheque with a note to say he was in Torgau prison camp; and one of an officer, missing since September, who was not heard of until February the following year, through the American consul general in London. All of these accounts encouraged Hazel to write that 'in spite of the long silence, I feel Angus is safe somewhere'.[54]

The anguish of not knowing whether a loved one was wounded and in hospital, a prisoner of war, or dead, was compounded by the delays in receiving news: typically a matter of weeks for privates and NCOs. Some families waited far longer, however, the farther they were from the theatre of war. It was over six years before the family of New Zealander Augustine Bond finally learned of his fate. In June 1915 his father heard that Augustine had been wounded at Gallipoli but was 'progressing favourably'. After attempts to trace him had failed, a military inquiry concluded a year later that he had probably been killed; but only in February 1922 was his body 'removed from an isolated grave' and buried in a military cemetery in Gallipoli.[55]

In making their judgements, the searchers had to scrutinise the evidence and compare it with previous information, unravelling, as the Australian searcher Vera Deakin put it, the 'confused threads of the tangled skein of mystery which surrounded the fate of the "Missing" '.[56] They usually reached a conclusion. 'Little by little the contradictions are sifted down and good evidence built up,' wrote Harley Granville-Barker in his 1916 history, *The Red Cross in France*. 'The stark facts will appear quite suddenly sometimes.'[57]

Once their final decision was made – dead or alive – the Wounded and Missing Enquiry Department would send a report to the War Office, as well as to the soldier's family. 'Sometimes, to the joy of the searcher, the report advised, 'there may dawn a day when he is traced, and happiness comes again to the house of mourning, through a letter from the Department'. But just as often, 'a man is found who can give exact information as to how another reported "missing" met his death. His story puts an end to further inquiry, and at least the sorrowing family know the worst.' Hundreds of thousands of families received letters written by a searcher but signed by the Earl of Lucan, that concluded: 'I fear we can no longer doubt the fact, and desire to close the case with our deep sympathy in your bereavement.'[58]

There were many cases, however, where the department could not come to a definitive conclusion, and there were no eyewitness accounts. In these circumstances, the best it could do was to provide a general picture of battle conditions around the time of the soldier's disappearance, leaving the enquirers with nothing left to cling to but unreasonable doubt. Such was the case of Private H. Dean of the East Surrey Regiment. In a letter from the department to Private Dean's father, dated 5 March 1920, it was regretted that 'notwithstanding constant and careful enquiries, we have never succeeded in telling you anything about your son … His name was on our lists for months, and we asked all the men of his unit whom we were able to see, both in English hospitals and at the bases abroad, but none of them threw any light on his casualty. We have also questioned released prisoners but have learnt nothing. We can therefore only send you a General Account of the action in which he was last seen, with sincere regret at our inability to help you any further, as this Office is now closed. We wish at the same time to offer our sympathy to the family and friends.'[59]

The chances of an individual soldier's survival depended on the intensity of the fighting, and the ebb and flow of a battle at a particular moment: whether his company was pushing forwards, and taking new ground, or being driven back at the time of being wounded. In a lull in the fighting, search parties and stretcher-bearers would scour the battlefield for casualties, listening out for the moans or cries of the wounded or of those stranded in shell holes, scavenging water and rations from the packs of any corpses around. A soldier might even be able to stagger back to his own trenches, but only if he was within his own front line. If he was in no man's land, he was still at risk of being bombarded by artillery fire and might just be rescued – at night – by a search party. If the action had been unsuccessful, and he was now behind enemy lines, he was either dead or a prisoner.

That is why the questions asked by the searchers targeted the state of the action to determine whether the line was advancing or retreating; who held the ground where the soldier had last been seen; and whether therefore, if wounded, he was more likely to have been taken prisoner by the enemy or rescued alive by his own colleagues. The searchers' reports would assess the sorry statistical chances of survival in such circumstances. If the shelling had been particularly heavy, it was most unlikely that any body, alive or dead, would have survived intact under the deluge of falling earth – and would help to explain to enquirers why there was no marked grave.

Although further enquiries did occasionally result in good news – that a missing man was in hospital, like Robert Graves, or in a prisoner-of-war camp, like Maxwell Earle – the chances were loaded against survival, and it was the department's job to extinguish any false hopes by setting forth the grim facts. As

Rudyard Kipling, who lost his son John in 1915, reflected in his 1925 short story 'The Gardener': 'Missing *always* means dead.'[60]

The Red Cross regretted that the phrase 'tracing the Missing' was used in connection with its work, as it falsely implied that the department had the power to 'find': an expression that 'must often have led to disappointment'. 'The unhappy and unfounded rumour,' the Joint War Committee report concluded, 'that "hundreds of men were lying unidentified in hospitals suffering from loss of memory" was also responsible for much sad and useless correspondence. It can well be understood that most of the news to be passed on was painful, but certainly after weeks of suspense it was often a relief and better than continued anxiety. It was clear that Enquirers were touchingly grateful for small personal details which they could not possibly have obtained without the help of the Searchers.'[61]

The central records of the Wounded and Missing Enquiry Department were destroyed soon after the end of the First World War, and the reports it wrote, and the letters it sent survive only in the papers of the families of individual soldiers. The Australian records do survive, however, in Australia and in the archives at the International Red Cross headquarters in Geneva, and include 32,000 files. Since the Australian Bureau was modelled on the British department (and, as the bureau depended on British Red Cross searchers to write most of the reports, there being few Australian searchers in France and England), the role it played and the style of its reports give a fuller picture of the way in which the British department operated. The Information Bureau of the Canadian Red Cross, established after the arrival in France of the first Canadian troops in February 1915, performed a similar function. It, too, used the services of the British Red Cross and its searchers to get news of missing Canadians, and then relayed the information to the enquiring relatives. In her history, *The Maple Leaf's Red Cross*, published the year after the war ended, Mary MacLeod Moore wrote: 'It was, one need hardly say, of the greatest comfort to the sorrowing families, who had received only the terribly bald official notice. The little personal tributes brought the dead nearer; they broke the awful silence. They gave the mourners a vivid picture of the last moments of one of the heroes of the war; they put an end to that hope deferred which maketh the heart sick.'[62]

The handling of the reports received from the searchers, and forwarded to the enquirers, required great sensitivity. Whatever the outcome, it was vital to show that a personal interest had been taken in each case, beyond the curt, perfunctory and often frustratingly inadequate responses of the military. As the Joint War Committee report described: 'It quickly became established, therefore, that in writing to these correspondents official forms and methods should be, as far as possible, discarded so that each enquirer might feel that a certain personal interest was taken in his or her case ... this part of the work was, of course, the raison d'etre of the whole organisation; and it was abundantly proved that no labour was wasted which might convince the families of the missing of the wide and assiduous research which had been made on their behalf.'[63]

Despite the many disappointments it brought, the work of the Wounded and Missing Enquiry Department also gave profound psychological benefits to the people it tried to help. At the very least, it offered certainty, a relief from the anxiety of not knowing, an end to 'this awful suspense'.[64] In an appreciation of the work of the department, published in 1919, G. G. Buckler suggested that 'definite information, it may almost be said, was our highest ideal, and judging from the letters of thanks received, it can be positively stated that ninety-nine people out of every hundred choose agonising certainty rather than hope deferred'.[65] If the news was bad, the department might even be able to reassure a relative that the dead man had been given a grave – and where. 'We are all glad to know that he lies comfortable,' many of the enquirers wrote in thanks.[66]

Enquirers were often pathetically grateful for the personal touch. When people turned to the Red Cross, they were turning to an organisation that appeared to care. Lord Northcliffe observed that 'no department of State could hope to touch the human chord which gives this work its greatest value. It would be wrong to expect an already overworked War Office to busy itself collecting small personal details, yet it is just these details for which all those who have suffered the great loss yearn so wistfully.'[67]

These details had the ring of 'truth' – and it was 'truth' that most people wanted. The handwritten letter from an officer in the missing soldier's platoon that came a few days, or weeks, after the standard War Office communication was all very well. Such letters tended to follow a common formula, with a few stock phrases of sympathy. They stressed what a good soldier he had been; how loved he had been by his fellows ('He was one of my most reliable and trustworthy men and he will be very much missed by all officers and NCOs alike'); how significant his sacrifice had been to a noble cause ('I feel the deepest sympathy with you in your great loss. You have, at least, the satisfaction of knowing that he died a noble death while taking part in a most glorious deed'); and how painlessly he had died ('He did not say a word nor did he suffer').

The department believed that it owed the truth, or something close to the truth, to the bereaved. In many cases, the evidence it relayed would be the only description people would ever receive of their loved one's last moments. They would be able to share in these, to walk in the footsteps of the fallen, to see what he saw, to hear what he heard, to experience what he felt: 'to be with him in spirit', as if on a virtual pilgrimage.

This level of detail was needed in the searchers' reports for forensic reasons, to remove any doubt about the fate of the soldiers they had been asked to investigate. But it also satisfied the quest for information on the part of the bereaved, who were often – like Vera Brittain in her search for the circumstances of her brother Edward's death – 'driven and impelled by a remorseless determination'.[68] For some, only a full disclosure of the facts, however brutal, could facilitate such a feat of empathy; and it made any words of praise from a comrade all the more comforting for being genuine.

The verbatim eyewitness accounts, with their graphic details, were not always sanitised: 'Blown to bits', rather than the blander 'Killed by a shell'; 'Shot in the genitals', rather than 'Hit low down'. The reports did not always gloss over the more grotesque details: the body buried alive in a shell blast, the 'bullet that knocked an eye clean out' of its socket, the 'guts spilling between clasped fingers', the froth seeping out of the corner of a mouth, the screaming, agonised last minutes. Or should these fates, some people asked, have best been downplayed and described generically as a 'Blighty wound', with its comforting connotations of home, as in the official statements? There was a fine balance between tact and truth-telling.

The euphemisms associated with life and death at the front during the First World War were often what the authorities wanted people to hear, rather than what people wanted to hear themselves. Perhaps surprisingly, the reports were relatively free from official censorship, with *The Times* reporting in October 1915 that the Wounded and Missing Enquiry Department was 'unfettered by official restrictions' and that 'Direct communication between the Department and inquirers remains undisturbed'.[69]

The response from the department to the sister of Private A. C. K. Sibley of the 10th Hants is typical: 'We have been trying to obtain information for you about your missing Brother, but have not been very successful up to the present, which in itself is, I fear, a discouraging sign. One of the Officers of his Company, 2nd Lieut. J. I. T. Scallon … was interviewed three days ago at the 5th Southern General Hospital, Milton Section, Portsmouth, where he is a patient,' the searcher's letter continued. 'He gave a report about your Brother, which shows that in the stress of the fighting he became reckless of danger. This is what he said about him: – "We were on the Vardar front, and on September 1st [1918] had practically taken our objective, Black Rock Salient. We were under a concerted Barrage and Sibley was believed to have been wounded. He was also suffering from shell-shock, and threw away his rifle and equipment and ran laughing towards the Bulgar lines, waving a pickhandle." '[70]

In his account of the Red Cross in France, Granville-Barker noted: 'the supreme value of these simple stories is that they do sink to the sheer rock bottom of war. We can see in them fighting, as it was to the men who had to fight, in all its beastliness, in all its dignity. And, finally, that is all there is worth knowing about war.'

'In one office in London,' Granville-Barker summarised, 'and half a dozen others in France there is being built up a unique history of the war ... a soldier's war, a war of platoons, we are told, so that in one sense its truest story will be the stories that privates and corporals and sergeants tell of the things they did and the things they saw. That is the history which is being written in the Red Cross offices which search for the fate of the Wounded and Missing.' He concluded: 'From the time the work started ... every battle can be found described, not from its planning thirty miles away, not from the result of it as weeks later the journalists may tell, but from the hundred points of view grasped by and made vivid to the very men who were fighting it there on the field. You learn not what tactics are and leadership, but what crude fighting is and the luck of fighting and the ill-luck ... I would not want to go further for the truth. And if I were the men about whom some of the stories are told ... I would not ask a finer epitaph.'[71]

A couple of months after the First World War ended, it was estimated that the whereabouts of more than half a million British soldiers were unknown. Without a registered final resting place, there was still a chance, in the minds of some families, that their loved ones had survived. The Armistice, then, was not the final reckoning that many people thought, the day when a line was drawn between the living and the dead.

By the terms of the 11 November Armistice, the Germans were obliged to repatriate all Allied and US prisoners of war with immediate effect. The release was often orderly, as the prisoners were handed over to other Allied soldiers. But sometimes they were simply allowed by their guards, who had put on red armbands to express their sympathy for the Bolshevik revolution, to walk free, without food or money. They had to make their own way home across a starving and defeated country, as Germany was convulsed by near-civil war. Wherever they could, they hitched lifts on buses and trains to the Channel ports, hoping to catch a boat back to Blighty.

The Times History of the War, published in full in 1921, described the blue- and khaki-clothed refugees staggering along the roads:

At every town on the front, from the far north of Belgium
southward to where the mountains of Alsace overlook the
Rhine, those thinly clad, shivering warriors, whose arms had
not the strength of a child's, and who, if they could swallow
a morsel of bread, thought themselves fortunate, crowded
together in search of warmth and food. They had been let
loose by their captors the Germans, who having underfed
and maltreated them for months, cared nothing whether
they ever reached the Allied lines or died on the way …
A more melancholy and wistful procession, men seldom saw,
French, British, Belgians, Italians, Americans and Russians, all
shared the horrors of that march. With sunken cheeks, with
shoulders bent with fatigue and ill-treatment, with shrunken
frames that made their uniforms look ridiculously ill-fitting
in their abundant largeness, dressed in an amazing collection
of coats and caps, no distinction of nationality or speech was
recognised, for the helpless helped the helpless whether Russian
or Italian.[72]

Some died on the way, weakened by their years in prison, by the
lack of food and by influenza.

The prisoners were repatriated at the rate of several thousand
a day. By December, more than 70,000 prisoners had arrived in
Britain, with a further 60,000 by the new year. They landed to
enthusiastic welcomes at Dover, Leith and Hull, but also to the
pathetic sight of women lining the docks, carrying pictures of
missing sons, husbands, brothers, with the question: 'Have you seen
this man?' From the ports, the men were transferred by special trains
and motor vans to reception camps, where they were registered,
medically examined, and asked to report any ill-treatment of which
they or their fellow prisoners had been the victims.

The reception camp at Ripon had accommodation for 14,000
men, with twenty-eight large dining huts hung with bunting, a
well-appointed club for officers, a hospital, and four theatres
where the returnees were entertained with variety shows. During
the thirty-six hours that, typically, they stayed there, the soldiers

would exchange their lousy dark-blue prisoners' uniforms and underclothes. They would be issued with new kit, before being sent home, with £2 10s. in cash (officers got a bit more), a railway pass, a printed letter from King George V, welcoming them 'on your release from the miseries and hardships which you have endured with so much patience and courage', and instructions to report back to their regimental depot in two months' time.[73] While at the reception camp, they might be interviewed by one of several searchers about prisoners from the same battalion who appeared as 'missing'. There were even cases of repatriated prisoners finding their own names on the searchers' lists.

Inevitably, there were discrepancies between the numbers of British prisoners of war reported by the Germans and those estimated as prisoners by the British themselves. In the spring of 1918 the Germans had advanced right across France, taking tens of thousands of prisoners in a matter of weeks; in the chaos, record-keeping was a lesser priority. The Allied counter-attack in August had been just as furious, as the Germans retreated across Europe. This led, in January 1919, to a demand by the Interdepartmental Committee on Prisoners of War that the enemy governments account for every British prisoner of war who had at any time been in their hands. 'Instructions have been sent to British representatives to make investigations at camps, mines, asylums, and elsewhere in enemy countries and wherever prisoners may possibly be found … It is possible, for instance, that some may have been temporarily "lost in the mines"; others may have taken up farm work in Germany and settled there … and a few others, again, may have been reported dead who are alive in German hands.'[74] Search parties, accompanied by motor ambulances, were sent to Germany to small, satellite prison camps, hospitals and work camps to look for stray prisoners. In February, Winston Churchill, the secretary of state for war, admitted that 64,800 such servicemen remained missing without trace. The search parties tracked down only 121 of these (all of whom were either too sick or wounded to travel home, or had stayed behind of their own volition). By the time the last prisoners were repatriated, it had to be assumed that the others were dead, and not just for the duration of the war.

The Wounded and Missing Enquiry Department continued to operate throughout the war, until March 1919. The Earl of Lucan estimated that, over the course of the conflict, its searchers had interviewed up to five million service personnel, and responded to almost 400,000 enquiries from relatives and friends of the missing. 'No letter, however trivial, remains unanswered; no enquiry, however difficult, is neglected,' ran one observer's account of the department, a bureaucracy run with the most humane of aims. 'This, then, is a labour of love,' it concluded: 'It is a labour which eases the sorest wounds of warfare and which indirectly brings great comfort to the fighting men themselves, many of whom are haunted by the fear of being numbered among the lost and so becoming a source of suffering to their friends.'[75]

2

E. M. Forster and a Labour of Love

Halfway through the First World War, the newspaper publisher and propagandist Lord Northcliffe assembled a collection of his writings about the conflict. The book, *At the War*, included pen portraits of Allied commanders Haig, Joffre and Cadorna; tributes to groups of unsung heroes, such as the women working in the munitions factories; and descriptions of the 'war doctors' tending the wounded at the front. There was a whole chapter on the Red Cross Wounded and Missing Enquiry Department in which he cited one of its dossiers – those 'human documents of rare interest which none can read unmoved' – as a real-life example of the department's work.[1] The dossier concerned the search for 'Flight Sub-Lieutenant C. G.' of the Royal Naval Air Service, who had been shot down on a mission to deliver food to the besieged city of Kut, in eastern Iraq, in April 1916. A couple of months later, a fellow airman, by that time in hospital in Bombay, reported that 'C.G.' had been taken prisoner, although his name had not yet appeared on any prisoners' lists.

It was an eyewitness report, dated 27 July 1916, given by an informant in hospital in Alexandria, Egypt to a searcher there, that provided the definitive detail. C.G. had been shot down over Turkish lines, wounded, and taken prisoner; at the request of the Turks, his kit was then taken upriver by motorboat and delivered to an agreed rendezvous with his Turkish captors. The searcher noted that this was 'a more detailed account than the last we sent you' and went on to 'hope that when we obtain full lists of the prisoners in the hands of the Turks we shall find his name in them'. The following day, the pilot's father wrote to thank the searcher for his report and 'all those who work so unselfishly for others', and enclosed a donation of £25 towards the department funds. In September, the Wounded and Missing Enquiry Department finally informed the parents that their son had been released 'quite well' by the Turks, as part of a prisoner exchange in Baghdad, and was now sailing to India in a hospital ship. This, then, was the department's 'labour of love', Lord Northcliffe concluded, 'which eases the sorest wounds of warfare'.[2]

'C.G.' was, in fact, Flight Sub-Lieutenant Gasson, and the anonymous searcher in Alexandria, who tracked him down remotely, was the writer E. M. Forster. In a letter to his mother, written 'full of [his] own abilities', a few days before Christmas, Forster described the 'recent excitement' of having 'lived to be praised by Lord Northcliffe … speaks of the case of Flight-Lt. Gasson as one of the many Red Cross enquiry successes. Mine was the report, and what is more to the point Gasson's people have sent £25 in consequence'.[3]

Forster had been fretting for much of the first year of the war about the role he should play. At the suggestion of the historian G. M. Trevelyan, who commanded an ambulance unit, he had considered joining the Red Cross on the Italian front. What appealed to him about this proposal, as his work in Alexandria was later to show, was the opportunity 'in this world of maniacs … to pick up the poor tortured broken people and try to mend them'.[4] His mother, Lily, was against the idea, however, and she was 'the deciding influence'[5] in his choosing not to go. Malta, he told his mother, would be 'pleasant in the winter and absolutely safe which is a comfort, as I should know Mummy wouldn't worry – or at least have no excuse for doing so'.[6] In the end, it was Egypt which claimed him – but only just.

In October 1915 Forster was interviewed by Gertrude Bell, now in charge of the newly established London hub of the Red Cross Wounded and Missing Enquiry Department. 'Miss Gertrude Bell was not sympathetic,' Forster later recalled, 'she was hard and severe ... and while willing to give all relevant information she had not time for trimmings. I remember asking her what the inhabitants of Alexandria would be like. She replied I should have no opportunity to find out. I should only see them in the streets as I went to and fro on my work.'[7] Forster had not impressed Bell either. 'Feeling that I had been too deferential towards her, I reacted, became uppish and impertinent at the wrong moment (it's called initiative when it's at the right moment) and I nearly never got sent to Alexandria at all.' Fortunately for Forster, Bell was not the head of 'the Red Cross hierarchy' ('a mistake into which she had allowed me to fall') and thanks to his King's College, Cambridge contemporary Percy Lubbock, who also worked at the Red Cross headquarters in London and overcame Gertrude Bell's opposition, Forster got the job.[8] 'I am leaving no stone a gentleman may turn to be sent to Egypt as a Searcher by the Red Cross,' he reported to Virginia Woolf. 'Miss Gertrude Loathly Belle [a play on her full name, Gertrude Margaret Lowthian Bell] was greatly against me, but I do fancy is silenced at last.'[9]

Forster left England for Egypt in November 1915, expecting to stay for around three months. He was thirty-six years of age and at a crossroads in his career. His first four novels, *Where Angels Fear to Tread*, *The Longest Journey*, *A Room with a View*, and *Howards End* had been published between 1905 and 1910, by the time he had just turned thirty. He had started writing *A Passage to India* before the war, but was stuck because, as he explained in a letter to his mother, 'all the details of India are vague in my mind':[10] it was not to appear until 1924, more than a decade after the publication of his last novel. Forster also confided to his diary that, as a homosexual, he had given up writing novels, because he was bored with 'the only subject that I both can and may treat – the love of men for women & vice versa'.[11] He had, in fact, written *Maurice*, a novel about the love of men for men, before the war, but because of its subject matter, this could not be published until after his death, in 1971.

Despite the great critical acclaim, Forster appeared to Virginia Woolf as 'timid as a mouse, but when he creeps out of his hole very charming'.[12] Blocked in his professional life and stifled in his private life, he was lonely and depressed when he arrived in Egypt: 'a very pale, delicately built young man, slightly towzled and very shy, with a habit of standing on one leg and winding the other round it', an acquaintance recalled.[13] The next three years were to have a profound effect on all aspects of his life.

Forster's job was to interview wounded men in military hospitals for information about any of their comrades reported missing. The Red Cross was a semi-military organisation so, although technically a civilian and unpaid, he wore a khaki uniform 'with some sort of rank sewn on to it, which later came out in the wash',[14] and enjoyed some of the perks of an officer, such as travelling at half-fare on the trams (where he was to meet his lover, Mohammed). He arrived in 'a slightly heroic mood', but as the threat of a Turkish invasion of Egypt receded, his mood changed. 'What had begun as an outpost turned into something suspiciously like a funk-hole, and I stuck in it for over three years, visiting hospitals, collecting information, and writing reports. "You are such a wonderful *sticker*," a detestable Red Cross colonel said to me scathingly. I was; and I dared not retort that it takes both stickers and climbers to make a world.'[15]

Throughout the war, Egypt was strategically important as a supply base for campaigns in the Dardanelles, Palestine and Mesopotamia, as well as being home to over a quarter of a million troops stationed there to defend the Suez Canal. Although it may have felt like a 'funk-hole', Alexandria had four hospitals, three convalescent camps, and five clinics for officers, to care for the soldiers wounded in those campaigns. In the first months of his work there, Forster interviewed some of the thousands of wounded men who had been evacuated from Gallipoli. From then on, his workload fluctuated with the flow of wounded men from successive campaigns. From the spring of 1916, convoys – with several hundred wounded soldiers on each boat – would arrive from Mesopotamia, and from the spring of the following year from Palestine.

At times Forster had so much work that he felt he was 'trudging on beneath [his] work like a camel through some boundless desert … conscious of an absence of enthusiasm'.[16] At the end of the war, he was kept busy interviewing repatriated prisoners from morning to night, going down to the docks to meet the arrivals. On one occasion, he 'went down to the boatful of P/Ws, and found on its list names of 23 men whom we thought missing or dead'. It was rewarding work, and the searchers gleaned much valuable information.[17]

On arrival in Alexandria he had checked into the comfortable, newly opened Majestic Hotel, which was a ten-minute walk around the Place Mohammed Ali from the Red Cross office, looking for a time 'neither to the right hand nor to the left in the streets, as Miss Bell had enjoined'.[18] Work started at 10 a.m., with a break back at the hotel for lunch, and then finished around 7 p.m. Forster would spend the evenings writing reports which were sent, eventually, to the London Office of the Red Cross (and the War Office) and then on to relatives in England. He liked the routine: 'the regular and definite work has stopped me thinking about the war, which is a mercy, for in England I very nearly went mad'.[19]

His first impressions of the city were not favourable. 'I do not like Egypt much,' he wrote to a friend in December 1915, '– or rather, I do not see it, for Alexandria is cosmopolitan. But what I have seen seems vastly inferior to India, for which I am always longing in the most persistent way, and where I still hope to die. It is only at sunset that Egypt surpasses India – at all other hours it is flat, unromantic, unmysterious, and godless – the soil is mud, the inhabitants are of mud moving, and exasperating in the extreme: I feel as instinctively not at home among them as I feel instinctively at home among Indians …'[20] He rather shocked himself with his hatred of the place, 'or rather its inhabitants'. He had come to Egypt, particularly after his experience of India, inclined to be 'quite free from racial prejudices', but 'in 10 months I've acquired an instinctive dislike to the Arab voice, the Arab figure, the Arab way of looking or walking or pump shitting or eating or laughing or anything – exactly the emotion that I censured in the Anglo-Indian towards the native there … It's damnable and disgraceful, and it's in me.'[21] Gradually, however, he began, 'furtively at first',[22] to adjust himself to the rhythm of the city and, particularly when he wandered Alexandria without his officer's uniform, to apprehend the 'magic and the antiquity and the complexity of the city, and determined to write about her'.[23]

His colleagues in the department were a curious mixture of volunteers washed up in Alexandria, a backwater of the war, as it had turned out. A Colonel Needham, a 'muddling fish' in Forster's opinion, was the Head Searcher. Then came Victoria Grant Duff, Forster's immediate superior, 'a youngish, slightly shrewish lady', Forster wrote to his mother, who brought to her role the assumptions, energy and 'slightly distingué' manner befitting the daughter of a former Governor of Madras.[24] Another of his colleagues, Denys Winstanley, a Cambridge historian, was also staying in the Majestic, and they often ate together or discussed wounded and missing news in the lounge. 'Everything threw us together,' Forster recalled in a lecture long after they had drifted apart, '– our jobs, our uniforms, our education, our humane outlook, we had many friends in common, it seemed a miracle that we had met.'[25] There were also two full-time searchers (plus a handful of elderly part-timers, some of whom 'do nothing but complain there is nothing to do',[26] according to Colonel Needham, and, according to Winstanley, did not accomplish much 'through debauchery and age'[27]). Nevertheless, Forster and Winstanley flattered themselves that very few of the wounded men escaped their nets. 'Mr. Spencer, the other searcher, also fishes diligently, but rather infrequently, and is set to watch the less frequented pools.'[28]

'I must try not to be muddly,' Forster began a detailed description of his work to his mother within days of his arrival in Alexandria. Winstanley was handing some of his hospital rounds over to his new colleague, and took Forster on a tour of introductions. At the San Stefano and Bombay Presidency Hospital, 'We wandered about from bed to bed till we dropped, then came away. All the soldiers most pleasant and some of them charming, but a great deal of talk seems to produce a very little information … I have a printed list of all the missing, arranged by Regiments, and after civilities have been exchanged one asks the man what he belongs to, and goes through the bit of the list that concerns him. The visiting hours are 2 to 6, but they don't seem to offer you tea, without which it's difficult to remain intelligent for more than 3 hours! The bad cases I don't see, so it isn't a depressing job: most of the beds have tins of cigarettes by their sides, and the corridors are full of amiable loafers in pyjamas.' The Syrian Convalescent Home for Officers, on the other hand, was 'a small and very luxurious affair'. They had never been 'inflicted with a Searcher' before, and Forster proceeded up the marble steps towards the porticoed building rather nervously, planning to handle them with great care – 'it is no joke tackling a Major who is recovering from nervous breakdown'. Nothing untoward occurred, however, and all were 'civil and some jolly', although they had very little information to impart. 'Two or three visits ought to polish off the Syrian Home, then,' he concluded.

After writing up his reports, Forster would take them to Grant Duff, whom he suspected was treating him 'as a new boy is treated the first day at school, for she did not sound so pleasant when talking to some of the workers'.[29] In a letter to his Aunt Laura, he provided details of a real case, in which a lieutenant who had been reported missing in August had been traced alive and well in hospital – through an informant interviewed by Forster. Although he had never had 'the supreme joy of confronting a Missing or Killed with his own name', this sometimes did occur, he told his mother. 'One man, describing it, said "My chum always was a regular comic and when we showed him his name he said "Oh! dead am I? First I've heard of it. I suppose I'd better go away and lie down." – They can be so amusing – and such loves.'[30]

Forster fell in with a small, slightly louche circle of friends and acquaintances which 'never coalesced into a set'. As he described in a lecture at the Aldeburgh Festival in 1956, he 'got to know the Swiss Director of the tramways and the French Director of Ports who thought he had discovered a prehistoric Harbour and an Englishman who had built an exquisite fortress for the Bedouin in the Western Desert and an Egyptian tram conductor and a Syrian Police Officer who was enthusiastic for George Moore, and an Italian composer who sang Tristan to me under the sea'.[31] His close friends included Robin Furness, an old acquaintance from King's College, Cambridge, who now ran the Press Censorship Department of the Egyptian Civil Service. It was Furness who had promised to introduce their fellow Kingsman, the economist J. M. Keynes, to 'all the attractions which made Gomorrah such a popular resort in the good old days',[32] when he had visited Alexandria in March 1913. And it was Furness who put Forster up for membership of the cosmopolitan 'Cercle Mohammed Ali', where Forster first met the poet C. P. Cavafy. Furness also introduced Forster to Aïda Borchgrevink, the American widow of a Norwegian judge, who sang Wagner at the top of her voice as she drove, and helped Forster find lodgings when he left the Majestic. There was 'nothing of club land or drawingroomia', Forster wrote of his new milieu. 'I have never been so free – it's an odd backwater the war has scooped out for me, and I don't know whether I most dread or long for England. Whenever I open a paper things seem filthier …'[33]

The most serious threat to his peaceable existence was a scare in the summer of 1916 that he might be forced to enlist. In March 1916 the government had introduced full conscription, announcing that it would replace – by the end of June – a previous arrangement, under which, fit, eligible men had been invited to 'attest' their readiness for service when needed at some point in the future. As a Red Cross volunteer, Forster had originally been excused from any pressure to attest; but in June 1916, three months after the introduction of conscription, the Red Cross decided to release its staff for military service. Forster was asked to have a medical examination, and to attest before the expiry date at the end of the month. He felt betrayed by the Red Cross, and dreaded being called up; or returning to England to put his case not to attest, on conscientious grounds, before a tribunal. In the event, his friends and supporters – including Victoria Grant Duff, who wanted to keep him in Egypt – rallied round and pleaded his case. One senior officer even told Sir Courtauld Thomson, the Red Cross commissioner, that the army did not want Forster in any case. 'I am quite shameless over this wirepulling,' Forster wrote cheerfully to his mother: 'If I can't keep out of the army by fair means then hey for foul!'[34] He would continue to do all he could 'to shirk soldiering', but would never protest against it on principle. What he liked about his work was that it was for the individual and not for 'that body-and-soul destroying machine, the state'.[35]

Every day, Forster would do the rounds of his hospitals, questioning wounded soldiers for news of their missing comrades. 'It is depressing in a way, for if one does get news about the missing it is generally bad news,' he wrote to his friend, Syed Ross Masood. 'But I am able to be of use to the wounded soldiers themselves in various unofficial ways – I lend them books, get their watches mended, write their letters, &c. They are so pleasant and grateful, and some of them quite charming.'[36] It was this contact with the men that made him so content. 'I am here become cheeriness itself and run from one little kindness to another all the day,' he told Leonard Woolf.[37] He would play chess, compile deeds for the sale of houses in Australia, scatter cigarettes about, proffer advice on practical matters. On one occasion, he took chocolates and flowers to a 'poor fellow who is deaf, almost dumb, and weak of sight', probably from shellshock. It was not strenuous or difficult work, and many of his fellow searchers were dissatisfied by its monotony but, as Forster wrote to his friend Malcolm Darling, 'it has quite silenced me, silenced my thoughts I mean, which is what I wanted, and I forge ahead contented & often happy'.[38] It gave him pleasure to 'do the motherly to Tommies', as he described his bedside ministrations to 'Goldie', his Cambridge friend, the political scientist Goldsworthy Lowes Dickinson.[39] Forster was good at listening and very conscientious; and, all in all, the experience was therapeutic for everyone.

He also started to help organise entertainments for the soldiers in hospital – piano recitals, lectures and concerts of classical music – although it was hard to devise the programmes. 'Wounded soldiers make a difficult audience,' he wrote to his mother, '– you must be neither vulgar, unpatriotic, painful or dull, and when all four are forbidden what is left of Poppy?' – as he referred to himself by the pet name his mother had given him as a young boy.[40] 'Your child arose to address a howling mob of 700 Tommies on Classical

Music – how they mustn't suppose it was dreary dull stuff written by old men who died 300 years ago and were mostly German.'[41] He managed to quiet them down and talk 'sense about music instead of that damned superior art patronage', attributing his success to the fact that he loved them.[42] He also gave lectures on ancient Alexandria, which he eventually worked up into a book. These talks, as he mentioned in a letter to his mother, met 'with an amazing variety of fortune' as they did the rounds of the hospitals: on one occasion, to his great discomfort, the commanding officer, who was an ardent archaeologist, turned up with an escort of 'minor luminaries'. Masses of patients too, many too feeble to get away, were ranged row after row into the depths of the hall. 'I delivered myself execrably,' he confessed.[43]

Forster's love for these soldiers in general occasionally took a more particular, personal turn, and he would seize on these opportunities to 'do the brotherly', as well as the 'motherly'. One day, as he was leaving the bedside of a patient, whose interview had yielded no useful information, the patient called Forster back, and to his amazement, claimed that he was 'awfully interested in ideas … more interested in ideas than anything' – 'and blimey so he was', continued Forster, 'and amusing and charming too'.[44] This 'sensitive and intelligent fellow' was Frank Vicary, a ship's steward originally from a farming family in Herefordshire, who read voraciously, devouring 'masses of Dickinson and Shaw'.[45] The two became 'real friends', although Forster was troubled by his attraction to the young man. In a letter to the veteran social reformer Edward Carpenter, Forster groused about his 'physical loneliness' and the 'wretched fastidiousness' that went with it. 'I am sure that some of the decent people I see daily would be willing to save me if they knew, but they don't know, can't know … I sit leaning over them for a bit and there it ends – except for images that burn into my sleep. I know that though you have heard this and sadder cases 1000 times before, you will yet be sympathetic, and that is why you are such a comfort to me. It's awful to live with an unsatisfied craving, now and then smothering it but never killing it or even wanting to …'[46]

His frustrated love for his fellow man slipped into the homoerotic. One of the main convalescent hospitals was housed on the edge of the city, in the extravagant Orientalist palace built at Montazah by the former Khedive for his Austrian mistress. Forster was to get to know the hospital well, for in addition to his searching duties, he spent two spells inside as a patient himself: one for jaundice in December 1916, and the other for a sprained ankle in February 1917. The place made Forster proud of the Red Cross, 'whose show it is', he wrote to his mother, claiming that the wounded soldiers really did forget about the war while they were there: which was why the 'Military authorities do not like it, as too comfortable'.[47] Set amongst tamarisk groves and avenues of flowering oleander, the palace overlooked the bay, with its reefs and fantastic promontories of rocks and breakwaters with steps leading down through the rocks to the sea. He wished 'Goldie' was there with him one morning in July 1916, when he saw hundreds of young men at play, 'fishing, riding donkeys, lying in hammocks, boating, dosing, swimming, listening to bands. They go about bare chested and bare legged, the blue of their linen shorts and the pale mauve of their shirts accenting the brown splendour of their bodies; and down by the sea many of them spend half their days naked and unrebuked.' The sight of so many young men made him 'very happy yet very sad – they came from the unspeakable, all these young gods, and in a fortnight at the least return to it: the beauty of the crest of a wave'.[48] Waves of wounded young men arriving in convoys and then, if fit enough, being sent back to the front.

It was to one of these young gods that, at the age of thirty-seven, Forster eventually lost his virginity – or 'parted with respectability', as he described it in a letter to Florence Barger, his friend and confidante in matters sentimental and sexual: 'I have felt the step would be taken for many months. I have tried to take it before.' The casual encounter left him 'curiously sad', but confirmed for him that what really drove him, even more than a physical hunger, was a longing for intimacy. 'Perhaps – but I'm not hopeful – it may be better for the next generation, even for the men and women in it who are like me. My life has *not* been unhappy, but it has been too dam lop sided for words and physically dam lonely.' He was beginning to realise that, despite the practical difficulties, he had to seize opportunities for affection rather than to be fearful of them.[49]

This consciousness that future generations should not have to suffer as he had became even stronger during his 'anxious but very beautiful'[50] love affair with Mohammed el Adl, the young Egyptian tram conductor whom Forster met in 1917. 'When I am with him,' he confided to Florence, 'smoking or talking quietly ahead, or whatever it may be, I see, beyond my own happiness and intimacy, occasional glimpses of the happiness of 1000s of others whose names I shall never hear, and know that there is a great unrecorded history.'[51]

Alexandria, then, was the city where for Forster 'the last barrier'[52] had fallen, where he freed himself from the paralysis of desire, fear and fastidiousness. This Mediterranean city on the edge of the Arab world had a liberating effect on him, thousands of miles from the 'small and somewhat suburban'[53] home he shared with his mother in Weybridge, or the closeted, cloistered world of his Cambridge friends.

'In some ways I have never been so free,' he wrote to Goldie in 1916.[54] He was open to new experiences. He taught himself to swim. He visited a hashish den, sneaking up 'the pitch black stairs in a slum', before scratching tentatively at the door at the top; although Forster himself didn't smoke hashish, or succumb to the attentions of the extraordinarily beautiful young man who came to sit down beside him, he 'felt curiously at ease in that haunt of vice, and didn't even realise [he] was behaving priggishly till afterwards'.[55] And, in March 1918, he went flying for the first time: this experience, of what scientists had aimed at and poets dreamed of for centuries, filling him with awe. 'There is nothing mystic in aviation,' he wrote, 'but no earthly pleasure resembles it. It has opened a new kingdom of material beauty …'[56]

The city was the backdrop to his first proper love affair, and to the happiness and fulfilment he found with Mohammed. He did not even fear the separation when Mohammed was offered a job away from Alexandria, for although it was terrible to be parted from him, he was 'freed for ever from the burden of loneliness and failure that has oppressed me for so many years. I wish every one could have my luck and come at last into the light.'[57]

Forster grew to like the city that had so disappointed him on arrival, and he began to describe it. 'I never thought to write another book, and the mere fact of being able to concentrate is a pleasure,' he told his mother.[58] The researching of *Alexandria: A History and a Guide*, which had at first been conceived with the convalescent soldiers in mind, helped to unblock his writing. 'I'm constructing by archaeological and other means an immense ghost city,' he wrote to Siegfried Sassoon as his guide took shape.[59] In the book, he reimagined a city that had lived upon its past as much as its present, bringing to life its ancient glories architecturally, intellectually and spiritually. He was 'touring in time',[60] he told Florence Barger. 'The "sights" of Alexandria,' he wrote, 'are in themselves not interesting, but they fascinate when we approach them through the past.'[61] There was nothing to be seen of its lighthouse, one of the Seven Wonders of the Ancient World, its light long extinguished, except in the imagination, its pathetic ruins submerged beneath the waters of the harbour. But in his guide, Forster recreated the building, imagining the procession of donkeys going up and down its spiral stairway, night and day, to deliver wood as fuel for its blazing lantern. He also mentioned the ex-Khedive's summer palace at Montazah, through which had passed thousands of convalescent soldiers who, like Forster, 'will never forget the beauty and the comfort that they found there'.[62]

During these formative years in Alexandria, Forster also wrote what he described as 'imaginative sketches' about Alexandrian life. Most of these were published in the *Egyptian Mail*, an English-language newspaper, and then brought together in a collection published as *Pharos and Pharillon*. One of them captured a chance encounter with the poet Cavafy in the street: turning on hearing his name called, Forster saw 'a Greek gentleman in a straw hat, standing absolutely motionless at a slight angle to the universe'.[63] Another compared the pandemonium of the Alexandrian Bourse, or cotton exchange, to a vision from Dante's Inferno. These gently satirical vignettes signalled a move in Forster towards non-fiction, in the form of history, biography, and literary journalism after the war.

Forster found that he was rather good at his role as a searcher, reporting, in a letter to his mother, how Miss Grant Duff had described him as 'the best person she had got and so useful to her in other ways'. 'So there's for Miss Bell!' he gloated.[64] It was later that year that Lord Northcliffe quoted his report on Flight Sub-Lieutenant Gasson in *At the War*; and in 1917, the Red Cross's Annual Report singled out the Alexandria office for special commendation, with 'private words of praise' from 'our people in London' for Forster.[65] Not only did he find many aspects of his work satisfying, he also threw himself into office politics. For two years, 1917 and 1918 – with the exception of his writings on Alexandria and his reports for the Enquiry Department – the literary output of one of the finest writers of the early twentieth century was dominated, in letters to friends and family, by mordant descriptions of office life and his colleagues: Miss Penfold, for example, 'the typist from below stairs, [who] is to give two hours of her most incompetent assistance daily, while I am to be eased by the ponderous figure of Judge Cator, an overbearing and meddlesome old man. I have stowed him away to No. 19 Hospital (the road to which is infested with flies) and there I hope he will stop.' He was scathing, too, about the Cairo office, where a chaplain, who 'seems intellectually no great shakes', had become a searcher, producing reports such as 'some one told me he had heard Jones was wounded' – that were 'perfectly useless as evidence'. When the question arose of whether the chaplain's reports should be forwarded direct to London from Cairo or via Alexandria, Forster seized 'the malevolent opportunity of scrapping the Chaplain's reports should [he] think fit, and preventing them ever seeing the light of an English day'.[66]

More serious, though, was the row with Miss Grant Duff – or 'Miss Goose Duff', as she now became in his letters to his mother. Tensions began to mount in the summer of 1917, as Grant Duff's apparent inability to delegate exacerbated the build-up of work.

There were 'masses and masses of men to interview and to ask about',[67] and on top of that, there was all the report-writing, the typing and card-indexing, the answering of local enquiries, the organising of photographs of graves, and the daily cable to send to London. Forster, whose tricky relationship with powerful women tended at times towards the misogynistic, even considered asking Furness, 'who is rather efficacious with the ladies', for advice.[68] When Miss Grant Duff was in hospital with typhoid in August 1917, Forster was confused by the work she had left behind: 'Everything higgledy-piggledy,' he complained, '– she knew her way about the chaos but no one else does.'[69]

Matters came to a head in October 1917 when, in recognition of his obvious efficiency and the excellence of his reports, Forster was appointed 'Head Searcher for Egypt' over his erstwhile boss – with the additional duties of preparing lists for the other searchers, and revising their reports. Grant Duff regarded this as a 'slap in the face'[70] and threatened to resign. She wouldn't speak to Forster, and for months they worked together in frosty silence. 'Oh how tiresome it all is,' Forster lamented in a letter to his mother, 'and how it obscures our sole raison d'être – that of furnishing news to relatives. The love of power is a terrific thing, especially when conjoined with shattered nerves.'[71]

Forster was eventually forced to write to the London office of the British Red Cross Wounded and Missing Enquiry Department for help in resolving the stand-off. In a letter to Percy Lubbock, who had helped him get the job in the first place, he described how, since his appointment as Head Searcher, Grant Duff had become very difficult. 'Our intercourse has sunk to the minimum, and is largely conducted in writing.'[72] He was also now concerned by 'Miss Grant Duff's attitude to her own searching', as she had done no searching in the two hospitals assigned to her. The London office came down on Forster's side. Lubbock had shown Forster's letter to Lord Lucan, the director of the department, and they were agreed that they would not be inconsolable in the event of Grant Duff's resignation and departure, '& I can't think you will be either. It seems to all of us that she has really been there long enough.

Her own conception of her position has grown in her own head, unencouraged, out of all knowledge.'[73]

Although the affair dragged on, poisoning the atmosphere, Victoria Grant Duff continued to hang about the office, even after her resignation in March 1918. When, at last, she finally departed in June, Forster had no regrets. 'Life in our office is so pleasant since poor Miss Grant Duff left,' Forster wrote to his aunt Laura in August; 'I feel I have had my share of overbearing and intractable females since I worked for the Red X …'[74] To his mother, he acknowledged that she was 'of course in great pain – a tragic figure, but I have suffered too much from her to feel any pity. My sensations with regard to her have all dried up.'[75] She was just one of thousands, he felt, whose characters had fallen to pieces during the war. After the war, Grant Duff stayed on in Egypt, eventually dying of injuries sustained when kicked by the racehorse on whom she had spent what little money she had left.

During his lifetime, Forster published little or nothing about his war work; and it was not until 2008 that a ten-page section of the journal he kept throughout his life came out. The 'Incidents of War Memoir', as he called it, was written between November 1915 and July 1917 and consisted of notes taken from his interviews with wounded soldiers, of fragments overheard, with little or no commentary or reflection from the author himself. It was an abbreviated record of the days Forster had spent sitting beside hospital beds, teasing from the patients the jagged shards of their most traumatic memories and transcribing them into a notebook. 'Scraps' is how Forster starkly described his first entry from Alexandria, written after two weeks of working in the hospitals: 'The earth is full of dead – their arms and legs stick out. When a mine is exploded they are so mixed that when the digging recommences one had often to cut through corpses. They lie between the trenches after a charge and the smell of them is awful when there's a hot sun and a bit of wind. Sometimes a shot hits them, increasing their stench – they get blown all over the place. Two men, while sheltering from Turkish shells, came across a packet of them in a gully and preferred the shells.'[76]

This nightmarish scrapbook of experiences captured the sights and sounds and smells of the war, firstly during the disastrous Gallipoli campaign. The dead Tommies, as well as the Turks, still hanging from the barbed wire entanglements weeks after an action. The captain with 'two bullets in his Privates', and froth coming out of his mouth. The dead mules tossed into the sea that kept floating back, even when towed out again behind a rowing boat. The dead men, too, washed up on the beaches having been thrown overboard the hospital ships: only later were orders issued to weight them properly. The vision of the 'hellish Peninsula', provided by the wounded soldiers, fuelled Forster's rejection of the war, as he wrote to Goldie soon after his arrival in Alexandria. 'The war oppresses me in its viler aspects – I mean I am frightened of being conscripted or otherwise inconvenienced or hurt. I think too I am coming round to peace at any price – was never far from it perhaps, but here it's rubbed in day by day, and still more night by night that all the suffering and disease I see ought to be stopped at the cost of any humiliation.'[77]

The snippets provided by his 'informers' were dispassionate about the brutalities of everyday life and, literally, deadpan in their acceptance of death: the last words of a dying soldier reported by one of Forster's informants were 'Goodbye Sergeant. I'll turn over and die quietly.' He was 'Dead in ¼ hour', the informant concluded.[78] The soldiers were typically matter-of-fact in their recall of the horrors. The officer who had gone 'out of his mind' and insisted his men should bury a Turk alive rather than shoot him. The corpse so blown to pieces by a shell that he had to be shovelled into a bag. And the dead Australian who got in the way of a trench parapet, with the result that his comrades had simply to cut him at the neck and knees in order to fire through him.

Recorded verbatim, the entries captured the speech patterns of the soldiers, down to the stammered repetition of the shellshocked. For example, a Private Young of 8th Battalion, Manchester Regiment, 'after giving careful evidence for 20 minutes', got stuck: 'I never like any one to ask me about it – it leaves a bad taste in the mouth. I think of the days again, of the days again …'[79] Similarly, the private letters to mothers, wives and sweethearts, which Forster and his friend Aïda Borchgrevink extracted and transcribed, captured the vernacular of the soldiers' written words: the Christmas letter, for example, written by a private to his wife, which describes the army of bugs, 'as long as bats and stings worser than wasps and they bite sharper than crocurdiles [*sic*]'.[80]

The 'Incidents of War Memoir' provides a poignant oral history of the British Tommy, decades before such studies became popular. It gives voice to the working-class soldier, his culture and concerns, strengths and vulnerabilities. It records the things the Tommies said about the Turks ('you can understand them being so religious when you think of what they've got to look forward to – 8000 servants each'[81]); and about their British officers. One informer conceded that: 'Officers are all right in peace time but when it's sympathy they fail. "Excuse me, sir, is it correct my pal's been killed?" "I'm sorry my poor man, I'm afraid I don't know," and off to the canteen for a drink twirling his cane.'[82] Another informant recalled the officer, a religious man who was always trying to improve his men while incidentally treating them 'like dogs', who 'funked' at leading his men over the top: they bumped him over the parapet where he lay before coming back with a nervous breakdown. Such observations amount to a general cynicism about the officer class, leading on one occasion to the celebration 'of the one thing that "cheered the Regt. up that day and that was the Colonel getting killed. The fellows all waved and shouted."'[83]

Forster's Tommy is not particularly patriotic or self-consciously heroic. One of his 'heroes' 'didn't want no Turkey bullets', and so went sick before the charge; another 'hero', a Sergeant Corrigan of the Sussex Yeomanry, often thought as he lay in his hospital bed of all the foolish things he had done: 'Enlisting! King & Country! Godstrewth! I'll watch them! I don't want to go into battle any more. No place for me. They throw things at you and don't even say they're sorry. Nasty horrid things too. I don't care what country I belong to, provided I've my home. Once I get back to England – I'll watch them!'[84]

There is a short passage in the memoir specifically on friendship, and a strong sense of camaraderie throughout. 'Men are more than brotherly after the baptism of fire,' one of his informants told him.[85] They made crosses to mark the graves of fallen mates, wrote with sympathy to the sweethearts of dead men. As Forster concluded in a letter to his mother of February 1918: 'If I did not naturally like Tommies I could not bear it all, but they are so pleasant – not just to me, but to one another.'[86] It is this which Forster came to believe was the story of the war: a record, not necessarily of heroic events, but of individual experiences, of friendship, compassion, and solidarity between soldiers, of men who wanted peace just as their enemies did.

'I consort only with Tommies and others who have no interest in, or illusion about, bloodshed,' he wrote to Goldie after a few months in Alexandria.[87] The longer he stayed, the more he got to like them. 'They are neither intellectual [n]or sensitive, but their instincts are both good and strong and lead them to sensible and kindly conclusions, and they are brave without enthusiasm, which seems to me the finest type of bravery. They are in several ways a relief from the newspaper-fed middle classes from whom our officers are recruited now ...'[88] Forster was beginning to realise just how out of touch he had become with his own class.

Forster's sympathies lay principally with the common soldiers, and not with officers. 'I am sick to the death of the sight and sound of officers, and they seemed so unapproachable and romantic once,' he wrote to his mother after a visit to the Victoria Hospital, which was 'full of very hard cases' – men wounded at Gallipoli. 'Tommies, since I always meet them under such pathetic circumstances, appear different. ... The men are not only thankful to be off themselves but thankful every one else is off. "Death or victory" is to be found in English drawing rooms and pulpits, not at this end of the stick ...'[89] He shared with the poet and war hero Siegfried Sassoon a contempt for the officer class, and the corrupting effects of power: 'Give a man power over the other men, and he deteriorates at once. The "troops" are decent and charming, I believe, not because they suffer but because they are powerless. – And the devil who rules this planet has contrived that those who are powerless shall suffer.'[90] As a result,

Forster was beginning to wish that after the war the country could be governed by soldiers – 'by the young men who have been hurled against each other and have seen the filth and futility that results: not of course by the Staff Officers and militarist bureaucrats who probably will govern us, and to whom Socialism would be preferable …'.[91]

In his fury at the conduct of the war, Forster drew particular attention to the British censorship of military news. After a defeat by the Turks in Gaza in April 1917, which 'men who have fought at Gallipoli say [it] was more terrible than anything they knew there', he complained to his friend George Barger about the positive spin given to the official reports. Everyone in Egypt knows 'we have been knocked', he wrote. 'The sole result of the censorship is to conceal what has happened from England. The men are disgusted. "It makes one wild, knowing what it was, to be told you've won a victory" is a common remark; and one chap put it to the parson that it wasn't much to the credit of Christianity that our communiqués should lie more than the Turks!'[92]

Forster's distaste for the delusions practised by government and society was also directed at the fake 'cheeriness' of individuals, 'that shoots like a fungus from the decaying substance of the spirit, and convinces one that war also entails an inward death. It has taken the place of all the old healthy growths – love, joy, thought, despair – deluding men by its semblance of vitality, whether they be in the trenches or out of them, and tempting them "not to mind", either for themselves or for others, what ought to be minded down to such depths as one has of soul.'[93]

As he reproduced the words of the convalescent soldiers, and captured their feelings and preoccupations, Forster came to some conclusions. 'Sometimes I make notes on human nature under war conditions,' he wrote to the philosopher Bertrand Russell, reflecting on his first two years, 'harmless and unharmed', in Alexandria. 'I don't write, but I feel I think & think I feel … I love people & want to understand them & help them more than I did.'[94] Just as his own humanity and fellow feelings matured as a result of his daily contact with soldiers – finding expression in small practical acts of kindness – he came to believe ever more strongly and philosophically in the individual rather than the collective.

Forster's notes on 'Human Nature under War Conditions' concluded his 'Incidents of War Memoir': 'It is easier to personify an enemy nation than one's own owing to one's greater ignorance of the items that compose it. Only by believing in a Germany have we become patriotic, just as we remained religious only while we could believe in a Devil.' Forster was developing a horror of institutions and power structures. 'Privately most men attain to love and unselfishness and insight, and a priori one would expect them to display these qualities in their social life, for they certainly bring earnestness of purpose to it. But some psychological hitch takes place, and an observer from another planet who watched not only the earth's wars but its institutions would never infer what sweetness and nobility there can be in intercourse between individuals.'[95]

Underlying all these writings was a deep-seated desire for peace. One of the great paradoxical revelations of the war for Forster, as he wrote to Virginia Woolf, was that he talked about the war all day 'to people who can say "we fought as dirty as the Turks", and whose deepest wish is peace at once'.[96] Even after the end of the war he still worried that the peace was fragile: 'It's not my peace any more than it was my war, and I feel mortally aloof from the rejoicings. It's nice to see the soldiers' happy faces, and to think that the present slaughter has ceased, but the fear recurs that nothing has been learnt by the world and that it's incapable of learning …'[97]

Through his oral histories, Forster developed a greater understanding of himself, of humanity and of the very nature of history itself. This was less about the great and 'solemn' sweep of movements than about the actual lived experiences of individuals, as told to him by the Tommies. Forster suspected that, with the exception of Gibbon, all other histories would 'shatter into dust'. 'The Hospitals here are full of such dust – boys calling out "Oh Lord have mercy on me, Oh take this thing away", or even more terribly "I'm in a fix, I'm in a fix."' He felt 'a wave of helpless indignation that still shakes me so that I look down the ward at the suffering and the efforts of the able doctors and nurses to alleviate it and wonder how long the waste must all go on … Damn justice, damn honour. They were good enough trimmings for peace time, but the supreme need now is the preservation of life. Let us look after bodies that there may be a next generation which may have the right to look after the soul.'[98]

In 1922 Virginia Woolf painted a sorry picture of Forster returning to Weybridge one day: 'to come back to an ugly house a mile from the station, an old, fussy, exacting mother, to come back … without a novel, and with no power to write one – this is dismal, I expect, at the age of 43. The middle age of buggers is not to be contemplated without horror.'[99] But it was an unfairly dismal picture. For Forster's years in Egypt as a searcher, and the empathy he felt for the common soldier, had transformed his life. His quest for a connection with another human being, for an affection and intimacy that transcended race and class, was closer to fulfilment. He began to see the world through the eyes of the British Tommy – just as, in a parallel development, he began to see life in Egypt, with all its slights and injustices, through the eyes of Mohammed. When Leonard Woolf invited him to contribute to a Labour Party pamphlet on the 'Egyptian question', Forster's introduction on the historical, social and political conditions was critical of the continuing British occupation: he was writing it, he told himself, for Mohammed's sake.

Gradually, Forster acquired a new understanding of class and colonialism, a championing of the underdog, which would become ever more apparent in his writing, especially his non-fiction. His experience was just one example of how that most humane of bureaucracies, the Red Cross Wounded and Missing Enquiry Department, which eased 'the sorest wounds of warfare' for the families of the missing and for the 'fighting men themselves', also brought comfort and satisfaction to the individual searchers. His reflections also highlighted the twin threads, the individual and the collective, that were woven into the way in which the war and the war dead were to be remembered.

3

The Search for a National Shrine: The Cenotaph and the Tomb of the Unknown Warrior

In early 1916, a young army chaplain called David Railton had just returned from a burial service on the front line, when he had an idea that was to transform the way the British people remembered their war dead. At the bottom of the small garden of a cottage where he was billeted, at Erquinghem-Lys, near Armentières, he noticed a single grave with a plain, white wooden cross, on which was written in black pencil: 'An Unknown Soldier (of the Black Watch)'.

'It was dusk,' Railton recalled in an article on 'The Origin of the Unknown Warrior's Grave', 'and no one was near, except some officers in the billet playing cards. I remember how still it was. Even the guns seemed to be resting, as if to give their gunners a chance to have their tea.' All he knew was that the dead soldier was Scottish; but how he longed to see his folk. Who was he, and who were they? The more he thought, the more determined he became 'to ease the pain' of father, mother, brother, sister, sweetheart, wife and friend. 'Quietly and gradually there came out of the mist of thought this answer clear and strong, "Let this body – this symbol of him – be carried reverently over the sea to his native land."' Railton never thought at first that much would come of his brainwave, as so many good ideas were falling victim to 'the most common remark of those days – "There is a war on"'. But he could not dismiss the idea entirely.[1]

Life for chaplains on the front line was hard – and as dangerous as it was for any soldier (Railton was awarded the Military Cross in the autumn of 1916, 'for conspicuous gallantry in action', rescuing a fellow officer and two men under heavy fire[2]). It also presented huge theological challenges for which many chaplains were ill-prepared. Railton was not alone in having his faith severely tested by his experiences in France and Flanders. 'I have been out all day,' he was to write on 4 January 1917, 'tramp, tramp, tramp and of course – death and suffering somewhere or other as usual. If our Lord had not suffered on this earth on the Cross, I would blaspheme God all day if I believed in God at all. I only believe in God in this war because I believe in Jesus Christ the Crucified. Even then my thoughts – often – would not bear production. How old-time people believed in God, I cannot think – I mean people before the time of the Incarnation.'[3]

There were also the great pastoral challenges of coping with collective loss on such a scale. Railton did his best to comfort bereaved relatives searching for the whereabouts of their fallen loved ones. 'Every Padre,' he wrote, 'serving with infantry brigades was bombarded after each publication of casualties with at least this request. "Where – exactly where – did you lay to rest the body of my son? Can you give me any further information? I have been officially notified that he is "missing, believed killed". To all these questions we were allowed to send a "map reference" only. Oh, those letters of "broken" relatives and friends!'[4] It was these letters that prevented him from dropping the idea.

Railton noticed in these letters a phenomenon that psychologists have subsequently identified as the effects of 'ambiguous loss': that 'those who mourned relatives or friends who were in the casualty list as killed but who were unidentified or whose graves were unknown seemed to be more distressed for one reason or another than people who had been told the exact location of the grave upon which had been put a cross with the name of their loved ones inscribed'. He realised the therapeutic benefits of 'the reverent burial of the mortal remains' of those they had lost, or at least 'a service with some simple symbolism showing both honour to him who had fallen and voicing the hope of immortality and re-union'. How, he wondered, could the 'unknown' as well as the known 'be sufficiently honoured in the minds of Englishmen'?[5]

As the war came to an end, Railton considered writing to Field Marshal Haig, the Archbishop of Canterbury, the prime minister, and even the king with his idea for the Tomb of the Unknown Warrior, but he never thought the time was quite right. Most people, he feared, would accuse it of 'the luxury of idealism' and would 'simply laugh at the notion of taking the mortal remains of an Unknown Soldier or Sailor back to Blighty to be enshrined in the heart of London'.[6] He was confident that the king would consider the idea at least, but worried that 'His Majesty's advisers might suggest an open space like Trafalgar Square, Hyde Park, or the Horse Guards for the Tomb of the Unknown Comrade. Then the artists would come, and no one could tell what weird structure they might devise for a Shrine! There could be only one true Shrine for this purpose. The Unknown Comrade's body should rest, if it were possible, in Westminster Abbey – the Parish Church of the Empire. Sometimes I thought of sending this suggestion to one of the newspapers; but who is there that would risk so great a matter becoming a newspaper "stunt"?'[7]

Railton was finding it hard to adjust to peacetime England, recalling years later 'that dreadful year of reaction' after the end of the war. 'Men and nations stumbled back ... the endless shedding of blood ceased, but there was no real peace in the souls of men or nations. The mind of the world was in fever.' In August 1920, he asked himself once again whether the time was right. His wife Ruby, who had just given birth to twins, told him that it was 'Now or never!'[8]

And so, on 13 August, he wrote to the Dean of Westminster, the Right Reverend Herbert Ryle, asking him to consider 'the possibility of burying in the Abbey the body of one of our unknown comrades'. A soldier, he suggested, should be selected from the thousands of those who had no known grave, and brought back to England to represent all those who had fallen. He also 'made bold to suggest that a real "War" flag in [his] possession be used at such a burial, rather than a new flag of no "Service" experience'.[9]

The idea of commemorating the Armistice like this appealed to the dean, but he was on holiday in Harrogate at the time and needed time to allow it to 'germinate'[10] and to canvas opinion. In October, Dean Ryle wrote to the king's private secretary, Lord Stamfordham, asking him to approach the king, claiming at first that the idea was his own: 'There are thousands of graves, I am told, of English "Tommies" who fell at the front – names not known. My idea is that one such body (name not known), should be exhumed and interred in Westminster Abbey in the Nave.'[11]

The king was initially inclined to think that the two years since the last shot had been fired on the battlefields of France and Flanders was so long ago 'that a funeral now might be regarded as belated, and almost, as it were, re-open war wounds which time is gently healing'.[12] Support for the plan, however, from the prime minister and from Field Marshal Sir Henry Wilson, the Chief of the Imperial General Staff, encouraged him to change his mind.

As with so many good, simple, but hardly unique ideas, various people, as well as the dean, claimed it as their own. A *Daily Express* news editor, J. B. Wilson, had campaigned in September 1919 for an unknown soldier to be buried in Whitehall – and the idea was picked up the following month by Colonel Wilfrid Ashley MP, who raised the matter unsuccessfully in the House of Commons. In France, after a campaign led by the war veteran Jean-Auguste-Gustave Binet-Valmer, the French had decided to bury their own Unknown Warrior, or *poilu inconnu*, at the Arc de Triomphe: a ceremony that was to take place at the same time on Armistice Day 1920 as the British burial in Westminster Abbey of the Unknown Warrior.

In the 'Story of the Padre's Flag', a semi-fictional account by David Railton of his flag's adventures, the author assumed the voice of his flag to tell of some of these rival claims. These 'claimants', the flag observed, included editors of papers and even a Church paper.

'He [Railton] has told some of them that it doesn't matter a brass pin who first had the idea; any ideas that are good come from God who inspires men. So in any case there is nothing to brag about. But another time when any idea that concerns the public comes to you, first choose your time and then approach some great and sympathetic leader of the church. Don't scribble about it in the papers (not even church papers) or jabber about it in drawing-rooms or even in Parliament. But go to a man like the Dean of Westminster who will get a move on and carry things out beyond your wildest hopes.'[13]

Railton's idea had been presented to the right person at the right moment. It filled a void at a time when 'there was no real peace in the souls of men or nations'.[14] Two ceremonies the previous year had revealed a need for some public commemoration of the war dead as profound as for the celebration of the military victory. In July 1919 the prime minister David Lloyd George was planning a morale-boosting victory parade, as part of the Peace Day celebrations to mark the signing on 28 June of the Treaty of Versailles. He was well aware of the discontent of many demobilised soldiers, unemployed and wounded; and wanted to divert attention from the hard economic times and labour unrest. Lloyd George also wanted the rejoicing to be accompanied by some sombre recognition of the million British dead. He had, at first, considered commissioning a catafalque, a temporary structure carrying a coffin on the parade route, as he had learned the French were to do in their celebrations in Paris on 14 July; and had invited the architect Sir Edwin Lutyens to Downing Street in early July, with this in mind. Within hours, Lutyens had come up with sketches for a 'cenotaph' – literally an empty tomb in Ancient Greek – to represent those bodies that never returned from the field of battle. Although the concept and the architectural features were rooted in the classical world – wreaths, ribbons, cornices and a sarcophagus on top – Lutyens's cenotaph was modern in character. The architect always resisted any attempts to add figurative details, such as the life-size bronze sentries at the four corners of the cenotaph that others suggested. There were no overt political or social messages, no sentimental trappings. The only words his cenotaph bore were to 'The Glorious Dead' – a tribute to the fallen rather than a reference to a military triumph. Above all, his elegantly austere cenotaph was non-denominational. There were no signs of the Cross, no brooding angels or any other Christian iconography; nothing to alienate the faiths of those who had fought for the British Empire: Hindu or Muslim, Jew or Sikh.

Lutyens's design was swiftly transformed into a temporary structure, made like a stage set from wood and plaster painted grey to look like stone. It was this memorial to 'The Glorious Dead' which 15,000 troops from the fourteen Allied nations, accompanied by all the latest military hardware, saluted as they marched down Whitehall on 19 July 1919. Once the parade had passed, 'something unexpected happened'[15] – in the words of the architectural historian, Gavin Stamp. In the wake of the troops, thousands of people began to lay wreaths at the Cenotaph, with the result that what had been conceived as a military celebration had been transformed by the people's response into an act of commemoration. From being a war memorial, the Cenotaph had become a place – as the press described it for the first time – of pilgrimage (and one that was considerably easier and cheaper to reach than the Western front).

'No feature of the Victory March in London,' *The Times* reported, 'made a deeper or worthier impression than the Cenotaph erected in Whitehall, to the memory of "The Glorious Dead". Simple, grave and beautiful in design, it has been universally recognised as a just and fitting memorial of those who have made the greatest sacrifice; and the flowers which have daily been laid upon it since the march, show the strength of its appeal to the imagination. It ought undoubtedly to be retained, in a more permanent form among the monuments of London …'[16]

As many as half a million people visited the Cenotaph in the last week of July 1919, laying their wreaths at its base, and they kept on coming through the second of the two ceremonies of that year, the Armistice events of November 1919, and then over Christmas. The popularity of the Armistice Day commemorations took the authorities by surprise – with extra police having to be drafted in to control the crowds. As Lutyens himself observed, in his *Journal of Remembrance*: 'Time passed and the plain fact emerged and grew stronger every hour, that the Cenotaph was what the people wanted, and that they wanted to have the wood and plaster original replaced by an identical memorial in lasting stone. It was a mass feeling too deep to express itself more fitly than by the piles of good fresh flowers which loving hands placed on the Cenotaph day by day. Thus it was decided, by the human sentiment of millions, that the Cenotaph should be as it is now, and speaking as the designer I would wish for no greater honour and lasting satisfaction.'[17]

People were soon calling for the temporary monument to be made permanent – spurred on by the hyperbole of the newspapers which piled on the emotional pressure. An article in the *Daily Mail* championed the idea that the Cenotaph should remain in Whitehall as the memorial had already been 'consecrated with the tears of many mothers'.[18] Months before the Cenotaph was dismantled in January 1920 – by which time the flimsy monument had begun to fall apart – the decision had been made to rebuild it on its current site in Whitehall. Lutyens translated his design into Portland stone. The memorial's simplicity was deceptive. The 'vertical' sides of the Cenotaph taper almost imperceptibly towards the top, drawing the eye up towards the empty sarcophagus and focusing the viewer's attention on the death of a single, symbolic individual. Such optical effects are the result of detailed mathematical calculations that were said to have occupied thirty-three pages of notebook.

Some leaders of the established Church were deeply suspicious of the public's enthusiasm for a permanent, secular Cenotaph in Whitehall – the cult of 'cenotapholatry' the *Church Times* called it.[19] They welcomed Railton's idea for a rival, obviously Christian shrine next door, which could be used to appropriate the nation's grief. Railton's letter to Dean Ryle suggesting a Tomb of the Unknown Warrior arrived as the Armistice events for 1920 were being planned. The authorities had at first envisaged a great state funeral, as might befit a monarch or a military hero, with the public there as spectators rather than as participants. But the events of 1919, and the continuing public response to the Cenotaph, had caused them to think again. David Railton's idea had struck a chord.

On 19 October 1920, the dean wrote to Railton, who had by now almost given up hope of his vision being realised, to tell him that 'the idea which you suggested to me in August, I have kept steadily in view ever since'.[20] Over the past few weeks, he had been in touch with the War Office, the prime minister, the Cabinet and Buckingham Palace; and was expecting an announcement from the prime minister that afternoon, to show how far the government was ready to cooperate. Railton, for his part, was 'overwhelmed with joy'.[21]

With just over three weeks to go to Armistice Day, a Memorial Service Committee was established under the chairmanship of Lord Curzon. Its task was to organise the burial in Westminster Abbey with full military honours of the Unknown Warrior, in a ceremony to be combined with the unveiling of the permanent Cenotaph. The advantages of such a ceremony, the committee concluded, would be that 'it would generally be acceptable to the people; that it would do honour to the great mass of fighting men; that it would furnish a Memorial to them in Westminster Abbey, without singling out for such distinction any one known man. At present Westminster Abbey has no memorial of the Great War.'[22]

Railton was full of praise for 'this most noble Dean', without whose consent and aid, 'the Shrine could never have been in the Abbey'.[23] The dean also agreed to accept the padre's flag for use in the burial ceremony, 'provided that it is in a condition not unsuitable for the occasion'.[24] Railton's wife, Ruby, had to patch some tears before Railton took it up on the train to London from Margate, where he had recently been appointed vicar of St John the Baptist Church.

The only request the noble dean 'did not see his way to grant' was Railton's suggestion that the tomb should be described as that of the Unknown 'Comrade' rather than 'Warrior'. This may have 'seemed more homely and friendly'[25] to Railton, whose strong social conscience had been forged during the war. (He had, for example, promised Ruby in a letter from the trenches in January 1917: 'If God spares me I shall spend half my life in getting their rights for the men who fought out here.'[26]) But to some this suggestion reeked of Bolshevism. In any case, the word 'Warrior' was preferred to 'Soldier' as it included servicemen from the navy and air force as well as the army.

The selection of the body of the Unknown Warrior was a matter of great sensitivity. For the sake of the bereaved, there had to be complete anonymity. There needed to be just enough grounds for hope that the body might belong to their loved one, but enough certainty that the body could not, for example, be that of a German.

Such was the secrecy surrounding the selection that various conflicting accounts emerged; and an aura of mystery enveloped the process. The most authentic account is that of Brigadier General L. J. Wyatt, who was in command of British troops in France and Flanders in 1920, and had been tasked with the selection. It was Wyatt who issued the instructions for the body of a British soldier, which had to be impossible to identify, to be brought from each of the four main battle areas: the Aisne, the Somme, Arras and Ypres. Exhumation parties, each consisting of an officer and two soldiers equipped with shovels and sacks, were dispatched with orders to take a body from a grave marked 'Unknown British Soldier', preferably from the early years of the war. This would ensure that the bodies were decomposed enough to be unidentifiable, yet clothed and shod in shreds of uniform and boots that were evidently British. The bodies were then loaded onto field ambulances and driven to Wyatt's headquarters at St-Pol-sur-Ternoise. Here they were received by the Reverend George Kendall and inspected again for signs that they were British but otherwise unidentifiable. The four bodies, 'which were nothing but a collection of bones, placed in Sacks',[27] and lying on canvas stretchers, according to Wyatt's handwritten account, were then covered with Union Jack flags and left for the night in a chapel in a corrugated steel hut. At midnight Wyatt entered the chapel and selected one of the bodies at random (some accounts, but not his, suggest that he did this blindfolded). Wyatt and one of his senior officers, Lieutenant Colonel Gell, placed this body in a plain pine coffin that had been sent from England and screwed down the lid. The three other bodies were removed and reburied in a military cemetery nearby.

The following day, 9 November, began with a service in the makeshift chapel led by the Church of England, the Roman Catholic and the Nonconformist chaplains. The coffin was driven in an ambulance with a military escort to Boulogne, where it arrived at the medieval castle in the afternoon. A temporary *chapelle ardente* – the chapel where, traditionally, the bodies of the good and the great might lay in candlelit state before their funerals – had been created in the officers' mess. Here, the pine coffin was placed in a casket made of oak from the gardens of Hampton Court Palace. A Crusader's sword – a symbol of heroic sacrifice – from the king's collection at the Tower of London was placed on top, secured by the wrought iron bands which bound the coffin.

After its overnight vigil, the body of the Unknown Warrior (or *Tommy anonyme*, as the French called him) began his journey back to England. The coffin was carried from the chapel and placed on a military wagon drawn by six black horses. As it left the castle, it joined a procession about a mile long which set off down the hill towards the port to the strains of Chopin's *Funeral March*. The streets of Boulogne were lined with soldiers, citizens and schoolchildren, and festooned with flags.

A British destroyer, HMS *Verdun* (named after the ten-month battle in 1916 at which the French had resisted the Germans), lay waiting at the docks, with its Union flag flying at half-mast. In a voice thickened with emotion, Marshal Foch, the Allied Commander-in-Chief during the war, expressed 'the profound feelings of France for the invincible heroism of the British Army', and his deep personal regard for 'the body of this hero as a souvenir of the future and as a reminder to work in common to cement the victories we have gained by Eternal Union'.[28]

The eight bearers then carried the coffin on board. It was followed by six barrels of earth taken from the battlefields of the Ypres Salient, which were to be used in the burial of the Unknown Warrior in Westminster Abbey, 'so that the body should rest in the soil on which so many of our troops gave up their lives';[29] and by wreaths of white lilies, roses and chrysanthemums so big that some required four soldiers to carry them.

At 11.45 a.m., a nineteen-gun salute was fired, the national anthem played, and HMS *Verdun* set sail for home, escorted from the middle of the Channel by six British destroyers: HMS *Witherington*, HMS *Wanderer*, HMS *Whitshed*, HMS *Wivern*, HMS *Wolverine* and HMS *Veteran*. Soon after 3 p.m., HMS *Verdun* emerged slowly from the sea mist, and could be seen by the crowds lining the docks in Dover for a first sight of the vessel carrying the Unknown Warrior.

The programme of ceremonies that had marked HMS *Verdun*'s departure from Boulogne was mirrored on her arrival at Dover, with the firing of a nineteen-gun salute from the ramparts of the castle, and the playing of 'Land of Hope and Glory'. The Unknown Warrior was one of very few dead British soldiers to be brought back home. Ironically, the occupant of what was to become the war's most visited grave was the one dead soldier since 1915 who, flouting the Commonwealth War Graves Commission's protocols, had been legally repatriated, as hundreds of thousands had not.

Six bearers boarded the ship and carried the coffin down the gangplank on to Admiralty Pier, and off to Dover Marine railway station, where it was loaded onto a railway carriage. The passenger luggage van had been specially adapted to accommodate the coffin. Its roof was painted white on the outside, so that people along the way would be able to recognise the carriage; and inside its sides were lined with purple drapes. The massive wreaths were then manhandled into the carriage with as much difficulty as they had been loaded onto the ship. A report in *The Times* captured the mood of sombre respect: 'Thus, the Unknown Soldier returns to-day to English shores bearing with him the banner of a victory greater than any victory of the sword. All that man can do to honour the dead the nation will do for him to-morrow; for he, dead, returning in the name of all who died as he did, honours his country more than we, living, can honour him.'[30]

In the collections of the Imperial War Museum, there is a dried, pressed rosebud belonging to a boy whose father had been killed in the first months of the war. The flower had fallen from one of the wreaths accompanying the coffin of the Unknown Warrior, as it was being unloaded at Dover, and had been picked up by the dead soldier's brother, the boy's uncle, who was watching the event. He sent it to his nephew, with the note: 'In Loving Memory of your Dear Dad who arrived at Dover Nov 10th 1920 in the Destroyer *Verdun* ... I hope you will keep it and in years, you will be able to show it, in remembrance of your Dad.'[31] It was an indication of just how deeply people identified with the Unknown Warrior.

At 5.50 p.m. the train set off for London, rattling in the dark through the Kent countryside, to be greeted at every station through which it passed – Faversham, Gillingham, Chatham – by crowds waving flags. Just over two and a half hours later, the carriage was shunted onto Platform 8 at Victoria Station. 'Men wept as they saw the double railway carriage,' *The Times* reported, 'with one compartment full of soldiers and its other compartment, as it seemed, full of flowers. They knew not why they wept. But the great gloomy arches of the station and the rows on rows of white faces pressed to the barriers were a setting which might not be denied ... The silence deepened, for no one seemed to move. One heard a smothered sound of weeping. The smoke in the roof bellied and eddied round the arc lamps. The funeral carriage stopped at last.'[32]

The guard was changed, leaving two guardsmen at the luggage van door to mount their night's vigil; and the crowds, which had at one stage threatened to break through the barriers and police cordon and rush the carriage, gradually dispersed for the night. People, mostly dressed in black mourning clothes, started to turn up early the following morning, packing the pavements that lined the route from Victoria Station to Whitehall up to seven deep. A thick autumn mist hung over the capital, but this lifted during the course of the morning. 'The Unknown Warrior, in his daydreams in France,' *The Times* reported, 'never could have imagined a more lovely English day than was the day of his home-coming ... It was a perfect late autumn day in London, with a touch of frost in the air, a veiled blue sky, and sun that would soon break through in full splendour, but had as yet a foggy glory round it. There seemed something appropriate in the utter stillness of the air. The smoke from the chimneys went straight upwards. The few flags, at half-mast, clung in sluggish folds round their flagstaffs.'³³

At 9.20 a.m., eight Coldstream Guardsmen entered the railway carriage, placed Railton's Union flag, and the steel helmet of a private soldier, on the coffin of the Unknown Warrior, and carried it on their shoulders to a gun carriage drawn up near Platform 8. Twelve of the most senior officers in the British armed forces, admirals, field marshals and an air marshal, assembled either side of the gun carriage, which was pulled, once more, by six black horses, before setting off at a slow, sombre pace on its two-and-a-half-mile procession towards the Cenotaph and Westminster Abbey. The massed bands of the Household Division led the way, again playing Chopin's *Funeral March*, the sound of their drums muffled with black cloth. Four hundred ex-servicemen marching four abreast brought up the rear.

Shortly before 11 a.m., the coffin arrived at the Cenotaph, where the king was waiting, dressed in the uniform of a field marshal, the highest rank in the British Army. He saluted the coffin and placed a wreath of red roses and bay leaves upon it, with a handwritten inscription that read: 'In proud memory of those warriors who died unknown in the Great War. Unknown, and yet well known, as dying and behold they lived. George R I.'³⁴

On the last stroke of eleven from Big Ben, the king pressed a button releasing the two great Union flags that shrouded the Cenotaph; as they fell, they unveiled Lutyens's masterpiece. Everyone then stood in silence for two minutes, as they had done the previous year. A two-minute silence – that 'great awful silence', as *The Times* described it³⁵ – had been held for the first time in Britain on 11 November 1919 to mark the first anniversary of the signing of the Armistice at the eleventh hour of the eleventh day of the eleventh month. The idea had originated in Cape Town, where a three-minute midday 'pause' to commemorate the dead had been observed during the war. This had been noted by the South African politician Sir Percy FitzPatrick who forwarded the suggestion, via Lord Milner, to King George V who liked the idea that 'there may be for the brief space of two minutes a complete suspension of all our normal activities'.[36] (In May 1919, too, the Australian journalist Edward Honey had promoted the idea of a five-minute silence on Armistice Day in a letter to the *Evening News*.)

As people held their breath beside the Cenotaph on Armistice Day 1920, a woman's wail 'rose and fell and rose again', according to *The Times*, until the silence 'bore down once more'.[37] The *Daily Mail*'s account was even more emotive: 'Men and women among the crowds gathered for the London ceremonies sobbed uncontrollably. People with handkerchiefs to their eyes leaned back in taxicabs or wept unaffectedly in the street, in omnibuses, railway trains, tube trains, and on railway platforms. Each motor-driver stood by the bonnet of his car, each driver by his horse's head, either with cap off or at attention. Cyclists and motor-cyclists dismounted and stood beside their machines in military fashion.'[38]

It wasn't just the crowds gathered along the route the coffin had taken, and around the Cenotaph itself, who observed the silence. The *Manchester Evening News* reported that 'it was as if the world stood still'.[39] Trading at the Stock Exchange was suspended, law courts paused their proceedings, traffic came to a halt in the major cities, factories stopped work, operators in telephone exchanges did not put through any new calls for two minutes so that the phones didn't ring, operations in some hospitals were scheduled so that they were not in progress at 11 a.m., and the departure of trains scheduled to leave at eleven was delayed by two minutes.

'Nothing more simple, more beautiful, or more dramatic than the Great Silence was ever conceived,' the *Daily Telegraph* concluded. 'For the brief space of two minutes the Empire remembered the glorious dead. All movement was suspended, all business at a standstill, and perfect silence everywhere.'[40]

Fabian Ware, the visionary who did more than anyone to shape the way Britain remembered its war dead, was later to recall an image that made the million 'Glorious Dead' more real, that brought them to life: 'Imagine them moving in one long continuous column, four abreast; as the head of that column reaches the Cenotaph the last four men would be at Durham. In Canada that column would reach across the land from Quebec to Ottawa; in Australia from Melbourne to Canberra; in South Africa from Bloemfontein to Pretoria; in New Zealand from Christchurch to Wellington; in Newfoundland from coast to coast of the Island, and in India from Lahore to Delhi. It would take these million men eighty-four hours, or three and a half days, to march past the Cenotaph in London.'[41] Under the weight of such numbers, the Cenotaph acquired a mystical atmosphere, the *Daily Mail* claiming that 'you could scarce see the Cenotaph for the *aura*, the halo, the throbbing air that encompassed it'.[42] It was if the spirits of the dead hovered above the watching crowds, as in those fake psychic photographs that became popular in the 1920s. Here was a place where the living could commune with the dead.

From the Cenotaph on Armistice Day 1920, the procession of the living moved towards the gates of Westminster Abbey, where the pall-bearers lifted the coffin from the gun carriage onto their shoulders, and carried it into the church. The coffin passed between lines of soldiers, including a guard of honour consisting of ninety-six men who had been decorated for conspicuous gallantry, and past David Railton and his wife who were in the congregation. The abbey was packed with almost a thousand widows and mothers of fallen soldiers, dressed in black or grey, many of them wearing the medals, or medal ribbons of their loved ones, which provided splashes of colour.

The king, the Archbishop of Canterbury and the twelve military leaders were gathered around the grave as Dean Ryle conducted the service. The coffin was lowered into the grave, and as the dean intoned the words from the service for the Burial of the Dead, 'Earth to earth, ashes to ashes, dust to dust', the king sprinkled a silver saucerful of soil from Flanders over the coffin. These were the funeral rites that had been denied so many.

The service concluded with the singing of 'Recessional', a poem by Rudyard Kipling that had been set to music and included the refrain 'Lest we forget', the injunction that had come to characterise all commemoration of the dead. 'The great wave of feeling that hymn always arouses could be felt surging through the whole congregation, and seen in many a woman, and even some men, finding expression in tears,' *The Times* reported. Finally, the Last Post and Reveille were sounded by two buglers, 'acute, shattering, the very voice of pain itself – but pain triumphant', according to *The Times*. It described the service as 'the most beautiful, the most touching and the most impressive that in all its long eventful story, this island has ever seen'.[43] The king concurred, his private secretary congratulating the dean on his behalf: 'The King was deeply impressed with today's unique ceremony, the inception of which was your own. All the arrangements and the manner in which the service was conducted were in reverence, beauty and dignity worthy of an event unparallelled [*sic*] and imperishable in the Nation's life and of the Abbey's noble tradition. His Majesty sincerely thanks you and all concerned for the perfect manner in which everything was carried out.'[44]

It was extraordinary that, at the end of a war which had begun with *The Times* printing casualty lists only of officers, a soldier of no known rank should be buried with all the pomp and ceremony normally reserved for a field marshal. 'No one knows the "Unknown Warrior's" rank, his wealth, his education or his history,' Railton wrote. ' "Class" values become vanity there. He may have been wealthy, or one whose home was in a slum. He may have been a Public School boy, or a gypsy. Many people have not yet grasped the fact that he may have come from any part of the British Isles, or from the Dominions or Colonies … It is quite likely that he was a communicant of the Church, or a Roman Catholic, a Jew, a Salvationist, a Wesleyan, a Presbyterian, or a member of any other, or of no religious denomination.'[45]

Newspaper accounts focused on the deeply personal responses to the burial of the Unknown Warrior, the private acts of mourning at such a public event. The *Daily Mail* published an impression of the abbey service by Mrs John Macbeth of Balham, whose two officer sons had been killed on the same day on the Somme and buried in unknown graves: 'We tried all we knew to find their resting place, but those who were with them when they fell said the whole place was a shambles and unrecognisable. To add to our sorrow we could not find their graves. To-day brought the sadness of a revived sorrow, but with it a splendid consolation.' In the same paper, another mother described her bittersweet memories of the service, and the way it assuaged her grief. For years she had tried to remember the happy times she had had with her son as he grew up and before he went off to war, rather than the times since she had learned of his death. But questions kept obtruding: 'Where did he fall? How did he fall? If only I could have known where he lay so as to have something tangible for my thoughts. But to go out of my life, never to listen for the sound of his footfall, never to watch for his sunny smile, never to have long cosy talks, to have nothing, nothing. But now – my boy has come home and has been buried with honours in our Abbey.'[46]

After the congregation had left the abbey and its doors had temporarily been closed, Railton's flag – 'literally tinged with the blood of the men of London and of every part of England, Scotland, Wales and Ireland,' as he described it[47] – was spread over the grave on trestle tables, with the steel helmet, web belt and sidearm placed on top. The war reporter Philip Gibbs singled out 'the steel helmet – the old tin hat – lying there on the crimson of the flag, which revealed him instantly, not as a mythical warrior, aloof from common humanity, a shadowy type of national pride and martial glory, but as one of those fellows dressed in the drab of khaki, stained by mud and grease, who went into the dirty ditches with this steel hat on his head'.[48] It was the identification of the Unknown Warrior with the common soldier that people found so compelling and cathartic. The wreaths around the grave included one sent by the War Graves Inquiry Bureau, 'composed of laurel collected from the ruined gardens of Ypres and the cloisters of the cathedral'.[49]

Four sentries – one from each of the services, the Royal Navy, the Royal Marines, the Army and the RAF – were posted around the grave. The burial of the Unknown Warrior, the *Manchester Evening News* reported, was 'the prelude to a great pilgrimage' to the Cenotaph, led by two amputees riding on tricycles, followed by policemen and truckloads of wounded veterans in blue hospital uniform.[50] The doors of the abbey were now reopened to welcome the first of the pilgrims. By the end of the day, some 200,000 people had shuffled past the Cenotaph, inches at a time. Many of them went on to pay their respects at the Unknown Warrior's tomb in the abbey, where a team of organists provided round-the-clock musical accompaniment during opening hours.

It had originally been thought that the grave would be closed within a few days; but such was the enthusiasm of the public that – just as a year before the success of the temporary Cenotaph had taken the organisers by surprise and inspired the creation of a permanent national shrine – the opening of the grave to the public was extended beyond the weekend (Saturday was designated 'Children's Day'). The grave was not sealed until the following Thursday, 18 November – initially with a slab of York stone, simply inscribed: 'A British Warrior/who fell/in The Great War/1914–1918/ for king/and country/Greater Love Hath No Man Than This'.

People continued to come throughout the year, and into the next one. For many, as *The Times* reported: 'The Great Pilgrimage was transformed into a great test of endurance. Packed together in a dense mass extending half way across the broad thoroughfare, they were left standing there without movement for an hour and a half, and when a move was at length made, the scene at times bore more resemblance to a football scrimmage than to a procession of mourners honouring the fallen.'[51] The wreaths of lilies, roses and laurels piled up around the Cenotaph – some 100,000 wreaths had been laid by the end of the first week, burying the base of the monument. By the time the grave was sealed, up to a million people had paid their respects. 'There has never before in this country been such a pilgrimage to the grave of a hero or such a display of mourning around a memorial to the dead,' *The Times* reported.[52] The piles of wreaths, and heartbroken messages, belied the idea that the British psyche (or physiognomy, rather) was characterised by a stiff upper lip.

The press reported the hopes of many of those present: the elderly man who 'said, "I lost two sons out there, but the other ..." and the implied, though unuttered words, "may be here" merely expressed the secret thoughts of many more';[53] the small groups of bereaved women, searching for the missing body of their loved one, whispering consolations to each other as they watched the coffin pass, ' "It might be he! It might be he! they said – hoping and hoping';[54] the report by the editor of a veterans' publication, which claimed that: 'The Warrior was not unknown to us. He was "Ginger", "Smiler", "Nobby", "Spud", "Towny", "Smithy" … he vanished into the mist on that night raid. He came back to us out of the mist. We knew he would come back. As for me, I knew it was my brother.' As the writer Ronald Blythe observed in *The Age of Illusion*: 'What had happened was that this most stately public show was being observed with an intensely private emotion. The dead man who had set out without a name, a voice, or a face only a few hours before was being invested with a hundred thousand likenesses.'[55]

The following year, the simple slab of York stone was replaced with a piece of black Belgian marble, into which an inscription was inlaid in brass letters smelted from spent shell cases found on the battlefields. 'Beneath this stone rests the body/ Of a British warrior/ Unknown by name or rank/ Brought from France to lie among/ The most illustrious of the land', the lengthy and rather cumbersome inscription supplied by Dean Ryle began, trailing off into every cluttered corner of the gravestone. On Armistice Day 1921, David Railton and his wife once again attended the service in the abbey. Railton had seen his 'bold' suggestion for the flag to feature in the burial service realised the previous year. He was now to take part in the formal dedication of the flag, which had lain for the past twelve months at the foot of the grave of the Unknown Warrior. During the service, Railton handed the flag to Lord Haig, who presented it to the dean, who then placed it on the altar, dedicating it 'to the glory of God, and in personal memory of all who gave their lives fighting on land and sea and air for their King'.[56] 'The padre's flag,' which, according to *The Times*, had 'filled so glorious and so tragic a part in the war', was then hung from a pillar close to the tomb.[57]

This was the flag which had flown at Vimy Ridge and at the Messines Ridge, and 'at many other places made memorable for ever by the splendid daring and the invincible resistance of our troops; it was the frontal of rude altars where thousands took the Sacrament for the last time; it served as the last covering for numbers of our dead; and it yet bears the glorious stain of their blood. It has covered the grave of the Unknown Warrior, and now it is to hang near his resting-place under the venerable roof which still shelters the helmet and the blazoned shield of the Royal conqueror of Agincourt, for both are of our race. Many thousands will gaze upon it to-day in their pilgrimage to the tomb which has become the symbol of what the "plain folk" of the Empire have done for the land of their fathers and of their children.'[58]

David Railton had been given the flag within a couple of weeks of his arrival in France in January 1916, by his mother-in-law, Mary De Lancey Willson, or 'Dubby' as she was known in the family (she, too, attended the Armistice Day service in 1921). Through three years of war on the Western front, he had carried the flag in his pack, along with a small wooden cross and two candlesticks, to be used as an altar cloth – spread over a table in a dugout, a box, bucket, or bale of hay – in countless Communion services at the front. For Railton, the flag represented 'a symbol of our National life and a radiant colour in the midst of all the horrors in France'.[59] It was also flown at parades, regimental concerts and boxing tournaments.

One of the flag's most frequent uses was as a shroud with which to cover a corpse before it was lowered into the ground in a burial service at the front, in the dead of night perhaps or at early dawn. Railton's first such funeral was that of Private Travis of the Northumberland Fusiliers on 15 February 1916. As Railton recalled in the voice of the flag: 'I have not told you about the numerous times when the Padre wrapped me round the lifeless body of one of the "Boys" when there was no other covering, no "coffin", not even a blanket. In spite of the agony of it all, I am glad to have served in that capacity. As time went on Officers and men alike expressed their disappointment on a few occasions when I was not there. To bury a man without the Union Jack, they said, was to bury him "like a dog". But somehow they felt my presence spoke to them one and all of dear Old England, and to every one who was in any sense a Christian of the "sure and certain hope of the resurrection" and of the union of all brave men bye and bye.'[60]

The use of a third-person narrative, in the form of the flag's voice, may have helped Railton achieve some distance during the recall of the most terrible moments. One of the times that tested his faith most severely was the last Communion of a soldier, Private Denis Blakemore, who had been sentenced to execution by firing squad for desertion in July 1917. 'Indeed as long as I rest in the abbey,' he recalled in the flag's voice:

> I shall always remember how in the dead of a certain night
> the Padre got up and took me in his pack into the wood.
> I wondered where ever was he going for a service at such an
> hour … Then he came to me and spread me over the grass
> and laid upon me the chalice that he used always and the
> paten and together he and a Private Soldier joined in the
> central part of that wonderful Communion service … soon
> after that the padre left me and took the arm of his friend [the
> convicted man] and went into the wood. The next thing that
> I can remember is that there was a startling report of rifles and
> presently I heard footsteps rushing through the wood and all
> the twigs crackling and the padre snatched me off the ground
> in a way he had never done before. He did not fold me up.
> He just crushed me into his pack and ran through the wood
> and up a hill to a little dug out. He flung me on the floor and
> stamped up and down. I do not know all he said but the words,
> 'Devilment' and 'Blood' and 'Misery' kept on coming in and
> he vowed he would never use me again; that he was done with
> the Army and would go home. Then he folded me up and
> went out.[61]

For a second year running, on Armistice Day 1921, great crowds gathered at the Cenotaph and outside the abbey, and kept on coming throughout the following week. On Children's Day, according to *The Times*, 'Bunch after bunch of white chrysanthemums bore … no other words than the touching phrase, "To Daddy." '[62]

Many of the pilgrims still believed that the Unknown Warrior was not just a representative body but the real thing, the body of their lost loved one. *The Times* reported the 'strange incident' of an elderly woman from the north of Scotland joining the queue, with a bunch of chrysanthemums and heather in her hand, to lay at the foot of the Cenotaph. She was there, she said, on the advice of a clairvoyant who had told her that the body of her son lay under the tomb of the Unknown Warrior in the abbey. 'No one,' *The Times* was pleased to report, 'disturbed her faith.'[63]

The ceremony of 1921 was briefly interrupted by a march of thousands of unemployed ex-servicemen, with pawn tickets pinned to their coats in place of medals. By then unemployment figures had risen to more than two million. Britain was hardly the promised 'land fit for heroes', and the authorities were conscious of the need to honour the living as well as the dead, as Field Marshal Lord Haig had argued in an article, entitled 'Our Debt to the Living', in *The Times* the year before: 'The dead have our reverence and our gratitude for ever. That is much, but it is not all that they can claim. No small part of what we owe to our dead comrades is to do our duty to the living. It is only by discharging fully our obligations to living ex-Servicemen, and to the dependents of all who fought for us, that we can hope to square our account with those who gave their lives for us and ours ... To-day we honour the dead. Let us not forget the living. To both we owe a duty. To the gallant dead, that by heedless action we may not imperil the inheritance they have handed to us. To the living, that they may be allowed to share freely in that great inheritance.'[64]

David Railton saw for himself the plight – 'the real bedrock difficulties' – of these ex-servicemen. In the autumn of 1921, he set off from his mother-in-law's house in Cumberland on a 'tramp' across the county, dressed in an old coat and with just a shilling in his pocket, asking for work by day, and sleeping rough or in a doss-house at night. 'The Vicar, a fresh-complexioned, curly-haired, youngish-looking man,' told the *Evening Standard* that he hoped to get work, and 'return with more money, and a better coat than when he started.' But, although he was given small sums of money here and there, the only paid work he was offered was the cleaning out of a garage, for which he earned 2 shillings and *6d*. and a religious tract. The *Evening Standard* concluded that: 'His experiences induce the belief that the position of the ex-service man seeking work is well-nigh hopeless.'[65]

The importance of these commemorative rituals – to honour the living and the dead – persisted into the 1920s, with pilgrimages lasting for a week around Armistice Day, and pilgrims leaving flowers at the foot of the Cenotaph or poppies on the grave of the Unknown Warrior. A plan to end the annual event was ditched in 1923 due to public pressure; and when there were further calls to discontinue the services in the 1930s, David Railton, by then Rector of Liverpool, argued that: 'If you remove the service of Remembrance Day you will add another wound. The true mourner can never forget … These wounded mourners deserve their brief hour of justifiable pride and consolation. There is for them this thought: I am not alone in my grief … If you who read this only knew the pain that is caused to a relative and comrade if, by chance, one name is omitted from a war memorial, or if the padre should fail to read it when the Roll of Honour is read aloud, you would know how sacred is the service for those who mourn.'[66]

Remembrance Day became an established rite, although since the Second World War, it has been held on the Sunday closest to 11 November, rather than on the 11th itself. In Canada, too, Remembrance Day became the nation's main commemoration of those who had died in the Great War, while in Australia and New Zealand, it was superseded by Anzac Day on 25 April.

In time, the cult of the Unknown Warrior became common to all belligerent nations, commemorating as it did, in one anonymous individual, the collective grief of all. In October 1921, an American sergeant from an infantry battalion selected at random one of four coffins containing bodies exhumed from graves in France. The coffin was taken from Châlons-sur-Marne, via Paris, to Le Havre, from where it was transported by sea to the United States, for burial with full military honours on 11 November in Arlington Military

Cemetery in Virginia. The Italians buried their Unknown Warrior the same year, and other nations were to follow – Belgium, Greece, Czechoslovakia – over the hundred years following the end of the war. In 1993, after decades of lobbying, an unidentified Australian soldier was exhumed from a cemetery in Villers-Bretonneux and buried on 11 November in the Australian War Memorial's Hall of Memory. In 1999 the Canadian Unknown Soldier was disinterred near Vimy Ridge, flown back home and laid to rest in front of the Canadian War Memorial in Ottawa. And in 2004 New Zealand's Unknown Warrior was exhumed from a cemetery in the Somme and buried in Wellington.

On 17 November 1920, the prime minister had written to thank and congratulate Lutyens for his 'fine and generous service in designing and building the memorial [the Cenotaph] which has become a national shrine, not only for the British Isles but also for the whole Empire ... How well it represents the feeling of the nation has been amply manifested by the stream of pilgrims who have passed the Cenotaph during the past week.'[67] It was to become the best known of more than a hundred cemeteries and memorials designed by the architect to commemorate the war dead – from the civic to the corporate, the regimental (he designed a memorial for his father's old regiment, the Lancashire Fusiliers) to the individual. (Like almost everyone else, Lutyens's family was touched by the war, and he designed the grave of Derek Lutyens, the last of his five nephews to die in the conflict.) The Cenotaph was that very rare example of a state commission that captured the people's imagination.

In style, the Cenotaph was austere, abstract, modern and decidedly non-denominational. It was uncluttered by words or other visual references: a blank screen onto which the bereaved could project their individual grief, an empty tomb into which they could pour their emotions. The Tomb of the Unknown Warrior, on the other hand, was avowedly Christian, the gravestone lettered in the lofty language of godly sacrifice, king and country, the Crusader's sword buried with the coffin representing a muscular, medieval Christianity.

In November 1929, the *British Legion Journal* compared the two very different memorials, which stand about 500 metres apart, concluding: 'If there be any distinction between the symbolism of the Cenotaph and that of the Grave of the Unknown Warrior, it is in the fact that while the former represents, as an entity, the noble Army of those who died for their country, the latter represents one individual, and the mystery as to whose son he was makes him the son and brother of us all. The Cenotaph, it may be said, is the token of our mourning as a nation; the Grave of the Unknown Warrior is the token of our mourning as individuals.'[68] The wreaths and tributes left at the two memorials appeared to confirm this: those at the Cenotaph often addressed to the whole army of the glorious dead, rather than to named individuals. Many people visiting the Tomb of the Unknown Warrior felt they were visiting, for the first time, the grave their missing relative had been denied. This is what David Railton had intended ever since he had come across the grave of that unknown soldier in Erquinghem-Lys: 'Those whose loved ones were amongst the "unknown" know that in this Tomb there may be – there is – resting the body of their beloved' – their husband, son, father or brother.[69]

The universal appeal of both memorials – one a surrogate body, the other a symbolic void – contrasted sharply with the very specific, personal appeal of a name on a headstone. For many of us, it is the rows of these individual graves that represent Britain's commemoration of the war dead: these were the work of the War Graves Commission. The commission had very little indeed to do with the burial of the Unknown Warrior, which was managed by the Office of Works under Sir Lionel Earle (who had set off for France on his own search for his missing brother, Maxwell, in 1914). Indeed, the return of the body of the unknown soldier defied, in principle, the commission's ban on the repatriation of the dead. This difference in interpretation is yet another example of the many ways in which people searched for the bodies and souls of their loved ones after the war.

4

Rudyard Kipling and the War Graves Commission: The Search for a Place to Grieve

In 1992 a researcher at the Commonwealth War Graves Commission spotted an anomaly in its records. Almost a year after the end of the war, the remains of an unidentified body had been dug up in no man's land, near Loos, in September 1919, and reburied as an 'unknown lieutenant of the Irish Guards', in the St Mary's Advanced Dressing Station (ADS) Cemetery, Plot 7, Row D, Grave 2. What piqued the researcher's interest was the fact that the spot in no man's land where the body had originally been exhumed was miles from where the Irish Guards had been operating. Nevertheless, after exhaustive rechecking of the records and map references, it appeared more likely that the body belonged to John Kipling, the only Irish Guards lieutenant unaccounted for in the area. In July 1992 the headstone was duly, exceptionally and, it transpired, controversially, changed to read: 'LIEUTENANT JOHN KIPLING, IRISH GUARDS, 27TH SEPTEMBER 1915, AGE 18'.

This new attribution came too late for Rudyard and Caroline ('Carrie') Kipling, who had searched for years without success for information about their son's fate. The decades of namelessness were a cruel irony for Kipling, who had drafted the inscription on the Stone of Remembrance in almost every military cemetery, 'Their name liveth for evermore'.

On 2 October 1915, a telegram from the War Office arrived at Bateman's, the Kiplings' home in Sussex, announcing that their son John had been reported wounded and missing near Chalk Pit Wood on 27 September. He had led his platoon into action on the afternoon of the 27th, the third day of the Battle of Loos. The telegram was soon followed by a letter from the trenches from John's No. 2 Company commander, Captain John Bird, describing how two of his men had seen John 'limping, just by the Red House', and one of them had then seen him fall. 'Your son behaved with great gallantry and coolness and handled his men splendidly,' Captain Bird concluded; he was 'very hopeful that he is a prisoner'.[1]

Over the next few days, news continued to filter through – although it was often fraught with conflicting eyewitness accounts. There is general agreement that on 26 September, the 2nd Battalion of the Irish Guards moved up to the front, where they settled into trenches for the night. The ground over which they were going to fight was former coal-mining country – 'a jagged, scarred and mutilated sweep of mining-villages, factories, quarries, slag-dumps, pit-heads, chalk-pits and railway embankments', as Kipling was to describe it in his history of the Irish Guards.[2] At four o'clock in the afternoon of the 27th, John led his men through the shattered stumps and brambly undergrowth of Chalk Pit Wood, then, under heavy German machine-gun fire across the open ground beyond, towards a former mineshaft known as 'Puits 14 bis'. As with so many accounts of similar actions involving over a thousand men, there is less unanimity on how far John got, and exactly where he was last seen. Was he swept forwards with some Scots Guards beyond the pit-head 'Puits 14' buildings, before being driven back in confusion through Chalk Pit Wood? At what point was he wounded, and where in the body? Was he buried, or could he have been taken prisoner? The battalion commander, Lieutenant Colonel Lesley Butler, reported in a letter to Kipling that John had been shot in the foot or the leg and had last been seen near the enemy lines, beyond Puits 14, hobbling back towards a building that was soon to be occupied by the Germans. Like Captain Bird, Butler was optimistic: 'I do hope and pray that in course of time you may hear that he was carried off by the Germans and looked after by them. Meantime, you have my deepest sympathy for the anxiety you must feel and which I share with you.'[3]

A report forwarded by the Wounded and Missing Enquiry Department appeared to dash these hopes. In it, a 'Sergeant Kinnelly [sic]' of the Irish Guards claimed to have seen John leading his platoon, shouting 'Come on boys'; he was then hit in the head by flying shrapnel and fell. 'He was about the bravest Officer I ever saw,' stated Kinnelly, 'and would, I believe, have won the V.C.' Kinnelly himself was wounded and gassed, but when he came to, he made his way back towards a dressing station with the aid of a stick, and passed the fallen body of Kipling, who he was sure was dead. He went on to explain how it would not have been possible for Mr Kipling to have been taken prisoner, as he lay on ground that had been held by the British ever since. Why the body was not found and brought in at the time, Kinnelly attributed to the fact that the ground 'was very heavily shelled from the big guns; and men lying there might be buried in a crater or disappear in other ways. It is impossible to bring in even all the wounded men.'[4]

Kipling was irritated when the *Morning Post* reported John 'missing, believed killed', rather than just missing; and further incensed when the newspaper described John as 'a boy of delicate health' – he was 'as hard as nails', his father protested.[5] He comforted himself with reports of his son's courage, translating the image he had of John dying with an improbable smile on his face into 'A Son', one of the short verses known as the 'Epitaphs of the War':

My son was killed while laughing at some jest. I would I knew
What it was, and it might serve me in a time when jests
are few.[6]

The morning after the Kiplings had received the telegram, Carrie drove over to visit her neighbour and close friend Violet Cecil at Great Wigsell, a house that she had taken near Bodiam, while her husband Edward was posted to Egypt. Carrie knew that she would get a sympathetic hearing from her old friend, who had lived through the same experience the year before, when her only son, George (a friend of John's and a frequent visitor to Bateman's), had been reported 'wounded and missing' near Villers-Cotterêts. Kipling described in a letter to Andrew Macphail on 5 October 'the horrible see-saw' of emotions that Violet had had to go through:[7] she had been told at first that her son had almost certainly been taken prisoner, and was now in Germany; but this news was soon followed by a report from George's battalion that a returned prisoner had seen the lad blown to pieces by a shell.

Kipling had made enquiries into George's fate on behalf of the Cecils that foreshadowed his and Carrie's desperate search for John. In an attempt to piece together George's last hours, he had visited Gatcombe House, a convalescent home on the Isle of Wight, to interview three Grenadier Guardsmen, one of whom was quite clear that George had been shot dead. George's family were grateful for Kipling's meticulous researches, illustrated with a neatly annotated map (which he produced in his interviews with the soldiers and found very useful in jogging their memories and corroborating facts); and believed the account to be 'as clear as one could expect'.[8] However, Colonel Wilfred Smith of the Grenadier Guards cautioned in a letter to Violet that 'private soldiers' stories are generally misleading. They really see so little and have such fertile imaginations':[9] a problem that Kipling himself was to encounter the following year.

Like the Cecils, the Kiplings initially hoped that John was still alive and had been taken prisoner. In a reversal of the roles, Violet wrote to Princess Margaret, crown princess of neutral Sweden, to ask if she would contact influential friends in Germany – to no avail. A family friend contacted the Prince of Wales, who was attached to the Guards Division, to see if he could help. And Kipling wrote to the British Minister to the Vatican; to Henry van Dyke, the American ambassador to the neutral Netherlands; and to Walter Page, the American ambassador to Great Britain, to request he ask his counterpart in Berlin. Kipling enclosed a physical description of his son: 'When I last heard from him he had lost his identification-disc so I send a description of him over-leaf. He is dark with strongly marked eyebrows, small moustache, thick brown hair (straight) dark brown eyes with long lashes. Height about 5 ft 7½ [inches]. Small white scar on forehead and one front tooth slightly discoloured. He is short-sighted and is most probably wearing gold spectacles. He wears a small gold signet-ring with monogram J. K. All his clothes are marked.'[10]

Kipling was worried that, if John had been taken prisoner, the Germans would turn the capture of the son of a Nobel prize-winner into a propaganda coup. He therefore arranged for the Royal Flying Corps to drop leaflets, written in German, behind German lines, asking for information on whether John, the son of '*weltberühmten Schriftsteller* [the world-famous author] Rudyard Kipling', was alive. Carrie was terrified that the son of such a rabid 'Hun-hater' and polemicist as her husband would be treated vindictively: 'When one imagines one's son in such a prison it's best by far to believe him dead,' she wrote to her mother, having read an account of a German camp.[11]

In 'The Gardener', the short story written in 1925, Kipling reflected on his own experience in searching for John. When the subject of the story, Helen, received the official telegram informing her that her loved one was missing, she followed a ritual that had evolved, 'English fashion', in meeting the experience of war. She found herself 'pulling down the house-blinds one after one with great care, and saying earnestly to each: "Missing *always* means dead". Then she took her place in the dreary procession that was impelled to go through an inevitable series of unprofitable emotions. The Rector, of course, preached hope and prophesied word, very soon, from a prison camp. Several friends, too, told her perfectly truthful tales, but always about other women, to whom, after months and months of silence, their missing had been miraculously restored. Other people urged her to communicate with infallible Secretaries of organisations who could communicate with benevolent neutrals, who could extract accurate information from the most secretive Hun prison commandants.'[12]

As he had done in his search for George Cecil, Kipling started to solicit statements from soldiers who had received a 'Blighty

wound' in the same action as John, and were now back in England.
As Colonel Smith had warned, their stories were often unreliable,
and motivated principally by a desire to offer hope. Three Irish
Guardsmen, in hospital near Hythe, had little to add when the
Kiplings arrived in person to interview them; indeed, one of them,
'a delightful fellow' called Rafter, who had been in John's platoon,
claimed to have seen John at seven o'clock in the evening – 'of
course, that is a mistake', Carrie wrote to her friend, Violet.[13]
A Sergeant Davidson, in hospital in Wantage, at first claimed that he
had seen John wounded in the leg, though not seriously, but could
not answer any further, more detailed questions. In November, the
Kiplings received a statement from a Sergeant Cochrane, who was
now in a Red Cross hospital in Glasgow. Cochrane recalled how
he and John had attacked a German machine-gun post in one of
the pit buildings before being wounded himself; he suggested that,
since John's body had not been found, he was possibly a prisoner.
As Carrie described in a letter to Violet, the Kiplings remained
'more at sea than ever'.[14] Through the persistence of their enquiries,
John was to become one of the most widely searched for soldiers of
the First World War.

As the Kiplings pieced together John's final movements from
interviews and statements, Kipling marked them on a map, as he
had done for George Cecil the year before. The accounts continued
to contradict each other, but the very fact they did, gave the
Kiplings – paradoxically – grounds for hope.

Privately, Kipling was beginning to fear the worst. On 12
November 1915, he reported, in a letter to his old friend, Colonel
Lionel Dunsterville, how: 'Our boy was "reported wounded and
missing" since Sep. 27 – the battle of Loos and we've heard nothing
official since that date. But all we can pick up from the men points
to the fact that he is dead and probably wiped out by shell fire.'
Kipling, nevertheless, was putting on a brave front. He was proud
of his son's courage: John had certainly lived up to the virtues of
manliness that Kipling had imparted to his son in his best-loved
poem, 'If'. 'It was a short life,' he continued. 'I'm sorry that all the
years' work ended in that one afternoon but – lots of people are

in our position and it's something to have bred a man. The wife is standing it wonderfully tho' she of course clings to the bare hope of his being a prisoner. I've seen what shells can do and I don't.'[15]

According to his close friend and sometime Sussex neighbour, the author Rider Haggard, Kipling had 'practically lost hope' by 22 December, when they met in London. Haggard had taken it upon himself to make enquiries about John on the Kiplings' behalf. Just after Christmas, he interviewed a young Irish Guardsman called Bowe, who had been wounded. Bowe claimed that, as far as he knew, John had been 'blown absolutely to pieces by a large shell'.[16] For reasons of delicacy, Haggard omitted in his report the fact that Bowe had seen an officer, whom he could swear was John Kipling, crying with pain, as he tried to fasten a dressing around a badly shattered jaw.

The letters of condolence kept coming: from Arthur Conan Doyle; Princess Beatrice, whose youngest son Prince Maurice of Battenberg had been killed the previous year near Ypres; Lord Curzon ('I do not imagine that any two parents in England will more cheerfully make the sacrifice or more heroically bear the loss'); and Theodore Roosevelt, who observed, equally reassuringly, that 'there are so many things worse than death'.[17] Along with these letters were approaches from mediums offering their help in contacting, or at least locating, John.

Friends, such as Arthur Conan Doyle and Rider Haggard, who were interested in spiritualism, might have encouraged them to do so, as could Kipling's own sister. Rudyard and Alice – or 'Trix' as she was nicknamed by her brother for being 'such a tricksy little thing' as a baby – had been very close as children.[18] Like their mother, she claimed the gift of second sight, and was to become a noted practitioner of crystal-gazing to foretell the future, as well as automatic writing – receiving and transcribing messages from the spirit world without the exercise of any conscious control. In the early 1900s, after reading Frederic Myers's *Human Personality and its Survival of Bodily Death*, Trix had become interested in the work of the Society for Psychical Research. Under the pseudonym 'Mrs Holland', which she adopted to spare the feelings of her family, who loathed any reference to psychic matters, she wrote hundreds of pages of automatic script for the society. These were then collated and compared with the writings of other mediums for 'cross-correspondences', gradually building up and corroborating a complete picture or prophecy.

Although, in the depths of her grief, Carrie may have considered trying to contact John, the Kiplings did not turn to spiritualism, as so many others did during and after the war. Kipling had a certain wary fascination for the supernatural – as some of his stories show – but, in the end, he believed that it should be avoided 'like the plague'.[19] He blamed Trix's interest in spiritualism, rather than an unhappy marriage, for his sister's mental instability. When asked whether he thought there was anything in spiritualism, he replied 'with a shudder': 'There is; I know. Have nothing to do with it.'[20] He had 'seen too much evil and sorrow and wreck of good minds … to take one step along that perilous track'.[21]

Kipling rejected all such approaches, evoking a particular revulsion in his poem 'En-dor', written in 1918, for the gifts of those mediums, who 'at a price', at a typical séance, 'must twitch and stiffen and slaver and groan'. The poem refers to the story in the Old Testament (1 Samuel 28:7) where Saul asks the Witch of Endor to summon the spirit of the dead prophet Samuel for advice in his battles with the Philistines. The poem begins:

> The road to En-dor is easy to tread
> For Mother or yearning Wife.
> There, it is sure, we shall meet our Dead
> As they were even in life.

But concludes:

> Oh, the road to En-dor is the oldest road
> And the craziest road of all!
> Straight it runs to the Witch's abode,
> As it did in the days of Saul,
> And nothing has changed of the sorrow in store
> For such as go down on the road to En-dor![22]

Early in 1916, Kipling received John's personal effects – a bundle of letters and a wallet – that he had left behind, not on the battlefield, but in the last place where his battalion had been billeted. Although this had no bearing on John's fate, and provided no new information on his final movements, it was a poignant reminder of his disappearance. And yet, despite all the evidence to the contrary, the Kiplings would not give up. Carrie, in particular, kept on hoping that John would turn up, either in a German camp or in a remote cottage hospital in France or Belgium. At the very least, she wanted to know the truth. In a letter to Violet Cecil, on 1 September 1916, the anniversary of George's death, Carrie wrote: 'My thoughts have been with you every hour of this day and its [sic] only because I know no one can say or do any thing to help that I have made no attempt ... You will see what Hells one lives in knowing that there are these secret camps and that our Govt will not take one step to help the men in them. All day and every day I cry for some confirmation some real proof that John is dead and there are thousands of mothers who feel as I do.'[23] It was the harrowing uncertainty that drove her husband in his searches, too, and which he captured in 'My Boy Jack', a poem written in 1916 and referring to the death of a sixteen-year-old sailor called Jack Cornwell at the Battle of Jutland. In the poem, Jack's father asks for any news of his sailor son with the same aching insistence as Kipling's quest for John after his disappearance at the Battle of Loos the year before. All he receives is the unchanging refrain: 'Not with this wind blowing, and this tide.'[24]

On 14 September 1916, almost a year after John had been reported missing, Kipling received a letter from the War Office regretting that, since no further report had been received concerning John's fate, 'it will consequently be necessary for the Army Council to consider whether they must now conclude that this officer is dead'. In view of this, it was time to wind up John's accounts, and to remove his name from the Army List. This was too much for Kipling, who replied a few days later: 'I should be glad if you would postpone taking the course you suggest in regard to my son Lieutenant John Kipling. All the information I have gathered is to the effect that he was wounded and left behind near Puits 14 at the Battle of Loos on September 27th 1915. I have interviewed a great many people and heard from many others, and can find no one who saw him killed, and his wound being a leg wound would be more disabling than fatal.' The War Office accepted Kipling's argument and decided not 'to proceed with the official acceptance of death in opposition to the wishes of the next-of-kin'. No further action was taken, for the time being.[25]

One of the more compelling pieces of evidence – and the one that went furthest in persuading Kipling that his son was dead – was introduced by his young cousin, Oliver Baldwin. In October 1917, Oliver tracked down a Sergeant Farrell of the Irish Guards on behalf of the Kiplings. Farrell claimed that he had seen John on the far side of Chalk Pit Wood, calmly emptying his revolver into a farm building which was occupied by a dozen German soldiers with machine guns. John was then shot in the head, and fell. Farrell claimed to have placed John's dead body in a shell hole for shelter, which was, in turn, buried by another shell blast. He confirmed his story to Colonel Vesey, and later in person to Kipling himself. Apologising that these details had not come to light before, Vesey suggested that it was because 'N.C.Os. and men hardly ever discuss any events in France when they get back here. It is an extraordinary thing but it is so.'[26]

The Kiplings did not finally give up hope until after the end of the war. When the search in Germany for missing men had not revealed a trace of John, and his name had not appeared on any list of prisoners received from the German government, Kipling was at last prepared to accept the fact of his death. This time it was Kipling who, through his solicitors, initiated the process with the War Office. 'In view, therefore, of the lapse of time since he became missing,' read the reply from the War Office, dated 24 May 1919, 'and of the absence of any information concerning him, the Army Council are regretfully constrained to conclude that this officer died on or since 27th September 1915, and I am to express their sympathy with you in your bereavement'.[27] John Kipling was now officially dead – and Kipling could claim his pay arrears of £64 0s.

4*d*. The Kiplings received an official letter of condolence from the king and queen the following month.

In 'The Gardener', Kipling described Helen's gradual and gentle coming to terms with her loss: 'In due course, when all the organisations had deeply or sincerely regretted their inability to trace, etc., something gave way within her and all sensation – save of thankfulness for the release – came to an end in blessed passivity.'[28] This did not necessarily reflect the Kiplings' own experience of grief, which was far more ambivalent, and muddied, perhaps, by guilt.

Kipling had always hoped that John would join the Royal Navy. Writing proudly to W. J. Harding in 1897, he described his newborn son as 'one small craft recently launched from my own works'. He gave his weight '(approx.) 8.957 lbs', its h.p. '(indicated) 2.0464', and its fuel consumption 'unrecorded but fresh supplies needed every 2½ hours. The vessel at present needs at least 15 years for full completion but at the end of that time may be an efficient addition to the Navy, for which service it is intended.'[29] By his early teens, however, it was clear that John's poor eyesight (like his father's) would make such a career impossible.

As soon as war was declared (and shortly before his seventeenth birthday), John tried to enlist as an officer with Kitchener's New Army, but was turned down on account of his eyesight. His medical records indicate a visual acuity score in both eyes of 6/36 without spectacles, implying that he would struggle with the second line of a standard eye chart. John was even considering trying to enlist as a private, when Kipling contacted his old friend Field Marshal Lord Roberts, a former commander-in-chief of the armed forces and honorary colonel of the Irish Guards – and, arguably, helped to send his son to his death on the Western front. Roberts got John a commission, and on 14 September 1914 he reported for training at Warley Barracks in Essex, where the regiment's reserve was based. Carrie wrote to her mother: 'We sent John away yesterday to his new life with outward good spirits and inward misery.'[30]

John had to wait until he was eighteen before being sent overseas to fight. In the meantime, the 2nd Irish Guards had been officially designated a regular rather than a reserve battalion in July 1915, and was inspected by Lord Kitchener himself on 13 August. Carrie was phlegmatic about her son's fate, writing: 'There is no chance John will survive unless he is so maimed from a wound as to be unfit to fight ... We know it and he does. We all know it but we must all give and do what we can and live in the shadow of a hope that our boy will be the one to escape.'[31]

John left home, after a final visit, on 15 August, his mother describing in her diary how he 'looks very straight and smart and young, as he turns on the stairs to say: "Send my love to Daddo."'[32] The following day, he sailed from Southampton, docking in Le Havre on the 17th, his eighteenth birthday. His father happened to be in France at the time, reporting as a war correspondent on the terrible hurt inflicted, particularly by the Germans. The front of Rheims cathedral had been badly damaged by incendiary bombs, and was 'roasted to a horrible flesh colour. The towers are smashed, the windows most of 'em in little bits of tinkling lacery, the gargoyles maimed and defaced – the whole thing looks like some wretched mutilated human being. Inside, there is nothing ... Birds flew in and out of the windows making a noise like the whirring of a shell ...'[33] Kipling found the time to offer John some not very relevant advice on how to use netting in the trenches to guard against enemy hand grenades.

The first days of September were spent digging trenches and training. On 25 September, the battalion prepared to move to the front, and John wrote his last letter home: 'This is THE great effort to break through and end the war ... They are staking a tremendous lot on this great advancing movement as if it succeeds the war won't go on for long. You have no idea what enormous issues depend on the next few days ... This will be my last letter most likely for some time as we won't get any time for writing this week ... Well so long old dears. Dear Love, John.'[34] Two days later, he went into action for the first, and last, time.

The question of whether Kipling blamed himself for his son's death has divided opinion, with some historians citing his 'Epitaphs of the War', and in particular 'Common Form':

If any question why we died,
Tell them because our fathers lied.[35]

However, Kipling was not really questioning the righteousness of the war itself, or the courage of those for whom the call of duty resulted in sacrifice. He was directing his criticism at the politicians who had failed to appreciate the threat of Germany and prepare for war before 1914; at the unions who had opposed conscription; and at some of the generals who had blundered, rather than blaming himself. But somewhere he might have reserved a little guilt for himself as one of those lying fathers.

*

On 12 November 1918 the church bells in Burwash rang to confirm news of the Armistice the previous day; and Carrie wrote in her diary: 'Rud and I feel as never before what it means now the War is over to face a world to be remade without a son.'[36] John was the second child the Kiplings had lost, their daughter Josephine, for whom the stories in *The Jungle Book* had been written, having died of pneumonia, aged six, in 1899.

Bateman's became a very melancholy place after the war, with both the Kiplings dogged by depression. Kipling was particularly disillusioned with the post-war world, for which his son had given his life, and was also suffering from a stomach ulcer that he feared was cancer. According to his secretary, he had 'lost his buoyant step'.[37] He seemed to have shrunk, and his weight dipped well below nine stone, accentuating his most striking feature, his vast bushy eyebrows. The conduct of the war also confirmed Kipling's deep-seated distrust of politicians, which lay behind his refusal ever to accept an honour, such as a knighthood or an Order of Merit, from the state.

Kipling tried to ease the pain – and, some argue, to perform an act of atonement – by throwing himself into two monumental tasks, to the exclusion of almost everything else: the writing of *The Irish Guards in the Great* War, and his work for the Imperial War Graves Commission. 'I'm as busy as the Devil in a gale of wind at all sorts of jobs that don't seem to matter much,' Kipling told Dunsterville in July 1919. 'Nothing matters much really when one has lost one's only son. It wipes the meaning out of things.'[38]

In January 1917 (when there was still the slightest hope that John might be a prisoner), Kipling had been asked by Colonel Douglas Proby, the Irish Guards officer who had recommended John for acceptance in the regiment in the first place, to write the official regimental history, 'not as a business matter, but as a memento of your son's service in the Regiment'.[39] This two-volume, five-and-a-half year labour of love enabled Kipling to walk in his son's footsteps, as countless other grieving parents would do on their personal pilgrimages. Sifting through maps and interviewing hundreds of Guardsmen finally convinced him that John must be dead. Some of the material for the book was collected from the diaries of officers – 'mere scraps of paper stained with the mud of the trenches, or even flecked with blood'.[40] Kipling knew several of the officers from 2nd Battalion, Irish Guards and, once disbanded in 1919, they spent weekends at Bateman's, giving the author first-hand accounts of particular engagements. 'Kipling bent his whole genius to completing this masterpiece of the Great War,' his secretary Dorothy Ponton wrote. She recorded that, although he told her it was 'being done with agony and bloody sweat', he later declared: 'This will be my great work.'

If not quite that, he did succeed in presenting the war from the soldier's point of view, rather than from the purely tactical perspective, leavening the military history with details of daily life and routines. For example, as he traced John's final journey to the front in September, he described Acquin, the 'little village on a hill-side a few miles from St Omer, in a fold of the great Sussex-like downs', where the men were billeted in barns forty and fifty at a time: 'it was to be their first and only experience of comfort for any consecutive time, and of French life a little untouched by war'.[41]

Kipling was aware that the 'whirlpools of war', as he described them in his introduction and as he knew from personal experience of the conflicting accounts surrounding John's death, made it hard to reconstruct exactly what happened. There was always plenty of room for error. 'Witnesses to phases of fights die and are dispersed; the ground over which they fought is battered out of recognition in a few hours; survivors confuse dates, places and personalities, and in the trenches, the monotony of the waiting days and the repetition-work of repairs breed mistakes and false judgements. Men grow doubtful or over-sure, and, in all good faith, give directly opposed versions. The clear sight of a comrade so mangled that he seems to have been long dead is burnt in on one brain to the exclusion of all else that happened that day. The shock of an exploded dump, shaking down a firmament upon the landscape, dislocates memory throughout half a battalion; and so on in all matters, till the end of laborious enquiry is too often the opening of fresh confusion.' In view of all this, it seemed best to him, then, 'to abandon all idea of such broad and balanced narratives as will be put forward by experts, and to limit himself to matters which directly touched the men's lives and fortunes'.[42] And that included the life and fortune of his son.

Kipling worked methodically, writing by hand on a manuscript that the long-suffering Dorothy Ponton would then type up – going through five or six successive drafts which he then edited and expanded. His handwriting was sometimes difficult to make out; but when Kipling himself tried to type, the results were 'much more undecipherable', Ponton complained. 'The beastly thing simply *won't* spell,' Kipling replied.[43]

As Kipling finished writing in July 1922, Carrie noted in her diary that he looked exhausted, 'yellow and shrunken'.[44] Kipling himself recorded that 'never was I so thankful to put a thing behind me. God knows it isn't much *qua* book, but it was done as one fidgets a sore tooth (or turns a knife in a wound) and each day, almost each hour, was pain and grief to me. But, in sum, it's done.'[45] After the war, Kipling's creative output diminished sharply – there were no novels and considerably less imaginative prose – a drying up that reflected the exhaustion and despair of the man.

It has been suggested that the reference to John's part in the action near Chalk Pit Wood on 27 September 1915, in which Second Lieutenant Kipling was reported 'wounded and missing', is curiously dispassionate: as if Kipling was trying to immerse himself in the professionalism of his task, in response to his personal loss. The casualty count 'was a fair average for the day of a debut', he concluded, 'and taught them somewhat for their future guidance'. But the pain is apparent, too. There were a great many 'almost children, of whom no record remains. They came out from Warley with the constantly renewed drafts, lived the span of a Second Lieutenant's life and were spent.'[46]

Kipling's account of the action builds into a savage criticism of the conduct of the whole battle, and of the lack of preparation. 'Consequently, for the third or fourth time within a twelvemonth, England was to learn at the cost of scores of thousands of casualties that modern warfare, unlike private theatricals, does not "come right at the performance" unless there have been rehearsals.' One and a half hours' of artillery bombardment, against an enemy bristling with machine guns was simply not enough. 'The Battalion had been swept from all quarters, and shelled at the same time, at the end of two hard days and sleepless nights, as a first experience of war, and had lost seven of their officers in forty minutes ... Their show had failed with all the others along the line, and "the greatest battle in the history of the world" was frankly stuck.'[47] Kipling often referred to the Battle of Loos, ironically, as 'the greatest battle in the history of the world'. For this is how Lieutenant General Richard Haking, of the Guards Division, had described the forthcoming attempt to deliver a breakthrough on the Western front to officers of the 2nd Guards Brigade at a briefing in the days before the battle. The writer Robert Graves, on the other hand, heard it described by his comrades at the battle as a 'bloody balls-up',[48] as British soldiers, without sufficient artillery support, were cut to pieces by German machine-gun fire.

The other great work Kipling undertook after the death of, and possibly in memory of, John was his role as literary advisor to the Imperial War Graves Commission (IWGC). In September 1917 its vice-chairman, Fabian Ware, came to Bateman's to invite Kipling (the first Englishman to win the Nobel Prize for Literature) to join the commission. The two men shared many opinions, particularly on empire, and a great mutual respect: Ware was later to recall how Kipling and he were often referred to 'as the pen and sword respectively of the Commission'.[49] Kipling was to serve as a commissioner until his death in January 1936.

*

The IWGC, like the British Red Cross Wounded and Missing Enquiry Department (W&MED), had had its origins in the first months of the war. In September 1914, in response to an appeal by Lord Kitchener, volunteers with cars converted into motor ambulances joined the Red Cross search, under Ware, for British soldiers wounded in the retreat from Mons, and conveyed them to hospital behind British lines. In fact, Ware's Mobile Ambulance Unit cared, at first, for as many French soldiers as British – and by the end of the year had conveyed more than 4,000 of them to safety.

In the course of their work, Ware's volunteers started to share lists of wounded soldiers admitted to hospitals in France with the fledgling W&MED led by Lord Robert Cecil, and to cooperate over enquiries about missing soldiers. When they had spare time out in the field, or when the ebb and flow of the fighting allowed, the volunteers began to take an interest in the graves and their occupants. They would come across small clusters of British graves marked by flimsy makeshift wooden crosses, with no sign that these graves had been recorded, registered or were being cared for in any way. They would sometimes replace the pencilled inscriptions with something more permanent, using paint, stencils, or machine-stamped metal identification plates: anything to preserve the name for evermore. 'The experience gained in the search for British wounded has helped the Unit in taking up another most useful piece of work,' Ware wrote back to London, 'viz: the identification of places in which British killed have been hastily buried, and the placing of crosses on the spots thus identified, with inscriptions designed to preserve the rough records which in many cases are already in danger of becoming obliterated.'[50]

It soon became apparent, however, that Ware's unit needed the support and resources of the army for the reporting of graves – a task in which the military authorities had had little interest at first. Ware managed to convince General Sir Nevil Macready, the Adjutant General to the British Expeditionary Force, to create the Graves Registration Commission (GRC); and in March 1915 Ware's GRC was 'officially recognised as the only organisation authorised to deal with the question of the locating, marking and registration of the graves of the British officers and men in France'.[51] In March 1915, Field Marshal Sir Douglas Haig, echoing Ware's beliefs in the 'extraordinary moral value' of the work, reported to the War Office: 'The mere fact that these officers visit day after day the cemeteries close behind the trenches, fully exposed to shell and rifle fire, accurately to record not only the names of the dead but also the exact place of burial, has a symbolic value to the men that it would be difficult to exaggerate. Further, it should be borne in mind that on the termination of hostilities the nation will demand an account from the Government as to the steps which have been taken to mark and classify the burial places of the dead, steps which can only be effectively taken at, or soon after, burial.'[52]

Ware was put in charge of the new organisation, and given the rank of major. The GRC was effectively taken over by the army, with the army supplying rations and fuel, and paying for crosses and inscriptions, while the original ambulance service provided by Ware's unit was hived off, and became the responsibility of the Red Cross. By October 1915, around 27,000 graves had been registered.

Already, Ware was establishing some of the principles, and laying the foundations, of what would become his great work. From the first days of the war, as his Mobile Ambulance Unit moved British and French soldiers to hospitals around Paris, Ware had enjoyed good relations with the French authorities. He put this to good use in his negotiations over the use of French soil in which to bury the British Empire's dead. These resulted in a bill, promising 'perpetuity of sepulture', which was supported by the French minister of war, Alexandre Millerand, and passed into law in December 1915. The British government was allowed to appropriate French land for use as burial grounds, the cost of the land being borne by the French state, with a 'properly constituted' British authority – provisionally, the GRC – responsible for the creation and maintenance of the cemeteries. In similar fashion, in 1917, the Belgian government in exile granted land in perpetuity to Britain for use as cemeteries.

In these early days, Ware was also developing his stance on equality of treatment. He wanted to stop the practice of bodies being privately exhumed and returned to Britain for burial, which only the wealthy could afford. Despite army instructions forbidding the practice, and a proclamation from the French general Joffre banning exhumations on French soil for sanitary reasons, there was a particularly high-profile case of this in April 1915. The body of William Gladstone, a twenty-nine-year-old lieutenant with the Royal Welch Fusiliers, who had been killed and buried in the Ypres Salient, was exhumed and brought back for burial in the parish churchyard at Hawarden in north Wales. Lieutenant Gladstone was the grandson of the great Victorian prime minister W. E. Gladstone, and the Gladstone family had applied such pressure in high places (up to the prime minister and the king) that the War Office relented, and allowed it in this case.

Ware was furious, writing to Robert Cecil on 5 May: 'There is possible trouble ahead about some exhumations at Poperinghe. I entirely agree with your remark about Gladstone's body [Cecil had described the incident as 'a little unfortunate' in his letter of 26 April]. Incidentally, the exhumation was carried out by British soldiers under fire. Fortunately (?or unfortunately) nobody was hit. The impression it has created among the soldiers out here is to be regretted. The one point of view overlooked in this matter is that of the officers themselves, who in ninety-nine cases out of a hundred will tell you that if they are killed would wish to be among their men.'[53] Ware's ambiguous parenthesis – '?or unfortunately' – suggests the furore that would have been caused if someone had been hit in such a vainglorious exercise would have settled the question for good. There were no repeats, however, or at least no legal ones, and the commission's ban on repatriation was to persist after the war.

Equality of treatment was not the only topic on which the GRC was prescriptive – something that would later characterise the IWGC. There would be standard registration procedures, and precise instructions, as to the dimensions and spacing of graves – these were to be between nine inches and one foot apart, with a path not exceeding three feet between the rows. Graves should be properly marked to ensure clear identification; and there was already a sensitivity to other faiths. 'On no account should [Egyptian] Mohammedans be buried in Christian consecrated ground'; Muslim graves were to be 'at least 6 feet deep' and dug by Egyptian labour if possible; Jewish graves were to be marked with a double triangle on a stake; and on no account should a cross be erected over an Indian grave.[54]

In February 1916, the GRC became the Directorate of Graves Registration and Enquiries (DGR&E), and Ware was appointed lieutenant colonel: he was well on his way to acquiring the nickname 'Lord Wargraves'. By May, when the DGR&E moved to Winchester House in St James's Square, Ware's successive organisations had registered more than 50,000 graves, and selected sites for 200 cemeteries across all the battle fronts, from France to the Middle East. The Battle of the Somme – which claimed almost 20,000 British dead on the first day alone – had not yet even started. Raging for four months from July to November, it would threaten to overwhelm the DGR&E.

The job of the DGR&E, organised into Graves Registration Units, was to decipher the often sketchy records provided by chaplains and burial officers. In the heat of battle, the dead were buried haphazardly, sometimes in scattered individual graves, in small, improvised cemeteries, or in mass graves sometimes dug in advance of the action. During the Battle of the Somme, many bodies were even left out to rot in the open for months before being buried, which exposed the DGR&E to criticism (although it was the army, rather than the DGR&E, which was actually responsible for burials, as opposed to the registration).

The registration officers had to interpret records that might amount to little more than a note left in a bottle by a grave, or a list of names tethered to a stake. Many bodies were destroyed beyond all recognition; and even with the introduction of the new double identification disc, made of pressed fibre, in 1916, it was hard to identify many of the dead. The members of the DGR&E needed to be familiar with identifying features, such as regimental badges and buttons, or other personal effects, down to the particular shade of khaki or style of helmet issued to a particular unit at a particular time. Above all, they needed to be good detectives, with a certain background knowledge, as they had to piece together information about the fighting, in order to reconstruct what was likely to have happened that day: which regiments had been in action where, and what had happened next, as the front line shifted and the same ground was fought over again and again, with the old graves obliterated.

It was not the job of the GRC or the DGR&E to deal directly with the relatives of the dead, wounded and missing, for this was the responsibility of the War Office and the Red Cross Wounded and Missing Enquiry Department. Nevertheless, Ware believed that his organisation had some role to play in consoling the families of the fallen. It did so by responding to requests for photographs of the graves, which were sent back to the families in England, together with information on the grave's location and directions to the nearest railway station, in case relatives wished to visit after the war. By the end of 1917, the DGR&E had registered 150,000 graves in France and Belgium; and sent some 12,000 photographs to grieving families. These were often the only record they would have of their loved one's actual grave, since so many graves were destroyed in the ongoing fighting or relocated after the war.

From these amateur beginnings grew an organisation that transformed the way in which the country honoured its dead. In its early years, the story of what became the Commonwealth War Graves Commission parallels that of the W&MED, another vast bureaucracy run with the most humane of aims. What had started in a piecemeal way went on to fulfil a role that no one had foreseen at the start of the war.

*

The First World War marked a turning point in the way in which the country commemorated its war dead. When war was declared, the British Army had fewer than 300,000 regular soldiers. Over the next four years, more than five million Britons were deployed on the Western front, with up to two million serving in France and Flanders at any one time. Most of these service personnel had volunteered, or from 1916 been conscripted, in what was believed to be a patriotic cause; and this, combined with the unprecedented scale of the slaughter, fostered a new sense of debt and responsibility towards the dead, a duty to name and commemorate them. These were citizen-soldiers rather than professionals. People now expected that the war dead should be spared the oblivion that had characterised previous wars. At the Battle of Waterloo, the bodies of the officers had been transported home to be buried, while those of private soldiers were simply tossed into mass graves. A hundred years later, it was time to commemorate individual sacrifices.

In March 1917, Ware proposed that an 'Imperial Commission' should take over the work hitherto entrusted to the National Committee for the Care of Soldiers' Graves. The empire, he argued, must be 'spared the reflections which weighed on the conscience of the British nation when, nearly twenty years after the conclusion of the Crimean War, it became known that the last resting place of those who had fallen in that war had, except in individual instances, remained uncared for and neglected'.[55]

Ware was convinced that, although it had no immediate military significance, the work had 'an extraordinary moral value to the troops in the field as well as to the relatives and friends of the dead at home'.[56] It was particularly important to the soldiers themselves that their fallen comrades should be identified, named, and the spot where they were buried, recorded.

The IWGC was established by Royal Charter in May 1917, charged with the care of the graves of all members of the imperial forces who had died on active service. It was the first time in history that an organisation had been created to commemorate a nation's dead in war in this way. The IWGC's driving force, and vice-chairman, was Fabian Ware, head of the DGR&E, which for the duration of the war continued to fulfil most of its responsibilities, while the IWGC planned for the post-war future. For this purpose it was invested with powers to acquire, and care for, land for cemeteries, to keep records and registers, and to enforce rules, such as those preventing 'the erection by any person other than the Commission of permanent memorials' in any cemetery under its control.

In the summer of 1917, an advisory committee, comprising the architects Edwin Lutyens and Herbert Baker, and the assistant director of the Royal Botanic Gardens at Kew, Arthur Hill, travelled to the Western front to advise on the future treatment of the military cemeteries. It was a bringing together of some of the greatest talents of the time in design and horticulture, and a sign that vision, quality and attention to detail might, unusually, characterise this great national task of commemoration. Lutyens described the unbroken line of makeshift burial grounds and individual graves that stretched from the Ypres Salient to the Somme as 'a ribbon of isolated graves like a milky way across miles of country where men were tucked in where they fell',[57] while Hill was taken aback by the beauty of that 'desolate shell-hole region', the Somme. 'Picture to yourselves a vast undulating landscape,' he wrote, 'a blaze of scarlet [poppy] unbroken by tree or hedgerow, with here and there long stretches of white Camomile and patches of yellow Charlock, dotted over with the half-hidden crosses of the dead.'[58]

The architects could not agree on an approach, their differences inflamed by personal rivalries. There were also more fundamental disagreements across the country over how a nation should remember and honour its war dead. In particular, it was necessary to strike a balance between public and private sentiment that also recognised the new spirit of democracy. Sir Frederic Kenyon, director of the British Museum, was appointed by the IWGC in 1917 to set up a committee to resolve these issues as they applied to the design of the cemeteries. 'My endeavour,' he wrote, 'has been to arrive at a result which will, so far as may be, satisfy the feelings of relatives and comrades of those who lie in these cemeteries; which will represent the soldierly spirit and discipline in which they fought and fell: which will typify the Army to which they belonged; which will give expression to those deeper emotions, of regimental comradeship, of service to their Army, their King, their country and their God, which underlay (perhaps often unconsciously) their sacrifice of themselves for the cause in which they fought, and which in ages to come will be a dignified memorial, worthy of the nation and the men who gave their lives for it, in the lands of the Allies with whom and for whom they fought.'[59]

The Kenyon Report, which was adopted by the commission in February 1918, skilfully managed to reconcile these different interests. It became the blueprint for the work of the IWGC after the war. Following Ware's strongly held beliefs, the report stressed the principle of equality of treatment for officers and men. There was to be no distinction, in the form of different styles of memorial, for officers and other ranks lying in the same cemeteries. The commission believed, according to Ware, that 'the proper and only possible place for special individual memorials was in the homes, villages, etc. of those who had fallen and not in the military cemeteries abroad'.[60] The flourishing of such memorials after the war testified to the need for this expression of devotion: represented by the figures of weeping angels and kneeling knights throughout Britain, in stained-glass windows and parish churchyards. Had the commission allowed these expensive and elaborate monuments to be put up by the wealthy in commission cemeteries, 'the common sacrifice made by all ranks would lose the regularity and orderliness most becoming to the resting places of soldiers, who fought and fell side by side'. Across the country, at a local level – in churches, on village greens, outside workplaces – monuments were erected to individuals and to groups of individuals, to complement any national commemoration. There were to be regimental memorials, too, such as the Guards Memorial in London, whose opening ceremony the Kiplings attended on 16 August 1926 and Carrie described in her diary as 'the close of the War for so many of us'.[61]

The Kiplings were among those families who commissioned a private memorial for their son. An elegant oval bronze plaque, designed by the sculptor Charles Wheeler, hangs on the wall in the north aisle of Burwash church. It reads: 'To the memory of John Kipling Lieutenant Second Battalion Irish Guards the only son of Rudyard and Caroline Kipling of Bateman's who fell at the battle of Loos the 27th September 1915 aged eighteen years and six weeks: *Qui ante diem periit* [who perished before his day].' At the time, there was no memorial to him in France because he was still considered 'missing'. John's name, roughly incised, also features on the village war memorial on a patch of ground outside the church – with the date of death given incorrectly as 29 September. It was perhaps for this reason, or perhaps because he simply could not face the emotion of it, that Kipling refused to attend the unveiling of the Burwash memorial. (John's name was eventually commemorated on a wall at Dud Corner Cemetery at Loos – and then removed – and on the gravestone in St Mary's ADS Cemetery in Pas-de-Calais.)

In pursuit of the principle of equality of treatment, the Kenyon Report, and the recommendations that followed, stipulated that the headstones should be uniform in design: two feet six inches tall, by one foot three inches, by three inches deep, with the head slightly curved so that the rain would run off. Initial designs by Lutyens and by Baker were set aside, in favour of one that was to become a rare example of something successfully designed by a committee (comprising the keeper of the Wallace Collection, the director of the National Gallery, and the artist and designer MacDonald Gill). They were made of English limestone – generally Portland or Hopton Wood – and were to bear the name, rank, date of death and regiment of the deceased (the headstones of the Chinese Labour Corps had inscriptions in Chinese). As a concession to individual sentiment, the bereaved could choose to add an incised religious symbol – say, the Cross or the Star of David – and a short text, limited to sixty-six characters including spaces, of a personal nature, a prayer perhaps. This was how the report resolved the question of whether the gravestones should be in the shape of a cross, as were the French. Whether the cemeteries should be Christian or non-denominational in style was one of the most contentious issues. The genius of the Kenyon Report, and the architects who put its recommendations into practice, was to forge a compromise that had its own aesthetic integrity, that did not appear to have been designed by committee, and that succeeded in creating some order out of the destruction and chaos. Overall, the cemeteries were to achieve a simple, secular, understated style, that was rooted in the classical tradition, yet somehow timeless: a far cry from the more sentimental, Gothic style to be found in French cemeteries, or the overt modernism, which characterised other artistic endeavours after the war.

As well as the graves, every cemetery of any size would have a 'Stone of Remembrance' and a 'Cross of Sacrifice'. The Stone of Remembrance, an abstract monolith designed by Lutyens, had something of the spirit of an ancient sacrificial altar, while the Cross of Sacrifice, designed by Reginald Blomfield, consisted of a tall stone cross bearing a bronze sword. Blomfield later recalled that 'many of us had seen terrible examples of war memorials in France and were haunted by the fear of winged angels in various sentimental attitudes', and had wanted his cross to be as abstract as possible, free from 'any of the sentimentalities of Gothic'. Nevertheless, its martial and religious theme was designed to appeal to a nation of Christian soldiers (although this had not been Ware's intention). His cross became so popular that, as he complained in his memoirs, it was 'freely pirated all over the country'. He came across some 'horrible travesties of it in many local memorials apparently executed by the local mason from illustrations of the Cross given in the papers. There is a deplorable example, typical, I regret to say, of many others, in the market-place at Aylesbury. The local man has done his best, but he has simply murdered my Cross.'[62]

As literary advisor to the IWGC, Kipling came up with the words for all inscriptions used in the cemeteries. For Lutyens's Stone of Remembrance he chose a phrase from the Old Testament Book of Ecclesiasticus: 'Their name liveth for evermore'. As he wrote to the commissioners in November 1918: 'It was necessary to find words of praise and honour which should be both simple and well known, comprehensive, and of the same value in all tongues, and standing, as far as might be, outside the flux of men and things. After search and consultation with all ranks and many races in our armies and navies, as well as with those who had given their sons, it seemed to me that no single phrase could better that which closes the tribute to "famous men" in Ecclesiasticus:– "Their name liveth for evermore." '63 It was a terrible irony that the man who had chosen the phrase marking the cemeteries of so many hundreds of thousands should have no shrine, stone or grave at which to lay his own grief. For those who had originally been buried in a wartime cemetery, but whose graves had subsequently been shelled out of existence in the fighting, he chose a phrase from the previous verse in Ecclesiasticus: 'Their glory shall not be blotted out.' These became known as Kipling Memorials. And for the headstones of the 180,000 unidentified bodies, he provided the haunting inscription: 'A Soldier of the Great War Known unto God', which, unknown to him, was to mark the grave of his son in St Mary's ADS Cemetery from 1919 to 1992. The French, on the other hand, sometimes housed the unidentified bones in great ossuaries, such as that at Douaumont near Verdun, which contained the shattered, skeletal remains of at least 130,000 unknown, nameless combatants.

There was bitter opposition to what was seen as the heavy-handed, bureaucratic policies of the IWGC. In 1919 a petition organised by Lady Florence Cecil, the wife of the Bishop of Exeter and mother of three sons killed in the war, collected 8,000 signatures, mostly from mothers and widows (there was not a single woman, it is worth noting, on the commission). This was presented to the Prince of Wales, with the complaint: 'We have been deeply wounded by the decision of the Commission that no crosses (other than those engraved on the headstone, which time and the weather will soon deface) are to be allowed over the individual graves of those who gave their lives to preserve the lives and liberty of others.'64 Why shouldn't the bereaved be allowed to express their love and loss in their own way? And not have to submit to the tyranny of the IWGC? The fundamental conflict yet again was between individual choice, on the one hand, and the principle of equality of treatment and aesthetic uniformity, on the other. Lady Florence's sister-in-law, the Countess of Selborne, published an article in the *National Review*, titled 'National Socialism of War Cemeteries', in which she argued that the rights of the relatives to their loved one's body had

been 'abrogated' by 'pure Socialism of the most advanced School
... the conscription of bodies is worthy of Lenin'.[65]

The High Church lobby, arguing for crosses rather than
headstones, was led by the Cecil family. Five of the ten grandsons
of the Victorian prime minister, Lord Salisbury, including George
Cecil, had been killed in the war. Florence's brother-in-law, Lord
Hugh Cecil, doubted Kipling's qualifications for the job of coining
inscriptions, complaining that the writer was 'not a known religious
man'.[66] Hugh's older brother, Lord Robert Cecil, meanwhile,
demanded a parliamentary debate.

Kipling did not attend the debate in the House of Commons
on 4 May 1920, but his support for the IWGC's policy of 'equality
of treatment' was clear from a letter he wrote to a Colonel Lewin
the previous day: 'Lord knows I'm no democrat: but it does seem
to me that in such deaths as our men died they are all equally
under the Empire's care for ever; no man being favoured more
than his neighbour.' Kipling strongly defended the principle of
equal treatment, as it reflected 'equality of sorrow' and sacrifice.
There should be no privilege in the face of death. 'The thought,'
he believed, 'at the back of every poor mother's and wife's mind
is:– "My man was as much to me as any one's man was to them.
Why should them that can afford it seem to grieve more?" [i.e. by
putting up a more elaborate headstone].' In a postscript, Kipling
speculated how, if John's body had not been missing after Loos
but had had a grave, he could have commissioned a fine, specially
designed gravestone for his son, but in that case: 'I shouldn't care to
face my boy in the next world: or to look at the women and fathers
in Burwash (where we have lost 50) who had to put up with a War
Graves headstone erected after long delays.'[67]

Despite his absence on 4 May, another letter from Kipling,
implying support for the IWGC's policy of 'equality of treatment',
was read out by William Burdett-Coutts, the MP for Westminster
who was fighting the commission's cause. 'You see we shall never
have any grave to go to,' wrote Kipling. 'Our boy was missing at
Loos. The ground is, of course, battered and mined past all hope
of any trace being recovered. I wish some of the people who are

making this trouble realised how more fortunate they are to have a name on a headstone in a known place.'[68]

The debate confirmed that the uniformity of the headstones should reflect 'equality in death': that officer or private, rich or poor, the graves should be undifferentiated by rank. It also confirmed that there should be no private memorials in military cemeteries and no repatriation of bodies. Despite attempts by the War Graves Association, a pressure group of more than 10,000 members, to reverse the decision, the policy of non-repatriation prevailed. The nation, it was deemed, owned the body, and not the dead man's family.

This was in direct contrast to the United States government, which pledged in 1919 to repatriate the body of any dead soldier whose family so wished, which resulted in around 60 per cent of families choosing to have the bodies of their loved ones shipped home. Though the French government had originally banned exhumations within the war zones, it bowed to popular pressure and the impossibility of stopping a trade in illegal exhumations. It, too, allowed bodies (as many as 300,000) to be returned to native villages and towns across the country.

The need for a body to ease the grieving process drove some people to desperate lengths. Even after the ban, there continued to be clandestine exhumations, often carried out at night, with bodies being smuggled back to Britain. In May 1921 the grave of a Private Hopkins, a Canadian in the Tyne Cot Cemetery, was found to have been 'wrenched open, the body taken out and the coffin left in the grave'. An investigation by the IWGC revealed that it had been the soldier's parents who had effected the break-in. They were tracked down and apprehended in Antwerp, on their way back to Canada, with their son's remains in a 'valise'; and Private Hopkins was duly reburied in Belgian soil. The following year, Major General Frederick Adam arranged – with the help of the local mayor – for the surreptitious exhumation of his son Norman's body from an isolated grave near Arras in France and its reburial in the Glasgow Necropolis.[69]

The burial and commemoration of the dead after the war proved to be a huge undertaking both architecturally and logistically: how to remember, on gravestones and memorials, the names of the million soldiers, sailors and airmen of the British Empire who had been killed. By the end of the war, there were some 1,200 cemeteries strung out along the Western front in France and Belgium. The task of caring for these graves had been further complicated by the German Spring Offensive and the Allied counter-offensive of 1918, when the same ground was fought over time and time again, destroying many of the existing graves in the process. Some of those bodies continue to turn up to this day.

The job had to be tackled quickly as farmers would soon be returning to reclaim their lands in the battlefields of France and Flanders, and relatives would be crossing the Channel in search of the graves of their loved ones: it was feared that they would be appalled to see some of the isolated graves, or the ramshackle wartime cemeteries, whose makeshift wooden crosses tilted crazily at all angles, or, even worse, the unburied bodies that still lay about some of the battlefields. In 1919 and 1920, therefore, the commission focused on tidying up and fencing existing cemeteries, shovelling and carting earth, smoothing grave mounds and uprooting tree stumps in preparation for sowing, and painting signs to guide visitors. By the spring of 1921 almost a thousand cemeteries had been planted up, including some of the new ones.

Rudyard Kipling was a great admirer of the commission's gardeners. In 'The Silent World', a chapter he contributed anonymously to *War Graves of the Empire*, a special edition of *The Times* published on the tenth anniversary of the signing of the Armistice, he described their work in the cemeteries soon after the end of the war: 'early 1919 saw what were called "Travelling Garden Parties" – closed lorries, each with tents, tools, driver, cook, foreman, eight gardeners, and the inevitable trench-found small dog in charge of all, cruising into chaos with three days' rations and water (there was none on the road drinkable), and a supply of some elementary plants, seeds and shrubs … There was small comfort then on the Somme of winter afternoons, with gale and wet almost immobilising the lorries, and the great hollows of the downs delivering thunders and coloured smokes as the live shells were being exploded in the pits.'[70] The life of these pioneers in the wilderness of the Western front was a hard and lonely one. Living in old army barracks or disused hospital wards when not on the road, they had to walk miles every day between camp and cemetery, with their tools on their back. By March 1921, there were almost 900 gardeners working for the commission in France and Belgium.

They had a therapeutic role, too. 'As their grounds matured to beauty through the seasons,' Kipling continued:

> the gardeners found themselves recipients of many heartbroken confidences and the helpers, in every kind of trouble, of those who came their way. It was their business to know, point out, or, on a blind person's demand, lead up to any individual grave in their charge; to give the angle and the hour best fitted to photograph incised letters that vanish or stand out with the sun; to make a rest, sometimes, for an unsteady little hand-camera; to indicate the proper people to approach when it was explained to them that someone in their care had been awarded a posthumous decoration – which the worn cutting from the *Gazette* proved – but that 'it had not been put on his headstone, and we don't know who to tell'; to defer to broken petitions that some small plant that someone had specially loved should be worked into the low border at the foot of his headstone; and to take no heed of people who appeared once a year on a certain day, wet or fine, suffered their hour beside a certain grave and departed. In winter, when visitors were few, their company would be the grave-diggers and the chaplain, who read the service over the known and unknown borne in to rejoin their comrades. It is difficult to overstate how real an object, even passion, it was with those who served our dead that no man should be left to lie out alone.[71]

The massive post-war programme of search and exhumation was carried out by units of the British Army under the command of the DGR&E. Between the Armistice and the end of 1921, more than 200,000 bodies were exhumed and reinterred, many of them concentrated in new or expanded cemeteries. Kipling himself described the process in 'The Silent World', noting that a further 28,000 bodies had been recovered since 1921, of whom a quarter had been identified. In 1921 the responsibility for searching the battlefields, and exhuming, identifying and reburying the bodies, passed from the DGR&E to the IWGC, and in 1922 the directorate was closed. Kipling praised its officers in *The Times* article: 'The officers and men detailed for discovery and concentration of scattered graves gave to their heavy duty a skill, devotion, and unselfishness beyond praise. Their names will be unknown to history, but it is possible they did more than most to bring comfort to those whose kin had fallen by the wayside.' He was not aware, of course, that in September 1919, the unidentified body of his son John had been exhumed: one of 7,000 exhumations carried out on the Loos battlefield, of which 5,300 were unidentified.[72]

Wherever possible, the commission tried to concentrate graves, particularly those that were isolated and scattered over the battlefields, into larger cemeteries. The Tyne Cot Cemetery, for example, on the slopes beneath Passchendaele, consisted of 343 British and Canadian graves in 1917, a figure which grew to 11,900 during the 1920s, when bodies from the battlefields and smaller cemeteries nearby were concentrated there. Its proximity to England impressed John Dove, editor of the *Round Table*, a quarterly review promoting the idea of a British Commonwealth. 'From the great wall or by the cross on the pyramid on a clear day,' he wrote of a visit to Tyne Cot, 'and looking, as the Germans used to do, westwards, a faint gleam will catch your eye far away to the north. It is the narrow sea, which thanks to the men who lie there, the Germans never reached; and beyond lies England … If there are tears in things, it is here.'[73] It was not always possible, however, to concentrate graves in such large cemeteries – and even today there are 918 cemeteries along the Western front, between the North Sea and the Somme, and most bodies are buried very near to where they fell.

When bodies were moved to the new war cemeteries, or when existing cemeteries were simply upgraded, and the graves marked with headstones, families were allowed to ask for the original wooden crosses to be sent home at the state's expense. Vera Brittain, for example, recalled her brother Edward's cross being returned wrapped in canvas. Back in Britain, the crosses were then buried in parish churchyards, or hung on the walls of the church, or piled in the porches as treasured relics. In the porch of Burwash parish church, where John Kipling is commemorated, there hang a number of wooden crosses retrieved from the battlefields in 1924.

To develop the recommendations of the Kenyon Report, three 'Principal Architects' were appointed in 1918: Reginald Blomfield, Herbert Baker and Edwin Lutyens. The idea initially was that each of them would design an 'experimental' cemetery, but in the end, Blomfield designed all three, at Le Tréport, Forceville and Louvencourt. It was Blomfield, too, who had to explain to the commission the basic processes involved in building: specifications and quantities, obtaining orders, drawing up contracts, and so on.

'It is the simplest, it is the grandest place I ever saw,' *The Times* reported in 1920 of Blomfield's 'experimental' cemetery at Forceville on the Somme. 'The most perfect, the noblest, the most classically beautiful memorial that any loving heart or any proud nation could desire for their heroes fallen in a foreign land. Picture this strangely stirring place. A lawn enclosed of close clipped turf, banded across with line on line of flowers, and linked by these bands of flowers; uncrowded, at stately intervals stand in soldierly ranks the white headstones. And while they form as perfect, as orderly a whole as any regiment on parade, yet they do not shoulder each other. Every one is set apart in flowers, every one casts its shadow upon a gracious space of green. Each one, so stern in outline, is most rich in surface, for the crest of each regiment stands out with a bold and arresting distinction above the strongly incised names.'[74] Baker described a similar effect for which he was striving in his cemeteries as that 'homely sense of the English churchyard'.[75] The style was quintessentially English and understated, of grass lawns, yew hedges, shrubs and herbaceous borders – although, as early as 1917, Arthur Hill had advised on appropriate plants from the Dominions, too: maple from Canada, eucalyptus from Tasmania and shrubs from New Zealand.

The experimental cemeteries provided the prototype, for design, planning and procurement, and the subsequent mobilisation of monumental masons and stone-carvers. It was a massive task, with headstones being shipped from England to continental Europe at the rate of up to 4,000 a week. By 1923 the IWGC had more than 2,000 staff. Paying tribute to the unique achievement of the IWGC, Blomfield drew attention to the 'tact, tenacity and remarkable organising ability' of Fabian Ware, who had 'built up a Department which has given the Empire, in our Military Cemeteries, a memorial of those lost in the war such as never had been dreamt of before, and which has been a model to other countries as to how these things should be done'.[76] By the time it had finished, the commission would have created, and cared for, around 580,000 separate, named graves, and 180,000 unidentified graves; and commemorated the names of a further 530,000 who had no known grave. These figures accounted for what was acknowledged at the time to be the empire's million dead.

The construction of the Commonwealth war cemeteries was the largest and most ambitious architectural programme ever undertaken by a government not known for its enthusiasm for funding design projects. The commission's global reach was to stretch far beyond the Western front, and cemeteries in the UK, from Italy to Iraq, Turkey to Tanganyika [now Tanzania], Egypt (where Kipling visited the cemeteries in 1929), to Portuguese East Africa [now Mozambique]. As Kipling summarised in *The Graves of the Fallen*, a booklet published by the IWGC in 1919, its work 'covered every part of the world where the men of the Empire had served and died – from the vast and known cities of our dead in Flanders and France to hidden and outlying burial-grounds of a few score at the ends of the earth. These resting-places are situated on every conceivable site – on bare hills flayed by years of battle, in orchards and meadows, beside populous towns or little villages, in jungle-glades, at coast ports, in far-away islands, among desert sands, and desolate ravines.'[77]

It was an extraordinary achievement. In *The Immortal Heritage* (1937), his account of the first twenty years of the work of the IWGC, Fabian Ware recorded that 'in France and Belgium alone there are 970 architecturally constructed cemeteries surrounded by fifty miles of walling in brick or stone, with nearly a thousand "Crosses of Sacrifice" and 560 "Stones of Remembrance", and many chapels, record buildings and shelters; there are some 600,000 headstones resting on nearly 250 miles of concrete beam foundations. There are also eighteen larger memorials to those who have no known grave ... .'[78] Kipling once remarked to Ware that it was: 'The biggest single bit of work since any of the Pharaohs – and they only worked in their own country.'[79]

The introduction to *The Immortal Heritage* was written by the poet Edmund Blunden, who succeeded Kipling as literary advisor to the IWGC; in it, he expressed particular surprise, given the conditions of the Western front, that the individual should be honoured. 'In the clash and bewilderment of actual fighting, in the rapid ruin and chaos and oblivion of the front line with its enormous process of annihilation, perhaps not many soldiers retained the confidence that the dead – themselves, it might be, tomorrow, or the next instant – would at length obtain some lasting and distinct memorial.' Instead, he celebrated, 'the great design of interment and remembrance ... in every place that saw the British Empire under arms', noting 'that no previous war has been marked by anything like this fulfilment of piety towards those who gave their lives ... The ancients regarded the soldier in the mass, and felt no difficulty in consigning him accordingly without name or detail into some common sepulchre ... It has been the faith of the Commission that those who fought and died in 1914–1918 were – what we know them to have been – several and separate personalities, each in human measure "the captain of his fate", each claiming individual comprehension ... and so it is entirely laudable that the Imperial War Graves Commission has carried out its task with a vivid sense of the individual grave.'[80] This was its unique and uplifting achievement. Today the commission commemorates 1.7 million Commonwealth servicemen and women who died in two world wars. It manages 23,000 sites spread over more than 150 countries, employing 850 gardeners worldwide, of whom around 300 are in France, along with stonemasons for the headstones, carpenters for the doors and windows, and metal-workers for the railings and cemetery registers.

*

After the war, the Kiplings rekindled their love of France, combining it with Rudyard's passion for motoring. He described their annual tours in six notebooks, with comments, in his role as a commissioner of the IWGC, on the condition of the cemeteries, and, as a car enthusiast, on distances travelled, petrol consumed, and punctures caused by the potholed roads of war-torn France. They never found John's grave.

On their first recorded battlefield tour in July 1920 (they had already visited France in March that year, but there is no record of any visits to the cemeteries), he and Carrie drove almost 1,500 miles in 'the Duchess', as he was to call each of his success-ive Rolls-Royces. They visited around thirty cemeteries between Ypres, Amiens and Rouen, and saw George Cecil's grave in Villers-Cotterêts. On Sunday 25 July, they proceeded to Loos, where they visited Chalk Pit Wood, arriving 'about the hour that John fell',[81] and where the previous September, unknown to anyone, his body had been exhumed. At Rouen, as so often, Kipling was impressed by the 'extraordinary beauty of the cemetery and the great care that the attendants had taken of it, and the almost heartbroken thankfulness of the relatives of the dead who were there'.[82]

The following May, the Kiplings were back in France, and making a detour to Villers-Cotterêts, undeterred by a warning that the road was '*impropre pour autos*'. At 11.50 a.m. (the motoring diaries are most precise about times), they visited George Cecil's grave again in the village cemetery, where he was buried with three other officers in the 'Guards' Grave'. In April 1922, at the request of the families, the four bodies in this grave were exhumed and reburied in the Guards' Cemetery, in beech woods north of the village, with the rest of their comrades. Kipling found the site 'perhaps the most beautiful of all resting-places in France, on a slope of the forest off the dim road, near the Rond de la Reine';[83] and visited it again in May 1923, when he admired the Guards' memorial put up by George Cecil's mother, now Lady Milner.

The Kiplings' tour of 1922 coincided with King George V's 'Pilgrimage', organised by Fabian Ware. The Kiplings arrived in Calais on 10 May, and on the 11th set off for Vlamertinghe Military Cemetery in the Duchess. Here, he had to do a 'lightning' change into his official, morning dress – 'blacks and a white shirt' – in the bedroom of a cottage lent by an old lady, before being introduced to the king for the first time.[84] The king, Carrie noted in her diary, was 'very appreciative' of 'Rud' for the speech he had written.[85] After the ceremony, the king passed through Belgium on his way to France, via Vimy Ridge and the Somme battlefield cemeteries, while Kipling drove south, through la Bassée to Lens on 'a most awful stretch of road and the countryside so altered that we passed where John had disappeared. Red House, Chalk Pit wood and all smoothed out'.[86]

On 13 May, the Kiplings joined the official ceremony at Terlincthun Cemetery, overlooking the Channel, near Boulogne. It was a fine day, with 'brilliant light' and a 'keen wind'. The king and Queen Mary stood beneath the Cross of Sacrifice, facing the Stone of Remembrance. The king spoke the words that Kipling had been asked to draft for him 'with splendid delivery, and dignified bearing', Kipling reported.[87] The words reflected Fabian Ware's belief that 'we remember and must charge our children to remember, that, as our dead were equal in sacrifice, so are they equal in honour', and that the shared history of the war, and the commemoration of its dead, could draw nations together: 'in the course of my pilgrimage,' the king intoned Kipling's words, 'I have many times asked myself whether there can be any more potent advocates of peace upon earth than this massed multitude of witnesses to the desolation of war. And I feel that, so long as we have faith in God's purpose, we cannot but believe that the existence of these visible memorials will, eventually, serve to draw all peoples together in sanity and self-control, even as it has already set the relations between our Empire and our allies on the deep-rooted bases of a common heroism and a common agony.'[88] Kipling was once again presented to the king, 'who said to me what was seemly'. Kipling reciprocated by praising the king's delivery, 'which was also seemly'. 'The King also spoke to Mum [Carrie] at the railings … about John. Mum's curtseys nice to behold,' he added.[89]

When Kipling came to write the official, illustrated account of the king's pilgrimage, he made few references to the part played by Earl Haig who accompanied the king. He was criticised for this omission, but Kipling could never forget that Haig, as commander of the First Army in 1915, presided over the Battle of Loos, in which John was one of more than 20,000 British soldiers killed. The king wrote a foreword for *The King's Pilgrimage*, with any profits going to philanthropic organisations that assisted relatives to visit the cemeteries abroad. At the front of this best-selling souvenir edition, Kipling added a poem that was to become equally successful in its own right. It began in heroic terms:

Our King went forth on Pilgrimage
His prayer and vows to pay
To them that saved our Heritage
And cast their own away.

But it also included lines, in parentheses, that alluded to his and Carrie's loss and their longing, like hundreds of thousands of other parents, for a grave at which to grieve:

(All that they had they gave – they gave;
and they shall not return,
For these are those that have no grave
Where any heart may mourn.)[90]

The Kiplings were touring again in 1924. On 29 August, they visited Notre-Dame to see Rudyard's inscription on the memorial plaque; the 31st was 'Wet – wet – wet! An inauspicious day.' The heavy rain had created a mud slick on the chalky road and the car slithered off, half burying its rear wheel in the bank: all 'this on a Sunday, in an absolutely deserted landscape and with all the inhabitants in their best clothes at Mass!' Eventually, with some local assistance, they managed to extricate themselves and at 4.50 p.m., they visited St Mary's ADS Cemetery. No mention was made of the 'Unidentified British Soldier, Officer Lieut. Irish Guards', buried at Plot 7, Row D, Grave 2. Kipling noted in his motoring diary that the cemetery was, 'Spoilt by the Gardener's shed – but otherwise very good.'[91]

In the spring of 1925, the Kiplings were back in France on another tour. They visited Rouen cemetery on 13 March. 'All the place has been levelled up & looks sloppy & dirty,' Rudyard complained in his motoring diary.[92] While there, he 'collogued with the Head Gardener and contractors', as he described in a letter to his friend Rider Haggard. 'One never gets over the shock of this Dead Sea of arrested lives – from V.C's and Hospital Nurses to coolies of the Chinese Labour Corps. By one grave of a coolie some pious old Frenchwoman (bet she was an old maid) had deposited a yellow porcelain crucifix!! Somehow that almost drew tears.'[93] The following evening, after dinner in their hotel, Le Grand Monarque, in Chartres, he started work on his short story, 'The Gardener'. As he wrote to Rider Haggard, it gave him 'something to do at the day's end'.[94] By the time they reached Pau, just over a week and many sights later (including a visit to the cathedral in Le Mans to see his plaque to the million dead), 'The Gardener' was finished enough to send off to his secretary for typing. 'A good job not so badly done,' he wrote.[95]

In 'The Gardener', middle-aged spinster Helen Turrell is guided by the Christ-like figure of a gardener to the grave of her 'nephew', Michael. Slowly and subtly, it is revealed that Michael is, in fact, her illegitimate son, killed near Ypres by 'a shell-splinter dropping out of a wet dawn'. In a reimagining of the circumstances surrounding John's death: 'The next shell uprooted and laid down over the body what had been the foundation of a barn wall, so neatly that none but an expert would have guessed that anything unpleasant had happened.'[96] After being informed by the authorities post-war that

Michael's body has been found, identified and reinterred in a vast military cemetery, Helen sets off, 'now strong in the certainty that there was an altar upon earth' upon which – unlike the Kiplings – she might lay her love. Like hundreds of other pilgrims, she makes her way to Ypres and the offices of the authority 'in a board and tar-paper shed on the skirts of a razed city full of whirling lime-dust and blown papers'.

The cemetery, in which Michael's body lies is in the process of transition – as were so many of those that Kipling visited on his motor tours – evolving from an overgrown, unkempt wartime burial ground into an orderly IWGC cemetery. All Helen can see is 'a merciless sea of black crosses, bearing little strips of stamped tin at all angles across their faces. She could distinguish no order or arrangement in their mass; nothing but a waist-high wilderness as of weeds stricken dead, rushing at her.' As she moves forward, wandering hopelessly to the left and the right, she wonders how she will ever find the grave she is looking for; and then she spies, a great distance away, 'a line of whiteness', a block of some two or three hundred graves whose headstones have already been set, whose flowers are planted out, and whose new-sown grass shows green. 'Here she could see clear-cut letters at the end of the rows, and referring to her slip, realised that it was not here she must look.' It is then, providentially, that the gardener redirects her back to the black crosses, and to her son's grave.

It could be particularly difficult to locate a grave during this transitional phase, when the cemeteries were still in the making. *The Pilgrims' Guide to the Ypres Salient* (1920) had warned that: 'The work of arranging and recording graves and cemeteries is by no means finished, and any description or directions must necessarily be incomplete. The official list aims at registering as a cemetery any collection of more than 40 graves. In some cases, isolated graves or graves in difficult country have been concentrated into larger cemeteries. Any guide is therefore bound to be out of date.'[97] It was necessary, therefore, to make enquiries first about the official location of the grave: the name of the cemetery, the row in which the grave is situated, and its number in the row. 'A search undertaken in ignorance of these particulars,' a directive of the DGR&E advised, 'is likely to end in failure.' On his motoring tours, Kipling spotted hundreds of grieving relatives, like Helen, wandering helplessly in search of a grave; and became aware, at first hand, of the importance of providing such information. He lobbied the IWGC to fund local enquiry officers, which it did in September 1920.

During the war, as much information as possible about the location of graves was collated in London by a department of the DGR&E led by Captain Chettle; and by 1918 there were more than a hundred clerks working for the Enquiries Department. After the end of the war, the IWGC took over this work, with Captain Chettle transferring as its director of records. By the end of March 1921, he and his department had logged around half a million names – almost halfway towards the contemporary record of the empire's dead.

Equally important was the decision by the IWGC, following a recommendation of the Kenyon Report, to produce a printed register, arranged alphabetically by name, to be made available at each of the commission's cemeteries. The first two were published in 1920 and comprised the Le Tréport and Forceville registers, two of the 'experimental' cemeteries. A decade after the end of the war, 700,000 names had been printed. Not only did these help resolve the 'numerous searching and pathetically persistent enquiries'[98] from the bereaved, but also fulfilled the humane task of recognising and commemorating the dead by name.

*

Early on in the war, Sigmund Freud had begun to see that modern war was different: that it was capable of causing collective trauma that society found hard to confront. The scale of the bereavement in the Great War was unprecedented. By 1918 nearly 10 million people were dead across Europe, and hardly a single family was untouched by loss, or several successive losses.

There were particular ways in which, during the war, the established processes of mourning were interrupted or even reversed. Lengthy mourning (which had previously been prescribed as appropriate) was now sometimes seen as self-indulgent, as a betrayal of those loved ones who had been killed: some soldiers even asked in letters home for their relatives not to mourn unduly in the event of their death. To mourn, it was thought, might undermine the cause for which they had sacrificed themselves. This might explain why, towards the end of the war, there were fewer people to be seen wearing mourning clothes in the street, despite the relentless rise in the number of deaths.

The war also disrupted the natural order of death. It is generally accepted that the death of a child is particularly traumatic, as is the loss of a parent for a young child or adolescent. And yet this is what happened throughout the war, as the normal succession of generations was overturned, affecting a growing number of parents and children.

Nor did relatives have the chance to attend to, or comfort, their loved ones in their dying moments – except in those rare cases, where the wounded man died in hospital back in Britain. This act of consolation, which can help prepare people for bereavement, was simply not available. As a result, relatives were tormented for years by the fact that they knew so little about their loved ones' last moments. How had they been killed? Where had they been wounded? And had they suffered? Questions like these are a common feature of many searches for the dead: of the Cecils' search for George, and the Kiplings' quest for John, and the thousands of enquiries made to the Wounded and Missing Enquiry Department; anything to fill the void left by the lack of knowledge.

In many cases, of course, there was not even a body to mourn: no coffin, no funeral, and no grave, to ease the grieving process. The British steadfastly refused to allow bodies to be repatriated; attitudes and policy have changed radically since then, partly, but not exclusively, as a result of the difference in scale: only a very few of the British troops who died in the Falklands War of 1982 are buried on the islands; and the bringing home for burial of soldiers, killed in conflicts in Iraq and Afghanistan, now follows the American norm. In the First World War, there were the cemeteries, and the monuments and memorials, and opportunities to display bereavement collectively, as on Armistice Day, but was there a suppression of intimate grief, of allowing people to suffer in solitude? And, as a result of that, did the grief last longer?

The families of the missing dead were desperate for their loved ones to be commemorated, along with those whose 'name liveth for evermore'; and as close to the place where they had fallen as possible. In their search for an 'altar upon earth' at which to lay their grief, for that six-foot corner of a foreign field that was for ever England, some families wanted the name of their missing relative inscribed on a headstone – even if this marked a 'false' or 'fake' grave with no body. The IWGC opposed the idea, as did Kipling himself, whose son John would have fallen into this category, describing it as a 'dud' grave.

The question of how and where the missing should be commemorated, and how much money should be spent, was further complicated by the problem of working out exactly who the missing half-million were. The bodies of these 517,000 servicemen, which constituted almost half the British Empire's war dead, were too blasted, burnt, or mutilated ever to be identified.

Parallel to the demand for memorials to the missing, there had been some enthusiasm, ever since the war itself, for a national war memorial in London. This grew after the war, with many grand designs proposed for monuments across the country. Eventually, the two proposals – for national war memorials, including battlefield memorials, and memorials to the missing – were merged. At the very least, this conflation of individual and collective commemoration avoided the duplication of effort and expenditure. It may also have influenced the style of architecture to one that spoke of human tragedy as much as military triumph. In Britain, there were very few war memorials to provide a precedent. What was needed was a form of architecture that did not glorify war, nor celebrate victory, in the way that the monuments of Imperial Rome or Napoleonic Paris did, so much as reflect the sense of loss suffered by the survivors.

The IWGC was given the responsibility of building these memorials, including the naval memorials at Chatham, Portsmouth and Plymouth to those lost at sea. Eventually, it decided to build four memorials in France: Soissons, La Ferté-sous-Jouarre, the Somme memorial at Thiepval, and the Indian memorial at Neuve Chapelle (for which the Kiplings attended the opening ceremony on 5 October 1927); and a handful in Belgium, including Ploegsteert and Ypres. If a memorial could not accommodate all the names, then these would be transferred to memorials within existing cemeteries: on the curving wall at Tyne Cot Cemetery, for example, which holds almost 35,000 names; or the memorial in Dud Corner Cemetery at Loos.

On 4 August 1930, the sixteenth anniversary of the declaration of war between Britain and Germany, Rudyard and Carrie Kipling attended the ceremony at Dud Corner Cemetery, where the name of their son was commemorated, along with more than 20,000 others on the walls of the Loos Memorial. Kipling was to have spoken himself, but was so overcome by emotion that all he could do, in his role as a commissioner of the IWGC, was to introduce General Sir Nevil Macready and invite him to unveil this memorial to the victims of the battles of Loos and Béthune. The buglers of the Irish Guards sounded the Last Post, followed by a minute's silence – a daily practice which the Kiplings funded for a number of years, until their deaths, and the outbreak of the Second World War. Of the original names commemorated on the Loos Memorial, 221 – including that of John Kipling – were subsequently removed as they could no longer be classified as missing, their bodily remains having been identified.

In addition, the IWGC decided that memorial tablets honouring 'The Million Dead' of the British Empire in the war should be installed in churches and cathedrals in Belgium, France and Britain: in Notre-Dame in Paris, Westminster Abbey (the unveiling of which the Kiplings attended on 19 August 1926), Amiens, Arras, Bayeux, Beauvais, Ypres, and so on. All bore Kipling's inscription: 'To the glory of God/ and to the memory of/ one million dead/ of the British Empire/ who fell/

in the Great War/ 1914–18/ and of whom the/ greater part rest/ in France.'

The Menin Gate was the first – and the best known – of the great memorials to the missing dead. In the autumn of 1919, Sir Reginald Blomfield, the Principal Architect assigned to the district around Ypres, visited the salient and recommended the site of the old Menin Gate, partly 'because it was the way by which most of our men had gone out to fight'. However, when Blomfield inspected it, 'there was nothing but a great ragged gap in the ramparts, and the roadway which passed across the moat on a rough broken-down bank was all to pieces'. Building started, based on his design, in 1923, with completion in 1927.

Although the Menin Gate Memorial is a variation on a triumphal arch of the classical world, it is not bombastic, or triumphalist, but a dignified monument to the huge scale of human sacrifice. Blomfield was particularly cheered by an article published in a German newspaper in 1928 by the Austrian novelist Stefan Zweig: 'It is a memorial,' he wrote, 'offered not to victory but to the dead – the victims – without any distinction … In its really Roman simplicity this monument to the six and fifty thousand is more impressive than any triumphal arch or monument to victory that I have ever seen.' It was a perfectly fitting memorial for those 'whose graves could not be found, who lie somewhere crumbled together in a common grave, mutilated beyond recognition by shells, or disintegrating in the water, to all those who, unlike the others, have not their bright, white polished stone in the cemeteries round about the town, the individual mark of their last resting-place'.[99] For Blomfield, it was 'perhaps the only building that I have ever designed in which I do not want anything altered'. Such praise was echoed in *The Times*, which described it as 'the stateliest and the most fitting of all the Memorials which love and admiration have raised to the Glorious dead', adding that it was of 'that austere beauty which befits the grand but cruel memories which it recalls'.[100]

Siegfried Sassoon was one of only a few dissenting voices. Put off perhaps by the martial connotations of the recumbent lion, he described the memorial as 'this pomp' of 'peace-complacent stone' in a poem, 'On Passing the New Menin Gate', written soon after its inauguration:

> Was ever an immolation so belied
> As these intolerably nameless names?
> Well might the Dead who struggled in the slime
> Rise and deride this sepulchre of crime.[101]

On the inside walls of the Menin Gate there are panels of Portland stone bearing the names of almost 55,000 men who were killed in the Ypres Salient before 16 August 1917, but whose bodies were never found. There was no room for the names of those who fell later, for example at the Battle of Messines, and these were inscribed at Tyne Cot. Above the entrance to each of the staircases leading from the Hall of Memory to the ramparts is the inscription devised by Kipling, which could equally have applied to his son, killed in another part of the Western front: 'Here are recorded names of officers and men who fell in the Ypres Salient but to whom the fortune of war denied the known and honoured burial given to their comrades in death.' Most impressively, there are only a tiny number of errors – spelling mistakes or cases of a name being duplicated.

'He is not missing, he is here,' Field Marshal Plumer told the crowd, and the large radio audience who tuned in, at the unveiling ceremony for the Menin Gate on 24 July 1927. The Last Post was played, and resonated so well with everyone there that, from 1929, two buglers took up position beneath the gate every evening to sound the Last Post – a tradition that has, with the exception of the years of the Second World War, continued to this day, with the bugle call being sounded at 8 p.m. by members of the local fire brigade (only one bugler and no spectators were permitted during the Covid pandemic restrictions of 2020/21). Will Longstaff, the Australian painter, was so moved by this inaugural ceremony that, when he took a walk beside the Menin Gate later that night, he had a vision of the dead soldiers of the salient rising up and marching off. This became the subject of one of the most celebrated paintings of its time, *Menin Gate at Midnight*.

The Menin Gate commemorates the missing from all over the British Empire. However, the Dominions, with the exception of New Zealand, generally chose to erect their own memorials. This was a disappointment to Fabian Ware, who had hoped, through the IWGC, to reconcile imperial unity and cooperation with the national aspirations of the individual Dominions. The Dominions had automatically joined the war on Britain's declaration in 1914, and had suffered losses on all fronts. The South Africans commemorated their dead at Delville Wood; the Newfoundlanders at Beaumont-Hamel, where they had been all but wiped out in a single hour on 1 July 1916; the Australians at Villers-Bretonneux and Gallipoli. The Canadian Memorial at Vimy Ridge, which was unveiled in 1936, bore the names of more than 11,000 Canadians with no known grave. The figure of a grieving woman represents the young nation mourning for its dead.

Lutyens's great Memorial to the Missing of the Somme, which was unveiled by the Prince of Wales on 1 August 1932, was the largest of these memorials, a massive ziggurat, composed of interconnecting arches, of red brick and white stone, overlooking the valley. It stands near the top of a chalky ridge at Thiepval, which the British had attempted unsuccessfully – and with great loss of life – to take from the Germans on the first day of the Somme. Although a variation on ancient themes – including the Roman triumphal arch – it is not triumphalist in style. At the very heart of the memorial there is a stone altar inscribed with 'Their name liveth for evermore'. This sense of timelessness is reflected in the architecture, which rescues and preserves for eternity more than 72,000 British and South African soldiers, mostly volunteers, who disappeared on the Somme. It is a fitting monument to a battle that scarred the memory of all those who had fought in France, just as Ypres (and Passchendaele, in particular) scarred those who had fought in Belgium; and a humane commemoration of the individuals who died in an age of industrialised slaughter.

The memorial is also an example of Anglo-French cooperation. One of the poles on top of the central tower flies the Union Jack, the other the French tricolore, in recognition of the joint offensive. And in the cemetery below, an inscription on the Cross of Sacrifice, diplomatically worded by Kipling, proclaims: 'THAT THE WORLD MAY REMEMBER THE COMMON SACRIFICE OF TWO AND A HALF MILLION DEAD HERE HAVE BEEN LAID SIDE BY SIDE SOLDIERS OF FRANCE AND OF THE BRITISH EMPIRE IN ETERNAL COMRADESHIP'. The cemetery itself is divided in two: 300 French concrete crosses on one side, with tin labels stamped with the word 'Inconnu'; and 300 British headstones on the other side, bearing Kipling's phrase: 'A Soldier of the Great War Known unto God'.

The war graves and the memorials to the missing were indeed an extraordinary achievement. But they were not quite as comprehensive in their coverage of 'every part of the world', as Kipling had claimed in *The Graves of the Fallen*. For a start, they were concentrated in Europe. More than a million Indian soldiers, from all over the subcontinent, and half a million non-combatants – cooks, carriers, drivers, labourers – served with the Indian Army during the First World War: in France, Africa and the Middle East. Of these, the 4,700 Indian servicemen of all ranks who were killed on the Western front, but had no known grave, are commemorated by name on the memorial at Neuve Chapelle, the village where the Indian Corps fought its first major action in March 1915. Designed by Herbert Baker, the memorial appropriates to the farmlands of northern France the style and symbolism of Indian architecture, with the column at its heart topped by both the British Imperial Crown and the Star of India. King George V expressed the hope, at the time of its inauguration in 1927, that the memorial 'would be the means of bringing to their kin in India – most of whom can never visit the far distant scene of battle – vivid realisation of the loving care and profound homage with which all parts of my Empire have combined to perpetuate the memory of the Indian fallen'.[102]

Outside Europe, the recognition of individual Indian servicemen was more discriminatory. The Basra Memorial in Iraq, which was unveiled in 1929, lists the names of the Indian Army officers who were killed in Mesopotamia, the Indian Army's major theatre of war, and have no known grave; but only the total numbers (33,222), arranged by regiment, are recorded on the memorial for the non-commissioned officers and other ranks, although printed registers of these names were available. This was in line with Imperial War Graves Commission (IWGC) policy for the Indian Army, as Sir Arthur Browne, the principal assistant secretary at the IWGC, had written in 1924: 'bearing in mind that the memorials themselves will in all probability not be seen by any of the relatives of the rank and file, the memorials in question outside Europe will contain only the names of the regiments concerned, followed in each case by the names of the British officers (and non-commissioned officers, if any), the names of the Indian officers and the number of the native non-commissioned officers and men'.[103]

The African dead were commemorated with even less respect than the Indian dead. However progressive it may have seemed at the time, the policy of equality of treatment, regardless of military rank or social class, the democratisation of death that was enshrined in the Kenyon Report, did not extend to skin colour. It was in Africa that the first shot of the First World War by a soldier in British service was fired – in Togoland on 7 August 1914 – and the last shot, too – in what was then Northern Rhodesia, on 13 November 1918, two days after the Armistice. In the meantime, some 200,000 Africans had died in East Africa alone. And yet for the African soldiers, and labourers recruited to the imperial war effort, there was very little commemoration indeed, simply a stark distinction between the 'white graves', which were carefully located, identified and marked, and those of the 'natives'.[104]

In contrast to the static Western front, where the opposing armies got bogged down in the trenches soon after the start of the war, the war in Africa was a very mobile one, with a fluid front. Troops travelled long distances across the bush in extreme conditions, in an attempt to outmanoeuvre each other. They required continuous supplies of food and water, and as pack animals had been devastated by tsetse fly, transport was mostly provided by human porters. Hundreds of thousands of Africans were recruited, or coerced, into service in the 'Carrier Corps' in the five British territories bordering German East Africa. Rates of death were extraordinarily high, from malaria, dysentery and pneumonia, as a swathe of suffering spread over a large region. Most of the dead were hastily buried in the bush, with no proper records kept, and the graves were allowed, in the words of the commission, to 'revert to nature'. Commemoration, such as it was, took the form of memorial statues to the 'missing' in the centre of a region or a large town, such as Nairobi, Entebbe or Kampala – with no reference even to the numbers involved, as there had been in the case of the Indian soldiers at Basra. Rudyard Kipling was, as ever, responsible for the rather generic wording on these monuments: for example, the one in Dar es Salaam, reads: 'This is to the memory of the Native African troops who fought; to the carriers who were the feet and hands of the army and to all the other men who served and died for their King and country in Eastern Africa in the Great War, 1914–1918. If you fight for your country, even if you die, your sons will remember your name.'[105]

Sending 'the natives missing', as the commission's officials described the practice of referring to them in general terms on a central statue, was a far cheaper option than erecting individual headstones; in effect, the Africans were being treated as if they were as dispensable in death as they had been in life. The justification, Sir Arthur Browne advised, was that 'the stage of civilisation reached by most of the East African tribes was not such as would enable them to appreciate commemoration in this manner [headstones]'. Put even more bluntly by the IWGC director of works in 1924: 'Pagan Natives have no regard for graves.'[106] It was 'very unlikely' that people would visit the places where their family members fell, hundreds of miles from their villages, Major Evans, working with a graves registration unit in East Africa, observed; there was therefore no pressure, as on the Western front, from the prospect of visitors being appalled by the neglect of the graves of their loved ones.

The Africans, and to a lesser extent, the Indians became forgotten armies. Unlike the white Dominion and European soldiers, these colonial soldiers were largely illiterate and did not leave letters and diaries in the same profusion; and unlike the Dominion nations afterwards, which celebrated the war and wove it into a narrative of nation-building, India and the African countries were more ambivalent about their active participation in an imperial past: both of which factors did nothing to rescue the hundreds of thousands of war dead from oblivion.

In 2021 a report commissioned by the Commonwealth War Graves Commission acknowledged that 50,000 Indian and African casualties had been commemorated 'unequally', and that several hundred thousand more African casualties had not been commemorated by name at all. The commission apologised for its historic failure fully to carry out its policy of equality of treatment. It undertook to continue the search for the missing.

*

Rudyard Kipling died on 18 January 1936, ignorant to the last of the whereabouts of John's grave. Fabian Ware was one of the pallbearers at his funeral in Westminster Abbey. Poignantly, Mr Prynn, head gardener at Dud Corner, where John Kipling was commemorated, brought a wreath made of flowers from the cemetery.

It was only in 1992 that the Commonwealth War Graves Commission, on the basis of evidence that was 'beyond reasonable doubt', changed the inscription on the gravestone of an unidentified 'lieutenant of the Irish Guards' in St Mary's ADS Cemetery, to read John Kipling. John's name was subsequently removed from the Loos Memorial to the missing. But the debate rumbles on to this day.

The reattribution hinged on several key issues. Had mistakes been made by the army labour company unit, which cleared the battlefield, north and east of Loos, in September 1919, when the body had been exhumed and reburied in St Mary's ADS Cemetery? In particular, had the burial return filed by the unit on 23 September for 'U.B.S. [Unknown British Soldier] Officer Lieut. Irish Guards' got its map references in a muddle? The sub-square it recorded, G25.c., placed the body some three miles west of where John was fighting, and had last been seen. It has been argued that this grid reference must have been wrong, as it fell at the join between two map sheets and therefore never existed. It was more likely, then, that the remains should have been recorded at H25.c., around Chalk Pit Wood, which was near where John had disappeared, and where Sergeant Farrell remembered placing him in a shell hole: this was where the bodies of three identified men, who were reburied in the same row in St Mary's ADS as John, were found.

The other key question was whether the body was that of an Irish Guards officer (or, indeed, a soldier, from another regiment altogether) and if so, a lieutenant or a second lieutenant. The burial return described the body as that of an Irish Guards lieutenant – the regiment probably deduced from the arrangement of the brass buttons on the front of the jacket, and the rank from the two 'pips' sported on each shoulder – whereas John, although entitled to two, may have been sporting only the one 'pip', belonging to the second lieutenant. Or perhaps these distinctions were altogether too fine for the labour company soldiers filing the returns. Two other second lieutenants of the Irish Guards were killed between 27 and 30 September, Pakenham Law and Walter Clifford, and both were recorded as being buried elsewhere: so the body could not be theirs. Since no other full lieutenant of the Irish Guards was unaccounted for on the Loos battlefield, the commission assumed that the body of the unidentified officer must have been that of Lieutenant John Kipling.

The argument centred around the fact that John Kipling's promotion to lieutenant was only formally announced in the *London Gazette* on 11 November 1915, some six weeks after his death, although his increased pay as a full lieutenant was backdated to 7 June, the actual date of his promotion, more than three months before his death. Did John Kipling know that he had been promoted at the time of his death, and had he 'put up' his rank, as he was entitled to do – or was he still wearing the uniform of a second lieutenant? He had written to his father on 19 September, asking for a new aluminium identification disc from the Army and Navy Stores, as he had 'gone and lost' his,[107] giving his name and rank as '2nd Lieutenant John Kipling, C of E, Irish Guards'. On the other hand, it was highly likely that John would have been informed about his promotion by his battalion commander, Lieutenant Colonel Butler, before going into the battle that claimed his life.

In 2015 the CWGC confirmed that it was satisfied with the decision it had made in 1992 to change the name on the headstone. It ruled that the original identification 'remained sound, and that there was clear and compelling evidence to support the identification'.

5

Searching for Solace in the Afterlife

On the morning of 15 September 1915, Sir Oliver Lodge was playing golf at Gullane, on the east coast of Scotland. Although he had been greatly looking forward to the round, the eminent physicist, and founding principal of Birmingham University, 'was in an exceptional state of depression', and could barely hit the ball. 'Not ordinary bad play,' he recalled, 'but total incompetence; so much so that after seven holes we gave up the game, and returned to the hotel.'[1] At the time, he did not ascribe any particular significance to his mood that day; in retrospect, however, he interpreted it as one of several premonitions.

Two days later, on 17 September, Sir Oliver received the standard-issue telegram from the War Office: 'Deeply regret to inform you that Second Lieut. R. Lodge, Second South Lancs, was wounded 14th Sept. and has since died. Lord Kitchener expresses his sympathy.'[2] Raymond Lodge was the youngest of Sir Oliver's six sons and, he reminisced, the most like himself both as a child – in looks, in his dislike of children's parties, in the trouble he had pronouncing certain letters – and, as he grew older, in his passion for engineering and machinery. 'Being so desperately busy all my life,' Sir Oliver admitted, 'I failed to see as much as I should like either of him or of the other boys, but there was always an instinctive sympathy between us.'[3] The blow to the family, on learning of Raymond's death, at the age of twenty-six, was 'if it is permissible to say … a terribly severe one', his father wrote.[4]

The news was followed by letters of condolence from fellow officers at Hooge in Belgium. In the style of such letters, they praised his mechanical skills, his resourcefulness, his cheerfulness in the face of adversity: 'the best pal I've ever had ... whilst his men were awfully fond of him and would have done anything for him', according to Lieutenant Fletcher; 'a charming young fellow – always so very cheerful and willing, hard-working, and a bright example of what a good soldier ought to be', wrote his captain.[5]

There were descriptions, too, of his actual death – struck in the back by a piece of shrapnel from a shell blast. As was customary in letters sent after a soldier's death, particular attention was drawn to Raymond's courage. Before being hit, he had seen all his men back down the line from the front to relative safety in the communication trench to the rear. 'I understand that he lived for about three hours after being wounded,' wrote Captain Cheves on behalf of the colonel, 'and all the officers and men who were present speak very highly of his conduct during this time ... When his body was brought down in the evening the expression on his face was absolutely peaceful, and I think that he probably did not suffer a great deal of pain. He was buried on the same evening just outside the aid post.' In November, Sir Oliver was sent the specific location of his son's grave: 'Ref. Map Belgium, Sheet 28. Scale 1/40,000. Square 1. 16. B. 2. Near Ypres.'[6] During the mass exhumations and the creation of new cemeteries after the war, Raymond's bodily remains were disinterred from here, and reburied at Birr Cross Roads Cemetery, to the north-east of the village of Zillebeke.

Raymond had studied engineering at university and, shortly before the outbreak of war, had joined a company established by two of his older brothers to exploit the invention, patented by their father, of the spark plug. He volunteered in September 1914, and was waved off to northern France by his brothers at Waterloo Station on 15 March, almost six months to the day before he was killed. His engineering skills were soon being put to good use in the digging and repair of trenches, laying barbed wire, arranging the water supply – usually in no man's land at night, and at the mercy of German snipers and machine-gun fire.

Raymond would write home a couple of times a week. His letters were generally breezy in tone, describing the domestic routines and rituals of the trenches, how he spent his time reading the daily papers (a day late), devising acrostics for his family to solve, and preparing meals. He thanked his parents for practical gifts – a trench periscope and a pair of ear defenders – but also for parcels of 'comforts', such as asparagus and figs, cabbages and the kippers, whose arrival on 5 June had thrown the mess into the greatest state of excitement: 'How splendid!' As the summer progressed, the fighting became more intense, and everyone got 'fed up'. 'I have been having rather a bad time lately,' he wrote on 7 August, 'one of those times that reminds one that it is war and not a picnic.'[7]

Sir Oliver included these letters, and the letters of condolence, in the memoir he wrote about his son, *Raymond, or Life and Death*. Assembled in Part I of the book, they help to build up a lively, playful picture of Raymond, while at the same time preparing the reader for his seamless translation, equally alive, to another world. As Sir Oliver wrote, a fortnight after his son's death: 'He has entered another region of service now; and this we realise. For though in the first shock of bereavement the outlook of life felt irretrievably darkened, a perception of his continued usefulness has mercifully dawned upon us, and we know that his activity is not over. His bright ingenuity will lead to developments beyond what we could have anticipated; and we have clear hopes for the future.'[8]

Raymond's death made spiritualism a personal article of faith for Sir Oliver. Within a week of receiving the fateful telegram, his wife Mary was the first of the Lodges to attend a sitting with the medium Gladys Osborne Leonard. They had been introduced by a Mrs Kennedy, who had a psychic faculty for automatic writing. Over the coming months, the Lodges and two of their children attended sittings at least once a week with various mediums; most of the other children, however, remained sceptical of their parents' interest, reacting to their brother's death in a less extreme way.

Mrs Leonard was one of those mediums who, on going into a trance, began to speak or write in a style quite different from their normal manner: they fell, as Sir Oliver described, under the guidance of a separate intelligence technically known as a 'control', and displayed a degree of clairvoyance well beyond their normal consciousness or knowledge. 'The control, or second personality,' he continued, 'appears to be more closely in touch with what is popularly spoken of as "the next world" than with customary human existence, and accordingly is able to get messages through from people deceased.'[9] In order to communicate with the spiritual world, he wrote, most people need 'an instrument of reception … an organism trained to allow itself to be used by other intelligences … Mrs. Leonard is such a medium, and has proved herself in the past to be the best or one of the best that I have known.' She, in turn, acknowledged her great debt to Sir Oliver. 'Indeed, where would my work have been without Sir Oliver Lodge's help? I cannot imagine.'[10]

Mrs Leonard, who was to become the most celebrated medium of her time, was then in her early thirties, a handsome woman with piercingly blue eyes and a homely grace. She had discovered her gift as a young girl, while on a visit to friends in a neighbouring Lancashire town: her mother had appeared to her in a radiant vision at exactly the moment when, Gladys was soon to discover, her mother had died. As her family fell on hard times, Gladys went on the stage. In the dressing room between acts, she and a couple of colleagues started to experiment with table-tilting, sitting around a table with their hands placed on top, waiting for the piece of furniture to move in response to a series of questions. During one of these sessions at the London Palladium, she went into a trance, and submerged her identity, temporarily, to Feda, her 'spirit control'. Feda was a young native American woman who had been married – so Gladys Leonard revealed in her memoir – to Gladys's great-great-grandfather, but had died in childbirth.

In the spring of 1914, Mrs Leonard decided to become a professional medium and, on the outbreak of war, began to hold public sessions for people looking for messages from those who had been killed in action. She was soon to concentrate, instead, on holding two or three private sittings a day. 'I understood then the purpose for which I was needed,' she wrote. 'I was used to prove to those whose dear ones had been killed that they were not lost to them and that the dead had never died.' She felt an equally great responsibility for the spirits of the deceased as for the bereaved. 'I wonder sometimes if many people realised the extraordinary psychic conditions that prevailed during the war; so many thousands of young active men being suddenly shot from their accustomed earth conditions to entirely new ones, which must have been a great shock and surprise to many of them. One could feel the tremendous urge from all these thousands of enthusiastic and loving souls, who probably (I think, *certainly*) longed to come back to the loved ones whom they had left behind on earth … if only for an hour, to comfort those who mourned for them, and to tell them something of their new conditions and surroundings.' She did not like her new profession at all at first. 'Honestly I would rather have scrubbed doorsteps for a living. The sense of responsibility was overwhelming.'[11]

If Part I of *Raymond* was a personal memorial to his son, Part II was a supposedly scientific study of Sir Oliver's communications with him. From Sir Oliver's reports, and from accounts kept by Marguerite Radclyffe-Hall and Una Vincenzo Troubridge, who sat with Mrs Leonard every week for eight years, and recorded almost every word, a typical sitting would last a couple of hours. Mrs Leonard would draw the curtains of the bay window in her apartment in Maida Vale. The only light came from a red lamp placed on a small table in the middle of the room, and a fire smouldering in the grate, which made the atmosphere rather stuffy (although some people reported a draught of cold air presaging any psychic event). She would sit, in a hard-backed chair, a couple of feet in front of the sitter. Silence would fall, disturbed only by her slow, regular breathing as she appeared to fall asleep, or by the rustle of clothing. Mrs Leonard would then sigh, and the voice of Feda would come in whispers from her mouth.

On 24 September 1915, just a few days after her son's death, Lady Lodge reported, at the first of many sittings, how Mrs Leonard went into a trance and 'came back as a little Indian girl called "Feda", rubbing her hands and talking in the silly way they do'. Feda began to describe the features of a young man who could quite easily have been the dead officer, shakily spelling the name 'Raymond'. At this, and at subsequent sittings over the coming months, Feda was playful and 'dramatically childlike', jerking about on the chair, and squeaking or chuckling, 'when indicating pleasure'. She referred to Raymond as 'Yaymond', Sir Oliver as 'Soliver' and his wife as 'Miss Olive'; and had an irritating habit of pronouncing what she no doubt considered long words in a carefully articulated and drawn-out manner: 'in-tri-cate', 'ap-per-taining', 'pers-perpec-perspective'. All these mispronunciations and malapropisms must have jarred and seemed rather out of character, as they issued through the well-modulated mouth of Mrs Leonard.[12]

On 27 September, Sir Oliver had his first sitting with Mrs Leonard, alone and supposedly anonymously. Feda continued to describe, in very general terms, someone who was trying to make contact with her: 'a young man, rather above the medium height; rather well-built, not thick-set or heavy … He has not been over long. His hair is between colours. He is not easy to describe, because he is not building himself up solid as some do. He has greyish eyes; his hair brown, short at the sides; a fine-shaped head; eyebrows also brown, not much arched; a nice-shaped mouth, a good-sized mouth it is, but it does not look large because he holds his lips nicely together; chin not heavy; face oval.' She also remembered a letter associated with the young man: 'R, that is to do with him.'[13]

On the same day, Lady Lodge went by herself to Mrs Kennedy's house to meet another medium, Mr A. Vout Peters. As Mr Peters went into a trance, his whole body shook with sobs, his head and neck became 'suffused with blood', and his personality was temporarily submerged with that of his spirit control, 'Moonstone'. Like Feda, Moonstone made halting attempts at describing aspects of the young Raymond, claiming that when he was younger, he was 'very strongly associated with football and outdoor sports', and that the Lodges had several of his trophies at home (this was not the case, and Sir Oliver attributed the mistake to 'some confusion in record here'). 'Was he not associated with chemistry?' Moonstone asked. 'If not, some one associated with him was, because I see all the things in a chemical laboratory.' This suggestion was clearly nearer the mark, and Sir Oliver the scientist accepted it willingly. It was a common feature of séances that sitters tended to forgive mediums their mistakes, while seizing on the bits they got right, especially if the description appeared to flatter the loved one and, by extension, the bereaved.[14]

It was at this sitting with Mr Peters that reference was made for the first time to a group photograph featuring Raymond. The Lodges had had no previous knowledge of this, although there must have been thousands of such photos in existence. Moonstone drew particular attention to the swagger stick under Raymond's arm in the photo, and to a moustache (which Raymond did not have). Sir Oliver took notes of these observations, and nothing more was heard on the subject for a couple of months. On 29 November a letter from a Mrs Cheves, the mother of Captain Cheves, a fellow officer, arrived out of the blue. She had some photographs featuring Raymond. Would they like copies?

While they waited for Mrs Cheves to send them, Sir Oliver had a sitting with Mrs Leonard, alone at her house, on 3 December. Through the mediumship of Mrs Leonard, he took the opportunity to ask more detailed questions about the photograph before its arrival, which Feda then relayed to Raymond. According to Feda, there were maybe a dozen people in the picture, including 'some body called C ... some body called R [and] another called B'.[15]

'Was it out of doors?' Sir Oliver asked.

'Yes, practically,' she replied.

'Does he [Raymond] remember how he looked in the photograph?'

'No, he doesn't remember how he looked.'

'No, no, I mean, was he standing up?'

'No, he doesn't seem to think so. Some were raised up round; he was sitting down, and some were raised up at the back of him. Some were standing, and some were sitting, he thinks.'[16]

Raymond could not remember whether he had a stick, but he did recall being particularly irritated by the fact that 'some one was leaning on him'.[17]

On 6 December, Lady Lodge was reading Raymond's blood-stained diary, which had been returned with his kit from the front, when she found an entry referring to the taking of the photograph. The following day, the copies finally arrived. On examination, Sir Oliver found that 'every peculiarity mentioned by Raymond' in sittings with both Mr Peters and Mrs Leonard was 'strikingly correct'. The swagger stick was there (but not under his arm – it was lying across his feet), the vertical lines in the background, mentioned by Feda, were those of the roof of a shed ('yes, practically' out of doors). Those officers who could be identified had names beginning with B, C and R. Some of the group were sitting, while others were standing.[18]

'But by far the most striking piece of evidence,' Sir Oliver reported, 'is the fact that some one sitting behind Raymond is leaning or resting a hand on his shoulder.' Overall, Sir Oliver thought the group photograph 'a peculiarly good piece of evidence' for the survival of the personality after death. He was particularly impressed by the fact that the existence, and nature, of the photograph were unknown to anyone attending the sittings, and could not therefore have been deduced through telepathy between the medium and anyone at the séance.

As he would be sorry to rely for such an 'important conclusion on any one piece of evidence, however cogent', he continued to accumulate 'proofs' over the coming months from what he called 'evidential and verifiable sittings'. For example, when Feda described 'a canvas house' near the water and 'a boat with white sails' that ran along the ground, Sir Oliver immediately identified these as a tent and a sand boat on wheels, which his sons had made in their laboratory at home, and then played with on holiday at Woolacombe Sands. On another occasion, Raymond referred to some speculation over whether a certain officer, who had been declared dead, had 'come over yet'. Raymond felt that he might well still be 'on the earth plane' (i.e. alive), and that he had been taken prisoner. His father hoped that this was the case – he had 'identified' the officer in question as a colonel of their acquaintance by Raymond's reference to an initialled riding whip – but Raymond counselled against telling the colonel's folks for the time being for fear of raising any hopes.[19]

Although Sir Oliver tried to subject the evidence to scientific scrutiny, he did have some reservations about drawing too many conclusions from the sittings. Since so many soldiers and their families were suffering a common experience, it was relatively easy for a medium to ask leading questions or to venture vague, ambiguous statements: 'Have you anything to say to me?' 'You have had a lot of sadness lately.' 'Have you lost a loved one near France?' 'The man is a soldier – an officer' ... 'You heard of his death by telegram ... he settled his affairs before he left' ... 'Was he carrying a walking stick?' And so on, in a cumulative process, in which previous revelations were confirmed and elaborated upon in subsequent sittings.

It was also quite possible that the mediums had researched their sitters in advance: asking third parties for information; or, gradually, over a course of séances, getting to know more about the identity and personal histories of their clients. (This was a particular problem when so many people were aware of Sir Oliver and his interest in psychical research.) In such cases, the medium could fish for information by asking the 'right' questions, and then rely on the sitter's powers of auto-suggestion. 'He says it's someone's birthday in January' ... 'Someone beginning with the letter A is involved.' Sir Oliver would explain such statements retrospectively in his notes of the sitting: 'of course, as I realised later, this must be [so-and-so] ...'[20]

'Somewhere in the north' could be anywhere between Watford and Scotland. Generic descriptions of a holiday beach or a popular song would be seized upon and given a specific identity, as people would go to great lengths to convince themselves of evidence that was, according to Sir Oliver, 'surely quite beyond chance or guesswork'. Imperfect answers, on the other hand, could wishfully be excused on the grounds that 'it was little more than a month since Raymond's death, and new experiences and serious surroundings must have been crowding in upon the youth, so that old semifrivolous reminiscences were difficult to recall'.[21]

The problem of prior knowledge on the part of the medium explains the significance of the 'anonymous' sitting. It was Mrs Kennedy who had introduced the Lodges to both Mrs Leonard and Mr Peters; and who arranged most of their meetings, including the supposedly 'anonymous' sittings. Knowing that he was interested in spiritualism, Mrs Kennedy had written to Sir Oliver in August 1914 after the death of her son Paul. She wrote again the following year when she read the announcement of Raymond's death in the newspapers, to say that 'Paul' had been in touch with Raymond. She could, as a result, easily have briefed Mrs Leonard on the personal circumstances of the Lodges.

Once Sir Oliver had established Raymond's credentials, and the reliability of his memory, he started to ask him, through Feda, about his experiences in the spirit world. Raymond had been 'bursting' to tell him: 'my body's very similar to the one I had before. I pinch myself sometimes to see if it's real, and it is, but it doesn't seem to hurt as much as when I pinched the flesh body.' He has never seen anyone bleed; he has ears, eyes, eyelashes and eyebrows, and exactly the same tongue and teeth. One man he has met had lost an arm, but had grown another one. Most of the people wear white robes. Men and women relate to each other in a slightly different way to that on the earth plane, and there do not seem to be any children born here. Raymond himself no longer wants to eat, but he sees some men who do, and are given 'something which has all the appearance of an earth food'. He mentions 'a chap [who] came over the other day who would have a cigar', and they were able to manufacture what looked like a cigar, although it wasn't quite the same as 'on the earth plane'. When the chap started to smoke it, he didn't appear to get the same satisfaction out of it. 'He had four altogether and now he doesn't look at one.' The same was true of meat and strong drink. Some of the men, on arrival, would call for whisky sodas. 'Don't think I'm stretching it, when I tell you that they can manufacture even that. But when they have had one or two, they don't seem to want it so much.'[22]

This spirit world was known as Summerland. Raymond's new home was a pastoral paradise of family values and Christian commitment (not unlike Heaven) that reflected none of the anger of some war literature. It was remarkably similar to other spiritualist visions of the time, and even Sir Oliver acknowledged that Feda – not Mrs Leonard, mind you – might well have picked up some of her ideas from the flood of spiritualist accounts that were circulating. At a sitting with Mrs Leonard on 24 March 1916, Raymond told his parents that he had been attending lectures in the 'halls of learning', where 'you can prepare yourself for the higher spheres while you are living in lower ones'. [23] Summerland was evidently a place of spiritual education and development; and it pained Sir Oliver that his critics focused on, and ridiculed, the passage describing the free availability of whisky and cigars.

The purpose of these communications from 'the other side' was not simply to console the bereaved. They also had a role in reinforcing an almost messianic message – as Raymond told his father. Lots of people 'over here' were saying that through the war Sir Oliver was now doing the most wonderful work of his life. 'People are ready to listen … now it's the great thing to think about the after-life. I want you to know that when first I came over here, I thought it was a bit unfair that such a lot of fellows were coming over in the prime of life.' But now Raymond sees that for every one who has come over, dozens of people will open their eyes, and want to know where he has gone, and then pass this knowledge on to others; 'ten years from now the world will be a different place … about fifty per cent of the civilised portion of the globe will be either spiritualists, or coming into it'.[24]

Sir Oliver concluded, at the end of Part II of his best-selling book, that: 'The number of more or less convincing proofs which we have obtained is by this time very great … every possible ground of suspicion or doubt seems to the family to be now removed.' Not only was there proof that personality persisted after death, but 'it is legitimate to say, further, that partly through Raymond's activity a certain amount of help of the same kind has been afforded to other families'.[25]

The message in Part III of the book was that death was not to be feared any more than birth. 'The dead are not dead, but alive,' he claimed, and 'the change called death is the entrance to a new condition of existence – what may be called a new life ...' 'I am as convinced of continued existence, on the other side of death, as I am of existence here ... [and] reasonably convinced of the existence of grades of being, not only lower in the scale than man but higher also, grades of every order of magnitude from zero to infinity.' Sir Oliver believed in the seamless progress of the spirit, through 'the barrier' of death, towards perfection. His faith in spiritual evolution went some way to reconcile the principles of Darwin with his spiritualism, and science with his belief in Christ.[26]

Sir Oliver claimed that he would not have written *Raymond* were it not for the 'premature and unnatural bereavement at the present time', which was 'so appalling that the pain caused by exposing one's own sorrow and its alleviation, to possible scoffers, becomes almost negligible in view of the service which it is legitimate to hope may thus be rendered to mourners, if they can derive comfort by learning that communication across the gulf is possible'.[27] But, as further reassurance, he wanted it to be known that the dead continued to work in the service of others. 'It must be remembered,' he wrote in 'A Message to the Bereaved', 'that, from the point of view of the individuals who have gone over, there are many mitigating circumstances ... Good friends are waiting for them; their help can be utilised, and is much wanted, for their fellows who are coming over; and they themselves will continue in the joy of service. They would like their friends here to recognise that, and not to mourn them unduly; above all, not to consider them as gone out of existence ... Sorrow at their departure is inevitable, but grief which is excessive causes them pain.'[28] It was a sentiment echoed by a writer in *the Occult Review*, who claimed that the dead were

Vera Deakin (right) sifts through the files of the Australian Red Cross Society's Enquiry Bureau for the Wounded and Missing in London, 1919.

Graves, belonging to the missing and marked 'Known unto God', lie scattered across the battlefield of Pozières in France, 1917.

The palaces of Cairo and Alexandria served as hospitals during the First World War. Here, the Heliopolis Palace Hotel in Cairo receives the wounded from Gallipoli.

The writer E. M. Forster, photographed in the gardens at Montazah, a former palace converted into a hospital, in 1917, the year he was appointed Head Searcher for Egypt.

British soldiers parade past the Cenotaph in the Peace Day celebrations of July 1919.

The grave of an unknown soldier of the First World War.

Lutyens' sketch for the Cenotaph, a temporary structure initially made of wood and plaster.

The coffin of the Unknown Warrior is pulled in procession through the streets of London on the way to its final resting place in Westminster Abbey on Armistice Day, 11 November 1920. Twelve of the nation's most senior military commanders march either side of the gun carriage.

The coffin of the Unknown Warrior rests on a cloth in the nave of Westminster Abbey before the ceremony.

Officers. 2nd Battⁿ Irish Guards, Warley, 1915.

John Kipling (with thick spectacles, third from left) poses with a group of fellow officers during training in 1915.

Rudyard Kipling, with his wife, Carrie, attends the ceremony in August 1930 at Dud Corner Cemetery where the name of their son, John, was commemorated on the walls of the Loos Memorial to the missing.

The bodies of Australian soldiers, killed during one of the final battles on the Western Front in September 1918, await burial in a cemetery being constructed at Guillemont Farm.

Australian soldiers make grave crosses for their fallen comrades amidst the ruins of Ypres, October 1917.

The coffin of a Canadian soldier, killed at Passchendaele, is draped in a Union flag at a military funeral in Poperinghe, August 1917.

'helping to form a Britain or Empire beyond the grave, a better Britain or Empire than exists now on the material plane'.[29]

Sir Oliver's vision was an immensely reassuring one, in which the dead continued to be the same people they had been 'on the earth plane' – with the same characters, emotions, and appetites. There was no brutal cutting short of life, but rather a gentle transition to a similar, if idealised, world, where they experienced profound contentment and continued their spiritual development. One of their principal concerns was to reach out and comfort those they had left behind, letting their loved ones on earth know that they were happy, well, and surrounded by friends.

There was also some practical advice for the bereaved. Communication with the dead is not easy, he acknowledged, but 'humanity has reason to be grateful to those few individuals who, finding themselves possessed of the faculty of mediumship, and therefore able to act as intermediaries' can restore 'some portion of the broken link between souls united in affection but separated for a time by an apparently impassable barrier'.[30] He wasn't advising everyone to attempt to communicate with the dead, but simply to be aware 'that their loved ones are still active and useful and interested and happy'. Peaceful assurance, such as this, must depend on the individual. 'Some may get it from the consolations of religion, some from the testimony of trusted people, while some may find it necessary to have first-hand experience of their own for a time. … What people should not do, is to close their minds to the possibility of continued existence.' They should not deny the fact of death, nor give themselves over to grief. 'Now is the time for action; and it is an ill return to those who have sacrificed all and died for the Country if those left behind do not throw off enervating distress and helpless lamentation, and seek to live for the Country and for humanity, to the utmost of their power.' This sounded like a clarion call to a reformed religion.[31]

For some people, Sir Oliver was constructing a metaphysical system that flew in the face of science. But he never saw the contradiction himself. 'I have been engaged for over forty years in mathematical and physical science,' he wrote, 'and for more than half that period in exploration into unusual psychical development, as opportunity arose; and I have thus been led to certain tentative conclusions respecting permissible ways of regarding the universe.'[32] Sir Oliver saw the universe as one, 'not two. Literally there is no "other" world – except in the limited and partial sense of other planets – the Universe is one. We exist in it continuously all the time ...'[33] In his autobiography *Past Years*, he confirmed this: 'For myself, I do not believe that physics and psychics are entirely detached: I think there is a link between them.'[34]

Sir Oliver had been interested in science from a young age. Although he had left school at fourteen to work in his father's business, selling clay and glazes from the West Country to the Staffordshire Potteries, he had been inspired one winter by a series of lectures he attended in London on a visit to his aunt. On his return to Staffordshire, he managed to study at evening classes – working up to thirty hours a week on top of his day job, and winning a place at University College London. 'At an early age,' he was to write in *Past Years*, 'I decided that my main business was with the imponderables – as they were then called – the things that worked secretly and have to be apprehended mentally. So it was that electricity and magnetism became the branch of physics which most fascinated me.'[35]

His research into electromagnetism led to an interest in wireless telegraphy. In August 1894, at a meeting of the British Association (for the Advancement of Science) in Oxford, Sir Oliver became the first person to transmit a message by wireless signal from one room to another: an experiment he was to replicate across a quadrangle in Liverpool. Although he did not quite appreciate at the time the significance of what he was doing, Sir Oliver filed his first wireless patent in 1897, and set up the Lodge–Muirhead Syndicate with his friend, the electrical engineer Alexander Muirhead, to exploit its commercial potential. This was before Guglielmo Marconi, who had been attempting something very similar, had established his patent. In the longer term, Marconi was to achieve greater practical, commercial success – possibly because Sir Oliver had a tendency to get sidetracked by other interests, spreading himself too thinly. In

1912 the Marconi Company paid the Lodge–Muirhead Syndicate more than £20,000 for Sir Oliver's tuning patent, effectively buying the company out.

By the time of Raymond's death, Sir Oliver was internationally recognised for his research into electromagnetism and wireless telegraphy. His work had brought him great academic success in England, first as Professor of Experimental Physics and Mathematics at the University College of Liverpool, and then as principal of Birmingham University. His had been a Victorian tale of enquiry and industry, and its material rewards included Mariemont, a comfortable house in Edgbaston, with a flower garden and a paddock, a suite of large sitting rooms on the ground floor, and plenty of bedrooms for his twelve children upstairs.

In his scientific research, Sir Oliver embraced the materialism of the nineteenth century; but parallel to that ran a strong interest in spiritualism. His research into electromagnetic waves in the late nineteenth century confirmed a belief in the existence of an ether that filled the universe: a belief that was to dominate both his scientific thinking and his spiritual beliefs for the rest of his life. Although he could never prove its existence, Lodge took the nineteenth-century view that the ether was the invisible medium, a sort of cosmic glue, which binds the universe together, and makes it a coherent whole instead of a chaotic collection of independent isolated fragments.[36] It was the medium, he contended, through which electromagnetic waves travelled, in much the same way as other waves, such as shock, sound or water waves, travelled through the more tangible media of solids and fluids. He continued to uphold the idea of the physical existence of ether – in a material world, it was argued, electromagnetic waves had at least to be supported by some medium – long after most scientists had embraced relativity and quantum physics, which rendered the existence, or not, of ether as irrelevant.

Sir Oliver, however, went further still: he believed that the ether supported spirit communications, too; that it was the sublime medium which united the material and spirit worlds, which made them complementary. The ether underpinned his philosophic understanding of the universe. Spiritualism and materialism were thus reconciled through the language of experimental science, in the idea that waves of thought and feeling and spirit behaved in a similar way to other invisible waves, like electromagnetic and radio waves. Just as listeners would eventually tune in to wireless broadcasts, Sir Oliver described a world in which mediums would tune in to 'the other world'.

In the first instance, Sir Oliver had been attracted by the scientific challenges of psychic research, and especially the type of investigation undertaken by the Society for Psychical Research. In 1882 a group of intellectuals, including Frederic Myers, Edmund Gurney, Henry Sidgwick and other members of the Cambridge Ghost Club, had founded the Society for Psychical Research 'for the purpose of inquiring into a mass of obscure phenomena which lie at present on the outskirts of our organised knowledge'.[37] Their aim was to apply scientific methods to the study of psychic phenomena, such as table-tilting or automatic writing, and to test extraordinary human faculties, such as hypnotism and clairvoyance. Membership did not automatically imply a belief in spiritualism. Early members and associates of the SPR included a future prime minister, Arthur Balfour; the man of letters and father of Virginia Woolf, Leslie Stephen; the art critic John Ruskin; the naturalist A. R. Wallace; the clergyman Reverend C. L. Dodgson, better known by his pen name Lewis Carroll; the psychologist (and brother of Henry) William James; and the poet Alfred, Lord Tennyson. It was by no means a lunatic fringe.

In 1884 Sir Oliver agreed to act as a scientific observer for experiments into thought-transference among workers in a Liverpool drapery business. Some of the young women working there seemed to have an uncanny knack for being able to name or draw words or scenes imagined by a third party. In his report for the SPR, Sir Oliver concluded that: 'to the best of my scientific belief no collusion or trickery was possible under the varied circumstances of the experiments'.[38] Thought-transference by extrasensory means, or 'telepathy', was a reality.

He joined the SPR that year, and would conduct investigations for the society throughout the 1880s and 1890s, bringing the supposedly scientific rigour that underpinned his study of other 'imponderables', such as electromagnetic waves, to the mystery of psychic phenomena. In 1889, he met the celebrated American medium, Leonora Piper, off the boat from Boston, and helped to arrange her onward travel from Liverpool to Cambridge, where he attended his first sitting with her at the home of his friend, Frederic Myers. Sir Oliver was convinced when his much-loved, late aunt Anne took control of the medium and 'spoke a few sentences in her own well-remembered voice'. Next, he invited Mrs Piper to his home in Liverpool, putting away the family photograph album before her arrival, and temporarily engaging new household staff, to ensure that she could not glean any background information on the family. This time an old uncle of Sir Oliver's communicated through Mrs Piper, giving details of his early life that were unknown to any of the sitters but were subsequently confirmed to be true. These experiences left Sir Oliver 'thoroughly convinced not only of human survival, but of the power to communicate, under certain conditions, with those left behind on the earth'.[39]

He was less impressed by Eusapia Palladino, the Italian 'physical' medium, who claimed to be able, when in a trance, to cause furniture to move, tables to levitate, musical instruments to play themselves, and sitters to feel the ghostly hand of another upon them. When Eusapia came to Cambridge in 1895 for investigations, she managed to pull off some of these effects – or conjuring tricks – despite the fact that a couple of observers held her hands, and her feet, while another grasped her neck from behind to prevent her from moving objects about. Even so, Sir Oliver was not convinced – and on a trip to the United States in 1910, Eusapia was eventually exposed as a fraud.

Sir Oliver managed to combine his two interests, in science and spiritualism, so successfully that he was elected president of the Physical Society and president of the Society for Psychical Research in successive years. In his presidential address to the SPR in 1902 (the year he was knighted), he claimed that he was, 'for all personal purposes, convinced of the persistence of human existence beyond bodily death ... it is a belief which has been produced by scientific evidence; that is, it is based upon facts and experience'.[40] His progression from psychical researcher to full-blown spiritualist was almost complete. War, and the loss of Raymond, simply accelerated this process.

Raymond, or Life and Death was published in November 1916, and chimed with the mood of the time, when almost everyone in the country had lost a close friend or relative. It went to six editions before the end of the year; and Sir Oliver received thousands of letters from those who had found solace in the book for their bereavement. The *Daily Mail*, however, described *Raymond* as 'Sir Oliver Lodge's Spook Book; Half a Guinea's Worth of Rubbish'; and claimed that the distinguished scientist was 'as easily credulous as the sad creatures who fall a willing prey to soothsayer and fortune-teller'. Its criticism was part of the newspaper's campaign to purge London of 'clairvoyants, psychic healers, palmists, massage and hypnotic specialists, psychometrists, astrologers, mediums, phrenologists, crystal-gazers and divine healers'.[41]

In *The Menace of Spiritualism*, Elliott O'Donnell, the author and self-appointed authority on the paranormal, conceded that Sir Oliver Lodge and Sir Arthur Conan Doyle were geniuses, but that 'geniuses are always more or less abnormal' and susceptible to spiritualism. He was particularly unimpressed by *Raymond*, and by the vagueness of the descriptions of people that passed for evidence. At a private sitting, he complained, 'the medium can always count on receiving no inconsiderable amount of help from the client. She has only to give the broad outlines of a face for her client to fill in the features. The tall, thin man in khaki, pressing a handkerchief or photo to his heart, is at once metamorphosed by the agonised young widow client into the most accurate description of her dead husband, though goodness alone knows how many other sons and husbands the same description – which became a very common stock-in-trade with mediums during the war – has previously furnished.'[42]

Many of Sir Oliver's critics complained that he had not demanded the same standards of scientific evidence in his psychical research as he would have demanded of his university students in their research; that he had been derailed by grief. The psychiatrist Charles Arthur Mercier argued that Lodge's eminence as a scientist had been exaggerated, or was at least irrelevant, in such a different field of enquiry; and warned that: 'We see what we look for. We overlook what we are not looking for.'[43] One contemporary philosopher, Paul Carus, condemned the 'silliness of its [*Raymond*'s] revelations', regretting that 'the saddest part of it consists in the fact that a great scientist, no less a one than Sir Oliver Lodge, has published the book and so stands sponsor for it'. The biologist Sir Edward Poulton, whose son Ronald was killed the same year as Raymond, probably reflected the feelings of the silent majority, writing that he had no time for the 'supposed instances' of communication with the dead. He simply suffered what most parents felt: the numbness of despair and 'the awful silence that grows deeper and deeper'.[44]

*

Second Lieutenant Raymond Lodge was one of three-quarters of a million British soldiers killed in the First World War – over a million if losses from the empire are included. Britain became a nation of the bereaved. Sigmund Freud had predicted, in 1915, the emotional impact of war in a lecture, which was later published in 'Our Attitude Towards Death': 'It is evident that war is bound to sweep away this conventional treatment of death. Death will no longer be denied; we are forced to believe in it. People really die; and no longer one by one, but many, often tens of thousands in a single day. And death is no longer a chance event.'[45] People would need to find new ways of coping.

The Church struggled to answer some of the most frequently asked questions. How could an all-powerful, benevolent God allow such slaughter and suffering? And whose side was He on anyway? What was the nature of life everlasting? And how was our boy faring on the other side? Chaplains were often ill-equipped to cope with such theological challenges, let alone the practical ones of performing battlefield burial services. There were even reports of séances being held in the trenches.

The experience of the trenches was a hell on earth: a fertile breeding ground for apocalyptic legends and tales of the supernatural, with the spirits of the dead returning to help the living. In one popular story of the time, a phantom army of medieval archers protected the British soldiers in their retreat from the Battle of Mons in the summer of 1914. Were the killing fields of France and Flanders, people asked, the great battlefield of Armageddon at the end of the world – with the Kaiser's armies the forces of the Devil? And would the war end in the Second Coming of Christ?

When Margaret Brown's only son was killed by a sniper's bullet in France in 1915, she wrote to the parapsychologist James Hewat McKenzie (who had, incidentally, introduced Mrs Leonard to Mrs Kennedy) to say that her faith had 'received a great shock'. 'I feel heart-broken and hopeless … I receive no comfort from the church which I attend, nor can my minister give me any light as to whether my boy lives a conscious existence beyond death.' So typical was her letter of the many McKenzie received that he published his reply in a pamphlet entitled 'If a "Soldier" Die shall he Live Again': 'They may be well-meaning, but are hopelessly behind the times … these clergymen, with kindly intentions no doubt, speak of bereavement as an experience common to all, and counsel resignation, or refer you to ancient writings, which is really about as satisfying as offering the menu card to a hungry man who asks for bread, expecting that the reading of the bill of fare will fill his stomach.' He reassured the Liverpool woman that her son's soul would have passed from his body at death, and would have been guided 'by helping hands to a place of rest some considerable distance from the battlefield', before waking up in its new home. This place had 'the appearance of the ideal country home', with a garden outside, and books and musical instruments within. Like Sir Oliver's vision, McKenzie's Summerland was essentially pastoral, a place where the dead soldier continued to 'rise to high perfection through his own effort and the helpful influence of noble teachers ever ready to assist him'.[46]

The scale of the slaughter on the Great War battlefields came as a profound psychic shock. Although many people had been interested in spiritualism before 1914, many more were drawn towards it during the war, because it addressed some of the fundamental questions that the Church had failed to answer. According to the political philosopher J. Neville Figgis, spiritualism had become 'a Nemesis on the Church for its neglect'.[47]

Even when people had accepted that their loved one had died – and this was hard enough in the absence of a body or a grave – they wanted to believe that they existed in the afterlife. Spiritualism offered this belief, and the hope that contact could be made. In the words of the hymn 'Abide with Me', which became an anthem of the cause, spiritualism robbed death of its sting: as a denial of death, it proved very popular. The number of spiritualist societies and churches grew, as did the membership of the Society for Psychical Research. Spiritualism became something of a craze, with 'seekers' trying to contact the dead using Ouija boards, table-tilting, and through mediums, whether, in the words of Charles Mercier, in 'sumptuous Persian-carpeted and beflowered apartments in Bond Street, or the dingy antimacassared room over the suburban greengrocer's shop'.[48] They flocked to hired halls, or clustered in dimly lit rooms, straining to hear about the journeys on the other side of their husbands, fathers and sons.

Some Church leaders attempted to accommodate the appeal of spiritualism, using language in prayers and liturgy, and descriptions of the afterlife, that were not so different from those of the spiritualists. The idea that the dead had passed into another, happier life but still hovered around those they had left behind, rather than being consigned to hell and damnation, was not, after all, so different from heaven. But other Church leaders went on the attack, reinforcing the ban on communicating with the dead and condemning 'these sham sciences', in the words of William Ralph Inge, Dean of St Paul's, 'these companion sciences of astrology, witchcraft, and other mischievous delusions, [which] have once more stalked out [into] the light of day, and are unsettling the reasons of hundreds'.[49] They joined the press in drawing attention to fraudulent mediums and fortune-tellers, and to their prosecution under the antiquated witchcraft and vagrancy laws. 'It is surely nothing less than criminal,' complained the Sunday newspaper the *Umpire* in August 1916, 'that these harpies of humanity should be permitted without practical protest to trade upon the mental crucifixion of those whose loved ones have fallen to die upon the war-wasted fields of France and Flanders.'[50]

Sir Arthur Conan Doyle, the creator of Sherlock Holmes, had supported Sir Oliver on the publication of *Raymond*, praising 'the unflinching courage and honesty of the man who chronicled it',[51] in the face of hostile reviews. 'Every ignoramus,' he wrote to his sister Ida Foley in August 1917, 'seems to think himself at liberty to make … criticisms of this great man who has worked for 25 years at this subject with all his power of scientific analysis, and has for the moment shaken his whole professional position by his brave frankness'.[52] He and Sir Arthur had been friends and regular correspondents for years and had been knighted on the same day in 1902. They shared a desire to comfort others through the solace of spiritualism, and even sat with some of the same mediums, such as Mr Peters.

Conan Doyle had trained and practised as a doctor; and, like his friend, had grown up embracing the scientific materialism of the nineteenth century. 'When the candle burns out the light disappears,' he wrote. 'When the electric cell is shattered the current stops. When the body dissolves there is an end of the matter.' He had originally regarded spiritualism as 'the greatest nonsense upon earth'.[53] Around 1886, however, he began to take part in the odd table-moving séance, and to take an interest in telepathy and hypnotism. As a member of the Society for Psychical Research, he continued to study these subjects and other psychic phenomena from a scientific standpoint, and became increasingly open to the possibility of life after death after hearing the accounts of people who had communicated with the dead through mediums.

Then came the war. As Sir Arthur admitted, he 'might have drifted on for [his] whole life as a psychical researcher' had it not been for the impact the war had on his beliefs. 'In the presence of an agonised world … I seemed suddenly to see that this subject with which I had so long dallied was not merely a study of a force outside the rules of science, but that it really was something tremendous, a breaking down of the walls between two worlds, a direct undeniable message from beyond, a call of hope and of guidance to the human race at the time of its deepest affliction.'[54]

It took a personal revelation, however, to transform his deep interest in spiritualism into an obsession. As Sir Arthur explained in *The History of Spiritualism*, writing of himself in the third person: 'Evidence of the presence of the dead appeared in his own household, and the relief afforded by posthumous messages taught him how great a solace it would be, to a tortured world if it could share in the knowledge which had become clear to himself.'[55] As with Sir Oliver, to whom Conan Doyle dedicated his two-volume history, this evidence of the presence of the dead involved his nearest and dearest.

During the war, Lily Loder-Symonds, a friend of Sir Arthur Conan Doyle's second wife, Jean, came to stay and work as a nanny at Windlesham, their house near Crowborough. Lily spent much of her time receiving messages from the 'other side' through automatic writing, including messages from three of her brothers who had been killed at Ypres in 1915, and from Jean's brother, Malcolm Leckie, who had fallen at Mons in August 1914. What had particularly impressed Sir Arthur was Lily's detailed recall of a conversation he had had with his brother-in-law Malcolm long before his death.

As he wrote to his mother in May 1917, Conan Doyle did not fear death for his son, Kingsley, who was serving with the Hampshire Regiment, 'for since I became a convinced Spiritualist death became rather an unnecessary thing, but I fear pain or mutilation very greatly.'[56] Kingsley did not die in action, but of pneumonia, brought on by influenza, in hospital in London in October 1918, just two weeks short of his twenty-sixth birthday – at much the same age as Raymond. Nevertheless, his father blamed the war for his son's death, attributing his ill health to his failure to recover fully from a wound he had received on the Somme.

Sir Arthur had already come to believe that death was not an impassable barrier; but on 7 September 1919, he finally broke through that barrier and made contact with Kingsley. He and his wife were in Portsmouth to attend a lecture by a Welsh medium called Evan Powell. They invited Powell back to their hotel room, along with some friends, searched him for any props, turned out his pockets, and strapped him to a chair with stout twine to prevent any shenanigans. As the room was plunged into darkness, Powell went into a trance, groaning, muttering and snoring; objects started to move around the room; and a voice emerged from Powell's mouth, claiming to be his 'control', a native American spirit called Black Hawk. Sir Arthur then had 'the supreme moment of [his] spiritual experience': 'It is almost too sacred for full description, and yet I feel that God sends such gifts that we may share them with others.' A voice in the darkness whispered: 'Jean, it is I', and his wife felt a hand upon her head, and cried out: 'It is Kingsley.' Sir Arthur then had the sense of a face very near his own, breathing, and heard a voice that had all the depth and intensity of his son's. 'Forgive me!' pleaded Kingsley, to which Sir Arthur replied eagerly that he 'had no grievance of any kind'. 'Tell me dear, are you happy?' he asked his son. There was a pause and then, very gently, Kingsley (who had, in life, always been sceptical of his father's spiritualist beliefs) replied: 'I am so happy.'[57]

Sir Oliver Lodge was chairing the meeting of the London Spiritualist Alliance when Conan Doyle had come out in person, publicly, as a spiritualist, in a talk entitled 'The New Revelation'. This formed the basis of a book, which was to become a spiritualist classic. In *The New Revelation* (1918), Sir Arthur claimed that death brought no sudden change to an individual's spiritual development, but simply provided an easy and painless passage into the spirit world. The spirit body was the exact counterpart of the old one, 'save that all disease, weakness, or deformity has passed from it'.[58] Like Sir Oliver and James Hewat McKenzie, he described a place called 'Summerland': an idealised version of the contemporary world – which some critics thought resembled Hampstead Garden Suburb rather than Heaven.

Sir Arthur's journey from materialist to messiah was more dramatic even than Sir Oliver's, and his tone became intensely emotional and apocalyptic. In *The New Revelation*, for example, he cited Mrs Piper's pre-war prediction that a terrible war would 'cleanse and purify' the world and reform 'the decadent Christianity of today', revealing the truth of spiritualism to all.[59] Sir Arthur explained the causes of the First World War in religious rather than geopolitical terms; and his analysis led him to propose what was effectively an alternative, spiritualist version of Christianity.

'IS CONAN DOYLE MAD?' demanded a headline in the *Sunday Express*.[60] How could this avuncular, pipe-smoking, eminently sensible man, the creator of that cool and calculating investigator Sherlock Holmes, be spouting such nonsense? Or perhaps it was not so surprising, after all, the critics joshed, since he had already managed to bring his hero Holmes back from the dead.

On 27 April 1919, more than six months before the first Armistice Day service at the Cenotaph, the Spiritualists' National Union held a National Memorial Service for the fallen in the Royal Albert Hall. The 5,000 or so congregants who packed the hall had been asked by the organisers to wear white – the colour associated with spiritualism – in the form of white rosettes. The weather echoed the dress code for the evening by producing an unseasonally icy spring night. 'A blinding snowstorm clothed all London in a mantle of white,' the spiritualists' journal, the *Light*, reported. 'Not a man or woman who ventured out of doors could escape wearing our insignia.'[61]

The ceremony was similar to a church service, with hymns, addresses and deeply invocatory language. But as Sir Arthur, the evening's most prominent speaker, observed, it was a 'joyous reunion' rather than a memorial service, 'an event unique in the history of the world … We believe in the depths of our souls that they are here with us tonight. It matters not whether they died in the mud of Flanders, whether they died in the chalk of Picardy, whether it was on the sands of Kut or Mesopotamia or Palestine, or whether they left their young lives among the swamps of Equatorial Africa.'[62]

There was an idea that a new age was dawning, when spiritualism, with its core belief in life after death, was 'going to be the leading

power in the social and political reconstruction of the world.'⁶³ Even
the *Evening Standard* acknowledged that spiritualism had spread
through every class and rank in society, the vast majority being
ordinary people, although there were, of course, a number of the
'pallid, long-haired persons whose appearance suggested the occult.'⁶⁴

Conan Doyle embarked on a crusade to visit every major
town in Britain, marking them on a map that hung in his
study: Birmingham, Cardiff, Glasgow, Doncaster, Huddersfield,
Manchester, Leicester, Northampton … By the middle of 1919, he
had lectured, he calculated, to well over 50,000 people. Like Sir
Oliver, he was driven by a sense of God-given duty to alleviate
the misery around him by sharing his experience and evidence.
'He had this knowledge locked up in his heart,' his friend John
Lamond wrote in a memoir of Sir Arthur, 'which he knew would
be a source of comfort and enlightenment to the thousands who
were sitting in darkness.'⁶⁵ At the Connaught Hall, Worthing, in
July 1919, he answered those who questioned the point of all these
psychic phenomena and thought it 'puerile that tables turn round
or chairs go up in the air'. The point, he contended, was the 'many
people in this land needing consolation so badly … [the] Rachels
mourning and without comfort'.⁶⁶ After such events, he would
often receive letters from the bereaved, whom he'd then refer to a
medium: of seventy-two such referrals, sixty, he later claimed, had
been a 'complete success'.⁶⁷

It was a personal crusade that would expose him, like Sir Oliver,
to ridicule, and eventually undermine his reputation as a man of
letters, losing him friends and followers. Nevertheless, he embarked
on lecture tours of Australia and New Zealand, and North America,
covering 50,000 miles on his second tour to the United States and
Canada in 1923. Sir Arthur invested money, as well as time, on the
cause – around a quarter of a million pounds, it was claimed. In
1923 he helped to finance the founding of a spiritualist church in
London, a project about which Sir Oliver was sceptical: 'I rather
regret Doyle's decision … But that I suppose is a natural outcome
of his missionary activity. I suppose he regards himself as a sort of
Wesley or Whitefield.'⁶⁸

In the last chapter of his autobiography, *Memories and Adventures*, Sir Arthur admitted that the psychic quest had come to absorb the whole energy of his life: 'It is the thing for which every preceding phase, my gradual religious development, my books, my modest fortune, which enables me to devote myself to less lucrative work, my platform work, which helps me to convey the message, and my physical strength, which is still sufficient to stand arduous tours and to fill the largest halls for an hour and a half with my voice, have each and all been an unconscious preparation.'[69]

In his private – as opposed to his public – life, Sir Arthur continued to hold séances, at home at Windlesham, in the old nursery next to the billiard room. Here, he communicated with Kingsley, and with his younger brother Innes, adjutant general with the 24th Division, who had died of influenza in Belgium in February 1919: on one occasion, to everyone's amazement, Innes spoke in Danish, his wife's first language. Sir Arthur kept Sir Oliver updated in his letters.

Sir Oliver, too, continued to hold jolly family sittings at Mariemont at which, on occasion, he recorded, 'the table got rather rampageous and had to be quieted down', and 'things like flower-pots got broken'.[70] Although he had once witnessed, at a session with Eusapia Palladino, the appearance of 'a sort of supernumerary arm'[71] from her side, Sir Oliver was, in general, more scientific and reserved in his spiritualism, more responsive to 'mental' than 'physical' mediumship. Conan Doyle, on the other hand, was a very firm believer in the existence of 'ectoplasm', as such emanations from the medium's body were known, and was drawn to the further shores of spiritualism. Ectoplasm was a sticky, gelatinous material that appeared to flow from the medium, through eyes, nose, ears, mouth or vagina, forming a clammy, luminous cloud. This the medium would then mould into the form of a human face or limbs, to provide material evidence of the presence of a spirit. In his memoirs, the travel writer Norman Lewis described growing up in a spiritualist household in Enfield just after the war. One day his father, a 'prophet of the new awakening', took him to a hall in London to witness a demonstration by Miss Mildred Frogley, a 'materialisation medium'.[72] The lights were dimmed, a white-haired pianist in tails played sacred music on a grand piano to the accompaniment of a lady harpist, and Miss Frogley went into a trance – only for some people, suddenly, to rush the stage and drag her away, trailing a collapsed parachute of ectoplasm, which looked remarkably like curtain material when the lights were turned on.

As it was evidently possible for the medium to conceal the 'ectoplasm' about her body, in the form of a piece of gauze for example, they were sometimes subjected to intimate searches first. Conan Doyle had not witnessed these at first-hand, but he had read about experiments conducted by the German psychical researcher Albert Schrenk-Notzing, involving an attractive, young medium known as 'Eva C'; and was convinced by the rigour of the German's gynaecological examinations.

Sir Arthur was also impressed by the unearthly psychic photographs taken by Mrs Ada Deane during the two-minute silence on Armistice Day, 1922: in which, clouds of faces, purporting to be those of the dead, hovered over living mourners in Whitehall. A couple of years later, the *Daily Sketch* showed that, on microscopic examination, the so-called 'spirit heads' were, in fact, shots of famous sporting figures, including footballers, superimposed above the crowd at the Cenotaph. The 'armies of the dead' were – literally – still alive and kicking. In his book *The Coming of the Fairies*, Conan Doyle also endorsed some photographs, supposedly of fairies, taken by a couple of girls in Cottingley Glen in Yorkshire. It was an indication of his commitment to the reality of another world. Sir Oliver was less susceptible, however, advising his friend, when he first saw the photos, that they were fakes and that he should drop the matter.

In pursuit of his mission, Sir Arthur championed many spiritualist causes. Lester Coltman, a young lieutenant with the Coldstream Guards, had been killed at the Battle of Cambrai in November 1917. Five years later, his aunt, Lilian Walbrook, began to receive messages from him through the medium of automatic writing, just as Lily had done at Windlesham. These she transcribed into a book, *The Case of Lester Coltman*, for which Sir

Arthur Conan Doyle provided an introduction. Lester had always been interested in modern psychic developments – so it was only natural, wrote Sir Arthur, that he would 'give us psychic help from the other side'. Sir Arthur attempted to corroborate some of Lester's evidence, including his description of his death, concluding that 'it is the mental evidence, the similarity of style and thought between the living man and the dead, and the superiority of both to the intellect of the recipient [Lilian Walbrook] which has made the deepest impression upon my mind, and has convinced me that this splendid young man has, indeed, found his way back to give us the help and information which we need'.[73]

People were particularly interested in hearing about the experience of death itself, and about conditions in the afterlife. 'Please tell us more of your Actual Surroundings,' Lester was asked. 'Please tell us what you can of the pleasures of the world in which you find yourself.' What games was he playing, and what work was he doing in the science laboratories on the other side:

'Q. Are there any women working in your laboratory?'

'A. Yes, several, and they are most fitted for painstaking, minute detail work, which requires infinite patience and which certain workers are unable to cope with whilst engaged on big brain effort.'[74]

This is what the friends and relatives of Lester Coltman wanted to know; and what justified the mediumship of Lilian Walbrook and others. In one section of the book, she published a selection of letters written by Lester before his death 'to give them to the public as showing the character and mentality of their writer ... and bringing out the similarity to them in general style of the spirit-communications as imparted to the medium'. This is what had reassured Sir Arthur. The tone of these letters is jocular and breezy, in the style of so many letters from the front, including Raymond's: letters extolling the joys of a cream bun, which 'even as I speak it seethes and rumbles sublimely within me'; letters describing his everyday routines, thanking his family for sending cake and tobacco, or enquiring about Woggins the cat.[75]

These contrast in style with the 'philosophy of the beyond', vouchsafed to his aunt, in the third part of the book: 'The depletion of the universe is by complete exhaustion, and when all the matter conserved by mortals is etherealised a substitution is effected in the etheric fluids, which conglomerate and eventually habitate in the spheres' ... and so on for sixty pages.[76] Did Sir Arthur really believe that this had been written by a twenty-two-year-old second lieutenant (although twenty-seven if he'd allowed for a further five years of spiritual development)?

Spirit biographies, like *Raymond* or *The Case of Lester Coltman*, recounted the continuing adventures of fallen soldiers on the other side. Another example of this particularly popular genre, in which the living dead retained their personal identity and were passed as still fit for service, concerned Private Thomas Dowding. Major Wellesley Tudor Pole was walking by the sea, at Bournemouth, on 12 March 1917, when he sensed the presence of someone he felt was a soldier, trying to communicate with him. When he returned home that evening, he sat down at his writing table – and immediately his pen moved, transcribing messages from Thomas Dowding, a self-confessed 'crabby, selfish old bachelor' and schoolmaster of thirty-seven, who had been killed in the autumn of 1915.

Like the other spirit-soldiers, Dowding believed that his experiences might be useful to others. He had one overriding message of reassurance for the bereaved: 'Physical death is nothing. There really is no cause for fear.' Dowding was now in a place of no pain, where 'life' was strangely similar to earth life. He went on to describe his new surroundings, his lovely new home, a bungalow beside a brook, with 'mossy banks green and restful', and 'a wonderful view stretching across the gardens down the hillside over the tree-tops to a sapphire lake in the green valley below ... There were flowers and pictures everywhere and deep comfortable seats in alcoves.' *Private Dowding* evoked a paradise, but it was also a manifesto for a utopian future after the war, when extremes of wealth and poverty would disappear and democratic republics would rule the world – and, like Lilian Walbrook's book, a practical guide to contacting the spirit world.[77]

In a coda to the story, Sir Oliver left one final experiment to posterity: a test to divine whether he would himself be able to remember, after death, a message he had left behind, and communicate it to the living through a medium. On 20 June 1930 he deposited his message at the Society for Psychical Research, confident that it was so personal that no living person would be able to guess it and pass it on to the medium. The message was contained within a series of seven envelopes, which came to be known as the 'Posthumous Packet', each holding a clue to the next envelope. These were to be opened, one after another over a period of time, eventually guiding the medium towards the final, innermost message. In 1947, seven years after Sir Oliver's death, the first two messages were opened, and over the next few years more than a hundred sittings were held, until in 1954 the final envelope was opened. It contained 'a five-finger piano exercise which Sir Oliver had learned as a child'.[78] Although some of the sittings had hinted at messages that came quite close to the sense of this final message, the experiment must be deemed inconclusive in its attempt to prove the survival of memory and personal identity after death.

6

Pilgrimage: The Search for Meaning

The hundreds of thousands of visits made every year to the graves and battlefields of the First World War are no recent phenomenon. Even before the war had ended, people were planning trips, and publishers providing information. The French tyre manufacturer Michelin published the first in its series of *Illustrated Guides for the Visit to the Battle-fields* in 1917. Dedicated to Michelin workers who had died for their country, it struck a delicate balance between regional history, with a particular focus on the war years, and practical sightseers' guide, between encouraging rubbernecking and appealing for respect and reverence. In doing so, it set the tone and format for future guides, exhorting its readers to view their journeys as 'a pilgrimage', not merely a journey across the ravaged land. 'Seeing is not enough,' it advised, 'one must understand: a ruin is more moving when one knows what has caused it; a stretch of country which might seem dull and uninteresting to the unenlightened eye, becomes transformed at the thought of the battles which have raged there.'[1]

Some people made their way to the 'devastated regions' soon after the fighting had stopped, and many more – particularly those who could afford to – had followed by the summer of 1919. It was a short railway journey from the Channel ports to Ypres, and a person leaving London Victoria at 8.45 a.m. could arrive in Ypres at 8.17 p.m. via Dover and Ostend. One of the advantages of this route, in view of the fact that customs examinations had become much more rigorous since the end of the war, was that only one set of customs, the Belgian border in Ostend, had to be negotiated, rather than two sets of customs, the French and then the Belgian, via Dover and Calais. The advantage of the latter route, via France, was that visitors approached the Ypres Salient through Poperinghe, following the same fatal avenue through which millions of British troops had been funnelled to the front.

These early visitors did not expect luxury. When in the war zone, they stayed in one of the makeshift wooden 'bungalow' or 'baraque' hotels ('somewhat primitive in character', according to one of the guidebooks[2]) that sprang up on the outskirts of Ypres. By day, they made excursions into the wilderness, picnicking off tables assembled from old ammunition boxes. Although Ypres was closer to, and more convenient for, the battlefields, there was a higher standard of comfort in Poperinghe. 'Pop', as it was known to the British troops for whom it had represented civilisation, lay some six miles behind the front and had suffered less damage than Ypres. The town still bore the scars left by shrapnel and bomb splinters, and there were gaps in some streets where houses had been completely destroyed, but Pop had been relatively safe through the war. Life had continued in this small town of 11,000 inhabitants that became 'the hostess of the Salient'.[3] Children had still gone to school; the shops and cafes had stayed open, catering at any one time for up to a quarter of a million soldiers who were enjoying a rest from the front. Skindles Hotel had hot and cold water in the bedrooms. The visitor might even dine, or smoke a cigar, in the same establishment patronised by their loved one years before.

In March 1919, the Canadian journalist John Dafoe made a pilgrimage to Vimy Ridge that he predicted would be made in a more leisurely manner by thousands of Canadians in the coming years. Although the area was accessible then only with a military pass, he foresaw a time when generation after generation of Canadians would 'follow the Canadian way of glory over the battlefields of France and Flanders, with reverent hearts and shining eyes'. On the March evening he visited Vimy Ridge, it was 'bleak and cheerless beyond the power of words to express. The tide of war had flowed past and left the wrecked countryside vacant – the huts empty and the camps abandoned save for, here and there, a handful of men engaged in salvage work; the roadways, once swarming with life, deserted and silent! Over all desolation and loneliness rested like a pall.' Recognising that the storming of Vimy Ridge by Canadian troops in April 1917 would continue to hold a unique place in the Canadian consciousness, he reported on proposals to 'erect and maintain in perpetuity a number of battle shrines which would be stations on this pilgrimage'.[4]

In September 1919, the Hon. Alice Douglas Pennant visited her brother's grave, near Ypres, for the first time. 'Driving back to Ostend (for at that time there was nowhere one could stay in Ypres),' she described, in language that echoed that of the spiritualists, the impression she had had of the tens of thousands, the 'clouds of witnesses', hovering in the air. 'The level light of a beautiful autumn evening made the down of the masses of thistles which covered the devastated country shine like silver sheen, whilst the thistledown, floating away on some imperceptible zephyr, looked like souls updrawn from the earth, composed of their hallowed dust …'[5]

The writer Sergeant Joyce Kilmer had been killed by machine-gun fire in Picardy on 30 July 1918. The following spring his mother, Annie Kilburn Kilmer, asked permission from the US government to visit her son's grave in France: she and Joyce's widow had decided to respect the wishes expressed in his last poem, 'Rouge Bouquet', to leave his body undisturbed in France, rather than to have it repatriated:

> There is on earth no worthier grave
> To hold the bodies of the brave
> Than this place of pain and pride
> Where they nobly fought and died.[6]

Her request was refused on the grounds that, at this stage, no relatives of the dead were allowed to visit the battlefields. In 1920, however, citing business in England and France, Annie travelled to Europe; and on Thursday 9 September drove to Fère-en-Tardenois, where Joyce lay in the American Cemetery. She asked to be left alone as she placed her wreath of roses and pinks by the headstone and knelt to pray. Counting off her rosary beads soothed and quieted her that day 'more than anything else could have done. And I did not shed one tear.' On returning to the grave later, she took away a little of the earth from the burial plot, and made arrangements with the people caring for the graves for flowers to be put on Joyce's grave on his birthday (6 December) and on Christmas Day. It was only as she left France that she cried for the first time because she felt that she was leaving Joyce behind. 'But I don't feel like that any more,' she came to realise in time, 'for he is with me always!'[7]

Not all these early visitors were well-heeled. The soldier and writer Henry Williamson recounted the touching story told to him by an officer who had just returned from grave registration duties at Cambrai. It concerned the quest of a poor, elderly couple who travelled more than 7,000 miles from Canada in 1920 to view the grave of their son, a sergeant with a Canadian battalion. The only information the father and mother had was a letter from their son's company commander, stating that their boy's body had been buried in an old trench about 500 metres north of a farmhouse five miles from Cambrai; the officer regretted, however, that it would be impossible to find the grave as the place had been heavily bombarded. The couple insisted on undertaking their pilgrimage despite this warning and, accompanied by the officer, found the ruins of the farmhouse, and the stumps of trees that marked the whereabouts of the grave. For a time there was no sign of the grave itself – until, at last a small dark cross was found, bearing an inscription which, when deciphered, was found to mark the resting place of their son's body.[8]

In September 1921, the writer Vera Brittain left on what she described as a pilgrimage to Europe, to mourn at the graves of the two men who had been dearest to her. Her fiancé Roland Leighton had died of his wounds in a casualty clearing station, near Louvencourt on the Somme, in December 1915. The khaki vest and breeches he had been wearing when he was shot were returned to his family later, blood-stained, caked in mud, and 'reeking', as Vera explained, of the graveyard. Roland's mother had had the clothes burned immediately, to get rid of the smell of death. Then, two and a half years later, in June 1918, Vera's brother Edward was killed on the Italian front.

It was Edward's grave she visited first, in the small cemetery at Granezza on the Asiago plateau. 'Who could have dreamed,' she wrote, 'that the little boy born in such uneventful security to an ordinary provincial family would end his brief days in a battle among the high pine-woods of an unknown Italian plateau?' Later, on the same pilgrimage, she and her companion Winifred Holtby hired a car in Amiens and 'plunged through a series of shell-racked roads between the grotesque trunks of skeleton trees, with their stripped, shattered branches still pointing to heaven in grim protest against man's ruthless cruelty to nature as well as man'. She read the inscription on Roland's grave in the cemetery at Louvencourt, and plucked a bronze marigold from the ground to keep in her diary.[9]

Conditions in the devastated regions immediately after the war deterred all but the most intrepid travellers. In October 1919, the writer Wilfrid Ewart went on a pilgrimage to the Somme with his sister Angela in search of her husband's grave. Picking their way past shell holes treacherously overgrown with weeds, they were struck by the wreckage of the fighting all around. Fragments of letters and photos littered the ground. Tragedies lurked on either hand, he wrote: 'In this livid green, stagnant pool where a soldier's clothing and equipment, his respirator and rifle, lay adjacent to an oozing, battered grave; in that shell-hole where a blood-stained overcoat and steel helmet suggest what may have happened there.' As the blue and gold afternoon faded, Wilfrid and his sister carried on towards Butte de Warlincourt, near where they knew Angela's husband was buried. At every cross, they bent down to puzzle out the 'letters and numbers which time and weather have reduced to mere ciphers'. They never found the grave they were looking for among the fields of crosses. But as they paused in their search, a 'profound disappointment' upon their faces, they looked up and spotted – in one of those epiphanies that were such a feature of pilgrimages – 'against the roseate sunset glow three high crosses set upon a little hill'.[10]

These first visitors to the Western front after the war were shocked by the post-apocalyptic landscape. As Findlay Muirhead described in the *Blue Guide to Belgium and the Western Front*, 'the greatest volume of artillery fire' had fallen on the 'fateful strip' of no man's land, 'churning the surface far and wide into a wilderness of shell-holes, exposing the barren subsoil and wrecking everything that stood above the ground'. Forests were reduced to groups of shattered tree stumps, 'streams were obliterated or converted into swamps, and the trampled fields were strewn with the sinister debris of war'. Hardly any leaves were left on the trees.[11]

Guidebooks warned about the dangers of unexploded hand grenades or shells, which continued to cause serious injuries to the curious every year. One guidebook writer mentioned another hazard: he knew of a lady who, in stooping to pick up what she imagined was a 'souvenir', 'sustained a great shock' in discovering that it was really an old boot, and that inside the boot were human bones.[12]

There was always the inconvenience of developing a puncture on the rutted roads, and even, it was rumoured, of attack by gangs of deserters who roamed the battlefields. Enid Bagnold, in a novel chronicling the adventures of Fanny, an army driver, described how, immediately after the war: 'A certain lawlessness was abroad in the lonelier areas of the battlefields. Odds and ends of all the armies, deserters, well-hidden during many months, lived under the earth in holes and cellars and used strange means to gain a living … There had been rumours of lonely cars which had been stopped and robbed …'[13]

Conditions such as these limited the number of pilgrims and tourists to a trickle – and nothing like the one and a half million foreign tourists predicted by the Touring Club de France for 1919. Gradually, however, Britons did start travelling to the Continent, as they had done in the years before the First World War. Many of these opted for tours organised by travel agents. Thomas Cook, for example, offered packages to the Western front from £8 11*s.*, with luxury jaunts, featuring Pullman car seats on the train and ex-service officers as chauffeurs and guides, at 35 guineas. Although these trips were often promoted as pilgrimages – resembling visits to a shrine rather than to a show – they often threw in stops at the Belgian seaside or sightseeing excursions to Bruges, to complement the more gruelling time spent on the battlefields.

As Muirhead advised, the 'conducted tour' – whether by Thomas Cook, Dean & Dawson, Pickfords, Lazenby's Tours or the South Eastern and Chatham Railway Company – relieved the traveller 'of all trouble and anxiety with regard to transport and hotel accommodation. This advantage is of especial value in the present state of the devastated region …'[14]

By the 1920s, tens of thousands were making the journey every year. Guidebooks proliferated. Many of them struck the balance set by the early Michelin guides between the practical and the polemic, the historical and the contemporary. Photographs of battlefields, scattered with dead soldiers and horses, were counterpointed with others of statuary and stained-glass windows, as you would expect in a guidebook to the region. A common theme of these before-and-after illustrations was that of an ancient civilisation laid low by modern weapons and German vandalism. The idea 'that it was to preserve this heritage of history and beauty intact, that so many of our heroes have fallen', began to be seen as one of the justifications for the sacrifice.[15]

'Few names awaken more memories than that of Ypres,' claimed the Michelin guide to Ypres and the Battles of Ypres, published in 1919, 'a city of incomparable splendour in the Middle Ages, and of which nothing now remains but a heap of ruins. Of the last precious traces of this ancient prosperity, the rich and splendid buildings which filled the mind with wonder – the immense Cloth Hall, the beautiful cathedral, the churches, the sumptuous mansions, the sculptured houses – the German guns have spared nothing.' Almost revelling in the scale of the devastation, it urged readers to clamber up onto the Vauban ramparts. From the muddy path which ran along the top of the ramparts, you could see the semicircle of ridges from which the Germans had bombarded the city. But it was also the best vantage point for a 'magnificent panorama' of the ruins. Pictures of Biebuygk House before the war, when 'it was one of the handsomest houses in Ypres', were juxtaposed with 'Biebuygk House, as the war left it'; the 'Grande Place on Market-Day, before the War' and 'What the German Shells Left of It'; the Rue au Beurre before and after; and so on.[16]

Much of the detail in the English guides to the battlefields was practical, and geared towards the independent traveller: currency exchange rates, railway timetables for the boat trains, recommendations for local transport on arrival in Ypres, including car hire from the 'Wipers Auto Service'. Captain Poyntz of 12 Regent Street offered a first-class conducted tour by motor car; or you could take the light railway, which ran alongside the main Menin Road, from Ypres to Hooge, the scene of continuous fighting throughout the war, past the 'tank cemetery', where the wreckage of a dozen tanks was a popular sight. Sightseeing itineraries of the salient included the eighteen miles, best travelled by motor car, from Hooge to Gheluvelt, Zonnebeke, Passchendaele, St Julien and St Jean. As Muirhead observed, 'hundreds of humble village-names, scarcely heard of before 1914, have become household words throughout the world; familiar English names now dot the Flemish plains with reminders of triumph or disaster or of grim endurance; and everywhere are quiet spots with a sacred claim to be "for ever England" '.[17]

There was advice on the best time of year to visit (between March and October, as the byways were apt to be impassable during the winter months); and on where to snatch a light lunch of omelette and coffee at a small roadside *estaminet* in a battlefield village – usually no more than a shed made of rusty sheets of corrugated iron. For those planning on a picnic, a thermos flask was needed, along with a tin opener – travellers were advised not to forget any essential piece of equipment. Many of these guides were written by veterans and benefited, as Captain Atherton Fleming explained in his foreword to *How to See the Battlefields* (1919), from information collected 'in the course of over four years' campaigning in France and Flanders'.[18] Another veteran, Lieutenant Colonel T. A. Lowe, advised that the best way to see the battlefields was on foot, not least because the traveller 'will feel that he is tramping as they were obliged to tramp'.[19] For clothes, he recommended an old golfing suit, with stout boots and leggings to protect the shins against sharp ends of wire, of which there was still a lot lying about. Ladies should wear strong boots, thick woollen stockings and short skirts, with a woollen jumper or jersey. Other recommendations included a waterproof coat or cape, field glasses and a camera, and a small first-aid outfit containing antiseptic to dab on cuts and scratches.

However detailed the practical advice, these guides tended to stress their lofty intentions. In *A Short Guide to the Battlefields*, published in 1920, J. O. Coop conceded that many people were contemplating 'a pilgrimage to some sacred spot where all that was mortal of some relative or friend lies buried'.[20] It was for them that Fleming's book had mainly been written, too. 'There are many thousands of people who will want to see the ground over which the fighting took place; some, no doubt, out of pure curiosity, others with a much more pathetic object in view. To the latter their journeyings will be more in the nature of a pilgrimage than a mere round of sightseeing, and should the information contained herein prove of use to these pilgrims, I shall feel more than amply repaid for my trouble.'[21] Similarly, the introduction to *The Pilgrim's Guide to the Ypres Salient*, by Noel Mellish, VC, concluded that these trips were pilgrimages 'in memory of those who passed this way', and commanded visitors: 'You will tread reverently, for it is holy ground. It is the shrine of those who won the right for us all to have a country of our own.'[22]

Some of these guides urged visitors to hurry, as the process of reconstruction had begun, and the battlefields of northern France and Flanders were being reclaimed by local inhabitants returning to their farms. For the pilgrim there was no time to lose, wrote Wilfrid Ewart, as 'today a certain atmosphere may be recaptured – for the last time since tomorrow it will be gone'.[23] T. A. Lowe claimed in the introduction to *The Western Battlefields* that: 'Nature is hard at work on the battlefields', and soon 'the old familiar landmarks will be things of the past'.[24] The same was true of the cities. Ypres, a mound of rubble, a ghost town in 1918, was, by 1925, a 'newness of bricks and mortar', which can be 'very disconcerting for the Pilgrim'. What you have to do, it advised, was 'to picture the town of Ypres as you would have seen it soon after the Armistice'.[25]

One of the common features of these guides was to describe the battlefield trips made by veterans and the bereaved as spiritual quests or pilgrimages, thereby adding a layer of solemnity and meaning to their loss. Ypres, in particular, became 'holy ground', a 'high altar of sacrifice', 'the most hallowed spot on earth'. This high diction, resonant with religious expressions and archaic, often medieval, turns of phrase (soldiers became 'warriors') persisted through the 1920s and 1930s. Attempting to find a higher meaning in the experience of war, it acted as a conservative counterpoint to the bitter, ironic, modernist tone of the anti-war books, which flaunted their disillusionment with the values of 1914.

In 1920, Lieutenant Colonel Henry Beckles Willson, a Canadian journalist who had served during the war, observed in *Ypres: The Holy Ground of British Arms*, the first post-war guide specifically dedicated to the city: 'There is not a single half-acre in Ypres that is not sacred. There is not a stone which has not sheltered scores of loyal young hearts, whose one impulse and desire was to fight and, if need be, to die for England. Their blood has drenched its cloisters and its cellars, but if never a drop had been spilt, if never a life had been lost in defence of Ypres still would Ypres have been hallowed, if only for the hopes and the courage it has inspired and the scenes of valour and sacrifice it has witnessed.'[26] Beckles Willson had been appointed town major of Ypres while it was still under military jurisdiction – and had even built himself a small bungalow by the ramparts. His efforts to preserve the ruins of Ypres as a permanent memorial were supported by the mayor of Ypres, who placed a sign beside what was left of the Cloth Hall, with the instruction: 'This is Holy Ground. No stone of this fabric may be taken away.'

Beckles Willson took it upon himself to preserve Ypres as it had been when the war ended. He resisted attempts to turn Ypres's war celebrity into commercial profit, urging the Belgian government not to allow the city to become 'a cheap holiday resort or country fair', adding that: 'Ypres should be the one great and sacred repository of all the scattered dead in the Salient.'[27] Like some other veterans, Beckles Willson had a profound lyrical appreciation of the old front line, as vegetation returned in the summer of 1921. 'In the very early morning (before the trains and the char-a-bancs arrive) and in the evening (when, thank Heaven! they are gone) I love to wander in my garden,' he wrote of the battlefield. It was a place of enchantment, with 'thickets of roses and honeysuckle, a thousand torn and fretted beds of fuchsias, carnations, nasturtiums and violas …'.[28]

Whereas the French focused their emotional energy on Verdun, making it France's main memorial, there were several sites on the Western front which resonated with British communities. Pals battalions were composed of men who had enlisted during local recruitment drives, with the promise that they would serve alongside their friends and workmates: as a result, whole swathes of soldiers from towns such as Leeds, Bradford and Sheffield, had been slaughtered on a single day on the Somme, and specific sites became associated with particular towns. The Sunday closest to 1 July, the first day of the Battle of the Somme in 1916, became a date to remember, and the occasion for annual pilgrimages.

Ypres, however, was always the most popular among the British. This was partly because it was easier to access than the Somme. It was only a day's journey from London, and offered a host of sites in striking distance, whereas the Somme had no convenient centre from which to visit the battlefields: Amiens was a long way away; Albert was in ruins immediately after the war; and Peronne was 'still in a state of desolation'.[29] The battlefields of northern Italy and the Near East were initially for the very adventurous only. Guidebooks warned of 'adverse conditions' and 'uncongenial surroundings' in Turkey, Egypt and Palestine. Even in 1929, the writer Robert Byron was describing the bones of the British dead still littering the trenches in Gaza.[30]

The special significance of Ypres went far beyond its ease of access. The city became a symbol of everything that had been worth fighting for. Britain had entered the war in protest at the invasion of Belgium in the first place; and Ypres remained throughout the war the only major town in Belgium not to be taken by the Germans. Ypres and the salient, a shallow semi-circular bowl about six miles in diameter which bulged out from the front line, hindered German access to the Channel ports, and to that extent came to be regarded almost as an outpost of south-eastern England. The fact that the salient was surrounded on three sides by low hills, from which the Germans could bombard it, made this strategic town extremely vulnerable.

Compared with the Somme, where most of the fighting took place in 1916, Ypres was the scene of fighting in every single year of the war. Its successive major battles involved the greatest number of British soldiers, and resulted in more casualties than in any other war zone. In 1935, Beatrix Brice, who had served in the Voluntary Aid Detachment as a nurse and became one of the great champions of Ypres, confirmed how: 'For four years Ypres was an objective which the enemy never ceased to covet and never captured, the pivot of ceaseless fighting … the centre of a little patch of country which witnessed more intense and continuous effort and gallantry and agony than any other like-sized piece of land of which human history bears record.'[31]

The British lost around 254,000 men in its defence, of whom nearly 100,000 have no known grave, their bodies 'swallowed up in the abysmal mud of Flanders':[32] they are named on the memorials for the missing at the Menin Gate and Tyne Cot. The scale of the slaughter was justified in spiritual terms, so as to give comfort to the bereaved. The Menin Road, which led east out of Ypres into the salient, and along which hundreds of thousands of soldiers had tramped, was often described as the Via Dolorosa which Jesus Christ had walked, carrying the Cross, on the way to his crucifixion. Eventually, there would be three cemeteries for every square mile of the salient. As well as the great strategic significance of Ypres, therefore, there was a huge spiritual significance: Ypres became 'a synonym for sacrifice'.[33] What was the point of all those deaths, of all that bloodshed, if Ypres were surrendered? In a viciously circular way, the rhetoric of heroic sacrifice, as a spiritual ideal and a source

A stonemason engraves the headstone of a Canadian soldier killed in France (note the national symbol, the maple leaf).

Coxyde Military Cemetery in Belgium was designed by Sir Edwin Lutyens. In 1922, the cemetery was in transition, the wooden crosses on the left being gradually replaced by the uniform headstones on the right.

A special supplement of *Light*, the Spiritualists' journal, celebrates the national memorial service for the fallen at the Royal Albert Hall in May 1919, which featured an address by Sir Arthur Conan Doyle.

The medium Gladys Osborne Leonard with the scientist and psychic researcher Sir Oliver Lodge, whose dead son Raymond she helped him to contact.

The group photograph sent by the mother of a fellow officer to the Lodges on 7 September 1915 shows Raymond in the front row (second from right). The officer seated behind appears to be leaning or resting his hand on Raymond's shoulder – as described in a session with Mrs Leonard.

A St Barnabas pilgrim at the grave of a loved one in 1924.

In a picture taken by Olive Edis, Britain's first official female war photographer, Women's Army Auxiliary Corps gardeners tend the graves of the war dead at Etaples in France.

'This is Holy Ground', reads a sign placed at the Cloth Hall in Ypres. 'No stone of this factory may be taken away. It is a heritage for all civilised people, 30 August 1919, Town Mayor'.

The ruins of Ypres Cathedral dominate a scene of devastation a few months after the end of the First World War.

Thousands of British Legion Pilgrims gather for a ceremony, led by the Prince of Wales, at the Menin Gate in Ypres, August 1928.

Sir Fabian Ware (left), the founder of the War Graves Commission, accompanies the Prince of Wales at the unveiling of the Memorial to the Missing of the Somme. The memorial's architect, Sir Edwin Lutyens, can be seen further to the left, in the background.

The ceremony inaugurating the Memorial to the Missing of the Somme at Thiepval in northern France was held on 1 August 1932.

In the aftermath of the war, a line of soldiers moves steadily across the battlefield, searching for human remains.

The remains are then brought from the battlefield to a cemetery for burial.

Second Lieutenant Eric Francis Seaforth Hayter was killed in March 1918, but his body was not found for almost six years after the end of the war, and a grave was not registered.

In 1924, Eric's father commissioned a memorial for his missing son near the place where he had fallen. In an extraordinary twist of fate, Eric's body was unearthed as the contractor dug the foundations for the memorial.

'Souvenir King' Private John 'Barney' Hines displays his collection of trophies at Polygon Wood, near Ypres, September 1917.

of inspiration, became a reason in itself for the strategic importance of carrying on the struggle.

'The Ypres Salient,' the former war correspondent, Sir Philip Gibbs wrote in his foreword to *The Immortal Salient*, 'was the ground on which the quality of British manhood was put to the test, most often, in most frightful conditions, against heaviest odds, during the years of war. Every yard of it is sanctified for our race by the heroism of our men who defended it by their bodies and souls.' However much he welcomed the gradual return of normality after the war – the new buildings, the farming – he echoed the sentiments of many veterans when he claimed that: 'this ground will be for ever haunted by that noble youth of ours, by those muddy men in steel hats, by the surge of transport and guns, by the ghosts of a great army of youth, so cheery even on the edge of abominable ordeal, so valiant in the face of death itself, so patient in suffering, so stubborn in endurance, so simple and splendid by the faith that was in them and never told'.[34]

Tiny hamlets and hills, copses and crossroads became household names, the microgeography of Ypres projected onto the world stage: Poperinghe and Ploegsteert, for example, Zillebeke and Zonnebeke; with places and features of the landscape reduced to easily pronounceable names such as 'Pop' and 'Plugstreet', Clapham Junction and Piccadilly Circus, Hellfire Corner and Mouse Trap Farm, Stinking Farm and Suicide Corner. Different international communities identified with different places: the city of Worcester with Gheluvelt, the Germans with Langemarck, the Canadians with St-Julien, the Australians with Polygon Wood, and New Zealanders with Messines Ridge. Overall, the fighting around Ypres, particularly during Third Ypres in 1917, known as Passchendaele, came to represent the very essence of the Great War.

In the 1980s, the French historian Pierre Nora developed the concept of the '*lieu de mémoire*', a place invested with intense historical meaning and significance in the nation's collective unconscious. For the British, Ypres was that 'memory site' par excellence, a fact that had been acknowledged soon after the end of the war, in an editorial in *The Times*. 'Ypres is more than the name of a city or a battlefield. It is a symbol – and the fittest symbol – of the pride of the Empire in the achievements of its sons in the war.'[35] Fifteen years later, an article in the *Ypres Times* answered the question: 'What does Ypres mean to me?' by suggesting that there was no other place 'on the whole lengthy battle front from Britain to the furthest corners of the Seas [that] can be so utterly and completely a British memory as the half-dozen miles around Ypres we call the Salient'.[36]

In response to a plea by Field Marshal Lord French of Ypres, Sir Arthur Conan Doyle and Philip Gibbs campaigned for an organisation to preserve and manage the memory of Ypres and all it represented, and in September 1920 Beckles Willson founded the Ypres League. Membership was open to veterans of the battles of Ypres, and for those who had lost a loved one in the salient. The league's main objectives were to 'commemorate the Immortal Defence of the Salient, and to keep alive that spirit of fellowship which was so powerful a lever and so beautiful an element in the war'.[37] To that end, it aimed to provide special travel facilities and information for those interested in Ypres and the salient; the marking of historic sites and the compilation of charts of the battlefields; and the erection of a British church and school in Ypres.

Beckles Willson was helped in this task by the indefatigable Beatrix Brice. With Earl Haig as president and Princess Beatrice of the United Kingdom, who had lost a son during the First Battle of Ypres, as a patron, Beckles Willson wanted to make sure that people would 'never forget what their dead did and suffered in that enclave'.[38] Although, even in the 1920s, the Ypres League never had more than around 10,000 members, it became, in the hands of Beckles Willson, a powerful propaganda machine, with international branches in Australia, New Zealand and Canada.

The league published the first issue of its quarterly newsletter, the *Ypres Times*, in October 1921 (as distinct from the *Wipers Times*, a satirical magazine produced during the war by British soldiers on the front line). Over the following years, the league published books and guides as well, including *The Immortal Salient* (1925),

The Battle Book of Ypres (1927), and *Ypres: Outpost of the Channel Ports* (1929). On 31 October every year, it held a celebration, known as Ypres Day, to mark a turning point in the First Battle of Ypres in 1914.

It funded the erection of six of the 118 Demarcation Stones that marked the extent of the German advance along the Western front in 1918. It launched a successful appeal to build St George's Memorial Church in Ypres, which was designed by Sir Reginald Blomfield and consecrated in 1929, to serve both the pilgrims and the permanent British 'colony' in Ypres – the people working for the Imperial War Graves Commission, who maintained the cemeteries. The same year, the Eton Memorial School opened next door for the children of those British workers, fostering a permanent link between Britain and the town and, in line with one of the league's primary objects, helping to maintain 'cordial relations with dwellers on the battlefields of Ypres'.[39] To this day, there are Anglo-Belgian and Anglo-French families who have worked as gardeners for the commission over several generations since soon after the war.

But, most significantly of all, it organised the first league pilgrimage to Ypres in July 1922: 'a return of the "old crowd"', according to the 'Special Pilgrimage Number' of the *Ypres Times*, '– the men who served and suffered at Ypres – the old comrades-in-arms who *knew* Ypres – the parents, and widows and orphans of "pals" now sleeping on the Salient'. Some 800 pilgrims travelled direct from London – the men in medals, and the women in black – with others joining at Calais, Boulogne and Ostend, thereby swelling the numbers to nearly two thousand who took part in the proceedings in the Grand Place. For those who had fought around Ypres during the war, the first emotion was one of 'pure wonder', tinged with regret: 'Ypres had practically risen from its ashes while they unconsciously expected it to remain as it was three years ago.' Many were disappointed by the city and its gradual restoration – and horrified by the stalls selling relics and souvenirs. 'It was not OUR WIPERS,' one ex-Tommy remarked.[40] 'Ypres is unrecognisable: Wipers exists in memory only,' Henry Williamson complained.[41] And Wilfrid Ewart expressed a similar feeling in an article in *Cornhill* magazine: 'You may here see a city in ruins – but it is not the Ypres of the Great War.'[42] Nevertheless, these pilgrimages became annual events, with the league raising funds to help impoverished relatives of the dead make the journey. In 1928, for example, it paid for ninety-seven women, most of whom were 'poor mothers and wives whose sons and husbands are among the "missing"'.[43]

The Ypres League was one of several organisations which arranged and provided limited financial assistance for pilgrimages to the battlefields; others included: the Church Army, which converted wartime canteens into hostels for pilgrims; the War Graves Association, based in the north of England, which organised a pilgrimage every Whitsun; the British Legion, the Salvation Army and the YMCA, which helped 60,000 people between 1919 and 1923. The St Barnabas Society, named after the saint associated with consolation, was founded in 1919 by the Reverend Matthew Mullineux, a New Zealand army chaplain. It too arranged pilgrimages to the Western front, and also to Italy, Greece and Gallipoli, providing hostels for pilgrims and help in locating graves. In 1923, when the average industrial wage was £3 a week, a typical cut-price, comfort-free St Barnabas pilgrimage to the Western front cost around £4, with travel agents charging many times that amount. For bereaved relatives who could not afford to go on a St Barnabas pilgrimage, the society offered to lay a wreath by the loved one's grave.

Around 850 pilgrims travelled to Ypres for Palm Sunday 1923, and a similar number to the Somme at Michaelmas. Dressed in black, the parties set off from Victoria Station for Folkestone, where they boarded the ferry to Calais. For Mary Macleod Moore, writing in the *Toronto Saturday Night*, one of the most beautiful memories of Ypres came towards the end of the day: 'the station square was softly dark and mysterious when the people gathered at nine o'clock. Some were resting on the edge of the platform, others were sitting on their rugs, many were standing wearily. But very very softly the R.A. Band began to play "Abide with Me" and tired men and women rose to their feet to sing. People near me were crying, but I like to think they were tears without bitterness, for they no longer thought of their boys and men as lying afar off in a strange lonely country. They had seen their sweet graves, and … knew the resting places were cared for by tender hands.'[44] To this extent, the significance of the pilgrimages reached beyond those who actually went on them: for the reassurance provided by the pilgrims that the graves were well maintained gave great comfort and consolation to the bereaved back home.

The pilgrimages to the Somme were more dispersed than the Ypres pilgrimages, with different parties going to Boulogne, Etaples, Amiens, Albert, Béthune, Arras. Pilgrims were met by a St Barnabas 'lady worker', whose unselfish 'tact and sympathy', the organisation noted, 'has soothed many a Sorrowing Pilgrim, and brought a glimmer of peaceful sunshine into many a desolate and lonely heart'. They were then conducted by car or bus to the appropriate cemetery, before being taken back to a hostel for the night, in time for their return to England the following day.[45]

Whether it was to Ypres or the Somme, the impulses which inspired people to go on pilgrimages in the first place, and the therapeutic benefits they might expect to reap, were the same. As the preface to a souvenir edition of the 1923 pilgrimages explained: 'These War Pilgrimages do not reopen old wounds; they set hearts that have been too long aching at last to rest … No one who has seen these serried ranks of shining white stones, smelt the glorious profusion of multi-coloured flowers which surround these stones, or listened to the eternal choir of birds carolling above them, will ever forget, though he may be unable to communicate the amazing sense of content that steals over his senses as he stands in silent communion with the spirits of those who kept England free.'[46]

One of the more remarkable organisations to arrange pilgrimages was Toc H, which had been founded by the Reverend Philip 'Tubby' Clayton. 'Tubby' had opened a club for soldiers in Poperinghe towards the end of 1915, in premises rented from a wealthy Belgian brewer. He named the three-storey property in the Rue de l'Hôpital 'Talbot House', in memory of Gilbert Talbot (the brother of Tubby's fellow army chaplain Neville Talbot), who had been killed in July 1915 at Sanctuary Wood.

Tubby was the self-appointed 'inn-keeper', and he and his colleagues set about making the house weather-proof – its back had been ripped off by a shell fired from the Pilckem Ridge. Well-wishers sent gifts of furniture, curtains, books and pictures to make Talbot House feel like home: around half-a-million soldiers would pass through its doors during the course of the war. The name of the house was abbreviated to T. H., which then became Toc H in signallers' code. The extraordinary thing about Toc H was that it was open to all denominations and ranks, and run entirely on egalitarian, civilian principles. Over the door of the chaplain's room was a sign reading: 'All Rank Abandon Ye Who Enter Here – an injunction that must have seemed unique in the hierarchical, military world of the Western front. The discipline of the house was not enforced by army orders but by light-hearted little notions that arrested the reader's attention and won their cooperation. A hand-painted sign reading 'Pessimists, Way Out' pointed to the exit from the house onto the street, with other notices advising: 'If you are in the habit of spitting on the carpet at home, please spit here', and: 'The waste-paper baskets are purely ornamental'.[47]

It was a 'home from home', according to its rotund presiding genius, Tubby, where less was said about the war 'than probably anywhere else in Europe at the time'. 'Outside there were sharp words of command, feet moving together, the rumble of congested traffic, the narrow crowded pavements, the slatternly shop windows. Inside was comfort and warmth, and light, and music, and a touch even of home and of the love that came out to them thence.'[48] The Upper Room, in a hoploft in the attic, was reached by very steep wooden stairs that had been scuffed by the tramp of thousands of hobnailed boots. This was the chapel, a haven of inner peace, despite the intermittent sound of firing from the front line.

An old carpenter's bench served as an altar, with a frontal of green and gold cloth worked by some nuns from Haywards Heath. Above the altar hung a reproduction of Perugino's *The Crucifixion*, flanked by two wooden candlesticks carved from old bedposts. During services, the chapel was bathed in the warm glow from a great gilt candelabrum suspended from the loft's central beam, and hummed to the sound of music supplied by a portable harmonium. During the course of the war, some 20,000 soldiers received the Sacrament in this makeshift space, fifty grown men were baptised, and 800 confirmed. On one day alone – Easter Day 1916 – there were ten celebrations of Holy Communion from 5.30 a.m. onwards, which Tubby administered single-handedly, intoning 'This is my Body – This is my Blood' over and over again. On one occasion, Tubby found General Plumer sitting alone and thoughtful in the Upper Room, and enquired anxiously after his state of mind. 'A good place for rest and quiet after a particularly heavy day,' the general replied. General Cavan, a corps commander in the Ypres Salient who later became Chief of the Imperial General Staff, was another regular at Talbot House; he was to recall how his prayers in the Upper Room, after a particularly terrible day in 1916, gave him strength for the remainder of the war.[49]

The appeal of Talbot House was never limited by rank. In *The Pilgrim's Guide to the Ypres Salient*, published by Talbot House in 1920, F. R. Barry claimed, in a chapter entitled 'In Praise of Poperinghe', that 'Everyman's Club' offered a 'radiant history of light and fellowship and joy and laughter breaking into the darkness of the Salient'. Imagine, he continued 'what it meant to the British soldier! To be able to lie back in a real armchair, and sleep, or read, or talk as he felt inclined, not to be "pushed about" by anybody, to know he was expected to do as he would.'[50]

For Tubby, Christianity – 'the living Spirit of the Master [Jesus] suddenly made real to young men' – lay at the core of Talbot House. But for many it was the sense of brotherhood and peace that made it a place of joy and renewal. Those who had spent time in Talbot House during the war felt a great debt of gratitude towards it; and began to look towards 'Poperinghe as a holy place of pilgrimage' in the aftermath.[51]

When the house's owner, M. Coevoet Camerlynck, returned to live there in 1919, parties of ex-servicemen returned to visit Talbot House, although he was understandably reluctant to admit all of them. In 1926, however, Tubby armed himself with a letter of introduction from the Belgian embassy in London to the Burgomaster of Poperinghe, and pleaded so effectively with M. Coevoet Camerlynck that he eventually consented to admit a party of pilgrims into his house in relays of twenty. The doors were opened the next day, and Tubby led the first twenty people to the chapel in the attic, where a disused pram stood in one corner and some onions had been left out to dry on the floor. 'We all instinctively knelt as we entered,' one of the pilgrims recalled, 'for we knew that the ground whereon we stood was holy.'[52] This was destined to be the first of many pilgrimages to the well-loved shrine. The problem of access was resolved in 1929 by the purchase of Talbot House, on behalf of Toc H, from the owner by Viscount Wakefield. Toc H pilgrims could often be heard singing: 'He who would valiant be', the Pilgrim's Hymn originally written by John Bunyan, and – like Bunyan's pilgrims – sometimes carried pilgrims' staffs, as in *The Pilgrim's Progress*. Toc H developed into a worldwide Christian movement after the war, but its roots would always be in the salient, as its banner bearing the Ypres Cross proclaimed.

Even before the war, more people had been going on pilgrimages to religious sites, such as Lourdes. But, as an article in 1928 in the *Morning Post* noted: 'Since the War there has been a revival of that reverent and adventurous spirit which inspired the Pilgrimages of the Middle Ages. The Ypres Pilgrims have set an example that may well be followed for many generations.'[53] In the spirit of St Barnabas, pilgrimages offered consolation to those whose lives continued to be dominated by the war. For veterans, such as those of Talbot House, this might come from renewing old friendships, reminiscing about wartime experiences, and even recapturing and confronting the past. They often travelled in groups from the same area, or from the same company or battalion, returning year after year, as with the Old Contemptibles Association pilgrimage to Mons and Ypres. These personal acts of exorcism could be traumatic. Wilfrid Ewart expressed such an ambivalence in an article in the *Cornhill Magazine*. Passing the entrance to a dugout he had once occupied for weeks near the Menin Gate, he reflected: 'One cannot regret a nightmare, even the lucid intervals of it; and at the same time one cannot regret having experienced the nightmare.'[54] The salient, and nowhere more intensely than Ypres, continued to hold veterans in its grip, both attracting and repelling them. On a visit to Ypres in 1928, the writer Ralph Mottram claimed that the Menin Gate 'is the main passage to those fields of memory, whence come dreams that are nightmares, and others we would not part with for any consideration … In our minds, whatever the day, it is always raining, always dusk, always lighted by a greenish flicker, deafening with hideous noise, on that road.'[55]

The novelist Henry Williamson was similarly haunted by his memories of the war. Wounded on the first day of the Somme in 1916, he went on to serve at Passchendaele the following year. The scars he suffered for the rest of his life were emotional as much as physical. In 1927, the year in which his best-selling *Tarka the Otter* was published, he went on a personal pilgrimage to France and Flanders. He revisited the sites of his wartime experiences in the company of a friend, a former Tank Corps officer whom he called 'Four Toes' for having lost a toe from each foot from frostbite. 'I must return to my old comrades of the Great War,' Williamson wrote, '– to the brown, the treeless, the flat and grave-set plain of Flanders – to the rolling, heat-miraged downlands of the Somme – for I am dead with them, and they live in me again.'[56]

He contrasted his experiences a decade before with what he saw in 1927. The fields of the salient in 1917 were 'as shapeless as the ingredients of a Christmas pudding being stirred', and Ypres no more than a ruin. The city was now 'clean and new and hybrid-English', but however new the houses and freshly laid the tiles, they could never 'obscure the passing of the men'. Old memories kept flooding back. On a road near 'Av-er-loy Wood', where 'the young man of my old self used to walk … the dead still unburied in the shell-craters on either side', the trees were now green, and the new growth twelve feet high, rearing like 'verdant waves' against 'the black stumps of the trees which knew the lost generation that toiled along the road'.[57]

On the last night of his pilgrimage, Williamson stayed in a seedy *estaminet*, where damp patches caused by a leaking roof spread across the ceiling. Men and women danced to the blare of an

American hurdy-gurdy, but he could not bring himself to enter into the fun of their rowdy party: 'I was entirely a foreigner among the living, and half a foreigner to myself – a man who had lost part of himself, and was only now beginning to find it again. For years the lost part had lurked in the marsh, seeing wraiths of men in grey with coal-scuttle helmet and big boots, wraiths of men in khaki, always laden and toiling ... When I awoke the next morning the wraiths were fled ... I was filled with longing for my home; to see again the lanes, the sea, the barns, the hills, the eyes of my wife, the smile of my little boy ... the new part of myself, overlaying the wraith of that lost for ever.'[58] Williamson had started his spiritual recovery.

As with some other veterans, there was an underlying romanticism to Williamson's memories of the past, a nostalgia for a sense of comradeship that, as it faded with the end of the war, made the world seem a poorer and more dispirited place. What H. Harris remembered on his return to Gallipoli in 1936, more than twenty years after he had left, were 'the grim vessels of war, both British and French, belching forth flame and smoke as the shells scream overhead on their errand of destruction'; the dysentery cases who cared not whether they lived or died; those 'loathsome dead mules that would insist on coming ashore after they had been towed out to sea by the naval men (How they smelt!)'. But what sustained him, above all, were his memories of the 'happy cheerful comradeship of men'.[59]

Whereas most soldiers wanted to obliterate their memories of the war, for a few, it had – however improbably – been the backdrop to the happiest days of their lives. When it ended, they particularly missed the camaraderie. On pilgrimage, they went back to the same *estaminets* they had frequented during the war, for an omelette and a glass of 'plonk' (vin blanc) at twopence a glass – 'toot sweet and the tooter the sweeter', they would order, rehashing the old army Franglais slang. They might even feel moved to commune with the dead. 'I was only having a pipe with dear old Ted ... just as we used to,' one ex-serviceman observed as he was spotted talking to himself beside a grave.[60]

The story of a strange graveside meeting in 1932 between an ex-serviceman and a Miss Emily Causton was told by various Australian newspapers. Emily had, since the end of the war, made periodic visits to the grave of her fiancé who had been killed at Passchendaele in 1917. On several of these occasions, she met the same man beside the grave, but it was not until 1932 that they fell into conversation for the first time; and Emily discovered that she and the stranger, a German garage proprietor called Hans Klutzen, shared an interest that went beyond a mutual interest in the works of Shakespeare and George Bernard Shaw. It transpired that Hans had bayoneted Emily's former fiancé to death in hand-to-hand trench fighting fifteen years before. Haunted by the memory, Hans had visited the grave every year, on the anniversary of the encounter, to pay his respects to the man he had killed. The couple fell in love, and were married towards the end of the year. Emily claimed that her late fiancé would have approved, as both soldiers were 'victims of circumstance'. As she told the newspaper reporters, she had come to the conclusion that it would be wrong to throw away 'God's gift of love just because Fate had brought these two men together in deadly conflict … I believe that a union such as this will do more for the reconciliation of the two peoples than all the efforts of the world's politicians.'[61]

Bereaved relatives, too, felt that by visiting the battlefields and the cemeteries, where their loved ones lay, they came closer to the spirits of the dead. There was an idea – not just among spiritualists or in the writings of people like Alice Douglas Pennant – that the spirits of the fallen, the great army of the dead, hovered above the battlefields.

The bereaved also craved a close physical link with their loved one, kissing the name on the headstone, photographing it or tracing it onto a piece of paper to take back home. They had never seen the coffin, or derived any psychological comfort from a funeral, which would at best have been a makeshift affair conducted on the battlefield in the presence of a padre and a burial party. The pilgrimage, then, could be seen as a substitute for a mourning ritual that had been interrupted by the war.

One woman at the Menin Gate in 1927 spoke for thousands of mothers when, on seeing her son's name on the Memorial to the Missing, claimed: 'I feel so happy to have seen that name. He was killed in 1914 – thirteen years ago – and ever since I have wanted to tread where he trod. I am happy.'[62] For many pilgrims, the visit to the grave was cathartic, and completed a chapter in their life. 'I have had the dearest wish of my life'; 'We have had a great yearning fulfilled in having seen the last resting place of our beloved sons'; 'I came all the way from home for this; now I can die content': all of these sentiments were expressed time and time again.[63]

Some of the pilgrims wore their dead husband's or son's medals on their breast; and carried letters, or diaries, written by their loved one, to guide them on their way. As they followed the route he had made on his last journey, they came to experience something of what he had suffered. The harsher the conditions, the thicker the mud, the steeper the slope, some pilgrims felt, the closer and more authentic was the experience and the greater the consolation. Those who made the same journey year after year chronicled their pilgrimage in albums, lichen from the headstone or flowers from the graveside pressed between the pages. They returned home each time reinvigorated, radiant, fulfilled, the contours of their grief evolving with the changes in the landscape illustrated in the photographs. Gradually they came to accept their loss.

The Bickersteth family visited and revisited the old battlefields several times after the war, to commemorate the death of Lieutenant Morris Bickersteth, who was killed, aged twenty-five, on 1 July 1916, the first day of the Somme, on which 20,000 British soldiers were killed. Each trip was overlaid with the memories of previous pilgrimages made by members of the family, the parents Samuel and Ella and their surviving sons. The time of year was particularly poignant as, only days before his death, three of the five brothers, Morris, Julian and Burgon, were all in the same area of the Somme. In his last letter home, addressed to 'just the most perfect parents in the world', Morris described how, on 29 June, they had contrived to pull off 'the most historical meeting the family has ever had', at

Bus-lès-Artois.[64] His letter arrived the day after his parents received news of his death.

The family's search for Morris's grave started within days. On 3 July, Julian, an army chaplain, bicycled over to Serre, where the 15th Battalion of the West Yorkshire Regiment had been operating, to get first-hand news of Morris. A Private Bateson told him that he was with Morris, when Morris was hit in the head by shrapnel, and that he had died instantly. Julian was thankful to God for the fact that Morris had not been one of the thousands of cases of wounded men left out on the field of battle to die. 'The cries for water from wounded men left out in inaccessible spots are absolutely heart-rending,' he wrote.[65] Julian tried to return later in the month to locate Morris's grave, but was told to turn back, as the area was under heavy shell fire. Ella's diary records how 'our darling's body lies in "No Man's Land" unburied, & we have heard as late as to-day [23 July] that it still lies there'.[66]

Julian kept going back to the battlefield. In March 1917, his colonel asked whether he could find the bodies of any of those killed at Serre nine months before: Julian was amazed to report that a great number were still lying as they had fallen – in no man's land. He was back again the following month, to place a rickety wooden cross within a few yards of where – in the absence of an identifiable body and grave – he believed Morris must have fallen. 'In the midst of the desolation and the endless circles of shell holes,' Julian read the burial service aloud and scattered earth to the four corners of the world, when he came to the words of the committal. 'I felt that I was standing on holy ground,' he wrote, 'sanctioned forever by the blood of heroes. It was a privilege to be allowed to do even this, exactly nine months after the day.'[67] Although Julian had not found Morris's body – like many it would have been unidentifiable – he was sure that it was one of the many exhumed and buried somewhere in this consecrated cemetery.

Towards the end of June 1919, just days after both Julian and Burgon had received their Military Crosses from the king at Buckingham Palace, the two brothers accompanied their parents on the first of a series of family pilgrimages to the battlefields and to the place where Morris had died. The Bickersteths were one of the first families to make such a pilgrimage after the end of the war. At Villers-Bretonneux, where the German Spring Offensive was stopped in April 1918, Ella picked up a battered German helmet to bring home. 'It was thrilling,' she wrote, 'to be on a spot where a son of ours had actually taken part in a battle that saved Amiens and the Channel ports.' After Amiens, they made for Albert, where the desolation of its ruins beggared description: 'Nothing, absolutely nothing, remains standing of the Cathedral (where the hanging Virgin so long remained without falling) or houses, except for a few tottering walls.' Detachments of German prisoners were beginning to clear up the debris, and a good many people seemed to be living in the cellars beneath their ruined homes.

At Bus-lès-Artois, they identified the farmhouse where Morris had been billeted before the battle and the place where the three brothers had last met. Julian showed them the underground cellar that had served as a chapel at Hébuterne, and the advanced dressing station where he had helped out.[68] He then led his family across the battlefield to one of the three Serre cemeteries: an experience made all the more desolate by the relentless rain. At Puisieux they found the Queens Cemetery and the cross they were looking for. Samuel offered a few prayers, and Ella placed some roses from their Canterbury garden under the cross, before turning away to try to find the actual spot where Morris fell three years to the day before. As they viewed the higher ground near Serre, from which the Germans had machine-gunned the advancing British soldiers, Ella realised that her son and his comrades had stood 'absolutely no chance'; nevertheless, 'to see it all made one feel the glory of their advance against such hopeless odds, and their willing self-sacrifice filled one with a never-dying admiration and pride'.[69]

They were to repeat these trips throughout the 1920s, visiting Morris's grave and covering ground that had been known intimately to the boys during their war service. Burgon accompanied his parents on a trip to France in 1921. They visited the cemetery near Serre, which 'for our immediate family must always be the dearest and most sacred place of pilgrimage in the whole long battle-line'. They found it in good order, and threaded their way through wire and shell holes and bits of rifles to Morris's grave, where Ella laid her flowers. For Burgon, this was 'always the most moving thing to return to a part of France which was the scene of the most tremendous experience of my life'.[70] He particularly relished explaining the military actions in which he and Morris had been involved, thereby reassuring his parents that Morris had not died in vain.

Nothing had changed when the brothers made their next trip towards the end of June 1926. The wooden crosses were still in place, and little had been done to cultivate the soil in the immediate vicinity of the cemetery. They went straight to Plot 1, Row E, Grave 19, and – ten years to the day after the beginning of the Battle of the Somme – laid the flowers they had that morning procured in Arras on the grave.

When another brother, Ralph, visited Morris's grave with his wife Alison in 1929, the cemetery, along with its neighbours, had been rebuilt. 'The Cemeteries are lovely beyond all description,' she wrote '– perfectly kept and filled with flowers and the grass is mown and kept like velvet – English turf …' There was a dwarf rambler rose planted between Morris's grave and the next one, and they stood there for a long time, overcome 'not from the sense of sorrow, – but with the beauty and peace of the place'.[71]

To celebrate Samuel and Ella's golden wedding anniversary, and the fifteenth anniversary of Morris's death, Julian and Burgon took their parents on a final pilgrimage to France and Flanders towards the end of June 1931. In Poperinghe, they visited Talbot House, which had reopened that Easter. In Ypres, they took rooms at Skindles Hotel and heard the Last Post under the huge vault of the Menin Gate. Having toured some of the battlefields around Ypres, they journeyed southwards along the old front line, where Julian and Burgon had spent much of the war, revisiting old sites: Hébuterne, Bus-lès-Artois, where the three brothers had said goodbye for the last time on 29 June 1916, and on to Serre, where a path led over the fields to the cemetery which was the object of their pilgrimage: the Queens Cemetery.

Much of the land over which they walked was still uncultivated, rough and scarred by shell holes. Although various members of the family had visited Morris's grave several times before, it was the first time Samuel and Ella had seen the cemetery since it had been finished; and they found it 'supremely beautiful'. They had brought some red and white lilies, but the cemetery was already so full of flowers, with a small bush of red roses nestling against Morris's headstone, and below it a bed of pansies, that these were almost redundant. Samuel placed a copy of the memoir of Morris's life that he had written and published. 'The whole scene was one of extraordinary peace,' wrote Burgon. 'The countryside was bathed in the warm sunshine of a perfect summer afternoon.' Farmers were bringing in the freshly cut hay; and the family lingered by the grave as 'for us it was the holiest ground in all the long battle front'. At last 'the lengthening rays of the sun bid us be moving and we slowly made our way back to the high road'; and on to Serre and Albert. 'Always a hideous place,' Burgon remarked caustically, 'Albert rebuilt is more hideous still. The new church is execrable, a monument of bad taste. The Germans would be doing the world a service if they knocked it down again.'[72]

Earlier that year, on Maundy Thursday, a group of eighteen ex-servicemen assembled at Battersea Town Hall, where they had all worked for the Borough Council, to begin a pilgrimage – of a very different type – to the Western front. On their return, one of their number, Private Newbery, a former private with the London Regiment, compiled 'a slender record', or memoir, of their trip.

Les Dix-Huit, as they called themselves, also comprised Nobby Booth, who was 'famous for his moustache'; Tommy Brace, a Scot with a 'convivial nature' who could be 'pugilistic on occasions'; Harold Godfrey, a 'strong silent man – fond of rabbits and confectionery'; William Kelly, an Irishman 'with a liking for spicy stories and songs'; Harry Adam Smith, who spun 'like a top when dancing'; William Turnbull, a good after-dinner speaker, who liked a nap after lunch; and Bertie Woodruff, the club secretary, who was 'generally of good habits but sometimes out until three in the morning'.[73]

The object of their trip – somewhere between a works outing and a pilgrimage – was to visit areas and towns with which they had become familiar during the war: 'not to stand about, and groan, and curse the evil days which had originally sent us there, but rather to be there in our freedom, and endeavour to obtain every ounce of enjoyment to be had'. And, as Private Newbery explained, 'We got it!' They spent their nights in a 'riot of noise and song', drinking and dancing; and their days visiting the cemeteries, sightseeing, and nursing their hangovers from the night before.

Near Ypres, they visited Canal Bank and Hellfire Corner – 'memories of which are better sealed'. In Poperinghe, they just missed Tubby Clayton, who was due to preside at the official opening of the recently acquired Talbot House the following day. The group was constantly struck by memories of fifteen years before: in Arras, when they were entrenched on one side of the Rue de Strasbourg, while 'Jerry' occupied the cellars of the shops on the other; and on the way from Arras to Bapaume, by the sight of steel helmets, barbed wire and sheets of iron still lying beside the road and across the fields.

They were 'spellbound' by the 'wonderful work' of the Imperial War Graves Commission, by the splendour and magnificence of the cemeteries. Over the course of 300 miles in the battlefields area, they also visited the graves of several former colleagues from Battersea Borough Council, who had lost their lives on the Western front: Privates Greatorex, Roberts and Dean, and Rifleman Lloyd.

As Private Newbery's memoir concludes: 'midst all that enjoyment, we did not fail in our duty to those of our former colleagues who had made the great sacrifice. At their graves, tributes were paid with a fervency and zeal, with which I personally was profoundly impressed. The Grave and the Gay were certainly mixed; but after all, 'tis often but one short step from the sublime to the ridiculous, and in this case we made it short indeed.'[74]

*

Pilgrims – whether veterans or bereaved relatives – considered themselves somewhat superior to tourists, representatives of the sacred rather than the profane. They had particular personal links with the dead, to whom they wished to pay homage and prove that their deaths had not been in vain. The pilgrims were united in finding some aspects of battlefield tourism distasteful.

Only a year after the end of the war, Rudyard Kipling was imploring readers of *The Times* to behave reverently on the battlefields. Other writers complained about 'morbid seekers after sensation. Vandals. Ghouls of the battlefield.'[75] Tourists had been heard to complain that some memorial stones, marking a significant point on the battlefield, were inaccessible. 'But why did they put it here of all places, right off the beaten track?'[76] Tourists, as E. F. Williams observed in the *Ypres Times*, 'come with a rattle and a clatter through the Menin Gate, all packed together in huge char-à-bancs, and after a raucous voiced guide has pointed out the very obvious Cloth Hall ruins, they are whirled away again to one of the show places, perhaps Hill 60, and when they get back home, they think they have seen Ypres and the salient, and perhaps begin to wonder what all the fuss was about'.[77] It was an insult, Stephen Graham felt, that 'very few knew over what terrible ground they had passed and fewer still understood just where it was they were so contentedly munching ham sandwiches and tomatoes'.[78]

John Gibbons was particularly struck by 'one young Conservative Lady' among the tourists in Poperinghe and wondered 'why on earth she had to wear rather highly coloured beach-pyjamas to Do Our Heroes' Graves', but simply supposed, after all, that 'it was the Gay Continent and all that …'.[79] And Wilfrid Ewart complained that, although the devastating evidence of war was all around, 'this made no difference to the 1920 "flapper" who eyed the young mechanics in blue overalls and "got off" as frequently as in the Bois de Boulogne'.[80]

On the fifth day of his pilgrimage, Henry Williamson had visited Hill 60, where you could buy the 'souvenirs' dug up every day: wooden pipes, well preserved in the light sandy soil, fragments of rifles, bayonets, regimental badges, buttons, bully-beef tins, pistols, bombs, revolvers, boots. Some of the souvenirs were more macabre. When Rowland Feilding showed an American army doctor around the old Cuinchy–Loos battlefield, he was horrified by the doctor's preoccupation with collecting them: the man, Feilding described in a letter to his wife, would pick up a bone and 'call out, "Oh, look, a human tibia!" – or whatever kind of bone it might happen to be'. However horrifying it was to see the ground 'desecrated in this way', Fielding reflected, it would be, 'still more so to think of what will happen when the cheap tripper is let loose'.[81]

Some of the souvenirs being turned out after the war had a therapeutic quality. Made from debris found on the battlefields by local or Chinese labourers, who risked life and limb unearthing them, they were a tangible link with the places and landscapes where the spirits of the dead resided. Letter-openers were crafted from scrap metal, cigarette lighters from cartridges, ashtrays and photograph frames from shrapnel, and crucifixes from bullets. For the tourist, these holiday souvenirs had a certain novelty, but for the pilgrim they had a great sentimental value, particularly if the relevant regimental badge or button salvaged from the battlefield was soldered on. Some of the items were quite elaborate: vases fashioned from brass artillery shell cases and decorated with pastoral scenes, Chinese women in flowing traditional robes, or floral art nouveau designs, representing the flowering of 'Trench Art' from the scrap waste of war. In homes across the country, the very act of polishing them was both a permanent reminder and a relief. Henry Williamson was a little shocked when he saw a bishop buying one of these flower vases in the Grand Place in Ypres from a burly man dressed in blue jerseys and blue trousers, with a tray of brass souvenirs slung round his neck … and no arms.[82]

In 1935, twenty years after the death of his father, Frank, Christopher Isherwood visited Ypres to find his name on the Menin Gate Memorial. He, too, was offended by the vulgarity, writing in his diary: 'The towers of Ypres, which looked grand in the distance against the sunset, in the cup of the plain, are new and quite meaningless, like London County Council architecture, when you see them close. The Menin Gate – ugly enough, in any case, to be an entrance for the Wembley Exhibition – is made merely absurd by being piled up against the end of the street, on to which it doesn't fit. We searched for Daddy's name and finally found it, high up in a corner, heading a list of Addenda.' The town, he concluded, 'is certainly "for ever England" – the England of sordid little teashops, faked souvenirs and touts'.[83]

Pilgrims – particularly veterans – were sometimes disappointed when places were not as they remembered. When John Gibbons returned to France twenty years after the war, with the idea of 'trying to reconstruct [his] memories', he found it all very puzzling. He had difficulty working out where he was: the fields had been ploughed; the barbed wire cleared up; and the trenches no longer there (apart from those that had been artificially preserved for the tourists and for which a local farmer would charge). The line between the preservation of a battlefield site – the stretch of trenches at the Newfoundland Memorial Park at Beaumont Hamel, for example, or the crater left by a mine explosion on the Messines Ridge in 1917 – and its trivialisation, between the sacred and the profane, was always a fine one. Gibbons was astonished, time and time again, by not being able to find evidence of the war that once had filled his whole life. It was a tragedy that, after the waste of 'millions and millions of men', there was so little to show for it: 'We had not even permanently blasted the land, for everything was growing again just as if nothing had happened.'[84]

Ralph Mottram, too, revisited the Western front almost two decades after the end of the war, in an attempt to 'recapture the past in the present'. But he found all semblance of the past gone, 'irretrievably gone'. Particularly perplexing was his Flemish taxicab driver's desire to take him to what he called the 'Monument to the Egyptians', as Mottram was unaware that there had ever been Egyptian troops in the front line at Ypres. When the taxi stopped at a monolith on the Menin Road, Mottram noticed the design on it of a Sphinx, which not only explained his driver's Egyptian reference but also confirmed to Mottram that it must be the memorial to the Gloucestershire Regiment, whose crest was a Sphinx. 'That mistake of my driver's,' wrote Mottram, 'seems to epitomise something which is happening, and to provide the reason for this book. Our

War, the War that seems the special possession of those of us who are growing middle-aged, is being turned by time and change into something fabulous, misunderstood and made romantic by distance, as it recedes into the Past.'[85]

W. E. Stanton Hope had had a similar experience on a pilgrimage-cruise on the *Duchess of Richmond* in 1934 which featured sightseeing in Naples, Constantinople and Athens, as well as three days on the battle sites of Gallipoli. 'Anticipation,' he found, 'is sometimes a more vivid pleasure or pain than the reality.' He had expected that setting foot on the soil of Gallipoli for the first time in almost twenty years would be 'one of the great emotional experiences of [his] life …' But he was disappointed, finding it impossible to relate 'this peaceful little plateau with the Hell's acre of August, 1915!' The tang of brine and the fragrance of growing flowers had helped 'remove the memory of the putrescent stench which once had belched from the land and contaminated even the sea' – so effectively that one 'tourist who had come solely for a pleasure cruise expressed keen enjoyment of this sunlit, scented land and thought that everything was "very nice"'.[86]

Some of the bereaved feared that, as the landscape recovered, the scale of the sacrifice would be forgotten. Writing in the *Manchester Guardian* in 1930, Vera Brittain noted that: 'Time has a deceptive habit of blurring our pain while preserving the glamour of our larger-scale tragedies … And Nature herself conspires with time to cheat our recollections; grass has grown over the shell-holes at Ypres, and the cultivated meadows of industrious peasants have replaced the hut-scarred fields at Etaples and Camiers where once I nursed the wounded in the great retreat of 1918.'[87]

Many of the first pilgrimages after the war were relatively small-scale journeys to the battlefields, arranged by individuals or organised by associations and charitable societies. The first mass pilgrimage, which almost everyone could afford, was to London – to the Cenotaph and the grave of the Unknown Warrior. These became places where the millions of private individuals whose lives had been shattered by the war could identify with a common experience, and come together to grieve and remember the dead.

Right up until the Second World War, this pilgrimage became an annual event in the week around Armistice Day.

Members of the royal family were similarly moved, too, to go on a pilgrimage. On 11 May 1922, King George V, dressed as an ordinary officer, 'with no trappings of state nor pomp of ceremony, and with only a small suite', went as a private pilgrim, 'to visit the tombs in Belgium and France of his comrades who gave up their lives in the Great War'. His journey was recorded in an illustrated souvenir guide – the profits from which went to organisations that helped relatives – and helped to popularise the idea that pilgrimages could bring together people from all walks of life. The king's encounters were very public. He would stop to chat with the gardeners working in the cemeteries, who lived in camps and mobile caravans, or with other pilgrims 'because they were on the same mission as he was, of gratitude and reverence'.[88] He met representatives of the Dominions, such as the high commissioners for Canada and New Zealand, and French dignitaries such as Marshal Foch. In Ypres, he stood silently by the grave of his cousin, Prince Maurice of Battenberg.

The sun was shining and blossom covered the old battlefields as he visited the cemeteries of Tyne Cot, Vlamertinghe, Brandhoek and Lijssenthoek, making 'this corner of Flanders seem a fair and human country ... But the King knew all that it had been in the long dark winters of the war, when the very abomination of desolation brooded over it, and in its pools of slime his soldiers struggled and choked that the fields of England might be kept free of the foe.' From Belgium, the king's whistle-stop tour proceeded to France. On 12 May, he visited the Somme cemeteries: Warlencourt, Warloy-Baillon, Forceville, Louvencourt, Picquigny, Crouy, Longpré-les-Corps-Saints. At the cemetery in Etaples, which had been the main hospital centre during the war, the king performed 'an act of simple homage' at the grave of a soldier that expressed 'his feeling of kinship with those comrades of his who had fallen in the war'. A woman from the West Country had written to Queen Mary, as one mother to another, begging her to place a spray of forget-me-nots, which she enclosed, on the tomb of her dead son,

Sergeant Matthew, RASC. The queen did not arrive from Belgium until later, but she confided the mission to her husband, who carried out 'the pious task, taking care ... to find the grave and, bending down in homage, to place upon it the mother's flowers'.[89]

His last stop was Terlincthun Cemetery on the cliffs above Boulogne, where he was joined by Queen Mary. Standing at the Cross of Sacrifice, the king addressed the assembled crowd, 'his voice vibrant with emotion, but under rigid control'.[90] Never before, he noted, had people dedicated and maintained individual memorials to their war dead as were to be found in these cemeteries.

By the mid-1920s, pilgrims were travelling farther afield than the Western front, to the war cemetery on Mount Scopus in Jerusalem and to Gallipoli. On 25 August 1926 a party of almost 300 men and women assembled at Victoria, the boxes containing their wreaths piled high on the station platform. They were bound for Gallipoli on a pilgrimage organised by the St Barnabas Society. 'We were of all grades and walks of life,' recalled the novelist Ian Hay in *The Ship of Remembrance*. Some had paid for their passage in full, others had paid for a part, and some had travelled as guests of the St Barnabas Society, paying nothing at all: 'for that is the principle in which St. Barnabas works ... you give what you can afford'. One of Hay's fellow travellers was a 'peeress', going out to visit her husband's grave near Suvla Bay; another was a 'poor seamstress from the north of England', who had lost all three sons in the war.[91]

The pilgrims boarded the SS *Stella d'Italia* at Marseilles, split roughly between bereaved women and veterans. Although their motivations were rather different, they did come together for the various entertainments on board, the dance nights and, later, for the paddling and picnics on the beaches at Anzac Cove. As Trevor Allen, one of those veterans, described in *The Tracks They Trod*, around a third were Salonika or Gallipoli men, revisiting 'those barren hinterlands of war in which, for good or ill, we lived the epic of our younger years'. Why on earth should anyone want to return? he asked? 'We hated those arid countries with a blasphemous hate when we had to campaign in them, and swore never to set foot in them again. But Time, that wily trickster, has been stealthily at work all these years, smoothing out the bad memories and gilding the good.' Stopping off in Salonika, where they visited the graves of those who had died from disease, he found the city a little disappointing, not as fun as it used to be. It had lost 'its hectic flush of wartime prosperity'; and modern shops had replaced most of the tawdry little *estaminets* in the Rue Egnatia, 'where garish women used to sprawl uninvited on your knee'.[92]

On 2 September the pilgrims landed at Cape Helles, where British troops had disembarked on 25 April 1915, for a service by the memorial. With the Aegean below sparkling in the sun, and the long grim peninsula stretching into the distance, there was a ceremonial laying of wreaths and the singing of 'O, Valiant Hearts', a hymn which compared the sacrifice of soldiers with that of Christ. In the minute's silence between the Last Post and Reveille, nothing could be heard, according to the St Barnabas edition, 'but a weeping as quiet as the rustle of wind in the thistles'.[93] Afterwards, the pilgrims moved on to what Ian Hay described as 'more private business', as they searched for the graves of their loved ones. 'To wander through one of these cemeteries,' he wrote, 'and note the diversity of names recorded – names of men, of ranks, of regiments, of counties, of countries – is to read in miniature the roll call of the Empire. The first name recalls some drowsy village in Hampshire; the next a grimy industrial city of the north; the third a Highland glen; the fourth some far-distant sheep-farm in Australia or New Zealand.'[94] The pilgrims admired the cemeteries as 'things of sheer beauty', their architecture 'simple but impressive'.[95]

Among them was a 'spirited, indomitable little woman of seventy-five', who brought to the grave of her officer son a sprig of lavender from an English garden he loved; and an aged doctor and his wife from Hemel Hempstead, who had come to Lone Pine Cemetery to find their son's headstone.[96] For many, however, the long journey's end was no more than a name inscribed on a roll of honour for 5,000 of the missing – from which they might make a lead-pencil tracing on a scrap of paper to bring back to England.

On 5 September, the party put in at Kelia Bay. Sister Jessie Holmes who had, with Reverend M. Mullineux, played a leading role in organising the pilgrimage, was one of the first women to disembark, alongside a Mrs Aitken, who had lost four sons in the Great War. They then moved on to Gallipoli and Anzac Cove. On the return journey, as the ship stopped off Skyros, a memorial service was held on board for the poet Rupert Brooke.

The emotions expressed, at the end of their 5,000-mile round trip and visits to twenty-six cemeteries, had several common strands, irrespective of any particular walk of life. Consolation and relief, certainly, but, as Ian Hay observed, there was for many, for the first time, 'something akin to genuine pride in their own contribution to the common cause'; gratitude to those whose lives had been sacrificed; and also great hope and inspiration for the future, to live up to the ideals for which these men had died.[97] Ten years later, H. Harris was returning from a pilgrimage cruise to Gallipoli on board RMS *Lancastria*, along with 150 other veterans. On the way to Salonika, they crowded the ship's rails to scan the beaches where the landings had been made, their memories quickening at the sight of that familiar coastline. It was an almost mystical experience. 'We had a strange feeling,' he wrote, 'that the spirits of the thousands of magnificent men who died were parading the cliffs, silently bidding us farewell, and, as the sun set across the Aegean Sea, it was as though we saw those spirits illumined by rays of golden light … .'[98]

Whereas the first pilgrimages had generally been undertaken individually or in relatively small groups, the second half of the 1920s witnessed some mass pilgrimages, reflecting a range of motives and messages. By 1927, 7,000 mothers, fathers, sons and daughters had already been on pilgrimages organised by the St Barnabas Society to graves on the Western front. But the society believed that one further duty remained, to honour those who had no known grave, whose names were among the 55,000 'listed under the simplest and saddest of all categories – Missing' on the Menin Gate Memorial.[99] The society roused itself for a final effort, its last pilgrimage. On the evening of Saturday 23 July, 700 pilgrims, many subsidised by the society, left Victoria Station. The following day they were in Ypres, at the opening of the Menin Gate Memorial.

During the ceremony, Lord Plumer addressed the wives and mothers, clutching their wreaths of English flowers, in words that resonated, via radio, far beyond the town, touching the hearts of hundreds of thousands of grieving relatives around the world. 'Now it can be said of each one in whose honour we are assembled today: "He is not missing; he is here".' One mother was so happy to see the name of her son, killed thirteen years before in 1914, that she wanted to kiss it immediately. Many others believed that their loved ones would 'lie more peacefully' now that they had seen him. 'He knows that I have been with him to-day.'[100] The playing of the Last Post and Reveille in the closing moments of the ceremony, their mournful notes rending the evening silence, so moved the local police superintendent that the following year it was decided to sound the Last Post at the Menin Gate every evening at 8 p.m.

In September 1927 around 20,000 people went on a pilgrimage to the French battlefields arranged by the American Legion. This inspired the British Legion Pilgrimage the following year. Of the 11,000 who left England as part of the organised pilgrimage (although perhaps twice that number travelled independently), around 3,000 were women: the 'March of the Widows', as some newspaper accounts described it. Many proudly displayed rows of medals, belonging to husbands or sons, on their chests. One woman in Ypres wore four complete sets of war medals from her husband and three sons; another the ribbons of two VCs, won by her husband and son. More than half the pilgrims were ex-servicemen, converging in different parties and contingents from all over the country: the East Anglian Section, the Pilgrims of the North West, the Ulstermen in France, the Yorkshire Contingent and so on. They travelled 'not in uniform nor holiday garb, but in the mufti of their everyday life, not to raise the paean of victory, not to stage a triumph; but to show to the world that their loved ones are not forgotten, and, above all, that the purpose for which they died is still remembered'.[101]

The first in a flotilla of steamers left England on 4 August 1928 (the fourteenth anniversary of the outbreak of war). On arrival on the Continent, the pilgrims were put up, at the legion's expense, by families in France and Belgium, or billeted in army barracks. There were tours of the battlefields and cemeteries, including Beaumont-Hamel, where Major Younger of the Royal Artillery observed one 'stalwart on crutches', who wondered whether his 'blinkin' leg is still up there?' E. T. Pinnington, describing the Scottish contingent, captured the sentiments of many, as they visited Beaumont-Hamel on 6 August and Vimy Ridge the day after. Grass, splashed with poppies and patches of yellow mustard, was growing in profusion on the muddy waste of no man's land; and the buzz of grasshoppers had replaced the inferno of 10,000 guns. They closed their eyes in an endeavour to capture something of the past. 'But now it was in vain.'[102]

Around four thousand individual visits were arranged for trips by car to specific graves or battlefield sites, where many of the pilgrims experienced some happy epiphany that gave meaning to their lives. One woman found her husband's handwriting on a trench wall, alongside his name, number and regiment. 'I have had the dearest wish of my life'; 'We have had a great yearning fulfilled in having seen the last resting place of our beloved sons'; 'You enabled us to visit our son's grave and thus end our life's ambition'; these were just some of the oft-repeated phrases. Major Younger commended 'one dear little old lady in tight-fitting bodice and black bonnet from some quiet English country cottage' for her patience, as she waited for hours in the heat for a car. ' "God bless you, Sir," she said with tears in her eyes. "I came all the way from home for this; now I can die content." '[103]

Mr and Mrs Butler came from St Ives in Cornwall in search of their son, Private Butler of the 1/5th Warwicks, who had been reported missing on 18 August 1916. Just a few months before the pilgrimage, they received notice from the War Graves Commission that their son's body had been found in an old shell hole and reinterred; and so they decided to register for the pilgrimage and visit his grave. 'After all those years of uncertainty,' wrote Mrs Ralph

Blewitt, who was in charge of all special visits, 'to have been and seen that grave with its cross bearing their son's name, has filled a void in their hearts …'[104]

On 8 August all the different parties, plus those who had travelled independently, met in Ypres for a service in memory of the dead at the Menin Gate Memorial, which had been opened the previous year. The pilgrims marched through cheering crowds, past the legion's patron, the Prince of Wales, who was wearing a lounge suit, to emphasise the point that he, like his father, King George V in 1922, was 'from first to last a Pilgrim like the rest of us, an ex-Service man travelling to France and Belgium to pay homage to his comrades who slept on foreign soil'.[105] In his address, the Archbishop of York claimed that the sacrifice had been worthwhile – a message which gave meaning to, and reassured, the pilgrims.

In contrast to Britain, where it was illegal to repatriate the bodies of the dead either during or after the war, American families were given the option from 1919 of bringing the bodies of their loved ones back home for burial. Around a third of the next of kin involved, about 30,000 families, chose to leave the bodies buried overseas. One of the first couples to do so were former president Theodore Roosevelt and his wife Edith, whose pilot son Quentin had been shot down over the Marne in July 1918. The Roosevelts had lobbied for his body to remain in France even before the official policy offering this option was introduced – on the grounds that: 'We have always believed that where the tree falls, there let it lay.'[106] In February 1919, three months after the Armistice, Edith and her eldest son, Theodore Jr, visited Quentin's grave at Chamery (her husband Theodore had died the month before). The grave was to become a magnet for American pilgrims before its removal, three decades later, to the Normandy American Cemetery, so that 'Quinikins' could lie beside his brother Theodore Jr, killed during the D-Day landings.

By 1924 around a thousand relatives, like the Roosevelts or Annie Kilburn Kilmer, had made private journeys to Europe, often relying on help from the US Graves Registration Service to locate the grave. More accompanied the American Legion Pilgrimage in 1927, at their own expense or sponsored by fund-raising. In 1930, however, the US government issued invitations to mothers and wives for a four-week trip to the graves of their loved ones.

The only large-scale, state-sponsored pilgrimages to the Western front were those organised and paid for by the US government. Between May 1930 and September 1933, 6,654 women travelled from the United States to cemeteries in Europe. They were known as the Gold Star Mothers, after the gold star, the symbol of mourning for a family who had lost a loved one in war, that they sported at the centre of their red-and-white service flags and armbands. The pilgrims travelled cabin class on the Atlantic crossing, and were given first-class accommodation in Paris for a night or two, with all expenses paid, including money for laundry, and tips for bell-boys and maids. The parties were then split into groups of around thirty women each, wearing their Gold Star Mothers Pilgrimage badges at all times, and escorted by army officers to the American cemetery – one of eight in France, Belgium and England – where their sons lay.

The government also provided complimentary wreaths of flowers – roses, carnations, daisies and ferns – to lay at the headstone, a touch that one mother appreciated was 'the most beautiful and consoling feature'. Some mothers also brought a little bag of earth from home to sprinkle on the grave. Pilgrims were taken to visit the cemetery several days in a row, spending around an hour by the grave each time, kneeling or sitting on a specially provided camp chair. There were nurses in attendance, although four women – far fewer than had been feared – passed away during the trips: one woman had an apoplectic fit at her son's graveside and died a few days later. Another – Anna Platt from Florida – had a mild heart attack at the cemetery and recovered. She was for ever grateful to have gone: 'I'll never be able to make the trip again but I've seen the place where my son lies and I know he's resting. Nothing else matters.'[107]

Mrs Mann from Illinois, whose son Willard was killed on 9 August 1918, travelled in May 1930. She was struck on arrival at

the Somme American Cemetery, where Willard was buried (Row
15, Grave 4, Block D), by the gravelled driveways and the 'flowers
everywhere blooming in season, beds of pansies, forget-me-nots,
daisies and baby's breath bordered with foliage of all colors'. As she
'marched silently and reverently to the final resting place', she was
moved by the beauty of the day. Not only was it one of the most
affecting days of her life, but the pilgrimage, as she wrote at the end
of the trip, 'stands out as one of the greatest achievements of our
honored and beloved Nation'.[108] It was perhaps the most ambitious
exercise by any nation after the war to assuage private grief at public
expense.

From Canada's baptism of fire at Ypres in 1915, and Australia
and New Zealand's at Gallipoli the same year, the Dominions
had been fully committed to the First World War. Canada and
Australia lost 60,000 men each, and New Zealand 16,000. For
the bereaved from the British Dominions, travel to Europe to
visit the graves of their loved ones was prohibitively expensive;
and many of them made do with trips to local war memorials,
which became the focus for 'pilgrimages'. Nevertheless, there were
also national memorials in Europe, proudly commemorating
the heroic performance of Dominion troops at Vimy Ridge,
Villers Bretonneux and Messines, in pursuit of a universally
acknowledged 'just' cause. These memorials provided a focus for
individual grief, as well as celebrating the young nations' coming
of age. Writers, such as Australia's official war historian C. E.
W. Bean, promoted the image of a rugged, self-reliant, frontier
folk, in contrast to the supposedly decadent, class-bound leaders
of the mother country; and the monuments, too, developed the
myth of a national character to match the emerging aspirations
of a nation which, after the war, was claiming an independent
place on the world stage. There were always subtle variations in
the ways different nations emphasised individual mourning and
national identity. Australian pilgrimages, for example, tended
to be dominated by ex-servicemen, such as those who marched
every year on Anzac Day to the Shrine of Remembrance in
Melbourne, while Canadian commemorations were split, as

with the British experience, more equally between veterans and bereaved relatives.

Soon after the war, a trickle of pilgrims from the Dominions – like Henry Williamson's elderly Canadian couple – began to visit the battlefields independently. During the late 1920s, however, these pilgrimages became more organised. In 1929, around a hundred pilgrims took part in the First Australian War Graves Pilgrimage, which included a visit to the cemetery in Jerusalem; to Gallipoli, where a service was held at the memorial to the missing at Lone Pine Cemetery; and to the battlefields of France and Belgium. Between them, they brought thousands of artificial sprigs of wattle, on behalf of the bereaved back home as well as themselves, to place beside the grave or memorial. When one widow was asked why she was placing her small wattle and laurel wreath on a specific 'unknown' grave, she answered, quite simply that: 'It might be his.'[109]

In 1934 the British Empire League of South Africa organised a pilgrimage for 350 ex-servicemen and bereaved women to travel at their own expense to Europe, to lay a wreath at the Tomb of the Unknown Warrior in Westminster, and to revisit the battlefields of France and Flanders. And then, in July 1938, around 400 Australian ex-servicemen (most of whom were living in England) went on a pilgrimage to the unveiling of the Australian National Memorial at Villers-Bretonneux in France.

By far the largest pilgrimage organised by a Dominion country, however, was the Canadian pilgrimage in 1936 to the unveiling of the Vimy Memorial. The memorial, which bears the name of every Canadian soldier without a known grave who had been killed in France, commemorates the heroic capture, against all the odds, of Vimy Ridge from the Germans on Easter Monday 1917.

On 16 and 17 July 1936, five ocean-going liners left Montreal, carrying more than 6,000 pilgrims – roughly half of them veterans, wearing khaki berets, the other half bereaved women wearing floppy blue berets. 'Every foot of ground along the docks,' it was reported, 'was taken up by cheering crowds that waved Godspeed to the big steamers, and every ship in the harbour, every dredge and tug – every floating thing that boasted a whistle – joined in a blasting farewell.' It was 'the greatest send-off Montreal's water-front has ever known'.[110]

On arrival in France, smaller groups of pilgrims split off to attend ceremonies on their way to Vimy: in Arras, for example, Mons, Valenciennes. On the afternoon of 25 July, the day before the unveiling of the memorial on Vimy Ridge, a ceremony was held in Valenciennes to rename a street after the late Sergeant Hugh Cairns, VC, from North Saskatoon. Sergeant Cairns had died of wounds sustained during fierce fighting in Marly, a suburb of Valenciennes, during the liberation of the city in November 1918. The naming ceremony, at which L'Avenue de la Tourelle became L'Avenue Sergent Cairns, was carried out in the presence of Mr and Mrs George Cairns, the aged parents of the dead hero.

On 26 July, the pilgrims, who had been joined by a further 1,500 Canadians travelling directly from Britain, congregated at the memorial for the unveiling. In his address to the crowd, which had now swollen to 100,000, King Edward VIII referred to the permanent gift from the French nation of the ground on which the memorial stood. Echoing a line from Rupert Brooke's poem 'The Soldier' he described this plot of 248 acres as a corner of France that is 'forever Canada'. Back in Canada, hundreds of thousands more tuned into the radio broadcast.

After the event, many of the pilgrims travelled, via ceremonies in Ypres, to England for a few days, for a service at the Cenotaph and a garden party at Buckingham Palace. On 29 July the prime minister Stanley Baldwin, speaking to a gathering of pilgrims in Westminster Hall, recalled a visit a few years before to 'those wonderful gardens in France and Belgium where our dead lie'. In particular, he remembered walking along the Menin Road, 'on which every regiment in the British Army at one time or another marched through the Valley of the Shadow of Death'. There, he had a 'consciousness', which he had never had before or since, but which would have resonated with so many of those who went on pilgrimages: 'that the vibrant air was full of something, and the roads were full, and I seemed to be pushing my way along. I know that that feeling must have been with you at Vimy, that feeling that you were being watched by an unseen cloud of witnesses; and those witnesses are our dead, who are speaking to us to-day. Never can we feel that companionship and that communion more closely than at those solemn moments.'[III]

7

Systematic Searching

People often described the landscapes of northern France and Flanders at the end of the Great War as post-apocalyptic, like the end of the world. Even four months after the last shots had been fired, the putrid smell of rotting flesh from humans and horses hung faintly in the air. The poet John Masefield pictured the area around Serre in the Somme, where Morris Bickersteth had lost his life, as 'skinned, gouged, flayed and slaughtered, and the villages smashed to powder, so that no man could ever say there had been a village there within the memory of man'.[1]

In the countryside around Ypres, the swampy wasteland of the salient stretched flat and featureless as far as the eye could see, like a choppy sea formed by the crests and troughs of the shell holes. The city itself was a ghost town, laid waste by four years of continuous fighting, covered by a layer of dust deposited by the swirling winds. Many of its houses were now no more than empty shells, with the windows blown and doors hanging haphazardly on their hinges. Some had no facades at all, exposing – as in a doll's house from which the front has been stripped away – the gaping interiors, the sagging floors and ceilings, and revealing every now and then the pathetic echoes of a formerly peaceful life: the wedding photo of a man and woman, its glass cracked and frame splintered, tacked to a bedroom wall; an armchair with its once-crimson velvet cover now sprouting a bloom of mould; a naked cherub, its pudgy stone cheeks chipped, holding a garland of flowers, that must once have graced a fountain in the courtyard of a wealthy cloth merchant's house.

There were some signs of life, however, among the ruins. By 1919, people had started to return in dribs and drabs to their former homes and blasted fields. These were the '*sinistrés*', or disaster victims, as they were often known in French; or the '*revenants*', a word used literally to mean they were 'returning', but also figuratively to evoke the pitiful spirits of the dead come back to terrorise the living, to haunt the places where they had once lived. Some of these people took up residence beneath their former homes, leading a troglodytic existence in cellars. Others lived in prefabricated Nissen huts originally erected by the army, or in lean-tos made of wooden planks propped against ruined walls, with roofs nothing more than flimsy cardboard coated in tar.

The first visitors to the battlefields after the end of the war would come across pathetic parties of people involved in salvage work in the countryside: gangs of German prisoners of war refilling the trenches, dugouts and shell holes, and levelling the fields for cultivation; Indian soldiers and Chinese labourers clearing rubble and removing tangled thickets of rusting barbed wire, and pointing out the unexploded ordnance that still littered the battlefields and was then taken away to be detonated by explosives experts. But there was one particularly gruesome sight that struck many of these visitors: parties of men moving steadily in lines across the fields, like the figures in a police search, staking the places where human remains had been found, and then carrying out the exhumations and reburials.

'The desolation is complete,' Lady Londonderry wrote on a visit to Belgium in April 1919, 'and as far as the eye can see devastation reigns.' On the Menin Road, 'The only sign of life were salvage parties of men exhuming dead bodies, or burying them, or else digging cemeteries. Two bright splotches of colour caught the eye in the near distance. Flags! Yes. They were Union Jacks which lay over the floor of two wagons, they covered poor shapeless lumps of clay carefully placed in sacks, the remains of those who had fought their last fight on this famous field.'[2] She would have preferred it herself if the dead had been left to lie in peace where they fell, but she understood that the bodies were being brought for burial into the large cemeteries agreed with the Belgian government.

Olive Edis, Britain's first official female war photographer, described how, travelling in Flanders in 1919, she scrambled, up to her ankles in slimy yellow mud, across the cemetery at Hooge, a mass of small white crosses packed tightly together, some of them marked by a tin hat, a scrap of clothing or a pair of men's boots. Sliding about on a path of duckboards, she reached the top of the field where she was tempted to look inside a tiny hut. Here she was confronted by: 'A pile of spades – two stretchers with long suggestive forms swathed in sacking mats – a pair of boots at one end – and one realised that the salvage workers had had a "find" in some shell hole, and had brought the poor remnants of humanity here to give them burial.'[3] The body was labelled: 'Unknown British Soldier, West Yorkshire Regiment'. A couple of years later, the novelist Elinor Glyn observed a similar sight at Hooge: the body of a uniformed headless corpse folded in sacking. He was, she observed, one of many bodies brought in, with their crosses, from the surrounding battlefields. She felt that he would now not be 'so lonely as scattered there'.[4]

In 1920, the former soldier Stephen Graham made a trip to the battlefields, when, as he described in *The Challenge of the Dead*, 'they still smelt of explosion and death'. Time and again, he would meet parties of exhumers at work and engage them in conversation. It was 'ghoulish work', Graham observed, 'but they have become as matter of fact as can be'. They got by with black humour, or a terrible fatalism. 'Lying in an old trench behold a skull! It is clean and polished – a soldier's head, low and broad at the brows, high at the back ... The more you look at the skull the more angry does it seem – it has an intense internal grievance. This one does not grin, for the mouth has been destroyed. It is just blind and senseless for ever and ever.' Death and the ruins completely outweighed the living, concluded Graham. 'It would be easy to imagine someone who had no insoluble ties killing himself here, drawn by the lodestone of death. There is a pull from the other world, a drag on the heart and spirit. One is ashamed to be alive.' These were Graham's bedtime thoughts as he tried to get to sleep in a prefab hotel in Ypres, to the sounds of an amorous couple next door.[5]

The war had left a terrible gash, over 300 miles long and up to fifteen miles wide, running through northern France and Flanders; and had turned some of the finest farming land in Europe into a desert. The reconstruction of this area was to prove an enormous task. On maps of France, the scale of the devastation was indicated by zones of increasing intensity, from blue and yellow to red (the most severe, where more than 80 per cent of the land had been destroyed). By the end of 1921, three years after the Armistice, around 2.5 million hectares of land had been cleared, about 250 million square metres of barbed wire had been removed, and 21 million tonnes of unexploded munitions had been destroyed. In order to prepare the land for cultivation, the bodies needed to be moved.

When the war ended, there were more than 1,200 cemeteries of varying sizes along the Western front, as well as a 'ribbon of isolated graves', as the architect Edwin Lutyens had described it during his visit in 1917.[6] It was estimated that around 160,000 graves, especially around Ypres and the Somme, had to be relocated. Pressure to clear the battlefields came from the farmers as they reclaimed their lands for cultivation, but also on behalf of the relatives of the dead soldiers. There was an added urgency as the authorities prepared for the first waves of visitors (the first commercial tours were organised in April 1919). The bereaved were hoping to find the graves of their loved ones identifiable and well tended, and were not expecting to see desolate and makeshift cemeteries with rickety crosses or even worse, corpses left out in the open.

During the war, the sight of unburied bodies, particularly on the Somme battlefields, had been considered bad for military morale and a potential public relations disaster back home. Lieutenant Colonel Neil Fraser-Tytler, an artillery officer who saw action on the Somme between July and November 1916, had been very sorry to see the 'Body Snatcher' or 'Cold Meat Specialist', as they referred to the burial officer, leave to rejoin his battalion. 'The latter was a very cheery Irish boy,' Fraser-Tytler wrote in his diary, 'who had messed with us for ten days; we never learnt his real name, since he always answered to the above pleasant soubriquets. He was in charge of our area and was most useful in removing our pet aversions, which otherwise might have remained unburied for months.'[7] One Australian soldier with the Graves Detachment described in a letter to his mother in April 1919 how an English lady came to Villers-Bretonneux looking for her son's grave. A load of bodies had just come in, and the exhumers had not had time to bury them before they knocked off work for the day. As a result, she found the body of her son lying in a bag on the ground, and 'fainted when she saw him & is in hospital suffering from shock …'.[8]

Many men had been buried where they had fallen, their final resting places marked by makeshift crosses, singly or in clusters on the battlefield, or buried in small, provisional cemeteries just behind the front line, often near casualty clearing stations. Sometimes the bodies had simply been left in shell holes with a light covering of earth. These original cemeteries may themselves have been disturbed by the ebb and flow of the fighting, particularly after the German Offensive of 1918, when more than 50 per cent of registered British graves and cemeteries fell into enemy hands, and many graves were blasted out of existence or confused with German graves. If possible, these bodies needed to be retrieved, identified, and then reburied.

The challenge after the war was to gather together, or concentrate, these scattered graves into larger, new, permanent cemeteries. Once more, this was against a background of continuing pressure from some bereaved relatives for the bodies of their loved ones to be exhumed and repatriated, 'to bring my boy home'. The Imperial War Graves Commission (IWGC) reiterated its argument that 'to allow removal by a few individuals (of necessity only those who could afford the cost) would be contrary to the principle of equality of treatment'.[9] In any case, to empty some 400,000 identified graves would be 'a colossal work'. The commission believed that a higher ideal was enshrined in these war cemeteries in foreign lands than in private burials at home, that 'those who fought and fell together, officers and men, lie together in their last resting place, facing the line they gave their lives to maintain'. It even went so far as to express the belief that the dead themselves 'would have preferred to lie with their comrades'.[10] These British cemeteries in foreign lands would be the symbol for future generations of 'the common purpose, the common devotion, the common sacrifice of all ranks' in a united Empire that included the Dominions of Australia and Canada.

Though in the immediate post-war years, France, Belgium and the United States, like Britain, all forbade the exhumation and return home of the bodies of the dead, public opinion was turning. The exposure of a trade in clandestine, cloak-and-dagger exhumations in France and Belgium – with French newspapers exposing the illegal profits made by 'Les Marchands de la Mort' – led to demands for the law to be relaxed in order to stop this cruel trade. In the summer of 1920, the French government allowed the bodies of those who had fallen for France to be brought back, at the state's expense, from their resting places on the battlefields, and reburied in cemeteries near their homes. The first removals started in December. Although the French originally estimated that 400,000 French bodies might be moved, it became apparent that the figure would be less than that, and take up to two years to complete, with many families opting to leave their loved ones where they lay. Nevertheless, it represented a mass uprooting and moving of bodies across the country. Belgium permitted the transfer of bodies from March 1921.

The position of the United States was beginning to embarrass the British government, too. From 1919, American families were given the option of bringing the bodies of their loved ones back home for burial. Around 46,000 families took this option. At Calais docks, Stephen Graham viewed with disapproval the boxes bearing the embalmed American bodies waiting to be repatriated. He felt that the mass transference of the dead across the Atlantic was out of keeping with European sentiment, and a reflection of America's belief in the nation's moral superiority: 'To be one in death with Frenchmen, Italians, Negroes, Chinamen, Portuguese, does not suit her frame of mind.'[11]

The Directorate of Graves Registration and Enquiries (DGR&E) attempted to reassure the British public that, even if the bodies of their 'kith-and-kin' had been moved and concentrated in large, convenient cemeteries, the exhumation and reinterment would have been 'most reverently, carefully and conscientiously executed', and carried out in a very good cause. Their final resting place would be 'for ever British soil'.[12] It was essential, however, that travellers planning a tour to the battle area should first ascertain whether the particular grave they were seeking had indeed been moved to a neighbouring cemetery.

Immediately after the war, the task of clearing the battlefields, and concentrating the graves, fell at first to soldiers who had yet to be demobilised. As a report to the War Office, written in March 1919 by Major General Burnett Stuart, acknowledged: 'The work is of necessity slow; the shell craters full of water, mud and tangled belts of barbed wire render it difficult to find graves which are known to exist and the ground has to be carefully searched to discover others which have been registered.'[13] As an example, in one thousand-yard square alone, where eleven isolated graves had been reported, a careful search revealed a total of sixty-seven. It took around six men one whole day to exhume, transport and rebury a body.

The pace of work was further hampered over the winter by the hard, frosty ground and by a lack of manpower. By the spring of 1919, only 1,750 exhumations had been carried out, and it was evident that more labour was required. The possibility of using prisoners of war was discussed but rejected, in deference to the sensitivities of the bereaved families. And so it was decided to recruit around 15,000 paid volunteers, some of whom were demobbed soldiers and could therefore claim to be former comrades of the fallen, into the exhumation companies of the Labour Corps, with a bounty of 2s. 6d. a day on top of their ordinary rate.

The systematic search of the battlefields now began. Under the DGR&E, the battlefields were selected for searching on the basis of wartime burial records. The survey officer divided them into 500-yard squares, marked by flags at the corners, to define each specific area of search. The exhumation companies were split into squads of thirty-two men under the command of a lieutenant, and supplied with enough stakes to mark the position of as many bodies as would provide them with two to three days' work. Guidance issued to the exhumers noted that experience was the most useful factor in determining where bodies were most likely to be found. Characteristic signs included: rifles or posts, toting helmets or equipment, to mark the location of an existing grave; stakes marked with an 'E' [for *Englisch*] burnt into the wood, showing spots where British soldiers had been buried by the Germans; rat holes revealing small bones or pieces of equipment brought to the surface by rodents; and discolouration of the grass, earth or water – grass was often a vivid bluish-green with broader blades where bodies were buried, while earth and water turned a greenish black or grey.[14] Some of the exhumers carried hollow sticks, one end of which they would sink into the ground, while sniffing at the other end for any whiff of human decomposition that might alert them to a body below.

Post-war conditions were not conducive to rapid work, as the guidance notes concluded: the battlefields were covered with rank grass and nettles, in places almost waist high, which often concealed the more obscure traces by which bodies, and even crosses, could be discovered. 'In consequence an area must be swept and re-swept before it is definitely decided that no graves have been overlooked.'[15]

Once the area had been thoroughly searched and staked out, the actual exhumations began. The squads of thirty-two men were further divided into parties of four under a NCO, and supplied with shovels, rubber gloves, canvas and rope with which to wrap and tie up the bodies, stretchers, cresol as a disinfectant, and wire cutters and shears. Each party started digging around the spots that had been staked out – taking care not to disturb the body or to miss any other bodies buried at the same spot. Once the bodies had been exhumed, a careful search was made for any effects that might lead to their identification. Pockets were searched, and a close examination made of the neck, wrists, and braces, where identity discs were most usually tied.

The human remains themselves were then placed on the canvas, which had been soaked in cresol, and wrapped. The body was labelled, with the following particulars, if its identity had been established: the map reference where the body had been found; whether an existing cross had been found, marking the grave; the name, number, rank and unit of the deceased; the list of personal effects found, and sent on in a ration bag attached to the body, particularly where a paybook or a will was found.[16] The same particulars, as written on the labels, were entered in a notebook kept by the officer in charge. The body was then sent by field ambulance or lorry, on to the cemetery for reburial and registration by the Graves Registration Unit; and any kit or equipment considered superfluous for the purpose of identification was chucked back into the grave, doused in cresol, and the grave filled in.

'The keynote of the whole work,' the guidance note concluded, 'is of course identification, and it is essential that the searching should be carefully and systematically done. It has been found advisable to impress upon reinforcements that their extra pay is not given them because the work is dangerous, but because it is of vital importance, having regard to the number of men still missing, many of whom can be found and identified if the work is carefully done. Furthermore, it is found that the greater the stress laid upon the need for identification, the greater the interest the men take in their work.'[17]

Identification was the overriding concern of the bereaved; and the quest for certainty – for a grave, for a place to grieve – is what continued to obsess the families of the fallen. The most important tool in this quest was the identity disc, though other personal effects, such as pay books, visiting cards, letters, boots, cigarette cases, spoons, watches, prayer-books, tattoos and markings on handkerchiefs also proved valuable aids to identity.

*

It had been the need for identification that had driven the very first searchers of the British Red Cross's Wounded and Missing Enquiry Department. In October 1916, for instance, Second Lieutenant

Farquharson of the Royal Fusiliers had been reported missing.
The news was followed by a series of letters from the W&MED,
with inconclusive and contradictory evidence about the nature
and location of his death, which only gave the family continued
grounds for hope. In December 1917, they heard from the DGR&E
that he had been buried near Bapaume, and his grave marked by a
durable wooden cross. It was not until more than two years later,
in March 1920, that the family received another letter from the
DGR&E, informing them that his body has been removed and
reburied in Grass Lane AIF (Australian Imperial Force) Burial
Ground, at Gueudecourt, south of Bapaume – in accordance with
the policy to concentrate all scattered graves and small cemeteries
containing less than forty graves. 'You may rest assured that the
work of re-burial has been carried out carefully and reverently,' the
letter concluded.[18]

The experience of the Briggs family, too, is typical of tens of
thousands of grieving families during and after the war. In October
1917, they received notification from the War Office that their only
beloved son, Private Claude Briggs, had been killed in action near
Ypres, between 20 and 28 September. This news was followed a few
days later by an egregiously uplifting letter from the army chaplain,
regretting the loss of their son: 'It was a terrible battle but a glorious
victory on Sept. 20th & those who laid down their lives on that
day have done so for the good of their comrades & the benefit of
the world. Nevertheless their loss is bound to be very deeply felt by
their dear ones at home. By their noble & brave acts the fallen have
earned a martyr's crown which now they wear in the safe-keeping
of their Saviour whom they have imitated.'[19] The chaplain went on
to explain that, from the enquiries he had made, it appeared likely
that Private Briggs had been buried on the battlefield with many
of his comrades, although, as in so many cases, there was no record
of his grave. Enquiries continued, and in February 1918, the family
received a letter from the W&MED suggesting the whereabouts
of Briggs's death, near Shrewsbury Forest. The family took some
comfort from this advice, and stuck a pressed flower picked from
Shrewsbury Forest in their photograph album. In June 1921 they

received a letter from a Sergeant Major Roberts of 68th Labour Company, confirming that the remains of a body had been found by a pillbox on the edge of Shrewsbury Forest, and identified as belonging to Private Briggs by a piece of his named groundsheet and the buttons of his tunic. Four months later, the IWGC wrote officially to confirm that, in line with the policy of concentration, it had been found necessary to exhume bodies buried in certain areas, and that during the course of this work, Private Briggs's remains had been retrieved and reinterred in Bedford House Cemetery 'carefully and reverently' (Cemetery No. 4, Plot 7, Row A, Grave 24).[20] His grave was renumbered – to Grave 32 – in 1923. The Briggs' photographs of what became an annual pilgrimage charted both the resolution of their own grief, and changes in the landscape of the battlefields: from scenes of total devastation to the rebuilding of Ypres, and from the first cemeteries to neatly ordered gardens of remembrance. The photograph of Claude's grave with its wooden cross, taken on Armistice Day 1924, contrasts with the one taken on Christmas Day 1926 of his shining new headstone with its crisp lettering.

The task of retrieving and identifying bodies may have evolved since the hasty wartime burials, but the experience of rummaging around a muddy, mangled corpse in search of an identity disc was as horrible as it ever had been. Second Lieutenant W. N. Collins, a burial officer, had described in November 1916 the clearing of Beaumont-Hamel of soldiers killed on the first day of the Somme, four months before: 'The flesh had gone mainly from the face but the hair had still grown, the beard to some extent. They looked very ragged … and the rats were running out of their chests. The rats were getting out of the rain, of course, because the cloth over the rib cage made quite a nice nest and when you touched a body the rats just poured out of the front … [to] think that a human being provided a nest for a rat was a pretty dreadful thing.'[21] Army chaplains were particularly exposed to such horrors. David Railton, the young padre whose idea for the Tomb of the Unknown Warrior was to transform the way the British remembered their dead, described in September 1916 how many men who had 'stood it all, cannot stand this clearing of the battlefield ... This Battalion was left to do that, and several men went off with shell-shock ... caused not just by the explosion of a shell nearby, but by the sights and smell and horror of the battlefield in general. I felt dreadful, and had to do my best to keep the men up to the task.'[22]

The task of retrieving bodies inevitably took a psychological toll on those who carried it out, although it is hard to determine how long-lasting this would be. Post-traumatic stress disorder (PTSD) was first identified only in 1980, and later used to define symptoms experienced by military personnel during and after the Gulf War, including those involved in mortuary work. It is likely, if anachronistic, that the 'cold meat specialists' would have suffered from something similar. For better or worse, they would have resorted to the coping strategies and mechanisms of the times – silence and the 'stiff upper lip', rather than the verbalisation and outpouring of emotions that would be considered more helpful today. Others would have distanced and distracted themselves from the horror with black humour or drink, or taken comfort in ritual and religion.

Julian Bickersteth, who lost a brother, Morris, on the first day of the Somme, wrote to his eldest brother, Monier, the same month, describing the sights and sounds of 'the last few days which will live with me to my dying day, and filled me with an agony of sympathy for those suffering indescribable things'.[23] In his diary, he referred to the 'piteous work' of collecting the dead, and how it tested people's nerves and caused 'a curious kind of irritability which was quite infectious – all the party being cross and out of temper, and it was quite easy to find oneself heatedly arguing some trivial point for no apparent reason'.[24]

It was the smell which lingered in his nostrils for months after he had been demobilised, tainting the taste of food, that Private John McCauley recalled. A soldier from the Isle of Man, McCauley had been attached, towards the end of the war, to a company of about 150 men, whose task was to search for dead bodies and bury them. Two issues of neat rum were served daily, 'to kill the dangerous germs which we might inhale' – and also, presumably, to numb the horror. 'It was a ghastly job,' he wrote in his diary, 'and more than ever I learned what war meant.' They would start their 'grim work' early in the morning, setting out in skirmishing order to search the ground for identity discs. 'Often have I picked up the remains of a fine, brave man on a shovel. Just a little heap of bones and maggots to be carried to the common burial place. Numerous bodies were found lying submerged in the water in shell holes and mine-craters; bodies that seemed quite whole, but which became like huge masses of white, slimy chalk when we handled them. The job had to be done; the identity disc had to be found. I shuddered as my hands, covered in soft flesh and slime, moved about in search of the disc, and I have had to pull bodies to pieces in order that they should not be buried unknown … .' By the end of the morning, rifles and barbed wire stakes would mark the places where they had buried their 'gruesome discoveries' – accompanied, on occasion above the grave, by small epitaphs crafted in stones and pebbles that he and his chum had collected, 'as a last worldly tribute to men who would probably be living to-day if the world had really striven for peace in the opening years of this century'.[25]

For the first couple of weeks, McCauley 'could scarcely endure the experiences' he encountered, but he gradually became hardened to the task, as many did, and carried on in the job for another three months. Before receiving his demobilisation papers after the end of the war, he was asked by the colonel of his battalion if he would stay on in the army for another year, at a higher rate of pay, as men with his experience of collecting dead bodies and burying them were desperately needed. McCauley 'gently but firmly declined', and returned to the Isle of Man to work in a foundry.[26]

The months before demobilisation were times of great demoralisation for the troops. In his diary, Captain J. C. Dunn, a medical officer with the Royal Welch Fusiliers mentioned by both Robert Graves and Siegfried Sassoon, described the reluctant resumption of daily routine duties and drills after the end of the war, and a 'vegetative existence' that was only partially relieved by organised games and recreation. The area around Villers-Bretonneux had gone 'completely Aussie', as large numbers of troops were engaged in burying or reburying their numerous dead, left where they had fallen the previous year. Much of the work was done by troops freshly drafted from England – men who had not previously been in France. Their battle-hardened NCOs and the veteran rankers called them Rainbows, as 'they had come out after the storm'. On his return to England at the end of May 1919, Dunn was surprised to discover in the hold of the transport ship a large gang of Australian military prisoners under armed guard, convicted of acts of indiscipline ranging from disorderly conduct and assault to desertion. 'Such tough-looking desperadoes I've never seen,' he observed, 'they looked capable of any crime.'[27]

Private William McBeath might have qualified as one of these 'Rainbows'. He had enlisted in June 1918, aged nineteen, 'to serve his country and expand his horizons'. After a few months in England, he arrived in France with the Australian Imperial Force, a couple of months after the war had ended. Years later, his daughter Norma compiled a record of his experience as a Graves Detachment Digger from his diary, letters and memorabilia, as 'not many have heard of the young men who had the task ... of digging up the bodies from the temporary graves of the battlefields and laying them to rest in the War Cemeteries'. Her father was certainly not one of the 'desperadoes' Dunn had spotted. A God-fearing young man, he soon fell in with 'some steady cobbers', none of whom had ever 'touched drink'. In April 1919, he wrote to tell his mother that he had 'started work last Monday & I can not say I am exactly in love with the job'. He preferred digging graves in the cemetery, which although very demanding as the ground was so hard, was at least a cleaner job than digging up the bodies. In May, he was working at the Chalk Pits Cemetery, near where John Kipling lost his life, and telling his mother about the hundreds of bodies they were moving: 'You would hardly think there were so many graves in the fields, still there are hundreds to come in yet.'[28]

Although McBeath did not dwell on the dark side of his experiences, showing a greater enthusiasm for the wonderful European buildings he visited when on leave, and for playing cricket and swimming in the canals of the Somme, he did describe some of his comrades, the Australian exhumers, as 'the roughest mob I have ever seen, they would just as soon down tools as not'.[29] Within a couple of weeks of starting work in April, they had already had two strikes, refusing to work any more until they had better tools for handling the bodies, better food and had stopped ceremonial parades.

In the first months after the Armistice, as soldiers waited impatiently for demobilisation, there was inevitably some indiscipline – and this was compounded by the nature of the work. But there was also trouble among those who had actually volunteered for the Labour Corps. Papers in the Imperial War Museum relating to 83rd Labour Company reveal how, during the summer of 1919, two privates were sentenced to two years' hard labour in a military prison. In September, the commanding officer, Captain Southgate, was having problems with a Second Lieutenant Elwood in his company, who had claimed that when he came to pay his men, the wind had simply blown the notes away, and he was now 200 francs out of pocket. When Southgate refused to reimburse Elwood for this loss, Elwood lost his temper. The following month, Southgate had another run-in, this time with a Lieutenant Dickinson, who had asked for a transfer as he was uneasy with Southgate's leadership – in particular, with Southgate's insistence that the Standing Orders for Officers be posted in the sergeants' mess (where they had no business): orders, for example, that gambling was forbidden in the officers' mess, and that officers and other ranks contracting venereal disease would 'ipso facto' be placed at the bottom of the leave roster. Captain Southgate also complained that a lack of resources, which he had repeatedly requested – especially canvas, picks and shovels, and access to a motor ambulance – had meant that his company had not met its targets, and was therefore being unfairly criticised for poor performance. His men were, as a result, underemployed and demoralised.[30]

The failings of the exhumation companies were highlighted – perhaps unfairly – by a number of enquiries. In March 1920 a series of complaints about the behaviour of soldiers in the Australian

Graves Services (AGS), which worked alongside the DGR&E and the British exhumation companies in France and Flanders, with specific responsibility for the collection and reinterment of the Australian dead, led to an inspection by a Major Phillips. This revealed that two members of staff in the Amiens office were running bars in the city, one of which was a brothel. Major Phillips was generally very dissatisfied with the way things were being managed, and told Lieutenant Lee, the inspector in charge of the Amiens office, that his services were no longer required. There were also complaints that Captain Kingston, who ran the AGS in Villers-Bretonneux, was a drunk, and that his staff used official cars for their own use, ferrying them to houses of ill-repute, and that they sold off supplies and spare parts for personal gain. One allegation described how, when a fire broke out in the Australian camp, some ten young local women, who had been living in the soldiers' huts, ran outside in a state of undress – some 'nearly quite naked'. On another occasion, drunken members of the AIF had returned to camp late at night, 'wantonly discharging many shots from a revolver to the imminent danger of others'.[31]

In April, a court of inquiry in London confirmed Major Phillips's findings, deciding that Captain Kingston was 'wholly unqualified and unfit' for the command of the unit at Villers-Bretonneux, and that he should be relieved of his duties and returned to Australia. Lieutenant Lee, too, had 'behaved himself in a scandalous manner, was guilty of conduct unbecoming the character of an officer and gentleman, was unfit for the post at Amiens and should be returned to Australia'. In conclusion, the court found that: 'The appalling condition apparent in March 1920, must come as a warning for the future guidance of those in charge, that unless immediate and drastic action is taken for proper control, this effort to honour the dead shall only be the means of bringing shame and disgrace upon the good name, fame, and reputation of Australia.'[32]

The Australian Graves Services was, as a result, completely reorganised, and the 'disreputable' elements weeded out. Major Phillips, a former governor of Lewes Detention Barracks, and a noted disciplinarian, was put in charge. Many of the Diggers (as

Australian soldiers were often known in celebration of their mining heritage) feared that Phillips would pack the AGS with military policemen, and that representatives of this hated corps of the AIF would now be caring for the graves of their fallen comrades. Discipline was eventually re-established, and new officers, all of whom had seen active service, were appointed.

The disgraced Lieutenant Lee, however, protested against his dismissal, and pressed for another court of inquiry, arguing that the first one, in London in April, had been rigged. He also claimed that some of the exhumations, under Major Phillips and Major Alfred Allen, who was in charge of the AGS around Poperinghe, and whose work was considered exemplary by his superiors, had been 'hoaxed' or falsely recorded. Lee also alleged that Major Phillips had committed a 'diabolical action' earlier in the year, when he was said to have passed around a photograph of the skull of a deceased Australian Digger, wearing an AIF hat, with a cigarette inserted between his jaws.[33] This second court of inquiry, which opened in London in January 1921 before being adjourned to Australia, found no evidence of any conspiracy by Majors Phillips and Allen to prejudice the first court of inquiry against Lee. It also decided that the exhumation at the heart of the 'hoaxing' allegation had been carried out properly.

In many ways, the care taken in conducting these inquiries, and into making sure that things were done properly and reverently, was a tribute to the way in which the nations honoured their dead. It was not long before Major Allen was involved in yet another inquiry. In October 1920 it had been discovered that crosses bearing the name of a 'Private Williams' had been erected both in Underhill Farm Cemetery, Ploegsteert and in Hooge Crater Cemetery. In order to clear up this duplication, Major Allen was given permission to have the grave in Hooge Crater Cemetery opened, which duly revealed the body of a Private Hamilton. Major Allen was worried by this result, and had the grave beside it opened, too. Although the cross marking the grave bore the inscription 'Unknown Australian', the body within bore an identity disc with a regimental number that could not have been that of an Australian soldier.[34]

When Brigadier General Wyatt, who was in command of British troops in France and Flanders, heard of these mistaken identities, he gave permission for the further exhumation of Australian graves at Hooge, with a view to confirming or amending existing identifications. It is something of an irony that the following month, from his headquarters at St-Pol-sur-Ternoise, Wyatt was to order the exhumation of four bodies in such a way as to guarantee that they were unidentifiable. Anonymity was paramount in the final selection of the body which was to become that of the Unknown Warrior.

Towards the end of October, Captain Coghlan and members of 126th Labour Company carried out further test exhumations on 135 graves at Hooge, of which eighty had previously been recorded as unknown and fifty-five as having a definite identity. This was, in effect, an inspection of the work of 68th Labour Company, who had been responsible for clearing the battlefields in the area soon after the war. Major Allen reported the findings revealed by 126th Labour Company to Australia House. The identity of three of the eighty unknowns was established for the first time, and five of the fifty-five so-called identifications were disproved. Some of the graves were found to be empty or to contain sandbags filled with earth; there was one example of a German soldier buried as a British soldier; and another of an identifiable Australian soldier being buried as an unknown British soldier; and so on.

In its defence, 68th Labour Company was one of the pioneering companies. When it had started work in January 1919, speed was more important – not least for sanitary reasons – than minute accuracy in establishing the identity of the bodies found. On the other hand, by the time 126th Labour Company conducted the exhumations at Hooge in October 1920, the company was highly proficient at identification, and may have displayed a not unnatural eagerness to find fault as it reviewed the work of another company, the 68th. The procedures it followed were those that had been developed by 68th Labour Company in the six months between January and July 1919, and later adopted by the DGR&E. In a sense, the performance of the 68th was being judged against precisely the protocols it had helped to adapt. It is also possible, after a lapse of twenty months from the time 68th Labour Company started digging up the bodies, and very nearly two years from the day the last shot was fired, that the task of identification had become easier. The extra months of decomposition may have made a more careful examination of the remains less disagreeable, and also have revealed clues to identity that had previously been invisible. It was not uncommon for a soldier's identity disc to be driven into his flesh, and buried, by the force of the projectile, only to be exposed later with the passage of time and decomposition.

A committee of enquiry, including Major Phillips amongst its members, assembled at St-Pol in January 1921. Its brief was to report on the recent exhumations at Hooge Crater Cemetery, and to advise on how any mistakes might be rectified, and avoided in future.[35] The public needed to be reassured that there were not tens of thousands of graves that had been wrongly attributed, and that grieving relatives would not, in fact, be mourning at the gravesides of strangers or, even worse, Germans.

The Army Council decided that the margin of errors (well under 10 per cent) did not justify further, wholesale exhumations in the cemetery. There were any number of stages at which errors could have been introduced. Some discrepancies might have been due not to 68th Labour Company, but to the unit which had erected the wooden crosses to mark battlefield graves during the war. As the area had come under very heavy shellfire, these crosses may have been blown from their places many times over, and replaced each time over spots that were further and further away from the original graves; or labels might have been eroded by the weather. It was concluded that the 'heavy crop of errors' had not always been preventable. 'War will not wait for the correct burial of the dead, and a battle has no respect whatever for a grave.'[36] The findings did not endorse the assertion made by one Australian officer at the inquiry that British soldiers had resorted to chopping bodies in half in order to double their body returns. Just as the British often disparaged the Australians, so the Australians tended to point to the carelessness of British work, bringing the spice of national rivalry to the politics of bereavement. The truth of the matter, probably, was that both the Australians and the British were doing very satisfactory work, but as Colonel Percy Buckley, the military adviser at Australia House had observed in 1921, the work was so 'disagreeable in all its aspects' that it was not easy to 'keep the men satisfied and contented' and to stop them going off the rails.[37]

*

Underlying these investigations and inquiries was the deep psychological need to recover, identify and bury the dead that characterised Britain's commemorative effort. It was the 'sentimental value' of the task that guided developments into the 1920s.[38] Just as, during the war, it had been important for soldiers to see that their comrades had been buried properly, so after the war the bereaved demanded that the bodies of their loved ones were handled with reverence, and preferably by soldiers who could have been their comrades, and not by German prisoners of war or by Chinese labourers. Ideally, around Courcelette and Vimy Ridge, the Canadians would bury their own dead, with the Australian Graves Service operating around Villers-Bretonneux and Pozières.

It had been the intention, since it was founded in 1917, that the Imperial War Graves Commission (IWGC) would eventually assume sole responsibility for war graves, assuming the duties of the DGR&E. The process began in 1919, as the IWGC took over the enquiries work, answering letters from the public about the location of graves. For this, the IWGC was dependent on records compiled by the DGR&E, and the work was necessarily interlinked, with the two organisations sharing a building. Gradually, during the course of 1921, the IWGC took on more responsibilities, including registration, with the task of exhumation left till last.

As preparation for the handover, it was necessary to establish how much work had been done, what areas required further work, and how this might be accomplished. By the summer of 1921, it looked as if much of France might be considered 'closed', the task completed. 'From lonely graves, and from shell craters and broken trenches all over the vast battlefield of France and Flanders,' the

Evening News reported in August, 'the bodies of the great company of British dead are being borne to the new cemeteries, to lie together in soil that our Allies have given to us for ever. The work of gathering in the dead is now well in hand.'[39]

A report the same month by Colonel J. K. Dick-Cunyngham claimed that, during the past three years, the whole of the battlefield areas in France and in Flanders had been thoroughly searched and re-searched for isolated graves and bodies.[40] The search had been carried out systematically, map square by map square, and in those areas where a lot of bodies had been found, some squares had been re-searched on two or three occasions (or as many as twenty, according to the secretary of state for war). Dick-Cunyngham acknowledged that further isolated graves and bodies would be found for years to come, as farmers worked their land, or gangs of civilians levelled the devastated areas, cutting drains, roads, or filling in craters – work that sometimes entailed digging to a depth of up to six metres. He also warned that, as several hundred bodies were still surfacing every week, the IWGC would need to be prepared for this.

New arrangements had to be made for the retrieval of bodies by the IWGC. First, though, Rudyard Kipling, one of the IWGC commissioners, believed it should be made clear to the public that it was the War Office, rather than the IWGC, who had stopped the systematic searching of the battlefields. The IWGC argued that its success in clearing the battlefields of isolated graves after the handover depended 'entirely on the technical experience of the men employed to undertake the work, and the knowledge of the local conditions for Exhumation': ideally, the organisation would employ British personnel with at least six months' previous experience of searching for bodies (or 'spotting') and looking for identifications.[41] It was decided, however, that the IWGC could not justify retaining the exhumation companies. Instead, the work should be carried out, at IWGC expense and under the supervision of British officers, by contractors, employing gangs of local, Polish, or even British, labour, who were also working for the French or Belgian governments. As it took on its new responsibilities, the

IWGC stressed that its registration officers had been carefully selected for their knowledge and experience, and were fully 'qualified to deal with the abstruse problems which meet them at every turn'.[42] There had been an idea that the IWGC gardeners might do the work, but Sir Fabian Ware did not want commission staff involved in the actual exhumation work.

On 9 September 1921, shortly before the official handover, Colonel Dick-Cunyngham signed a certificate on behalf of the DGR&E to the IWGC: 'I certify that the whole of the battlefield areas in France and Belgium have been cleared of such isolated British and German graves … as were marked in any way above ground which was accessible; or could have been found by reasonably careful search. Graves so found have been concentrated, and all available particulars of identity and full information of the places of original burial and re-burial have been furnished to the Imperial War Graves Commission.'[43] By October 1921, the DGR&E had exhumed and reburied more than 200,000 bodies, which left around 300,000 people unaccounted for – either missing or buried as an unknown soldier.

There were several circumstances under which the IWGC would need to retrieve bodies after the handover in September. There were, for example, specific areas around Ypres and in the Somme that required further work. Sometimes the French authorities would request the removal of British bodies from predominantly French or German battlefield cemeteries. This might be for reasons of public health or reconstruction, or because the presence of German cemeteries on French soil was 'obnoxious' to the French population – a form of 'occupation', it was argued, of French territory under a different name.[44] It might be precipitated by the rearrangement of French cemeteries, as the bodies of French soldiers were exhumed and transported back to their home towns or, if buried in Belgium, taken back to France. Or it might be to establish the identity of an 'Unknown' soldier, buried in an isolated grave or in a cemetery, in the case of a request by relatives: there had to be a good prima facie case for such a search – for example when a soldier appeared to have two graves registered in his name.

It was crucial to reassure the bereaved that their loved ones would not be forgotten when the DGR&E was disbanded, as Sir Laming Worthington-Evans, the secretary of state for war, observed: 'If this were done the public would not be left under the impression that no steps were being taken to fill the gap caused by the abolition of the exhumation companies.'[45] If the relatives could make a good case for an exhumation – and an official form, known as a WGR1 had been completed, along with an assessment of costs and risks – the IWGC might authorise an exhumation. But, as the following cases illustrate, it could be a long haul.

*

On 15 May 1918, twenty-two-year-old Captain Francis Mond was on a bombing raid with the recently formed Royal Air Force, 'laying eggs' as he described it, when he was shot down in a dogfight over northern France. There was little doubt about his death. His parents received an eyewitness account of his crash landing and an account of how his body and that of his observer, Lieutenant Edgar Martyn, had been retrieved from no man's land by an Australian officer, Lieutenant Hill, and identified. His body was then sent by boat down the Somme, away from the front line, to a village called Vaire-sous-Corbie. Traces of Francis then petered out, propelling his mother, Angela, on a five-year quest for her son's grave: a quest which the historian Richard van Emden describes in his book, *Missing*.

Enquiries through official channels yielded little. The DGR&E could find no records of his burial, and hopes that he might have been buried in the cemetery at Corbie were dashed when it was established that the only RAF grave was that of another man. The Monds were wealthy – Francis's father, Emile, was a director of a chemical engineering company that in the 1920s merged into ICI – and after the war Angela made several trips to France, tramping the cemeteries in search of the stencilled label on a temporary wooden cross that might bear her son's name. She placed notices appealing for information in *The Times*, and wrote to all the officers in her son's squadron. But, by 1921, more than two years after the end of the war, all lines of enquiry had reached a dead end.

It was not until 1922 that questions were raised about the deaths of another two airmen on 15 May: Captain John Aspinall and Lieutenant Paul Dornonville de la Cour. The records showed that the bodies of Aspinall and de la Cour had, like Mond and Martyn, been retrieved and brought to Corbie, but that they had then been taken away for burial at the Doullens Communal Cemetery. German accounts, however, including the combat report of the officer who had brought them down, established that Aspinall's Bristol Fighter had been shot down in flames behind German lines (whereas Mond's De Havilland 4 had crashed in no man's land near Bouzencourt, where its wreckage still lay in a field). Could Mond and Martyn have been mistaken for Aspinall and de la Cour, as it would seem more likely that their bodies would have been retrieved from no man's land than from enemy-held territory?

Angela Mond continued to press the IWGC for answers, requesting that the graves at Doullens be opened, and the bodies exhumed and identified. Eventually, it was established that a prima facie case had been made for exhumation, a WGR1 was submitted and an 'Authority for Exhumation' granted. On 20 March 1923, Angela watched with Captain Aspinall's father Herbert, as the first of the graves – registered as that of de la Cour – was opened. The body showed no signs of charring, however, as it would have done had his plane gone down in flames. The second grave revealed a body which Herbert Aspinall immediately stated was *not* that of his son. Although there was no identification disc or personal effects, an examination of the jaw matched the dental records of Francis Mond; and Angela identified the body as that of her son. Angela visited the cemetery again that autumn, once new headstones had been erected to commemorate Francis and his flying companion, and the names of Aspinall and Dornonville de la Cour were removed to the Arras Flying Services Memorial for the missing. Angela and her husband went on an annual pilgrimage to visit their son's grave until the outbreak of the Second World War.[46]

An even more extraordinary tale of parental grief and determination concerns Second Lieutenant Eric Hayter. An Australian by birth, Eric was serving with the Royal Field Artillery (RFA) during the German Spring Offensive in March 1918, when he was shot through the head with a rifle bullet, and killed. His father, Colonel Frederick Hayter, enquired about the location of his son's grave, only to be informed by the DGR&E that it might well be found during 'the final clearing up of the battlefields', among the many graves that had so far not been reported and registered. The following year, the Hayter family received, unsolicited, a package from a German soldier containing Eric's paybook and a tracing of a map. This showed where his body had been found, with those of two other English soldiers, and buried by the Germans, on a sunken road between Lagnicourt and Morchies, very close to the forward position of Eric's battery, the 87th.[47]

Colonel Hayter was a man of means, and embarked, like Angela Mond, on a personal search. He trawled the battlefields for the grave of his only son, sometimes in the company of former German soldiers who had fought against Eric. He also continued to ask the DGR&E for information, sending them the particulars of his son: twenty-five years of age, just over six feet tall, dark brown hair and, of 'special notice', the fact that several of his molars were crowned with gold. In April 1920 the colonel received a letter from the DGR&E expressing the hope that the grave of an 'Unknown British Officer' at Queant Road Cemetery might prove to be that of his son: 'It appears to be extremely likely that this is the grave of your late son and I therefore write to ask if you would like to have this grave marked with a Cross bearing his name.'[48] Colonel Hayter was dubious, because the original location of this body, before it had been brought into the cemetery, was some way from where he knew his son to have fallen.

Towards the end of the month, the body was exhumed and Colonel Hayter's doubts were confirmed: there were no marks on the skull to indicate a rifle bullet, and there were no gold crowns on the teeth. This was the first of many exhumations authorised in the search to identify Eric: in particular, the opening on 6 August 1921 of twelve graves marked as 'German' in the Lagnicourt Hedge Cemetery, which the colonel believed to contain British soldiers, including his son, buried by the Germans after the battle. In fact, the exhumations revealed twenty bodies, of which five were British but not one of these was Eric's.

Throughout 1922 and 1923, Colonel Hayter continued to visit France, and to supervise digging on land owned by a local farmer. He was beginning to give up hope and, in June 1923, proposed to erect a memorial to Eric on the spot where he thought his son had fallen, although this was not necessarily where his body lay. Over the following months, negotiations for the plot of land, five metres square, broke down over the price demanded by the landowner; and Colonel Hayter decided to buy a plot, just a few metres away on the other side of the sunken road, for a nominal sum from a sympathetic French countess.

In September 1924, six and a half years after Eric's death, as the contractor started digging for the foundation of the stone memorial, he came – amazingly – across a body three feet beneath the surface, probably buried in a hurry when the Germans overran Eric's battery. The RFA regimental buttons and badges of rank and the five gold crowns established the identity of Second Lieutenant Eric Hayter; his father was present to confirm the identification. Colonel Hayter decided that the body should not be moved and had a concrete coffin placed around the body with the memorial stone on top. Sir Fabian Ware, on being informed by his friend Colonel Hayter of the discovery, replied that his letter was 'one of the most remarkable that I have read in connection with our work', and agreed in an easing of the commission's policies, that the IWGC would maintain the privately commissioned grave and memorial at Colonel Hayter's expense until his death. An article in the *Dundee Advertiser* described the serendipitous discovery: 'The story of a father's undying faith, of a strange battlefield meeting, and of a coincidence so miraculous that I should hesitate to write of it were not the facts fully substantiated, has caused an almost superstitious wonder among the inhabitants of this part of France.'[49] In March 1970, long after his parents' deaths and in the absence of any living relatives, Eric's body was exhumed and transferred to Lagnicourt Hedge Cemetery.

*

As the DGR&E was disbanded, people began to worry about what would happen when military staff were sent home. Would their sacred duty to their fallen comrades be discontinued, and the link between home and away, between the living and the dead, be severed? An Australian businessman, Edward Hempenstall, cabled his concerns in a letter to the *Daily Mail*. He claimed that in the summer of 1921, bodies were still being recovered at the rate of several hundred a week. In future, would they simply be ploughed into the earth by farmers or covered over by builders? Of particular concern was the fact that 'twenty-five per cent of the recoveries are Australians'. Hempenstall argued that this was a job for the military and not the IWGC, and feared that hundreds, perhaps thousands, of bodies would be lost, left unidentified on the battlefields, when the exhumation companies were withdrawn. 'I consider the London handling of this national matter an utter disgrace,' he concluded.[50]

What would happen if work on the recovery and reburial of the fallen came to an end? Newspaper reports had long encouraged people to believe that missing bodies might be found. In an article in the *Daily Mail*, titled 'The Grave Finder', the writer John Oxenham cited the work of Major Allen, the same officer who had been accused of hoaxing in the court of inquiry earlier in the year. Allen, an architect by profession, who had been engaged to oversee the construction of cemeteries and memorials, had turned out to be 'a discoverer of missing men', who eight times out of ten 'solves the mystery and sets the seal of certainty on lingering hopes and doubts at home. For lack of knowledge is more agonising than assurances of death.' Oxenham claimed that ceasing recovery work would, at the least, create a very bad impression. 'If the work stops,' he wrote, 'it will mean the withdrawal of Major Allen of the Australian War Graves Service – one of the finest characters produced by the war. It is a maxim in Northern France and Belgium that if a missing Australian cannot be found by Major Allen he cannot be found by anyone. With the slightest of clues he has set the seal on lingering hopes and has supplied knowledge the lack of which was more agonising than death.'[51]

The Australian people were especially concerned by the prospect of the Australian Graves Service being disbanded. Around 46,000 Australians had been killed on the Western front, of whom almost 20,000 had remained unaccounted for at the time of the Armistice. Unlike the Americans, the Australians tended to accept IWGC policy that they should remain where they had fallen, thousands of miles on the other side of the world. But they did expect them to be tended and cared for by their former comrades – and had entrusted the locating and reburying of Australian soldiers to the Australian Graves Detachment and its successor organisation, the Australian Graves Service, which worked alongside the DGR&E. Relatives back home received photographs of the graves of their loved ones, which reassured them they were being well maintained. Much was made, in the domestic press, of the devotion and spirit of the Diggers, who had, the *Herald* claimed, stayed on in France and Belgium after the war to 'perform a labour of love for their dead comrades'.[52]

In December 1921, Lieutenant Colonel E. A. S. Gell, the assistant director of records at the IWGC, went on a tour of the battlefields in Belgium and France to report on progress. Gell had been at St-Pol with Brigadier General Wyatt just over a year before for the selection of the Unknown Warrior; only a few months ago, he had been sent away on a couple of weeks' leave as, according to his superiors, he had been showing signs of a breakdown under the stress. Gell's report painted a vivid picture of conditions on the battlefields three years after the end of the war.

It was growing dark when the colonel arrived at the cemetery at Villers-Faucon to find three British labourers burying seven bodies that had just been brought in. The next day, they found three graves at Lempire, near the 1917 front line, two of which were identified. On 16 December, they went to Bourlon Wood as large numbers of bodies had been reported missing there during the war. They worked their way through a part of the wood, but soon the tangled undergrowth became so thick that progress was impossible. 'Brambles grow in such profusion,' wrote Gell, 'that I give it as my opinion that no systematic search is possible. I do not believe the wood has ever been searched properly, let alone re-searched.'[53] At Railway Wood, a body was partially identified by the initials 'A.B.' on the cigarette case, a shoulder title indicating the Cheshire Regiment, and a whistle, which suggested he was an NCO.

Some sights continued to surprise: the coloured silk handkerchief on a corpse at Tower Hamlets was remarkably well preserved, whereas all the other bits of clothing were completely decayed. Similarly, at Polygon Buttes, an Australian body Gell watched being lifted from a shell hole had on him a pocket Gillette razor set with a nickel case of blades: each blade came in its own green paper covering, and was not at all rusty. He was shown two bodies at Shrewsbury Forest – one British, one German – which looked, from the position in which they lay, as if they had killed each other, and had then been buried by a shell. At Tyne Cot, an artillery officer was found entombed in his observation post after a shell blast, his telephone and receiver beside him.

As predicted, bodies kept surfacing throughout the 1920s and 1930s, turned up by the plough, or by builders digging the foundations of new buildings. Others were found by people searching for scrap metal on the battlefields in their spare time – who were encouraged to report to the IWGC by a two-franc reward for every body (although this might be rather less than what might be scavenged by way of personal belongings). There continued to be reports, too, of clandestine exhumations, of collusion between desperate relatives and furtive villagers. In April 1923, the *Daily News* reported a frequent visitor to the battlefields, an old man who was nearly blind, groping around a derelict battlefield, searching hopefully for the body of his only boy. The spirits had told him, he said, where his boy lay, and he came to dig and dig.[54]

Between the autumn of 1921, when the IWGC took over from the DGR&E, and the start of the Second World War, more than 38,000 bodies were found in northern France and Flanders, with rates of identification varying but generally under 25 per cent. Cemeteries, such as Bedford House Cemetery near Ypres, were regularly extended to accommodate these new arrivals. Lieutenant Colonel Gell had acknowledged in April 1922, in response to a claim by an Englishman living in France, that there were 'hundreds, possibly thousands' of British bodies that had never been recovered, that it was inevitable that some identifications had been lost. 'The limited staff at the disposal of the Commission,' he wrote, 'makes it quite impossible to watch without intermission the work of each individual of the hundreds of reconstruction workers employed in different areas from time to time. No effort is spared however, in keeping in touch with the different gangs and impressing upon them the necessity of reporting the presence of any remains that may be uncovered.'[55]

What was clear and consistent throughout was the demand for respect to be shown to the dead. In a memo, dated 22 October 1925, Gell continued to insist that registration officers employed by the IWGC should observe all the proprieties: 'The body must be reverently laid in the coffin at the place of exhumation, and from that time on until it is covered in, at the concentrations cemetery, it should be covered with a Union Jack. Registration Officers should warn exhumers constantly on the need of reverence, and attention to those small details of behaviour, the absence of which may cruelly wound the susceptibilities of relatives who may chance to see the work in progress.'[56]

This concern for the relatives inspired the search of the battlefields for the bodies of the dead, particularly in Europe, just as it had inspired the efforts of the Wounded and Missing Enquiry Department. It spawned a massive bureaucracy, of burial returns and records; but however great the challenge, and how inevitable some of its errors – many of them due to human frailties – it aspired to that most humane of aims: the need to identify and name the dead.

8

Fromelles and Beyond:
The Search Goes On

During the First World War, soldiers searched the battlefields for souvenirs so enthusiastically that at times: 'No Man's Land on a misty morning resembled nothing so much as Margate sands in August, only instead of happy children building castles there were men digging for [artillery-shell] nose-caps.'[1]

Over the last few decades, battlefield archaeology has grown from being a hobby, or '*souveneering*', as it was once called, to a discipline that is more professional and academically rigorous, encompassing anthropology, forensics, history, geography and geology. The landscapes of the First World War have been recognised as an integral part of the world's heritage. Archaeologists have become the new searchers, using a range of sources from the military records and war diaries in archives, to aerial photographs, letters and artefacts. Their skills may be those of the scientist, but the focus of their work is primarily humanitarian.

As fields were ploughed and trenches filled in after the war, the work of clearance and reconstruction preserved the battlefields under a thin layer of earth. Archaeologists did not have to dig that deep beneath the surface of a field to reveal a world that was previously invisible. They were increasingly called in to evaluate the archaeological impact of major construction projects: urban development, for example; the TGV railway line between Paris and Calais; or the A19 motorway extension, whose projected route through the heart of the Ypres Salient battlefield was diverted as a result of preliminary archaeological investigations.

During the 1990s, a Belgian amateur group started excavating, under professional supervision, in preparation for the extension of an industrial estate around Boezinge, near Ypres. Their work opened up just some of the hundreds of miles of buried trenches and tunnels, dugouts and shelters – subterranean cities almost – that lie relatively intact beneath the fields of Flanders and the Somme. In 1998 they came across steps leading down to an underground warren of rooms and passages: a dugout, known from a 1917 trench map, as the Yorkshire Trench. The dugout had been named after units of the 49th West Riding Division from Yorkshire, who had dug and held it in 1915, but two years later, during Third Ypres (Passchendaele), it became the headquarters of the 13th and 16th Royal Welch Fusiliers – the regiment which counted, among its members, the war poets Siegfried Sassoon and Robert Graves.

Scattered all around Boezinge, on the site of what had once been no man's land, was the detritus of war, well preserved in the waterlogged soil – cartridge belts and barbed wire, bayonets and telephone cables. Between 1992 and 2000, the archaeologists also discovered the remains of 155 soldiers, some of whom fell in 1917, with others killed in the Second Battle of Ypres in April–May 1915.[2] Although around half of them were British, only one of the 155 has been identified by name: a French soldier killed in May 1915. A further two British soldiers, identified by their regimental badges as from the Royal Welch Fusiliers, were discovered in 2001, caught almost at the moment, the time and place, of their death. One of them, or the skeleton at least, was still wearing his steel helmet and boots.[3]

Between April 2001 and September 2002, in preparation for the construction of a car factory at Point du Jour, north-east of Arras, archaeologists started to excavate an extensive network – more than sixty miles long – of German trenches and dugouts. One of the soldiers they unearthed was identified by the metal identity disc he had privately purchased as Private Archibald McMillan of the 15th Royal Scots. His body was handed over to the Commonwealth War

Graves Commission (the successor organisation to the IWGC), who reburied him at the nearby Point-du-Jour Military Cemetery. The service was attended by his son (then in his eighties) who had barely known the father he had lost as a one-year-old.

In total, the archaeologists came across the remains of thirty-one British soldiers, twenty of whom had been buried in a mass grave, probably by their comrades. Most of them were buried on their backs, with their heads facing north, and their hands on their abdomens. The discovery of regimental badges suggested that most of the men had belonged to 10th Battalion, Lincolnshire Regiment – a closely knit pals battalion known as the Grimsby Chums – killed during an attack with the 15th Royal Scots, on the well-defended Hindenburg Line in April 1917.[4]

Other discoveries included the remains of five Australian soldiers, from among the 7,000 Australians killed during Third Ypres, found in a shell-hole grave near Polygon Wood during the laying of a gas pipeline in September 2006. Overlooked during the systematic searching of the area after the war, they came to be known as the 'Zonnebeke Five'. Three of them were later identified by name. One, Private John Hunter, whose identity was confirmed through a DNA match provided by his niece, had apparently been buried with greater care than the others; which corroborated a family story that he had been laid to rest by his younger brother, Jim. John was reburied in Buttes New British Cemetery, and his name duly removed from the Menin Gate Memorial to the Missing.

In August 2007, archaeologists started excavations at Ploegsteert-St-Yvon. Bodies had already been recovered and identified from the Ploegsteert area in previous digs, including those of Private Harry Wilkinson and Private Richard Lancaster of 2nd Battalion, Lancashire Fusiliers, both of whom had been killed in November 1914. The devastation two and a half years later was more shocking: on the morning of 7 June 1917, a great ripple of explosions along the strategically important ridge between Messines and Wytschaete signalled the start of the Battle of Messines. Specialist tunnelling companies, recruited from mining communities in Britain, Canada and Australia, and from the labourers who had dug the London

Underground, had tunnelled up to a hundred feet deep beneath the German lines. There they planted a series of nineteen mines, which were detonated in the early hours, erupting in flames like volcanoes and spewing masses of earth into the air. The shock waves caused the dugouts to collapse, and thousands of German soldiers were buried alive. The plan was then for the advancing Allied troops to capture and occupy the German front line, turning it round so as to face the enemy.[5]

In August 2008 archaeologists found the remains of a soldier just forty centimetres below the ground surface, near Ultimo Crater, one of the enormous holes on the old German front line created by an exploding mine. He had evidently been killed in action, by a massive shell blast, and was still grasping the stock of a Lee–Enfield rifle in his left hand; he was surrounded by his equipment – a gas mask, a bayonet, parts of a medical kit, and some personal items in his pack, including a German *pickelhaube* spiked helmet that he clearly cherished as a souvenir. The 'Rising Sun' badges on his collar and shoulder identified him as an Australian, probably of 33rd Battalion, AIF, which was in the centre of the attack that day, but unfortunately his privately acquired identity disc was illegible. Whoever he was, his name was still remembered only on the memorial to the missing on the Menin Gate – until it was decided to test the DNA extracted from his teeth and bones against a shortlist of possible surviving relatives. This confirmed his identity as Private Alan Mather from New South Wales, and in July 2010 he was buried, with full military honours, in Prowse Point Military Cemetery, and his name subsequently erased from the Menin Gate.[6]

*

In 2009, work started near Fromelles in France on the largest project to recover and identify the bodies of First World War soldiers since the systematic clearance of the battlefields immediately after the war. The forensic archaeologists involved had at their disposal techniques considerably more advanced than when the body of an 'unidentified' Irish Guards lieutenant had been unearthed in 1919, or when he had been identified as Lieutenant John Kipling in 1992.

Clues to the existence of mass graves at Fromelles had, in fact, lain unnoticed for almost ninety years in the proceedings of the second court of inquiry, which had opened in London in January 1921. One of the allegations made then against Major Phillips and Major Allen of the Australian Graves Services (AGS) was that they had intended to 'hoax' or hoodwink a Mr Smith into believing that the grave of his wife's cousin Lieutenant Robert Burns had been located when it had not. Lieutenant Burns, an Australian with the 14th Machine Gun Company, had been killed at the Battle of Fromelles in July 1916, as he desperately fought his way back towards the Australian lines after the rout. He was the son of Colonel Sir James Burns, co-founder of Burns Philp & Company, a major shipping and trading company in the Pacific. In early 1919, the grieving businessman, who had received his son's identity disc as proof of his death but no further information, pressed the Australian authorities for help in locating the grave of his son. He was eventually informed that the AGS would investigate. As became apparent in evidence submitted by Major Phillips during the court of inquiry, the AGS had been advised in a communication from Germany that there were 'five large British collective graves … at Pheasants Wood near Fromelles and another at the Military Cemetery at Fournes'.[7] This was the first public reference to the existence of graves containing the bodies of British soldiers. Major Allen was instructed to conduct a search and, over the following months, he tramped extensively around Pheasant Wood and Fournes in search of any collective graves, but without success. He may even have stood on the very spot that would eventually be revealed as the resting place of 250 soldiers. Despite his celebrated skills as a grave-finder and 'discoverer of missing men',[8] he must have overlooked them.

By March 1920, Major Allen thought it possible that a collective grave in the German cemetery at Fournes might contain Lieutenant Burns's body, and was asked to carry out an exhumation. Mr C. A. Smith, acting on behalf of the Burns family, was initially denied permission by Major Phillips to attend the exhumation – in line with government policy on civilians attending exhumations at the time. In any case, as Phillips claimed in evidence at the inquiry, 'at no time was Mr Smith given the information that the body of this officer had been definitely identified'. After pressure from Smith and the Burns family, however, Phillips was overruled by the War Office, and Mr Smith was grudgingly granted permission to attend. A disgruntled Major Phillips asked Allen, in what was described at the inquiry as a 'tactless' private letter, to hurry the exhumation along before Smith's arrival. Phillips thought better of his fit of pique and cancelled his instruction to Allen by telegram. On 20 May 1920, Smith was present at the exhumation at Fournes, when five bodies were disinterred, all of them British. Lieutenant Burns's body was not among them. Far from being an attempt to falsify the result of the exhumation, or shut Smith up, the inquiry found 'that the exhumation in question was carried out in a perfectly straightforward normal manner and that no deception or hoodwinking of a relative was attempted by the Graves Services in France'.[9]

The case of Lieutenant Burns was one of several where official records, when examined carefully for the first time decades later, explained something that had puzzled people like Lambis Englezos. Englezos, a retired teacher from Victoria, the home state of many of the Australian 15th Brigade who had fallen at Fromelles, made the first of many visits to the site in 1996. It was the eightieth anniversary of the battle in which Australia had suffered its greatest loss of life in a single day, with almost two thousand killed. On a subsequent visit, in 2002, Englezos was struck by the discrepancy between the number of Australians listed as missing after the battle, on the memorial wall at the back of VC Corner Cemetery (1,294), and the number of unidentifiable Australians (1,131) recovered and buried in local cemeteries in the spring of 1920 during the searching of the battlefields.

Of the 'unknown' Australian soldiers, 410 had been buried in graves at VC Corner, the only all-Australian cemetery in France; and a further 721 had been buried at nearby cemeteries: Rue-David (266), Ration Farm (142), Aubers Ridge (120), Y Farm (72), Le Trou Aid Post (52), Rue-du-Bois (27), Rue-Petillon (22), Anzac (10) and

Sailly-sur-la-Lys (10). In 2003 the Commonwealth War Graves
Commission confirmed the discrepancy between the two numbers
(1,294 less 1,131) as 163. After further scrutiny, the 'official' figure
of Australians 'missing' after the Battle of Fromelles was revised
upwards to 191 with the addition, for example, of names from the
memorial panel to the missing at Villers-Bretonneux.

This arithmetical conundrum in the accounting for death
prompted Englezos to trawl through the files of the British Red
Cross Wounded and Missing Enquiry Department (W&MED) for
each of the 'missing' soldiers on the wall at VC Corner Cemetery.
Those buried by the Germans typically had a document recording
their name and battalion (from the ID discs the Germans had
retrieved, and from records of personal items returned to the
families of the dead). The number of these documents began to
tally with the number of 'missing'. Lieutenant Burns's file in the
Australian Red Cross Society Wounded and Missing Enquiry
Bureau files confirmed that his name had appeared on a German
death list, dated 4 November 1916: which is how the family knew,
by December of that year, that he was dead, fallen at Fromelles, but
not where he was buried.

The W&MED had stepped into the vacuum left by a War
Office overwhelmed by the scale of the slaughter and the volume
of enquiries from grieving relatives. The first Australian office had
been opened in Cairo in 1915 by Vera Deakin, the daughter of
a former prime minister of Australia, to trace those missing at
Gallipoli. When the focus of the war shifted to the Western front,
the Australian office transferred to London, where it created files on
around 32,000 servicemen reported wounded or missing. Whereas
the central records of the British W&MED were destroyed soon
after the First World War, when the department was closed, and
most of the enlistment records were lost to fire in 1940 during
the Blitz, the Australian records are much more complete. Red
Cross files at the Australian War Memorial include information
from German lists forwarded to the International Committee of
the Red Cross on Allied soldiers who had been killed in failed
attacks and found behind German lines, including Prisoner Lists,

Hospital Lists, Property Lists, Death Lists (*Totenliste*) and Graves Lists. When, for example, a body was retrieved by the Germans after a battle, with an identity disc or some other identifiable personal effect, his name might feature on a Death List and a Property List, and his possessions might be eventually returned to his family. This information, combined with eyewitness accounts by survivors locating the death of a 'missing' soldier behind enemy lines, suggested that he was likely to have been buried by the Germans.

Take the case of former bank manager Second Lieutenant John Charles ('Jack') Bowden of 59th Battalion, whose name appears on the wall of the VC Corner Memorial. Jack Bowden had gone over in the first wave of attacks at Fromelles, but was one of the 1,750 Australians reported missing soon after the battle. His family had hoped at first that he might still be alive – particularly as the Bureau for Wounded and Missing had mistakenly inferred from a reference on a German list of soldiers that he was a prisoner of war. The question of his fate was further complicated by the fact that there was also a Private Charles Bowden serving with 59th Battalion: since Jack had only recently been commissioned as an officer, and his identity disc may still have read Private John Charles Bowden, it was possible that the two had been confused. In January 1918, however, Jack's family received a letter, signed by Vera Deakin, officially recognising that Jack had been killed in action on 19 July 1916. There was another letter in his file, dated 20 June 1918, informing Jack's sister that the bureau had been informed by the German Red Cross via the Red Cross's international headquarters in Geneva that: 'After the battle near Fromelles on 19.7.16 the identity Discs were removed from all the fallen men and sent in. The name of Bowden is not reported in the lists of graves. It may be assumed that possibly Lieut. Bowden was buried in one of the five large British collective graves beside the Fasanen Wäldchen ['Pheasants' Wood] near Fromelles, or in the collective grave in the Military Cemetery at Fournes … .'[10] Although Jack's body has still not been found, it was this reference, in Jack Bowden's file at the Red Cross Wounded and Missing Collection at the Australian War

Memorial, that provided further evidence for the existence of mass graves at Pheasant Wood.

Gradually, the evidence for mass graves began to accumulate. Much of this had existed at the time, but had been overlooked for the sake of expediency or because of an exaggerated faith in the efficiency of the post-war searches. One of the circumstantial accounts that intrigued researchers such as Englezos was a report written by Australian infantryman Private William ('Bill') Barry of 29th Battalion, a plumber by trade. Barry had been knocked unconscious by a shell blast after he had reached the German trenches near Delangré Farm; when he came round hours later, he found that he been taken prisoner of war by the Germans and removed, with a leg wound, to a first-aid post behind enemy lines. 'It was the 21st of July,' he wrote, 'and the sun was shining brightly and when I was able to look around, and to my horror, I was in the place where all the dead men were. I was sitting on the edge of a hole about forty feet long, twenty feet wide and fifteen feet deep and into this hole the dead were being thrown without any fuss or respect. It was pitiful to see the different expressions on their faces, some with a peaceful smile while others showed they had passed away in agony.' This could well be a reference to a mass burial by the Germans. Barry was then taken by stretcher and horse-drawn ambulance wagon to a field hospital, before being evacuated to Germany where he had his leg amputated.[11]

In 2004 Englezos spotted differences in aerial photographs taken around Fromelles before and after the battle. In one, taken ten days after the battle, on 29 July 1916, there were signs of eight recently dug pits, arranged in two lines, next to the German light-railway track along the southern edge of a wood, Pheasant Wood; five of them had been backfilled. These pits did not appear in a photo taken a month before the battle, on 17 June. In a photo taken five months after the battle, on 20 December, three of the pits seemed still to be open and empty.[12] These findings tied in with documentary evidence from the case files of individual soldiers, and with German military records, particularly from the Bavarian Reserve regiments fighting in the area.

Englezos also learned in 2004 about a regimental history, published in 1923, by Major General Julius Ritter von Braun, who had commanded the Bavarian Reserve Infantry Regiment facing the Australians at Fromelles. This referred to the enemy dead being 'buried in mass graves behind the Pheasant Wood', and pointed to the fact that, once the Germans had reoccupied their front line after the battle, their first priority had been to rebuild their trenches, where necessary, and to clear the dead from the area.[13]

Researchers found further confirmation in the entry for 21 July 1916 in the war diary of the 21st Bavarian Reserve Infantry Regiment, and in a copy of Regimental Order No. 5220, which the new director of the Bavarian military archives in Munich unearthed in 2006. Headed 'Bringing up of materials and recovery of bodies', it included detailed instructions for the collection as soon as possible after the battle of all bodies in the front line.[14] The bodies were to be laid out in places, offering protection from the sun, near the light railway line, which connected the German front lines to their rear. German bodies were to be separated from the '*Engländer*' dead – a term which referred to both British and Australian soldiers. Bodies were to be stripped of personal items, such as letters and coins, and items that might identify them, such as any discs or pay books, so that there was some record, if possible, of those buried. Nobody, without exception, had the right to remove from the dead any kind of souvenir whatsoever. 'The misappropriation,' Braun warned, 'of even the most insignificant item of property from a body (German or English) constitutes robbery of the dead and will be severely punished.'[15] For the burial of the *Engländer* – to the south of Pheasant Wood, on the outskirts of the village of Fromelles – Braun ordered the excavation of mass graves for approximately 400 bodies.

*

The Battle of Fromelles had been designed as a feint, a diversionary action, to keep German troops from being transferred fifty miles south to the Battle of the Somme, which had begun almost three weeks before. It was the first major engagement for the Australians on the Western front, and it was to prove the most disastrous twenty-four hours in Australian military history, resulting in more Australian casualties in a single day than in the Boer War, Korean War and Vietnam War combined. The Australian 5th Division had only arrived in France earlier that month, after training in Egypt and England, and was relatively inexperienced.

In overall command of the British 61st Division and the Australian 5th Division was Lieutenant General Sir Richard Haking, the uncompromising and restless commander of the British XI Corps. Less than a year before, in September 1915, Haking had been responsible for the failure at Loos, ten miles away, at which John Kipling had lost his life. Thereafter, Rudyard Kipling often referred to the Battle of Loos, ironically, as 'the greatest battle in the history of the world';[16] for this is how Haking had described the forthcoming attempt to deliver a breakthrough on the Western front at a briefing before the battle.

Haking was obsessed with the idea of capturing a section of the Aubers Ridge, the only ground to rise more than a hundred feet or so above the low-lying farmland of French Flanders. Previous unsuccessful attempts had been made by the British to capture the ridge, including one in May 1915 on exactly the same spot; and British remains still littered the ground in no man's land, over which the Australians would now have to advance. This time, though, the underlying aim was more limited: to pin the German reserves down by encouraging them to think that a major offensive was in the offing.

The 6th Bavarian Reserve Division had been well entrenched in front of the ridge for months, arranged in lines up to a half a mile apart, with an intricate network of sturdy trenches and breastworks, or walls. Massive concrete 'blockhouses', bristling with machine guns, and reinforced dugouts, between the front line and the supporting lines, provided defence in depth and served as outposts from which German counter-attacks could be launched. Haking's plan was for the two infantry divisions to attack – the British 61st Division from the west and the Australian 5th Division from the east – along a line about two and a quarter miles wide. In the middle, the Sugar Loaf Salient projected out from the German line and into no man's land. If the German front line either side of the Sugar Loaf could be taken, and the tip of the Sugar Loaf itself captured by the converging British and Australian forces, then a new front line would be established. The Germans watched some of these preparations from the Aubers Ridge, and from an observation post in the church tower at Fromelles. They were waiting, with a sign above some trenches goading their adversaries: 'Advance Australia – If You Can!'

Things became a little confused before the start of the battle, as the British attack was postponed by a couple of days due to bad weather. At 11 a.m. on 19 July, the British began their artillery bombardment, aiming to cut through the German wire and break down some of the enemy defences, in particular the strong points, in preparation for the infantry assault. The effects of the barrage were limited – and, as events proved, it failed to silence the German machine guns in the Sugar Loaf Salient. Because of the artillery's relative inexperience, many of its shells fell short, inflicting 'friendly fire' casualties on the British and Australian troops. Hugh Knyvett, then a scout with 59th Battalion, described how British shells were bursting within their own lines: 'This made us very uncomfortable … Our first message over the 'phone was very polite. "We preferred to be killed by the Germans, thank you," was all we said to the battery commander. But as his remarks continued to come to us through the air, accompanied by a charge of explosive, and two of our officers being killed, our next message was worded very differently, and we told him that "if he fired again we would turn the machine-guns on to them." '[17] Knyvett was sent back to make sure the battery commander got the message, bearing an unexploded shell as evidence.

The first troops from the 14th Brigade (in the centre of the Australian attack) left their positions at 5.43 p.m., advancing across no man's land, and reaching and overwhelming the German front-line trenches. Supporting waves leapfrogged this first wave of troops and pushed on farther into the German defensive system. Or, at least, that was the idea. Aerial reconnaissance by the British before the battle had appeared to show further lines of breastworks a hundred yards or so beyond the first, but the photographs were misleading. The lines proved to be little more than ditches and provided scant protection for the Australian troops as they dug in in the zone beyond the German front line. Then came the German counter-attack. Those who had advanced farthest into German-held territory were now cut off, with the Germans reoccupying the trenches behind them. All the Australians could do was to try to fight their way back through the German front line, and across no man's land to the safety of the Australian trenches. The wounded and dead were left behind.

The 8th Brigade (on the left flank of the Australian attack) made good ground, like the 14th Brigade. They charged the hundred yards across no man's land, which was at its narrowest at this point, made it through the barbed wire, and reached and cleared the German trenches. But they, too, failed to locate the elusive German 'lines' beyond, supposedly shown in the aerial photographs, and were forced to dig in, in drainage ditches, and await the German counter-attack. Like the 14th Brigade, they were cut off as the Germans reclaimed their original trenches and attacked them from behind through the night.

The first waves of Australian troops from the 15th Brigade, on the Australians' right flank, 'hopped the bags' – as the Diggers described it – at around the same time as the other two brigades. The low-lying ground was waterlogged here in French Flanders, and soldiers tended not to dig deep trenches but to construct breastworks, two to three metres high and six to ten metres thick, out of sandbags filled with earth. They then launched their attack by clambering over the sandbags – 'hopping the bags' – or exiting through gaps or 'sally-ports', rather than by going 'over the top' of the trench parapet. The soldiers of 59th and 60th Battalions, 15th Brigade, were immediately cut down by German machine-gun fire. Very few of them made it across no man's land, which was at its widest at this point, to the German front line.

'Scores of stammering German machine guns spluttered violently, drowning the noise of the cannonade,' wrote Sergeant

Walter Downing – 'Jimmy' to his friends – of the 15th Brigade's reserve battalion, the 57th, watching the attack of 60th Battalion from the support line:

> The air was thick with bullets, swishing in a flat, criss-crossed lattice of death … The bullets skimmed low, from knee to groin, riddling the tumbling bodies before they touched the ground. Still the line kept on. Hundreds were mown down in the flicker of an eyelid, like great rows of teeth knocked from a comb … And then the 59th rose, vengeful, with a shout – a thousand as one man. The chattering, metallic staccato of the tempest of hell burst in nickelled gusts. Sheaves and streams of bullets swept like whirling knives. There were many corpses hung inert on our wire, but the 59th surged forward, now in silence, more steadily, more precise than on parade … It was the Charge of the Light Brigade once more, but more terrible, more hopeless – magnificent, but not war – a valley of death filled by somebody's blunder or the horrid necessities of war.[18]

When the attack on the Sugar Loaf from the west by troops of the British 61st Division faltered, and they were ordered to withdraw, the news was not relayed to the Australians until too late. The 15th Brigade pressed on alone into the night, only to be forced back across no man's land by the Germans, and subjected to an enfilade of machine-gun fire from front and side by enemy gunners in the salient.

The morning after the failed attack, the surviving, battle-scarred Australian soldiers sat, stunned, in their trenches. The scene was 'unexampled in the history of the AIF', according to the war correspondent Charles Bean, 'and was burned into the mind of everyone who saw it'.[19] For Hugh Knyvett, the sight of the trenches had a similar effect: 'In places the parapet was repaired with bodies – bodies that but yesterday had housed the personality of a friend by whom we had warmed ourselves. If you had gathered the stock of a thousand butcher-shops, cut it into small pieces and strewn it about, it would give you a faint conception of the shambles those trenches were.'[20] Brigadier General Harold 'Pompey' Elliott, commanding the 15th Brigade, was seen after the battle with his head in his hands, sobbing. He had had serious doubts about the action from the start, later describing it as a 'tactical abortion': he considered attacks over more than 200 metres of open ground unfeasible, and Major Howard, a member of Haig's own staff, had warned him of 'a bloody holocaust' if they went ahead. After the war, Elliott wrote the introduction to *To the Last Ridge*, thoroughly commending the devastating account of the battle by Downing, his former subordinate and now a co-founder of his legal practice, as a 'true picture'. Elliott took his own life in 1931.

Haking, the commander responsible for this valley of death, this 'blunder' in Downing's words, claimed that 'the attack, although it failed, has done both divisions a great deal of good'.[21] He was already known by some of the troops who had served under his command at Aubers Ridge and Loos in 1915 as a 'butcher'; and this failure at Fromelles did nothing to change that opinion. The British official war communiqué was equally bland and misleading: 'Yesterday evening, south of Armentières, we carried out some important raids on a front of two miles in which Australian troops took part. About 140 Germans were captured.'[22] In contrast, the official German communiqué observed: 'The brave Bavarian Division, against whose front the attack was made, counted on the ground in front of them more than 2,000 enemy corpses. We had brought in so far 481 prisoners.'[23] One of the German dispatch runners at Fromelles, with the dangerous job of finding out what was happening in the front line when the telephone lines were down and relaying the news back to headquarters, was a twenty-seven-year-old lance-corporal with the 16th Bavarian Reserve Infantry Regiment called Adolf Hitler. Memories of this particularly Bavarian triumph stayed with him. As soon as his generals had accepted the surrender of France to Germany in June 1940, which confirmed their conquest of most of Europe, one of the first places Hitler visited, in commemoration of his time there in 1916, was the battlefield at Fromelles. He found the house where he had been billeted that July, and visited the blockhouse where he had sheltered in the thick of the action.

For years, Australia's first full-scale – and calamitous – engagement on the Western front was barely dignified with the description as a battle in British histories: Fromelles was a 'subsidiary action', or sometimes known as the Battle of Fleurbaix, and for ever completely overshadowed by the Battle of the Somme.

Fromelles may have been relegated to a sideshow for the British, but it was never so for the Australians. The Australian official war historian, Charles Bean, described in his diary a visit to the battlefield at Fromelles on the day of the Armistice, 11 November 1918: 'We found the old Noman's Land simply full of our dead. In the narrow sector west of the Laies river and east of the corner of the Sugarloaf salient, the skulls and bones and torn uniforms were lying about everywhere. I found a bit of Australian kit lying about 50 yds. from the corner of the salient; and the bones of an Australian officer and several men within 100 yds. of it. Further round, immediately on their flank, were a few British – you could tell them by their leather equipment. And within 100 yds. of the west corner of the Sugarloaf salient there was lying a small party of English too – also with an officer – you could tell the cloth of his coat.'[24] These sights must have made some impression on Bean, as he assigned 120 pages of his official history to the 'Battle of Fromelles'.

Overall, the 5th Australian Division suffered 5,533 casualties, wounded, missing and killed, at Fromelles. Almost half the division had been incapacitated. Of these, more than 1,900 were killed – three times, at least, the number of British dead. The number of fatalities was probably exacerbated by the fact that there were only enough steel helmets for the first waves of Australian attackers, and subsequent waves had to face the Germans in soft slouch hats. More than 400 Australians were taken prisoner and marched to Lille on their way to captivity in Germany. Total German casualties, on the other hand, were less than 1,500. Very little was achieved at Fromelles: there were no tactical gains and, in any case, it had been apparent to some, even before the battle, that the Germans had no plans to move reinforcements to the Somme. The battle had made no difference to the overall course of the war.

Australian soldiers who had died in their own trenches were buried in battlefield cemeteries behind the lines, but a far greater number fell in no man's land or in advanced positions behind the German lines. Some of those who had fallen in no man's land were retrieved after the battle by forays of soldiers searching for bodies under cover of dark, often under fire. As Charles Bean had witnessed in 1918, most were left to rot in no man's land, which barely shifted for the rest of the war. During the clearance of the battlefields after the war, their remains were buried at VC Corner Cemetery. Those who had penetrated into the German section and died behind German lines, however, were cleared by the Germans in the days after the battle and hastily buried for health and sanitary reasons in mass graves: the bodies had begun to decompose in the summer heat and were covered in swarms of flies.

*

By 2006, the mounting burden of evidence assembled by Englezos and his fellow researchers suggested that all the dead had been stretchered off the battlefield by the Germans, and piled at collection points along the light railway, where they were separated. The Bavarian dead were taken by railway to the German military cemetery at Beaucamps; while the British and Australian dead were loaded onto flatbed wagons for transport elsewhere: there are photographs to show this. Initially, the bodies were taken to the cemetery at Fournes but, as this filled up, they were sent to a corner of Pheasant Wood for burial. Some of the collective graves at Fournes had been opened during the intensive exhumations after the war, and the bodies, or what remained of them, reinterred in new cemeteries. But no such search, it seemed, had been conducted of the supposedly undiscovered graves at Pheasant Wood.

In 2007, under intense media pressure, a panel of investigation recommended a non-invasive survey of the Pheasant Wood site. Consequently, a team from the Glasgow University Archaeological Research Division (GUARD) was commissioned that May to assess the probability of human remains being found. A topographical survey showed variations in the ground surface, consistent with the

1916 aerial photographs of the eight pits, with the light-railway line running alongside. The depth of each of the pits was estimated, after a ground-penetrating radar survey, at about two metres. Metal detectors revealed, lying just below the turf among a haul of buttons and buckles, two small copper-alloy medallions. One of these bore the letters 'ANZAC' (Australian and New Zealand Army Corps) and the other the letters AIF (Australian Imperial Force), with the words 'Shire of Alberton' and the date, 1914. Could the Alberton medallion, researchers asked, have belonged to Private Henry ('Harry') Willis of 31st Battalion? Willis had been born in Alberton, South Australia, and was known, like other soldiers from his district, to have been presented with a shire medallion before his departure for Europe in 1915; his Red Cross Wounded and Missing Enquiry file suggested that he, like Bowden, had been buried by the Germans (his name appeared on a Death List dated 4 November 1916), and his identity disc had been forwarded to his next of kin the following June.[25]

The GUARD report 'established beyond doubt that Australian troops at least had been buried on the site and also provided quite compelling evidence that the graves had not been discovered after the war and were therefore intact and undisturbed'.[26] Although it was highly likely that the graves had not been discovered, or disturbed, during the intensive searches by the Australian Graves Service in the years immediately after the war, there was still no 'absolute proof'. Several historians found it hard to believe that the site had been overlooked, despite the fact that Major Phillips himself had noted in 1927 that 'a great number must still be in the ground and too deep to be located by ploughing or probing'.[27]

In 2008, the GUARD team was invited back to carry out a more invasive search, with limited, sample excavations of the pits. Using a mechanical excavator, shallow, exploratory trenches were dug across the pits. Various items started to emerge from just below the surface, including buttons and eyelets, possibly from the waterproof groundsheets in which the bodies had been wrapped. The shape of the pits also became more evident. Below the grass and topsoil there was a mottled layer of blue and orange clay, which would normally have been found only at a greater depth. This, the archaeologists surmised, must be the earth with which the graves had been backfilled after the burials in 1916 and appeared to confirm GUARD's previous conclusion that the graves had remained undisturbed since then. The next step was to dig a series of metre-square test excavations, or sondages, into the pits, across about 16 per cent of the total surface area occupied by the graves. The modern-day 'diggers', like their Australian counterparts ninety years earlier, sifted by hand through the layers of soil, unearthing first of all the tip of a finger, which gradually revealed itself to be part of a hand. Over the coming days, the team discovered the remains of some fifty individuals, and a mass of artefacts, including two Australian Army 'Rising Sun' collar badges. Estimates suggested that there might be more than 400 bodies here – a figure which tallied with Braun's order.

In July 2008, the Australian government announced its intention to go ahead with the excavation, exhumation and reburial of the bodies at Fromelles. This would be overseen by the Commonwealth War Graves Commission (CWGC), acting for the Australian and British governments. Oxford Archaeology was awarded the contract for the excavation works under the management of the CWGC: the first time since the systematic clearance of the battlefields after the First World War that an attempt on such a scale had been made to recover missing soldiers. The project was to be carried out using the most modern scientific techniques; but however sophisticated these might be, Fromelles was above all a humanitarian project, focused on recovering and identifying individuals with living families. As such, it was inspired by the same underlying reasons that have driven other individuals and groups in this book: to restore humanity to the dead, and to give their relatives, whether wives or mothers, grandsons or great-nieces, the certainty of a named grave. To that extent, the project honoured the ideals set out by Fabian Ware almost a hundred years earlier.

As well as archaeologists and osteoarchaeologists – experts in the identification of human remains – the Oxford Archaeology team included explosives experts and forensics specialists, some of whom had worked on the mass graves in Bosnia and Iraq. Work started in May 2009. Once the topsoil had been removed to a depth of about twenty centimetres by a mechanical digger, the layers below were excavated by hand, scraping through the clay and silt. Over the next four months, the remains of 250 individuals were retrieved, along with 6,200 artefacts. This was despite the fact that the Germans had been ordered in 1916 to gather up all personal items, for return eventually to the Red Cross.

The team unearthed boots, buttons and brass belt buckles, and scraps of torn fabric from military uniforms that provided information on the army – Australian or British – for which the individuals had been fighting. Australian soldiers, for example, wore curved brass badges bearing the word 'Australia' on each shoulder, and Rising Sun badges on each lapel. Brass battalion shoulder numbers or regimental badges sometimes provided further information. The location of every item had to be recorded very precisely, in relation to the body next to which it had been found: objects shifted very little in the thick, heavy soil of the graves, and their context, their association with a particular individual, was crucial in making sense of the discovery. Typically, badges were worn on collars and shoulder straps, and would therefore be found near the neck or shoulder of the skeleton; and buttons from the front of the jacket would be located near the chest cavity.

All of the finds contributed something to an understanding of the soldiers' daily lives and concerns. Smoking paraphernalia included cigarette holders, a brass petrol lighter, and pipes – which, given the fact that they were often located near the chest of the corpse, indicated that they were typically carried in the soldier's breast pocket. Many of the artefacts – particularly those made from organic materials, such as paper, textile or leather – had been remarkably well preserved in the waterlogged, anaerobic (oxygen-less) soil. A 'Black Cat' English–French phrase book survived, with its useful instructions still legible: 'Bring me some cigarettes and cigars', 'Cut my hair quite short', and a pleading, hopeful 'Do not shoot'.[28] There was a purse containing French francs, British pennies,

Dutch guilders and coins from Ceylon; and a heart-shaped leather
pouch with tiny fragments of a lock of hair, presumably belonging
to a loved one, inside. Other finds included toothbrushes and a
shaving brush; glass ampoules of iodine from medical kits; pens and
lead pencils, including a fountain pen with a gold nib; and 'trench
art' rings made from the aluminium fuse of an unexploded shell.[29]
In much the same way as the bereaved of more than a century
ago yearned for some physical contact with the dead, people today
confess to a direct emotional connection with the past through the
objects which their ancestors carried. It is the material culture, as
archaeologists describe it, that illuminates the experiences of these
soldiers, the battlefields in which they fought, and the places where
they were buried.

Some of the items provided a poignant insight. An unused return
train ticket from Fremantle to Perth in Western Australia, folded
up inside a gas mask, hinted at a return journey that that soldier
was never going to make; likewise, a boomerang 'sweetheart' badge,
bearing the phrase 'Return to me'. But however touching these
might be, and evocative of a particular individual's personal story,
they offered no clues as to the owner's identity.[30]

The most telling aids to identification in 2009 were relatively rare
finds. After the battle, the Germans had been ordered to collect all
identity discs, for forwarding to the Red Cross. At the time, the
vast majority of British soldiers had only one disc, generally made
of compressed fibre and hung by twine around the neck; therefore,
even if the bagging, listing and forwarding of a disc by the Germans
was evidence of a soldier's death, the fact that it had been collected
made it impossible, in July 1916, actually to match a body with a
tag. Ironically, the German retrieval of the discs guaranteed the
anonymity of the body. The identification of the dead of Fromelles
in 2009 would have been simpler had the dual identity disc system –
introduced later in 1916 – been in operation at the time of the
battle. Some soldiers had paid privately, however, for more durable
identity discs, generally made of aluminium and worn round the
wrist or neck. Three of these metal discs, presumably overlooked
by the German burial parties, survived and were found during the

excavation. Similarly, there were several pieces of marked personal property that helped with identification: an engraved gold ring, with the inscription 'from Aunt Julie 1910', found on the ring finger of a soldier's left hand; a matchbox cover engraved 'Pt Cyril Johnston 1915'; a pipe scratched with the initials 'HEP' or 'HEW'; and dentures marked 'Weir'.[31]

The bodies themselves were contained in six of the eight pits, which were each ten metres long, about one and a half metres wide, and between one and two metres deep. Five of the pits were found to have between forty-four and fifty-two men each; one grave contained three men; and two pits were empty. Tattered remains of fabric and lengths of cable indicated that the bodies may have been wrapped in waterproof groundsheets, prior to moving, and the limbs tied together with wire. It appeared that the bodies had been buried across the width of the graves in two layers, one on top of the other, with a layer of earth in between. As with all mass graves, the archaeologists had to take particular care to establish, in the confusion of interlinked limbs, which bones belonged to which body. Evidence of fly pupae led investigators to believe that the bodies had been buried around a week after the battle; and the presence of lumps of chalk and lime suggested that the Germans had tried to disinfect the bodies by sprinkling corrosive chloride of lime on each layer of corpses.[32]

The men ranged in age from their teens to their forties, although most of them were in their twenties, and in relatively good health – apart from the poor state of their teeth and, of course, from their terrible battlefield injuries. All their characteristics were logged: estimated height and build, the shape of their face as determined by the jaw, and whether they were left- or right-handed. Chronic or congenital conditions were noted, as were any previously healed fractures from a bone broken, say, in childhood, that might have been recorded in the soldier's medical record on enlistment. Perhaps more revealing were the descriptions of their mortal wounds (whether, for example, they had been shot in the head or the chest), as these could be correlated with eyewitness accounts of their death in army reports or in their file at the

W&MED. The most common wounds were caused by projectiles, such as shrapnel or bullets, followed by wounds caused by shell blasts.[33]

Bone samples and teeth were sent off for DNA analysis in the hope that this might match that of a living relative, and hence identify the fallen. The ravages of time and decomposition had reduced the quantities of DNA found at Fromelles, but there was still enough viable DNA preserved by the anaerobic soil conditions to build a profile for almost every one of the 250 dead. Markers on the Y chromosome are passed from generation to generation only through the male line: so if a direct father-to-son line can be established, today's grandson or great-grandson, say, can provide a potential DNA match, even after almost a hundred years and several generations. The problem with the First World War, however, is that many of those killed were very young men who had no children; in those cases, the male lineage can only be established through male descendants of the dead soldier's brother or uncle. Alternatively – and additionally – a DNA match can be established through the mitochondrial DNA profile, which passes relatively unchanged through the female lineage. This can only be established via the female descendants of the dead soldier's sister or maternal aunt. The use of these markers, inherited through the paternal and/or maternal line, would not establish an identity 'beyond reasonable doubt' in a court setting but, taken into account alongside other pieces of corroborative evidence, they could indicate that 'an ID is substantially more likely than not'.[34]

Public appeals were made for living relatives of the missing soldiers to come forward, ideally from both the male and female lines. Attention focused on the list of 191 names published by the Australian government of soldiers whose remains might be among those recovered from the site. Detailed family trees were constructed, with the help of a small army of online amateur genealogists, to ensure that only 'informative' individuals – those on a direct male or female line – were invited to become DNA donors. By 2015 more than 3,000 people had registered, of whom a thousand were invited to provide DNA samples.

The tables were turned. It was now as if the bodies themselves were searching for their families to reclaim them, rather than the other way round. Within the first year of the project, by March 2010, ninety-four identifications of Australian soldiers had been made – using various types of evidence, including DNA profiling supported by personal items and other identifying features. Lieutenant Robert Burns was among them.

Whether they had been identified or not, all 250 soldiers were laid to rest with full military honours in a cemetery built especially for them. Its cross visible from the VC Corner Cemetery, the Fromelles (Pheasant Wood) Military Cemetery was the first Commonwealth War Graves Commission cemetery constructed in more than fifty years. And yet its design and feel echoed those guiding principles articulated by Sir Frederick Kenyon in his report in 1918:

The general appearance of a British cemetery will be that of an enclosure with plots of grass or flowers (or both) separated by paths of varying size, and set with orderly rows of headstones, uniform in height and width. Shrubs and trees will be arranged in various places, and sometimes as clumps at the junctions of ways, sometimes as avenues along the sides of the principal paths, sometimes around the borders of the cemetery. The graves will, wherever possible, face towards the east, and at the eastern end of the cemetery will be a great altar-stone, raised upon broad steps, and bearing some brief and appropriate phrase or text. Either over the stone, or elsewhere in the cemetery, will be a small building, where visitors may gather for shelter or for worship, and where the register of the graves will be kept. And at some prominent spot will rise the Cross, as the symbol of the Christian faith and of the self-sacrifice of the men who now lie beneath its shadow.[35]

The interments themselves were performed with all the care, dignity and respect on which Fabian Ware had insisted. Between 30 January 2010, when the first unnamed soldier was reburied (subsequent DNA testing revealed that he was Fred Dyson of 54th

Battalion), and 19 February 2010, 249 of the 250 soldiers were reburied. As the flags were lowered and the Last Post sounded, each of them was placed in an individual grave right next to the soldier whose body had lain alongside him in the mass grave for the previous ninety-three years. On 19 July 2010, the ninety-fourth anniversary of the Battle of Fromelles, the coffin of the 250th soldier – who is still to be identified – was brought to the cemetery on a gun carriage drawn by four horses and laid to rest. In the presence of several of the families of the missing soldiers, the new cemetery was officially opened and dedicated. From 2010 onwards, on 19 July, as each year's new identifications are acknowledged and honoured, the headstones on the graves of some of the previously 'unknown' soldiers are changed to reflect their newfound identity.

The final decision on the identity of a soldier or, failing that, on whether he should be buried as an Unknown Australian or British soldier, or simply as 'A Soldier of the Great War Known unto God', fell to the joint identification board. Where enough evidence tipped the 'balance of probability', other soldiers might further be identified, if not by name, by their regiment or rank. Comprising Australian and British officials and forensic advisers, this group met every year between 2010 and 2014 to consider recommendations on a case-by-case basis. After 2014, each country assumed responsibility for the identification of its own missing soldiers.[36]

By 2019, 166 Australian soldiers had been successfully identified, leaving eighty-four undetermined. Of these, fifty-nine are unknown Australian soldiers, two are unknown British soldiers, and twenty-three are Commonwealth soldiers of unknown nationality. No British soldier has yet been identified by name, partly because the British 61st Division suffered fewer casualties than the Australians, and partly because the Australian records are so much more comprehensive. Private Harry Willis was identified in 2010, through DNA testing, as having been buried at Pheasant Wood, and now lies in the cemetery at Fromelles. Other soldiers whose names featured in the Red Cross Society Wounded and Missing Enquiry files, with references to the German Death List of 4 November 1916, and whose bodies were later identified and reburied, included Corporal

Courtney Green and Lieutenant Colonel Ignatius Bertram Norris. Their relatives finally had a chance to pay homage to their ancestors and to claim some sort of closure.

*

Each year some fifty sets of human remains are recovered in France and Belgium. Some of these surface in fields during the ploughing season, in what the farmers refer to as the 'iron harvest' or the 'harvest of bones'. But the overall number of unearthed burial sites is growing as a result of works for infrastructure projects, such as the new hospital on the northern outskirts of Lens, and the Seine–Nord Europe Canal, where construction is due to start in 2024. The canal, an inland waterway link more than sixty-five miles long, connecting the Rhine to the Seine, will pass through many First World War 'hot spots', including Péronne on the Somme, potentially disturbing thousands of hitherto undiscovered bodies along the way.

When the CWGC is alerted to the discovery of a body by a developer, a mine clearance contractor, the local police, or a member of the public, it responds immediately. Members of the exhumations team, who are based at Arras, rush to the site before it is disturbed any further by the excavators or by amateur archaeologists, who might compromise the integrity of the scene, thereby depriving the bodies of a chance of identification. The team removes the bones and artefacts – a less grisly job now, when all that remains of the maggots that once infested the corpses are the shells, than for the exhumation squads a hundred years ago.

Back at the CWGC recovery unit, the team cleans the bones, and begins to assemble them, as with the four skeletons in the prologue to this book. Great care is taken to match the bones, and indeed the artefacts too, with the right body – a tricky operation when the remains are 'commingled' or jumbled together. The team looks, in particular, for any identifying features, such as badges and shoulder titles. Archival research is then conducted at the commission's headquarters: regimental war diaries, for example, sometimes describe specific actions in detail, citing the units that were at that precise location at the time, and naming the soldiers. The commission then submits its report to the Commonwealth member nations, in the case of the British to the Ministry of Defence's Joint Casualty and Compassionate Centre (JCCC). The so-called 'War Detectives' undertake further research and, as the final arbiters, decide on the identification and arrange the burial ceremony. Depending on their decision, a new headstone is crafted either for a named individual or for an 'Unknown Soldier'. The exhumations team, who were there at the start of the process, at the recovery, are there at the end, overseeing the burial itself and honouring the commission's pledge to 'care for their graves and those of their comrades in perpetuity'.

Within a few days of each other in June 2019, there were two rather different services. One was the funeral at Hermies Hill British Cemetery of Private Henry Wallington and Private Frank Mead of 23rd (County of London) Battalion, who were killed on 3 December 1917 during the Battle of Cambrai. Their bodies had been discovered in 2016, with only a 23rd Battalion shoulder title as a clue to their identity. After research into military activity in the area that day, the field was narrowed to a shortlist of nine possible names; and the JCCC constructed family trees to trace any possible surviving members for DNA testing. Two positive matches identified Henry Wallington, whose niece attended the burial, and Frank Mead, whose great-nephew attended. The personal inscription on Henry's headstone chosen by his family began: 'I am the family face ...', while Frank's ended, '... Never lost.'[37]

A few days later, on 19 June, a service of re-dedication was held for Captain William Kington, who was killed in the first year of the war, and was attended by several of his great grandchildren. More than a dozen of these ceremonies – at which the grave of a previously unknown soldier, such as John Kipling or Cecil Tuff, is identified retrospectively – take place every year. Kington's body had not been recovered until after the war, when he was buried, unidentified, in Tyne Cot Cemetery as an unknown captain of the Royal Welch Fusiliers. Meanwhile, his name appeared on the Menin Gate as one of the Missing. The redesignation of his grave at Tyne Cot came as the result of new evidence unearthed by private researchers and confirmed by the JCCC and the National Army Museum. His name has been removed from the register at the Menin Gate, and will not feature on the stone panel currently bearing his name the next time it is replaced.[38]

'I shall never believe,' wrote the mother of one of the hundreds of thousands whose bodies were missing, 'that my son is dead until his grave is found and it adds greatly to the sorrow of his father and me that we should be left in this awful state of uncertainty.' She was caught indefinitely in what Rudyard Kipling described as a 'horrible see-saw', a dreary procession of 'unprofitable emotions' – denial, anger, guilt – that was never to be resolved. The end of the war had failed to bring that certainty: only time, and the ongoing search to recover, name and commemorate the war dead, will draw that final line between the living and the dead.

Epilogue

During the pandemic of 2020/21, services of reburial and rededication were postponed, and the daily ceremony at the Menin Gate restricted. Recent months have added to our understanding of the collective trauma that followed the First World War. Most of the 150,000 and more who have died of Covid-19 in the UK passed away relatively suddenly, without their families to hold their hand or say a final goodbye. Among survivors, there is a legacy of fear and guilt that a loved one has died alone and in pain. In another echo of the past, the restrictions placed on mourning rituals have deprived families of a focus for their grief, of a chance to see the body and confront the reality of the death. Funerals provide the bereaved with an occasion for mutual consolation, eventually easing them back into normal life; and the absence of such rituals may delay grieving and derail the path to acceptance. Psychologists today predict that many of those bereaved by Covid-19 will develop a condition they call 'complicated grief', or prolonged grief disorder, stuck in a cycle lasting months or even years. Although the term had not been coined a hundred years ago, it describes many of the effects on those bereaved by the First World War.

The ceremonies on and around 11 November – Remembrancetide as it has come to be known – are still the focus of our commemoration of the First World War. Both the Cenotaph and the Tomb of the Unknown Warrior were inspired, and then shaped, by the public's need for a national shrine at which people were participants rather than onlookers. The genius of both memorials lay in the way they enabled individuals to come together in communal acts of mourning that the war had prevented – just as there is discussion now of how the nation might remember those who have died in the pandemic.

The November rituals were developed within three years of the end of the Great War. They have barely changed since then, although the thoughts and feelings of those who participate have naturally evolved. What goes through your mind, or do you imagine passes through the hearts and minds of others, during the two-minute silence on Remembrance Day every year? It's less likely to be the aching private grief that was given public acknowledgement in 1919; and more likely a general, abstract recognition of everyone who has ever died in war.

The mixed messages of the day – war and peace, the living and the dead – have their origins in the first post-war commemorations. The ceremony that takes place in Whitehall every November, first envisaged as a victory parade on Peace Day, 19 July 1919, was put together in a hurry. In the midst of what was primarily a military celebration, it was thought necessary to incorporate a reference to the dead. But on the day itself, something unexpected happened.[1] There was an outpouring of public feeling – what Lutyens called 'the sentiment of millions'. It was this which determined the overriding meaning of the day as one of regret for the loss of life, as much as one of celebration for a military triumph. The victory parade was transformed into a funeral march.

In the months following July 1919, people flocked to the temporary Cenotaph. On Armistice Day, 11 November 1919, the two-minute silence was observed there, and across the country, for the first time, to allow people 'to perpetuate the memory of the Great Deliverance' and 'those who had laid down their lives to achieve it'.[2] In response to public sentiment and campaigns in the press, the shrine was made permanent. The stone Cenotaph was unveiled on Armistice Day the following year, a few minutes before the Unknown Warrior, representing those who never returned, was buried in Westminster Abbey. There was at the time some doubt about the wisdom of such a tribute, that a funeral might reopen war wounds – a notion, as some people suggest today, that it would be better to begin to forget than to keep on remembering. What was absolutely clear, as the coffin passed, was the comfort many found in finding the grave for which they had been searching, in witnessing the funeral they had never had the chance to attend. Six years before, it would have been inconceivable that a humble soldier would be buried in Westminster Abbey, but the war had introduced some democracy to the nation's dead.

*

The year 2021 marks the hundredth anniversary of the adoption of the poppy as the emblem of British commemoration. Its symbolism, as one of the first plants to flower in the desolate killing fields of Flanders, has proved particularly powerful. It was as if the poppy leached its colour from the blood-soaked soil, where its roots lay among the buried dead, to flower in the world of the living above. The choice of the poppy was inspired by one of the war's best-loved poems – 'In Flanders Fields' by the Canadian army doctor John McCrae. Dashed off in twenty minutes the day after he had buried a close friend, the poem, and the poppy, quickly became established, catching on across the Commonwealth, and in America as well. Yet the meaning of both poem and poppy were open to interpretation. Was the warning in the third stanza – 'If ye break faith with us who die/ We shall not sleep, though poppies grow/ In Flanders fields'[3] – an injunction to keep on fighting the good fight, or was it a plea for peace?

The poppy contained the seeds of future ambiguities, with other variants being adopted more or less successfully. From the 1930s, the white poppy became an emblem of a commitment to peace. The purple poppy was introduced in 2006 to remember animal victims of war. And in 2010 the black poppy was launched to commemorate the contribution of black, African, Caribbean and Pacific Islander communities to the war effort. As the nation honoured its dead, Field Marshal Haig had, in his 1920 *Times* article, acknowledged the nation's debt of honour to the living[4] – to the injured ex-servicemen and to the widows and orphans of those who had been killed. The fund he established became the British Legion's Poppy Appeal, adding another dimension to Remembrance. Some 45 million poppies are sold every year in Britain to raise money for ex-service personnel, as originally envisaged. For many, however, the wearing of a poppy has come to mean something more: that you stand shoulder to shoulder in solidarity and support for those who currently serve (rather than once served) in the British armed forces, and for the causes in which they fight. Not to wear a poppy is considered somehow disrespectful, unpatriotic.

Watching the procession of choristers and clerics at the annual Remembrance Day ceremony nowadays, it is hard to believe that there were no prayers or hymns at the Cenotaph in 1919. The prime minister, David Lloyd George, and Lord Curzon, who organised the event, wanted it to be 'wholly secular', since it honoured those of several faiths; and Lutyens's memorial itself bore no traces of Christian iconography. Nevertheless, the views of the Church of England prevailed in 1920, and the language of Remembrance assumed its distinctly Christian tone – particularly from 1923, when Armistice Day fell on a Sunday for the first time. The redemptive sacrifice of the war dead – the notion that they died so that we might live, whether or not they had a choice in the matter – was used to soothe the suffering of the bereaved by giving meaning to their loss.

All the themes that are woven into our commemoration of the First World War had their origins in the hastily improvised aftermath of the war: public celebration or private sadness, religious service or secular remembrance. These themes soon became enshrined, with all their inherent contradictions, in the rituals we practise to this day. As early as 1923, there were discussions about ending the annual event, and throughout the 1920s and 1930s there were those who thought that interest in Remembrance would inevitably fade away altogether. But the ceremonies survived and, if anything, have grown more formal and elaborate: a great state function, led by the monarch, the leaders of the main political parties, and the heads of the armed forces. It is simply the meaning that people have attributed to the ceremonies that has shifted subtly. The mood at Remembrance in the 1920s was defiantly patriotic, whereas by 1930 it had become more concerned with peace, at a time when the purpose of the war and its disproportionate cost were under question. A new rhetoric evolved to justify the suffering and sacrifice of the war on the grounds that they had been in the cause of a lasting peace. By the end of the 1930s, it was apparent that the Great War was unlikely to be the 'war to end wars'; as international tensions mounted, pacifism became associated with appeasement, and the white poppy with the flag of surrender.

In 1945, the trauma of the Second World War overshadowed that of the First, and the government decided to commemorate the dead of both wars together. In Britain, Armistice Day was renamed Remembrance Day, and the main national ceremonies were moved to the Sunday nearest to 11 November, although in Australia and New Zealand, Anzac Day on 25 April has come to eclipse Remembrance Day in importance. New names, albeit generally fewer in number, were added to war memorials across the country. During the 1960s and 1970s, ideas about the futility of the First World War, which had first been propounded in the 1920s, took hold again, as fears of nuclear war escalated. There was also a feeling, particularly among the young, that the commemorative practices, however muted, were outdated, and appealed only to the relatively small proportion of the population who had a direct connection to the First World War. This is how I remember it as a teenager.

But the spirit of Remembrance is extraordinarily resilient. In the 1980s and 1990s, as the wars faded from living memory, Remembrance was reinvigorated by the Falklands War and began to take on a more nationalistic tone. It now includes other no less controversial conflicts: the Gulf War and conflicts in Afghanistan and Iraq – the 'war on terror'.

In recent decades, there has also been a renewed interest in battlefield tourism – a phenomenon that first emerged immediately after the war. As people with direct personal links to those who had died passed away themselves, there was, paradoxically, a growing number of descendants who wanted to find out more. Grandchildren and great-grandchildren were drawn by a pride in their inheritance, a sense that these soldiers in some way belonged to them; they were inspired by shared family stories, photographs and keepsakes that provided emotional and imaginative links to the past. The First World War affected every family in the country and it was almost reachable in a way that previous, less photographed wars had not been. Developments in online genealogy helped, as did the fact that the war was a triumph of bureaucratic endeavour, with reams of records for relatives to search.

In the late 1970s, the Commonwealth War Graves Commission – the first organisation in the world to commemorate a nation's dead – was receiving a couple of thousand enquiries a year about the location of war graves from both world wars; its website now receives 5,000 such searches a day. Hundreds of thousands of tourists, mainly from Commonwealth or former Commonwealth countries, visit the sites of the Somme and the Ypres Salient: Thiepval, Tyne Cot, the Menin Gate. Like the first pilgrims looking for their loved ones, many of them are following in the footsteps of their forebears, advancing across no man's land or taking shelter in a trench, in search of their past and a sense of identity.

The last British veteran of Passchendaele to visit Tyne Cot Cemetery was Harry Patch in 2004, eighty-seven years to the day after he was wounded by a grenade attack at Langemarck; he died in 2009. The last surviving combat veteran of the First World War, Claude Choules, who served with the Royal Navy, died in 2011. Now that the generation who fought has long since passed away, what does the war mean for subsequent generations? I had a grandfather and three great-uncles who fought in the First World War (all survived). My father fought in the Second World War, and my mother spent her teenage years in the shadow of war; and so, on Remembrance Day, I feel a connection to, and respect for, the suffering of people I know. But what do my children think, and what will my grandchildren make of these memories at third- or fourth-hand? The rhetoric of redemptive sacrifice, developed to soothe people traumatised by mass death, may seem empty when the experience is no longer traumatic.

Even more pointedly, what do Remembrance Day and the poppy mean, say, for those of other religions, for British Muslims, or for the Catholics of Northern Ireland? The military trappings of the ceremonies at the Cenotaph and at countless war memorials across the country, the choreography, the calling of the Last Post and the dipping of the flags, the hymns and the homilies, and the singing of the national anthem, all signal approval by the Church of England and state. But if the purpose of the day is to affirm a particular view of Britain's history and identity – of what it means to be 'British' – does this risk alienating, or at least detaching, large numbers of citizens?

There are very few people now who bring to the rituals of Remembrance Day the raw grief of recent bereavement: the type of grief that drove the Kiplings to search for their son's grave, or the Lodges to communicate with their dead son's spirit. But this does not mean that its obsolescence is inbuilt. Memory is notoriously slippery, and the strength of the occasion lies, as it has done since 1919, in its mutability, on the way it has assumed the meaning *du jour*, moulding itself or being manipulated to reflect contemporary thinking. Remembrance Day is a testament to the British talent for reinvention, and will continue to evolve, almost certain to be reinvigorated by the centenary of the Second World War in 2039.

Remembrance Day has always responded to the needs of the public and the private. Immediately after the First World War, the home was where the dead were mourned, where a dead soldier's personal effects became objects of devotion. When not obliterated in the same blast that killed their owner, these were returned by parcel to his relatives: a watch, a Bible, a cigarette case, a ring, even a comb, and some tattered scraps of clothing.

Other daily reminders of the dead included photographs fitted into lockets to hang from the neck, or into frames painted with forget-me-nots to grace the bedside table. Mantelpieces and sideboards across the country were turned into shrines, bearing copies of the standard-issue letter of condolence from the king and queen, or the bronze memorial plaque that came to be known as the 'Dead Man's Penny'. Some people planted wildflower seeds from the battlefields in their gardens back home, although few gardens were on the scale of the one created by the publisher Newman Flower. When the war ended, Flower decided 'to make a patch of remembrance in flowers – flowers that would go on and on, as one Summer succeeded another – to those who died'. In September 1919 he went out to the battlefields to gather seeds before the trenches were filled in, and the work of reconstruction began. On the battlefields of the Somme, at La Boisselle and Pozières, he harvested poppy seeds; in what remained of Delville Wood, he spotted lanky blue chicory flowers, whose roots had come to life again despite 'the havoc of four years'; and in the 'untouched trenches' of Vimy Ridge, he found that 'the wild antirrhinum was flowering as if in rejoicing that War had departed'.[5]

Carefully, Newman Flower collected the seeds, labelled them, and brought them home to Kent, where he created his 'War Garden'. To replicate the chalky soil in which the Somme flowers had flourished, he imported a load of chalk from ten miles away to mix with the local loam; and in the spring of 1920 he sowed the seeds. 'A blaze of blossoms came to me with the warming of Summer ... And every Summer they blaze again in remembrance,' he wrote. 'My War Garden is a pageant of scarlet and blue as I write, with the Vimy Ridge yellow antirrhinums as an undergrowth, and the scarlet-eyed creeping flowers from Trônes Wood, and a great flood of red Somme poppies sweeping over the whole.' When an article about Newman Flower's war garden appeared in a national newspaper, he was inundated with requests for seeds from people who had lost relatives on the Somme; he obliged by dispatching little packets of seeds to places as far away as New Zealand. 'And probably they have little gardens of remembrance by now.'[6]

While the public apparatus of the state responded to the needs of people in their search for a meaning to the war, for a story that made sense of the loss, for places and ways to mourn, it was still the little garden patches of remembrance, the household shrines, that provided this for many. The memories of the dead lived on in the inner recesses of the mind of the living.

So, what do you think, during the two-minute silence, as you search for answers, for a story, a connection, a meaning? The power of the silence, and perhaps the reason for its longevity, is that it invites introspection, a space where you can still the many voices competing for attention on Remembrance Day and ignore, if you wish, the language in which the commemorations are framed. Here, you can reflect on war and peace, loss and redemption, past and present, the living and the dead. Like the Cenotaph itself, the silence is a blank screen on which people can project their own emotions, pursue their own meanings, and recognise the value of being alive.

Notes

The following abbreviations are used in the Notes:

AWM	Australian War Memorial Archives, Canberra
BICK	Bickersteth Papers, Churchill College, Cambridge
Bodleian	Bodleian Library, Oxford
CHE	Cecil Papers, Hatfield House
CWGC	Commonwealth War Graves Commission Archive, Maidenhead
GBA	Gertrude Bell Archive, Newcastle University
KCC	Archives of King's College, Cambridge
IWM	Archives of the Imperial War Museum, London
NA	The National Archives, Kew
NAA	National Archives of Australia, Canberra
SAD	Sudan Archive at University of Durham (for Gertrude Bell letters)
SxMs	University of Sussex Special Collections, The Keep, Brighton

PROLOGUE

1 Quoted in Thomas W. Laqueur, *The Work of the Dead: A Cultural History of Mortal Remains* (Princeton University Press, 2015), p. 462.
2 Freud, Sigmund, *Civilisation, War and Death*, ed. John Rickman (Hogarth Press, 1939), p. 4.
3 Freud, *Civilisation, War and Death*, p. 24.

4 Major-General Sir Fabian Ware, 'The Work of the Imperial War Graves Commission', *Journal of the Royal Institute of British Architects* (Third Series), Vol. 36, No. 13, 18 May 1929, p. 509, quoted in Bart Ziino, *A Distant Grief: Australians, War Graves and the Great War* (University of Western Australia Press, 2007), p. 127.

5 The Imperial War Graves Commission's Royal Charter, quoted in Philip Longworth, *The Unending Vigil* (Pen & Sword Books, 2010), p. 28.

6 Michael Durey, 'The Search for Answers on the Missing in the Great War: Lt Hugh Henshall Williamson and His Parents' Struggle with Officialdom', *British Journal for Military History*, Vol. 2, Issue 1, November 2015, www.bjmh.org.uk.

7 Robert Graves, *But It Still Goes On* (1931), pp. 32–3, quoted in Paul Fussell, *The Great War and Modern Memory* (OUP, 1975), p. 207.

8 Durey, 'The Search for Answers on the Missing in the Great War', www.bjmh.org.uk.

9 'Missing or killed: The differential effect on mental health in women in Bosnia and Herzegovina of the confirmed or unconfirmed loss of their husbands' https://psycnet.apa.org/record/2010-17920-003.

10 Laqueur, *Work of the Dead*, p. 366.

11 Laqueur, *Work of the Dead*, p. 449.

12 Martin W. Stoneham, *West Kingsdown Remembers*, 2019, www.stoneham.org.

13 Martin W. Stoneham, *Captain Cecil Thomas Tuff and his Brothers*, 2019, www.stoneham.org.

I IN SEARCH OF THE MISSING: THE ENQUIRY DEPARTMENT

1 *The Evening News* (from November 1914), quoted in *Reports by the Joint War Committee and the Joint War Finance Committee of the British Red Cross Society and the Order of St John of Jerusalem in England* (HMSO, 1921), Part XVI, 323.

2 Quoted in David Crane, *Empires of the Dead* (William Collins, 2013), p. 31.

3 Letter from Violet Cecil to her first husband, Lord Edward Herbert Gascoyne-Cecil, 3 September 1914, Bodleian, VM 62, 207–79; VM 63, 280–359.

4 Letter from Violet Cecil to her first husband, 14 September 1914, Bodleian, VM 62, 207–79; VM 63, 280–359.

5 Letter from Rudyard Kipling to Andrew Macphail, 5 October 1914, in Rudyard Kipling, *The Letters of Rudyard Kipling*, Vol. 4: 1911–19, ed. Thomas Pinney (Macmillan, 1990–2004).

6 Letter from Violet Cecil to Colonel R. G. Gordon Gilmour, 1 October 1914, quoted in J. M. Craster, *Fifteen Rounds a Minute* (Macmillan, 1976), p. 62.

7 Letter from Robert Cecil to his wife, Nellie, 24 September 1914, CHE 5/139.

8 Letter from Violet Cecil to Colonel Gilmour, 1 October 1914, quoted in Craster, *Fifteen Rounds a Minute*, p. 62.

9 Letter from Violet to her first husband, 1 October 1914, Bodleian VM 62, 207–79; VM 63, 280–359.

10 Letter from Robert Cecil to his brother, Edward, 19 October 1914, Cecil Papers, CHE 55/148.

11 Letter from Violet to her first husband, 21 October 1914, Bodleian VM 62, 207–79; VM 63, 280–359.

12 Letter from Violet to her first husband, 23 November 1914, Bodleian VM 62, 207–79; VM 63, 280–359.

13 Letter from Killanin to de Vesci, quoted in Craster, *Fifteen Rounds a Minute*, p. 64.

14 Letter from Violet to her first husband, 3 December 1914, Bodleian VM 62, 207–79; VM 63, 280–359.

15 Letter from Killanin to de Vesci, quoted in Craster, *Fifteen Rounds a Minute*, p. 65.

16 Letter from Killanin to de Vesci, quoted in Craster, *Fifteen Rounds a Minute*, p. 68.

17 Quoted in Tonie and Valmai Holt, *My Boy Jack?: The Search for Kipling's Only Son* (Leo Cooper, 2001), p. 65.

18 Viscount Cecil, *A Great Experiment* (Jonathan Cape, 1941), p. 39.

19 Viscount Cecil, *All the Way* (Hodder and Stoughton, 1949), p. 127.

20 Sir Frederick Treves in *The Red Cross: the Official Journal of the British Red Cross Society*, February 1915.

21 Lionel Earle, *Turn Over the Page* (Hutchinson & Co, 1935), p. 102.

22 Earle, *Turn Over the Page*, p. 110.

23 Letter from Gertrude Bell (GB) to stepmother, Dame Florence Bell, 16 December 1914, GBA.

24 Letter from GB to father, Sir Hugh Bell, 23 December 1914, GBA.

25 Letter from GB to stepmother, 16 December 1914, GBA.

26 Letter from GB to stepmother, 16 December 1914, GBA.

27 Letter from GB to Sir Valentine Chirol, 16 December 1914, SAD 303/4/175.

28 Letter from GB to father, 23 December 1914, GBA.

29 Letter from GB to Sir Valentine Chirol, 12 January 1915, SAD 303/4/179.

30 Letter from GB to stepmother, 16 December, GBA.

31 Letter from GB to father, 30 December 1914, GBA.

32 Letter from GB to stepmother, 6 January 1915, GBA.

33 Letter from GB to stepmother, 12 January 1915, GBA.

34 Letter from GB to Charles 'Dick' Doughty-Wylie, 20 March, GBA.

35 Letter from GB to Charles 'Dick' Doughty-Wylie, 20 March, GBA.

36 Letter from GB to Sir Valentine Chirol, 1 April 1915, SAD 303/4/188.

37 Letter from GB to Sir Valentine Chirol, 1 April 1915, SAD 303/4/188.

38 Letter from GB to 'Dick' Doughty-Wylie, 26 March 1915, GBA.

39 Lord Northcliffe, *At the War* (Hodder and Stoughton, 1916), pp. 136–7.

40 *Reports by the Joint War Committee*, Part XVI, 345–55.

41 Melanie Oppenheimer and Margrette Kleinig, '"There is no trace of him": the Australian Red Cross, its Wounded and Missing Bureaux and the 1915 Gallipoli Campaign', in *First World War Studies*, Vol. 6, No. 3 (November 2015), p. 281.

42 *Continental Daily Mail.*

43 *Reports by the Joint War Committee*, Part XVI, 318–55.

44 *Reports by the Joint War Committee*, Part XVI, 318–55.

45 *Reports by the Joint War Committee*, Part XVI, 318–55.

46 *The Times*, 4 August 1916.

47 Robert Graves, *Goodbye to All That* (Cape, 1929), p. 281.

48 *Daily Graphic*, quoted in Richard van Emden, *The Quick and the Dead* (Bloomsbury, 2011), p. 184.

49 War Office note to newspapers, in January 1915, quoted in van Emden, *Quick and the Dead*, p. 185.

50 Letter from Enquiry Department, 10 April 1917.

51 *Morning Post* quoted in Angus Macnaghten, *Missing* (Dragon Books, 1970), p. 48.

52 Macnaghten, *Missing*, p. 58.

53 *Pall Mall Gazette*, quoted in van Emden, *Quick and the Dead*, p. 177.

54 Macnaghten, *Missing*, p. 39.

55 Rachel Patrick, 'Bereavement and Mourning (New Zealand)', in International Encyclopedia of the First World War, 1914–1918, https://encyclopedia.1914-1918-online.net/home/.

56 Oppenheimer and Kleinig, 'There is no trace of him', p. 282.

57 Harley Granville-Barker, *The Red Cross in France* (Hodder and Stoughton, 1916), Ch. IV.

58 Reports by the Joint War Committee.

59 Letter from British Red Cross Enquiry Department, 5 March 1920, IWM Docs. 14223.

60 Rudyard Kipling, 'The Gardener', in *Debits and Credits* (Macmillan, 1926), p. 405.

61 *Reports by the Joint War Committee*, Part XVI, para 342.

62 Mary Macleod Moore, *The Maple Leaf's Red Cross: The War Story of the Canadian Red Cross Overseas* (Skeffington & Son, 1919), p. 82.

63 *Reports by the Joint War Committee*, Part XXVII, 10.

64 Northcliffe, *At the* War, p. 140.

65 Reports by the Joint War Committee.

66 Northcliffe, *At the War*, p. 141.

67 Northcliffe, *At the War*, p. 142.

68 Vera Brittain, *Testament of Youth* (Gollancz, 1933), p. 441.

69 Eric F. Schneider, 'The British Red Cross Wounded and Missing Enquiry Bureau: A Case of Truth-Telling in the Great War', in *War in History*, 1997, 4 (3), p. 302.

70 Letter from British Red Cross Enquiry Department, 16 January 1919, IWM Docs. 9229.

71 Granville-Barker, *Red Cross in France*, Ch. 4.

72 *The Times History of the War: 1914–1919* (*The Times*, 1921), Vol. 21, p. 219.

73 *The British Prisoner of War* (a monthly journal published by the Central Prisoners of War Committee of the British Red Cross and the Order of St John), 1918, Vol. 1, No. 12, December 1918.

74 *The Times*, 4 January 1919.

75 Northcliffe, *At the War*, p. 148.

2 E. M. FORSTER AND A LABOUR OF LOVE

1 Northcliffe, *At the War*, p. 136.

2 Northcliffe, *At the War*, p. 148.

3 E. M. Forster, letter to mother, 22 December 1916, KCC.

4 Forster, letter to Syed Ross Masood, 29 July 1915, in Mary Lago and
   P. N. Furbank (eds), *Selected Letters of E. M. Forster,* Vol. 1, 1879–1920
   (Collins, 1983–1985), I: 147, p. 224.

5 Forster, 2 August 1915, in Philip Gardner (ed.), *The Journals and
   Diaries of E. M. Forster*, Vol. 2, 'The Locked Diaries', (Pickering &
   Chatto, 2011), p. 55.

6 Forster, letter to mother, 2 October 1915, quoted in Nicola Beauman,
   Morgan: A Biography of E .M. Forster (Hodder and Stoughton, 1993),
   p. 291.

7 Forster, 'The Lost Guide', a retrospective talk given at the 1956
   Aldeburgh Festival of Music and the Arts, in Miriam Allott (ed.),
   Alexandria: A History and a Guide; and Pharos and Pharillon (Deutsch,
   2004), pp. 354–5.

8 Forster, 'The Lost Guide', p. 354.

9 Forster, letter to Virginia Woolf, 17 October 1915, quoted in P. N.
   Furbank, *E. M. Forster: A Life* (Secker & Warburg, 1977–78), Vol.
   2, p. 20.

10 Forster, letter to mother, 19 March 1916, KCC.

11 Forster, 16 June 1911, in Gardner (ed.), *Journals and Diaries*, Vol.
    2, p. 27.

12 Virginia Woolf, letter to Margaret Llewellyn Davies, dated 31 August
    1915, in Nigel Nicolson (ed.), *The Letters of Virginia Woolf*, Vol. 2,
    1912–22, (Hogarth Press, 1976), p. 63.

13 Aïda Borchgrevink, quoted in Furbank, *Forster*, Vol. 2, p. 25.

14 Forster, 'The Lost Guide', p. 355.

15 Forster, *Alexandria: A History and a Guide* (Anchor Books, 1961),
    Introduction, p. xv.

16 Forster, letter to mother, 12 June 1917, KCC.

17 Forster, letter to mother, 14 November 1918, KCC.

18 Forster, 'The Lost Guide', p. 355.

19 Forster, letter to S. R. Masood, 29 December 1915, in Lago and
    Furbank (eds), *Selected Letters*, I: 152, p. 232.

20 Lago and Furbank (eds), *Selected Letters*, I: 152, p. 233.

21 Forster, letter to Malcolm Darling, 6 August 1916, in Lago and
    Furbank (eds), *Selected Letters*, I: 157, p. 238.

22 Forster, 'The Lost Guide', p. 355.

23 Forster, *Alexandria*, p. xv.

24 Forster, letter to mother, 24 November 1915, KCC.

25 E. M. Forster, lecture on A. E. Housman 1950, in Jeffrey M. Heath (ed.), *The Creator as Critic and Other Writings* (Dundurn Press, 2008), p. 128.

26 Forster, letter to mother, February 1916, KCC.

27 Forster, quoted in Furbank, *Forster*, Vol. 2, p. 23.

28 Forster, letter to aunt, dated 4 May 1916, KCC.

29 Forster, letter to mother, dated 24 November 1915, KCC.

30 Forster, letter to mother, dated 19 March 1916, KCC.

31 Forster, 'The Lost Guide', p. 355.

32 J. M. Keynes, quoted in Robert Skidelsky, *John Maynard Keynes: A Biography*, Vol. 1, *Hopes Betrayed, 1883–1920* (Macmillan, 1983), p. 274.

33 Forster, letter to Goldsworthy Lowes Dickinson, dated 28 July 1916, in Lago and Furbank (eds), *Selected Letters*, I: 156, p. 237.

34 Forster, letter to mother, 10 July 1916, quoted in Furbank, *Forster*, Vol. 2, p. 27.

35 Forster, letter to mother, 2 February 1918, KCC.

36 Forster, letter to S. R. Masood, 29 December 1915 in Lago and Furbank (eds), *Selected Letters*, I: 152, p. 232.

37 Forster, letter to Leonard Woolf, 12 February 1916, quoted in Furbank, *Forster*, Vol. 2, p. 25.

38 Forster, letter to Malcolm Darling, 3 February 1916, KCC.

39 Forster, letter to Goldsworthy Lowes Dickinson, 28 July 1916, in Lago and Furbank (eds), *Selected Letters*, I: 156, p. 237.

40 Forster, letter to mother, 4 February 1916, KCC.

41 Forster, letter to mother, 22 April 1917, KCC.

42 Forster, letter to Edward Carpenter, 23 April 1917, quoted in Furbank, *Forster*, Vol. 2, p. 34.

43 Forster, letter to mother, 13 April 1917, KCC.

44 Forster, letter to Goldsworthy Lowes Dickinson, 28 July 1916, in Lago and Furbank (eds), *Selected Letters*, I: 156, p. 237.

45 Forster, letter to Florence Barger, 2 July 1916, in Lago and Furbank (eds), *Selected Letters*, I: 155, p. 236.

46 Forster, letter to Edward Carpenter, 12 April 1916, KCC.

47 Forster, letter to mother, 27 July 1916, KCC.

48 Forster, letter to Goldsworthy Lowes Dickinson, 28 July 1916, in Lago and Furbank (eds), *Selected Letters*, I: 156, p. 237.

49 Forster, letter to Florence Barger, 16 October 1916, in Lago and Furbank (eds), *Selected Letters*, I: 160, p. 243.

50 Forster, letter to Florence Barger, 29 May 1917, in Lago and Furbank (eds), *Selected Letters*, I: 167, p. 256.

51 Forster, letter to Florence Barger, 25 August 1917, in Lago and Furbank (eds), *Selected Letters*, I: 174, p. 269.

52 Forster, letter to Florence Barger, 8 October 1917, in Lago and Furbank (eds), *Selected Letters*, I: 178, p. 274.

53 Forster, letter to Edward Joseph Dent, 1 October 1904, also quoted in Wendy Moffat, *E. M. Forster: A New Life* (Bloomsbury, 2010), p. 77.

54 Forster, letter to Goldsworthy Lowes Dickinson, 28 July 1916, in Lago and Furbank (eds), *Selected Letters*, I: 156, p. 237.

55 Forster, letter to Edward Carpenter, 18 May 1916, also quoted in Furbank, *Forster*, Vol. 2, p. 30.

56 Forster, 'Higher Aspects', *Egyptian Mail*, 5 May 1918, quoted in Furbank, *Forster*, Vol. 2, p. 43.

57 Forster, letter to Edward Carpenter, late October 1917, KCC.

58 Forster, letter to mother, quoted in J. H. Stape, *An E. M. Forster Chronology* (Macmillan, 1993), entry for 4 November 1918, p. 65.

59 Forster, letter to Siegfried Sassoon, 3 August 1918 in Lago and Furbank (eds), *Selected Letters*, I: 190, p. 293.

60 Forster, letter to Florence Barger, quoted in Furbank, *Forster*, Vol. 2, p. 44.

61 Forster, quoted by Frederick Williams, 'E. M. Forster's Alexandrian Quartet', *Hermathena*, Winter 2005, No. 179, p. 167.

62 Forster, *Alexandria* (Anchor Books, 1961), p. 188.

63 Forster, 'The Poetry of C. P. Cavafy', in Miriam Allott (ed.), *Pharos and Pharillon* (Deutsch, 2004), p. 245.

64 Forster, letter to mother, 7 March 1916, KCC.

65 Forster, letter to mother, 11 September 1917, KCC.

66 Forster, letter to mother, 12 June 1917, KCC.

67 Forster, letter to mother, quoted in Stape, *Forster Chronology*, p. 62.

68 Forster, letter to mother, 2 June 1917, KCC.

69 Forster, letter to mother, 13 August 1917, KCC.

70 Forster, letter to mother, 10 October 1917, KCC.

71 Forster, letter to mother, 3 November 1917, KCC.

72 Forster, letter to Percy Lubbock, 14 January 1918, KCC.

73 Forster, letter to Percy Lubbock, 11 February 1918, KCC.

74 Forster, letter to aunt, 23 August 1918, KCC.

75 Forster, letter to mother, quoted in Furbank, *Forster*, Vol. 2, p. 42.

76 Forster, 'Incidents of War' Memoir, 5 December 1915, in Gardner (ed.), *Journals and Diaries*, p. 10.

77 Forster, letter to Goldsworthy Lowes Dickinson, 5 December 1915, KCC.

78 Forster, 'Incidents of War', 3 April 1917, in Gardner (ed.), *Journals and Diaries*, p. 18.

79 Forster, 'Incidents of War', 6 March 1916, in Gardner (ed.), *Journals and Diaries*, p. 13.

80 Forster, 'Incidents of War', 6 May 1915, in Gardner (ed.), *Journals and Diaries*, p. 16.

81 Forster, 'Incidents of War', 21 May 1916, in Gardner (ed.), *Journals and Diaries*, p. 16.

82 Forster, 'Incidents of War', 3 April 1917, in Gardner (ed.), *Journals and Diaries*, p. 18.

83 Forster, 'Incidents of War', 21 May 1916, in Gardner (ed.), *Journals and Diaries*, p. 16.

84 Forster, 'Incidents of War', 21 March 1916, in Gardner (ed.), *Journals and Diaries*, p. 15.

85 Forster, 'Incidents of War', 27 September 1916, in Gardner (ed.), *Journals and Diaries*, p. 17.

86 Forster, letter to mother, dated February 1918, KCC.

87 Forster, letter to Goldsworthy Lowes Dickinson, 5 April 1916, KCC.

88 Forster, letter to mother, 3 July 1917, KCC.

89 Forster, letter to mother, 19 January 1916, KCC.

90 Forster, letter to Siegfried Sassoon, 2 May 1918 in Lago and Furbank (eds), *Selected Letters*, I: 188, p. 289.

91 Forster, letter to mother, November 1916, KCC.

92 Forster, letter to George Barger, 16 May 1917 in Lago and Furbank (eds), *Selected Letters*, I: 166, p. 254.

93 Forster, letter to Goldsworthy Lowes Dickinson, 9 October 1916, KCC.

94 Forster, letter to Bertrand Russell, 28 July 1917, quoted in Beauman, *Morgan*, p. 292.

95 'Incidents of War' Memoir, 8 July 1917, p. 18.

96 Forster, letter to Virginia Woolf, 15 April 1916 in Lago and Furbank (eds), *Selected Letters*, I: 154, p. 234.

97 Forster, letter to Goldsworthy Lowes Dickinson, 2 December 1918, KCC.

98 Forster, letter to Goldsworthy Lowes Dickinson, 5 May 1917, in Lago and Furbank (eds), *Selected Letters*, I: 165, pp. 252–3.

99 Virginia Woolf, *The Diary of Virginia Woolf*, Vol. 2 (1920–24), ed.,
     Anne Olivier Bell (Hogarth Press, 1978), 12 March 1922, p. 171.

3 THE SEARCH FOR A NATIONAL SHRINE: THE CENOTAPH AND THE TOMB OF THE UNKNOWN WARRIOR

1 David Railton, 'The Origin of the Unknown Warrior's Grave', *Our
    Empire*, November 1931, Vol. 7, No. 8, p. 34, in 'The Unknown
    Warrior: A symposium of articles on how the Unknown Warrior was
    chosen', IWM, LBY K60791.
2 *Supplement to the London Gazette*, 25 November 1916, quoted in
    Andrew Richards, *The Flag: The Story of Revd David Railton MC and
    the Tomb of the Unknown Warrior* (Casemate, 2017), p. 84.
3 Private Papers of Revd. D. Railton, IWM Docs.4760.
4 Railton, 'Origin of the Unknown Warrior's Grave'.
5 David Railton, *The Story of a Padre's Flag – Told by the Flag*, from the
    private papers of the Railton family, by the kind permission of David
    Railton QC.
6 Railton, *The Story of a Padre's Flag*.
7 Railton, 'Origin of the Unknown Warrior's Grave'.
8 Railton, 'Origin of the Unknown Warrior's Grave'.
9 Railton, 'Origin of the Unknown Warrior's Grave'.
10 Railton, 'Origin of the Unknown Warrior's Grave'.
11 Dean Ryle to Lord Stamfordham, 4 October 1920, RA GV O1637/1,
     quoted in Michael Gavaghan, *The Story of the British Unknown
     Warrior* (M&L Publications, 1995), p. 10.
12 Stamfordham to Ryle, 7 October 1920, RA GV O1637/2, also at
     Westminster Abbey 63774.
13 Railton, *The Story of a Padre's Flag*.
14 Railton, 'Origin of the Unknown Warrior's Grave'.
15 Gavin Stamp, *The Memorial to the Missing of the Somme* (Profile,
     2006), p. 42.
16 *The Times*, 26 July 1919.
17 Edwin Lutyens, *Journal of Remembrance*, quoted in Allan Greenberg,
     'Lutyens's Cenotaph', in *Journal of the Society of Architectural
     Historians*, Vol. 28, No. 1 (March 1989), p. 10.
18 *Daily Mail*, 23 July 1919, p. 5.
19 *Church Times*, 21 November 1919, quoted in Neil Hanson, *The Unknown
     Soldier: The Story of the Missing of the Great War* (Doubleday, 2005), p. 418.

20 Railton, 'Origin of the Unknown Warrior's Grave'.

21 Railton, *The Story of a Padre's Flag*.

22 Cabinet Memorial Services (November 11) Committee, Westminster Abbey 58671B.

23 Railton, 'Origin of the Unknown Warrior's Grave'.

24 Dean Ryle to David Railton, dated 25 October 1920, quoted in Richards, *The Flag*, p. 170.

25 Railton, 'Origin of the Unknown Warrior's Grave'.

26 David Railton to Ruby Railton, dated 19 January 1917, quoted in Richards, *The Flag*, p. 2.

27 Private Papers of Brigadier General L. J. Wyatt, IWM Docs.14122.

28 Marshal Foch, quoted in Gavaghan, *The Story of the British Unknown Warrior*, p. 30.

29 *Daily Telegraph*, 11 November, 1936, p. 6.

30 *The Times*, 10 November 1920.

31 IWM EPH 3232; the story is also told in van Emden, *Quick and the Dead*, p. 266.

32 *The Times*, 11 November 1920, quoted in Richards, *The Flag*, p. 188.

33 *The Times*, 12 November 1920, p. 25.

34 Gavaghan, *The Story of the British Unknown Warrior*, p. 50.

35 *The Times*, 12 November 1919, p. 15; Geoff Dyer, *The Missing of the Somme* (Penguin, 1995), p. 20.

36 King's statement, quoted in Juliet Nicolson, *The Great Silence* (John Murray, 2009), p. 177.

37 *The Times*, 12 November 1920, Armistice Day Supplement, pp. i–iii, quoted in Geoff Dyer, *The Missing of the Somme* (Penguin, 1995), p. 22.

38 *Daily Mail*, 12 November 1920, p. 7.

39 *Manchester Evening News*, 11 November 1920.

40 *Daily Telegraph*, 12 November 1920, p. 14.

41 Fabian Ware, *The Immortal Heritage* (The University Press, 1937), p. 27.

42 *Daily Mail*, 12 November 1919, quoted in Hanson, *The Unknown Soldier*, p. 418.

43 *The Times*, 12 November 1920, Armistice Day Supplement, pp. i–iii, quoted in Richards, *The Flag*, p. 195.

44 Stamfordham to Ryle, Westminster Abbey 58675.

45 Railton, 'Origin of the Unknown Warrior's Grave'.

46 *Daily Mail*, 12 November 1920, p. 7.

47 'The Story of a Padre's Flag', *The Times*, 10 November 1920 p. 14.

48 *Daily Chronicle*, 12 November 1920, quoted in van Emden, *The Quick and the Dead*, p. 266.

49 *The Times*, 10 November 1920, quoted in Hanson, *The Unknown Soldier*, p. 461.

50 *Manchester Evening News*, 11 November 1920.

51 *The Times*, 12 November 1920, quoted in van Emden, *The Quick and the Dead*, p. 264.

52 *The Times*, 16 November 1920, p. 14.

53 *The Times*, 12 November 1920, p. 25.

54 *Daily Mail*, 12 November 1920, p. 8.

55 Ronald Blythe, *The Age of Illusion: England in the Twenties and Thirties* (Hamish Hamilton, 1963), p. 10.

56 'The Silence and After', *The Times*, 12 November 1921, quoted in Richards, *The Flag*, p. 216.

57 *The Times*, 11 November 1921, p. 11.

58 *The Times*, 11 November 1921, p. 11.

59 Railton, *The Story of a Padre's Flag*.

60 Railton, *The Story of a Padre's Flag*.

61 Railton, *The Story of a Padre's Flag*.

62 *The Times*, 14 November 1921, p. 5.

63 *The Times*, 14 November 1921, p. 5.

64 *The Times*, 12 November 1920, Supplement, p. 27.

65 'Vicar's Pose as Tramp', *Evening Standard*, 19 November 1921, p. 3.

66 *Liverpool Echo*, 11 November 1935, quoted in Richards, *The Flag*, p. 169.

67 David Lloyd George, quoted in Allan Greenberg, 'Lutyens's Cenotaph', *Journal of the Society of Architectural Historians*, Vol. 28, No. 1 (March 1989), p. 11.

68 Herbert Jeans, 'In Death's Cathedral Palace', *British Legion Journal*, Vol. 9, No. 5, November 1929, IWM LBY K60791.

69 Railton, 'Origin of the Unknown Warrior's Grave'.

4 RUDYARD KIPLING AND THE WAR GRAVES COMMISSION:
THE SEARCH FOR A PLACE TO GRIEVE

1 John Bird, quoted in Frederick, Earl of Birkenhead, *Rudyard Kipling* (Weidenfeld and Nicolson, 1978), p. 268, Milner papers, Bodleian, VM 44 C396/36/2.

2 Rudyard Kipling, *The Irish Guards in the Great War* (Doubleday, Page & Company, 1923), Vol. 1, p. 109.

3 Lt. Col. L. Butler to Rudyard Kipling, 2 October 1915, Lieutenant John Kipling, NA, WO339/53917.

4 Statement of Sgt Kinnelly, 5 November 1915, Lieutenant John Kipling, NA, WO339/53917.

5 Rudyard Kipling to R. D. Blumenfeld, 6 October 1915, *Letters*, Vol. 4, p. 338.

6 Rudyard Kipling, 'Epitaphs of the War', *Rudyard Kipling's Verse* (Hodder and Stoughton, 1940), p. 387.

7 Rudyard Kipling to Andrew Macphail, 5 October 1914, *Letters*, Vol. 4, p. 259.

8 Quoted in Tonie and Valmai Holt, *My Boy Jack?*, p. 66.

9 Quoted in Tonie and Valmai Holt, *My Boy Jack?*, p. 66., VM27 C102/197/1.

10 Rudyard Kipling to Walter Page, 5 October 1915, *Letters*, Vol. 4, p. 337.

11 Caroline Starr Kipling to mother, 12 April 1916, quoted in Tonie and Valmai Holt, *My Boy Jack?*, p. 126.

12 Kipling, 'The Gardener', p. 405.

13 Caroline Starr Kipling to Violet Cecil, VM 44 C396.

14 Caroline Starr Kipling to Violet, VM 44 C396.

15 Rudyard Kipling to Colonel Lionel Dunsterville, 12 November 1915, *Letters*, Vol. 4, pp. 344–5.

16 Quoted in Martin Seymour-Smith, *Rudyard Kipling* (Queen Anne Press, 1989), p. 336.

17 Quoted in Tonie and Valmai Holt, *My Boy Jack?*, p. 99.

18 'Obituary of Mrs Alice Macdonald Fleming', *Kipling Journal*, J89 (April 1949), p. 7.

19 Quoted in Seymour-Smith, *Rudyard Kipling*, p. 333.

20 *Kipling Journal*, J204 (December 1977), p. 4.

21 Rudyard Kipling, *Something of Myself* (Macmillan and Co., 1937), p. 215.

22 Rudyard Kipling, 'En-dor' in *Rudyard Kipling's Verse* (Hodder and Stoughton, 1940), pp. 366–7.

23 Caroline Starr Kipling to Violet Cecil, 1 September 1916, VM44 C396/40.

24 Rudyard Kipling, 'My Boy Jack', in *Rudyard Kipling's Verse*, p. 216.

25 War Office correspondence, Lieutenant John Kipling, NA, WO339/53917.

26 Colonel Vesey, quoted in Tonie and Valmai Holt, *My Boy Jack?*, p. 162.

27 War Office correspondence, Lieutenant John Kipling, NA, WO339/53917.

28 Kipling, 'The Gardener', p. 406.

29 Kipling to W. J. Harding, 1897, quoted in Tonie and Valmai Holt, *My Boy Jack?*, p. 21.

30 Caroline Starr Kipling to mother, quoted in Tonie and Valmai Holt, *My Boy Jack?*, p. 60.

31 Caroline Starr Kipling to mother, quoted in Tonie and Valmai Holt, *My Boy Jack?*, p. 77.

32 Caroline Kipling's Diary, quoted in Harry Ricketts, *The Unforgiving Minute: A Life of Rudyard Kipling* (Chatto & Windus, 1999), p. 323.

33 *The Kipling Journal*.

34 John Kipling to parents, quoted in Tonie and Valmai Holt, *My Boy Jack?*, p. 92.

35 Rudyard Kipling, 'Epitaphs of the War' *Rudyard Kipling's Verse*, p. 390.

36 Caroline Kipling's Diary, quoted in Birkenhead, *Rudyard Kipling* (Weidenfeld and Nicolson, 1978), p. 287.

37 Dorothy Ponton, *Rudyard Kipling at Home and at Work* (1953), p. 27.

38 Rudyard Kipling to Dunsterville, 9 July 1919, *Letters*, Vol. 4, p. 560.

39 Douglas Proby to Rudyard Kipling, 8 January 1917, quoted in Ricketts, *Rudyard Kipling*, p. 334.

40 Ponton, *Rudyard Kipling*, p. 33.

41 Kipling, *Irish Guards*, Vol. 2, p. 4.

42 Kipling, *Irish Guards*, Vol. 1, pp. v–vi.

43 Ponton, *Rudyard Kipling*, p. 34.

44 Caroline Kipling, *Extracts from the Private Diaries of Mrs Carrie Kipling*, 27 July 1922, Book 4 (1919–23, ff.11), SxMs41/2/2.

45 *The Kipling Journal*, J324 (December 2007), p. 18.

46 Kipling, *Irish Guards*, Vol. 2, p. 14.

47 Kipling, *Irish Guards*, Vol. 2, pp. 12–13.

48 Robert Graves, *Goodbye to All That* (Jonathan Cape, 1929), p. 196.

49 Fabian Ware to Rudyard Kipling, 26 January 1926, quoted in Tonie and Valmai Holt, *My Boy Jack?*, p. 187.

50 *Spring Report*, 1915, quoted in Crane, *Empires of the Dead*, p. 41, CWGC MU1.

51 Fabian Ware, 2 March 1915, quoted in Longworth, *Unending Vigil*, p. 6.

52 Field Marshal Haig to War Office, March 1915, quoted in Crane, *Empires of the Dead*, p. 48, CWGC/1/1/1/44 (SDC 22).

53 Ware to Robert Cecil, 5 May 1915, quoted in Crane, *Empires of the Dead*, pp. 72–3, CWGC/1/1/1/26 (CWGC GRC1).

54 Memorandum, 1 February 1918, quoted in Crane, *Empires of the Dead*, p. 86, CWGC/1/1/1/38/1 (ADD3/1/3).

55 Ware's memorandum, 15 March 1917, quoted in Stamp, *Memorial to the Missing*, p. 76, CWGC/1/1/1/44 (SDC 22).

56 Field Marshal Haig to War Office, March 1915, quoted in Crane, *Empires of the Dead*, p. 48.

57 Edwin Lutyens to his wife, Lady Emily, 12 July 1917, in Clayre Percy and Jane Ridley (eds), *The Letters of Edwin Luytens to his wife Emily* (William Collins Sons & Co, 1985), p. 350.

58 A. W. Hill, quoted in Crane, *Empires of the Dead*, p. 103.

59 Frederick Kenyon, *War Graves: How the Cemeteries Abroad Will Be Designed* (HMSO, 1918), p. 4.

60 Statement issued by the IWGC in January 1918, quoted in Longworth, *Unending Vigil*, p. 33.

61 Caroline Kipling, *Extracts*, dated 16 August 1926, Book 4 (1919–23, ff.11), SxMs41/2/2.

62 Sir Reginald Blomfield, *Memoirs of an Architect* (Macmillan, 1932), p. 180.

63 Rudyard Kipling to the Commissioners, quoted in *The Times*, 28 November 1918.

64 *Petition to the Prince of Wales*, 1919, quoted in Crane, *Empires of the Dead*, p. 149, CWGC/1/1/5/14 (ADD4/2/7).

65 *National Review* 76, 3 July 1920, quoted in Laqueur, *Work of the Dead*, p. 471.

66 Lord Hugh Cecil, quoted in Longworth, *Unending Vigil*, p. 48.

67 Rudyard Kipling to Col. H. F. E. Lewin, 3 May 1920, *Letters*, Vol. 5, p. 17.

68 Letter from Rudyard Kipling to William Burdett-Coutts, MP, read out to the House of Commons and published in Hansard, 4 May 1920, quoted in Crane, *Empires of the Dead*, p. 157.

69 Private Papers of J. Sams, IWM Docs.12541.

70 Rudyard Kipling, 'The Silent World', in *The War Graves of the Empire* (The Times Publishing Company Ltd., 1928), p. 8.

71 Kipling, 'The Silent World', p. 8.

72 Kipling, 'The Silent World', p. 8.

73 Herbert Baker, *Architecture and Personalities* (Country Life, 1944), p. 92.

74 *The Times*, 2 September 1920, quoted in Crane, *Empires of the Dead*, p. 171.

75 Baker, *Architecture and Personalities*, p. 88.

76 Blomfield, *Memoirs*, p. 176.

77 Rudyard Kipling, *The Graves of the Fallen* (HMSO, 1919), p. 5.

78 Fabian Ware, *The Immortal Heritage* (Cambridge University Press, 1937), p. 56.

79 Ware, *Immortal Heritage*, p. 56.

80 Ware, *Immortal Heritage*, pp. 16–20.

81 Caroline Kipling's Diary, quoted in David Gilmour, *The Long Recessional: The Imperial Life of Rudyard Kipling* (John Murray, 2002), p. 280.

82 Rudyard Kipling, quoted in Longworth, *Unending Vigil*, p. 79.

83 Rudyard Kipling, *Irish Guards*, Vol. 1, p. 12.

84 Rudyard Kipling, *Rudyard Kipling's Motor Tours*, 11 May 1922, March 1911–August 1926, SxMs38/2/3/2/2/8.

85 Caroline Kipling, *Extracts*, 11 May 1922, Book 4 (1919–23, ff.11), SxMs41/2.

86 Rudyard Kipling, *Motor Tours*, 11 May 1922, March 1911–August 1926, SxMs38/2/3/2/2/8.

87 Rudyard Kipling, *Motor Tours*, 13 May 1922.

88 Frank Fox, *The King's Pilgrimage* (Hodder & Stoughton, 1922), Ch. IV.

89 Rudyard Kipling, *Motor Tours*, 13 May, March 1911–August 1926, SxMs38/2/3/2/2/8.

90 Fox, Frank, *The King's Pilgrimage* (Hodder & Stoughton, 1922).

91 Rudyard Kipling, *Motor Tours*, 31 August 1924, March 1911–August 1926. SxMs38/2/3/2/2/8.

92 Rudyard Kipling, *Motor Tours*, 13 March 1925, March 1911–August 1926, SxMs38/2/3/2/2/8.

93 Rudyard Kipling to Rider Haggard, 14 March 1925, *Rudyard Kipling to Rider Haggard: The Record of a Friendship* (Hutchinson, 1965), p. 152.

94 Kipling to Haggard, dated 19 March 1925, *The Record of a Friendship*, p. 156.

95 *The Kipling Journal*, J306 (June 2003), p. 28.

96 Kipling, 'The Gardener', p. 405.

97 *The Pilgrim's Guide to the Ypres Salient* (Talbot House, 1920), p. 66.

98 Longworth, *Unending Vigil*, p. 78.

99 Blomfield, *Memoirs*, p. 191.

100 Blomfield, *Memoirs*, p. 191.

101 Siegfried Sassoon, 'On Passing the New Menin Gate', *Collected Poems, 1908–1956* (Faber and Faber, 1961), p. 188.

102 Quoted in Michèle Barrett, 'Subalterns at War: First World War Colonial Forces and the Politics of the IWGC', *Interventions*, 9:3, pp. 451–74.

103 Barrett, 'Subalterns at War'.

104 Barrett, 'Subalterns at War'.

105 Michèle Barrett, 'Sent Missing in Africa', briefing paper for 'The Unremembered'.

106 Barrett, 'Sent Missing in Africa'.

107 John Kipling to his parents, 19 September 1915, quoted in Tonie and Valmai Holt, *My Boy Jack?*, p. 91.

5 SEARCHING FOR SOLACE IN THE AFTERLIFE

1 Sir Oliver Lodge, *Raymond, or Life and Death* (Methuen, 1916), p. 35.

2 Lodge, *Raymond*, p. 72.

3 Lodge, *Raymond*, p. 9.

4 W. P. Jolly, *Sir Oliver Lodge* (Constable, 1974), p. 201.

5 Lodge, *Raymond*, pp. 75–7.

6 Lodge, *Raymond*, p. 79.

7 Lodge, *Raymond*, pp. 45–59.

8 Lodge, *Raymond*, p. 10.

9 Lodge, *Raymond*, pp. 86–7.

10 Gladys Osborne Leonard, *My Life in Two Worlds* (Cassell & Co, 1931), foreword by Sir Oliver Lodge, p. vii; Gladys acknowledges debt, p. 59.

11 Leonard, *My Life in Two Worlds*, pp. 52–4.

12 Lodge, *Raymond*, p. 183.

13 Lodge, *Raymond*, p. 126.

14 Lodge, *Raymond*, p. 133.

15 Lodge, *Raymond*, p. 107.
16 Lodge, *Raymond*, pp. 107–8.
17 Lodge, *Raymond*, p. 108.
18 Lodge, *Raymond*, p. 109.
19 Lodge, *Raymond*, pp. 250–55.
20 Lodge, *Raymond*, pp. 250–55.
21 Lodge, *Raymond*, pp. 250–55.
22 Lodge, *Raymond*, p. 198.
23 Lodge, *Raymond*, 24 March 1916, p. 263.
24 Lodge, *Raymond*, 3 March 1916, p. 249.
25 Lodge, *Raymond*, p. 279.
26 Lodge, *Raymond*, Part III.
27 Lodge, *Raymond*, pp. vii–viii, quoted in David Cannadine, 'War and Death, Grief and Mourning in Modern Britain', in Joachim Whaley (ed.), *Mirrors of Mortality: Studies in the Social History of Death* (Europa, 1981), p. 229.
28 Sir Oliver Lodge, *Letters from Sir Oliver Lodge, Psychical, Religious, Scientific and Personal, Compiled and Annotated by J. Arthur Hill* (Cassell and Co. 1932), p. 108.
29 *The Occult Review*, xxiii (January 1918), quoted in J. M. Winter, 'Spiritualism and the First World War', in R. W. Davis and R. J. Helmstadter (eds), *Religion and Irreligion in Victorian Society* (Routledge, 1992), p. 189.
30 Lodge, *Raymond*, Part III.
31 Lodge, *Raymond*, Part III.
32 Lodge, *Raymond*, Part III.
33 Lodge, *Raymond*, Part III.
34 Sir Oliver Lodge, *Past Years: An Autobiography* (Hodder and Stoughton, 1931), p. 348.
35 Lodge, *Past Years*, p. 111.
36 Sir Oliver Lodge, *Ether and Reality: A Series of Discourses on the Many Functions of the Ether of Space* (Hodder and Stoughton, 1925).
37 Quoted by Cannadine in 'War and Death', p. 228.
38 Sir Oliver Lodge, *Proceedings of the Society for Psychical Research*, 30 June 1884, quoted by Jolly, *Lodge*, p. 57.
39 Lodge, *Past Years*, p. 279.
40 Janet Oppenheim, *The Other World: Spiritualism and Psychical Research in England, 1850–1914* (Cambridge University Press, 1985), p. 376.

41 *Daily Mail*, 24 January 1917, quoted in E. S. Turner, *Dear Old Blighty* (Michael Joseph, 1980), pp. 143–4.

42 Elliott O'Donnell, *The Menace of Spiritualism* (T. Werner Laurie, 1920), pp. 118 and 169.

43 Charles Arthur Mercier, *Spiritualism and Sir Oliver Lodge* (Mental Culture Enterprise, 1917), p. 26.

44 Sir Edward Poulton, *The Life of Ronald Poulton* (Sidgwick & Jackson, 1919), quoted in van Emden, *Quick and the Dead*, p. 203.

45 Sigmund Freud, 'Our Attitude to Death', quoted in Cannadine, 'War and Death', p. 218.

46 J. Hewat McKenzie, *If a Soldier Dies, Shall He Live Again?* (London, 1915).

47 J. Neville Figgis, quoted in J. M. Winter, *Sites of Memory, Sites of Mourning: The Great War in European Cultural History* (Cambridge University Press, 1995), p. 63.

48 Mercier, *Spiritualism and Sir Oliver Lodge*, p. 12.

49 Rene Kollar, *Searching for Raymond: Anglicanism, Spiritualism, and Bereavement Between the Two World Wars* (Lexington Books, 2000), p. 5.

50 Geoffrey K. Nelson, *Spiritualism and Society* (Routledge & Kegan Paul, 1969), p. 156.

51 Russell Miller, *The Adventures of Arthur Conan Doyle* (Harvill Secker, 2008), p. 367.

52 Jon Lellenberg et al. (eds), *Arthur Conan Doyle: A Life in Letters* (HarperPress, 2007), p. 629.

53 Arthur Conan Doyle, *The New Revelation* (Hodder and Stoughton, 1918), quoted in Kelvin I. Jones, *Conan Doyle and the Spirits: the Spiritualist Career of Sir Arthur Conan Doyle* (Aquarian, 1989), p. 59.

54 Conan Doyle, *The New Revelation*, quoted in Jones, *Conan Doyle*, p. 119.

55 Arthur Conan Doyle, *The History of Spiritualism* (Cassell, 1926), quoted by Winter, 'Spiritualism and the First World War', in Davis and Helmstadter (eds), *Religion and Irreligion*, p. 188.

56 Arthur Conan Doyle, dated 9 May 1917, in Lellenberg (ed.), *A Life in Letters*, p. 625.

57 Leonard, *Two Worlds*, quoted in Jones, *Conan Doyle*, pp. 134–6.

58 Conan Doyle, *The New Revelation*, quoted in Michael Coren, *Conan Doyle* (Bloomsbury, 1995), p. 155.

59 Conan Doyle, *The New Revelation*, quoted in Winter, 'Spiritualism and the First World War', p. 188.

60 *Sunday Express*, quoted by Miller, *Conan Doyle*, p. 374.

61 'The White Insignia', *Light*, special supplement, 3 May 1919.

62 'The White Insignia'.

63 'The White Insignia'.

64 *Evening Standard*.

65 Revd John Lamond, *Arthur Conan Doyle: A Memoir* (John Murray, 1931), p. 168.

66 Sir Arthur Conan Doyle, quoted in Georgina Byrne, *Modern Spiritualism and the Church of England, 1850–1939* (Boydell Press, 2010), p. 74.

67 Van Emden, *Quick and the Dead*, p. 198.

68 Sir Oliver Lodge, 31 August 1923, in Hill (ed.), *Letters*, p. 181.

69 Sir Arthur Conan Doyle, *Memories and Adventures* (Hodder and Stoughton, 1924), p. 395, quoted in Coren, *Conan Doyle*, p. 154.

70 Walter Cook, *Reflections on 'Raymond'* (Grant Richards, 1917), p. 18.

71 Lodge, *Past Years*, p. 301.

72 Norman Lewis, *Jackdaw Cake: an Autobiography* (Hamish Hamilton, 1985), pp. 43–4.

73 Lilian Walbrook, *The Case of Lester Coltman* (Hutchinson & Co., 1924), Introduction, pp. ix–xvii.

74 Walbrook, *Case of Lester Coltman*, Part I.

75 Walbrook, *Case of Lester Coltman*, Part III.

76 Walbrook, *Case of Lester Coltman*, Part IV.

77 Wellesley Tudor Pole, *Private Dowding: the Personal Story of a Soldier Killed in Battle* (Spearman, 1966).

78 Jolly, *Lodge*, p. 234.

6 PILGRIMAGE: THE SEARCH FOR MEANING

1 *The Marne Battle-fields: 1914* (Michelin et Cie, 1917), p. 2.

2 James O. Coop, *A Short Guide to the Battlefields* (Daily Post, 1921), p. 12.

3 *Pilgrim's Guide to the Ypres Salient*, p. 77.

4 John W. Dafoe, *Over the Canadian Battlefields* (Thomas Allen, 1919), pp. 13, 16 and 31.

5 Alice Douglas-Pennant, *The Ypres Times*, Vol. 1, No. 2, January 1922, p. 38.

6 Joyce Kilmer, *Scribner's Magazine*, September 1918 (Charles Scribner's Sons, 1887–1939), p. 351.

7   Annie Kilburn Kilmer, *Leaves from My Life* (Frye Publishing Co, 1925), pp. 130–3.

8   Henry Williamson, *Contributions to the Weekly Dispatch* (J. Gregory, 1969), p. 56.

9   Vera Brittain, *Testament of Youth* (V. Gollancz, 1933), Chapter 10.

10 Wilfrid Ewart, *Scots Guard* (Rich & Cowan, 1934), Chapter 9.

11 Findlay Muirhead, *Belgium and the Western Front* (Macmillan, 1920), lxiii.

12 Thomas A. Lowe, *The Western Battlefields* (Gale & Polden, 1921), pp. 3–4.

13 Enid Bagnold, *The Happy Foreigner* (William Heinemann, 1954), p. 187.

14 Findlay Muirhead, *Belgium and the Western Front* (Macmillan, 1920), lxxiii.

15 *Marne Battle-fields*, p. 2.

16 *Ypres and the Battles of Ypres* (Michelin et Cie, 1919).

17 Muirhead, *Belgium and the Western Front*, v.

18 Atherton Fleming, *How to See the Battlefields* (Cassell & Co, 1919), Foreword.

19 Lowe, *The Western Battlefields*, p. 2.

20 Coop, *Guide to the Battlefields*, p. 8.

21 Fleming, *Battlefields*, Foreword.

22 *Pilgrim's Guide to the Ypres Salient*, Introduction.

23 W. Ewart, 'Aubers Revisited', *Household Brigade Magazine* (1921), p. 15, quoted in David W. Lloyd, *Battlefield Tourism: Pilgrimage and the Commemoration of the Great War in Britain, Australia and Canada* (Bloomsbury, 2014), p. 117.

24 Lowe, *The Western Battlefields*, Introduction, ix.

25 Sir William Pulteney and Beatrix Brice, *The Immortal Salient* (Ypres League, 1925), p. 20.

26 Beckles Willson, *Ypres: The Holy Ground of British Arms* (C. Beyaert, 1920), p. xiii.

27 Willson, *Ypres: The Holy Ground of British Arms*, xiii.

28 *The Ypres Times*, Vol. 1, No. 3, April 1922, p. 67.

29 Coop, *Guide*, p. 68.

30 Reports quoted in Lloyd, *Battlefield Tourism*, p. 96.

31 *Over There: A Little Guide for Pilgrims to Ypres, the Salient, and Talbot House, Poperinghe* (Toc H, 1935), p. 15.

32 *Over There*, p. 16.

33 *Pilgrim's Guide to the Ypres Salient*, p. 5.

34 Pulteney and Brice, *The Immortal Salient*, Foreword.

35 *The Times*, 29 July 1922, quoted by Mark Connelly and Stefan Goebel, *Ypres* (OUP, 2018), p. 70.

36 R. H. Mottram, 'What does Ypres mean to me?', *The Ypres Times*, Vol. 8, No. 8, October 1937, p. 236.

37 Quoted in Lloyd, *Battlefield Tourism*, p. 36.

38 Quoted in Mark Connelly, 'The Ypres League and the Commemoration of the Ypres Salient', *War in History*, Vol. 16, No. 1, January 2009, p. 60.

39 'Primary Objects of the League', *The Ypres Times*.

40 *The Ypres Times*, Vol. 1, Special Pilgrimage Number, August 1922, p. 15.

41 Henry Williamson, *The Wet Flanders Plain* (Faber & Faber, 1929), p. 58.

42 Wilfrid Ewart, 'After Four Years: The Old Road to Ypres', *The Cornhill Magazine* XLIX (December 1920), p. 739.

43 Quoted in Connelly, 'The Ypres League and the Commemoration of the Ypres Salient', p. 63.

44 *St Barnabas Pilgrimages (Ypres-The Somme) 1923* (St Barnabas, 1924), p. 20.

45 *St Barnabas Pilgrimages*.

46 *St Barnabas Pilgrimages*, p. 2

47 P. B. Clayton, *Tales of Talbot House* (Toc H, 1934), pp. 20–1.

48 *Pilgrim's Guide to the Ypres Salient*, p. 87.

49 Tresham Lever, *Clayton of Toc H* (John Murray, 1971), p. 61.

50 *Pilgrim's Guide to the Ypres Salient*, p. 81.

51 *Pilgrim's Guide to the Ypres Salient*, p. 81.

52 Lever, *Clayton*, p. 147.

53 *Morning Post*, 6 August 1928, quoted in Lloyd, *Battlefield Tourism*, p. 33.

54 Ewart, *Cornhill Magazine* XLIX (December 1920), p. 738.

55 R. H. Mottram, *Through the Menin Gate* (Chatto & Windus, 1932), p. 2.

56 Williamson, *Wet Flanders Plain*, p. 19.

57 Williamson, *Wet Flanders Plain*, pp. 139–40.

58 Williamson, *Wet Flanders Plain*, pp. 143–8.

59 Private Papers of H. Harris, 'The Gallipoli Pilgrimage', IWM Docs.9355.

60 *Croydon Pilgrimage* (St Barnabas Society), p. 10, quoted in Lloyd, *Battlefield Tourism*, p. 146.

61 *Sunday Mail* (Brisbane), 22 January 1933; and *Mirror* (Perth), 4 February 1933.

62 Tony Walter, 'War Grave Pilgrimage', in Ian Reader and Tony Walter (eds), *Pilgrimage in Popular Culture* (Macmillan, 1993), p. 77.

63 *A Souvenir of the Battlefields Pilgrimage (August 1928)* (British Legion, 1929), quoted in Walter, 'War Grave Pilgrimage', p. 76.

64 Samuel Bickersteth, *Morris Bickersteth, 1891–1916, by his father* (CUP, 1931), p. 115.

65 John Bickersteth (ed.), *The Bickersteth Diaries, 1914–1918* (Leo Cooper, 1995), p. 95.

66 Ella Bickersteth's diary, 23 July 1916, Bodleian, Mss. Eng. D. 3024.

67 Bickersteth (ed.), *Diaries, 1914–1918*, p. 169.

68 BICK1/Vol. 10.

69 BICK1/Vol. 10.

70 BICK1/Vol. 10.

71 BICK1/Vol. 10.

72 Miscellaneous papers of Samuel and Ella Bickersteth, Bodleian, Mss. Eng. D. 6418.

73 Papers of W. H. Newbery, IWM Docs.16417.

74 Papers of W. H. Newbery, IWM Docs. 16417.

75 *Daily Express*, 23 September 1919, quoted by Lloyd, *Battlefield Tourism*, p. 41.

76 E. Swinton (ed.), *Twenty Years after: The Battlefields of 1914–18* (Newnes, 1936–8), quoted in Lloyd, *Battlefield Tourism*, p. 42.

77 E. F. Williams, *The Ypres Times*, Vol. 3, No. 6, April 1927, p. 153.

78 Stephen Graham, *The Challenge of the Dead* (London, 1930), quoted in George Mosse, *Fallen Soldiers: Reshaping the Memory of the World Wars* (OUP, 1990), p. 154.

79 John Gibbons, *Roll On, Next War!* (Frederick Muller, 1935).

80 Wilfrid Ewart, 'Vimy Heights to Aubers Ridge', *The Ypres Times*, Vol. 1, No. 4, July 1922, p. 94.

81 Rowland Feilding, *War Letters to a Wife* (Medici Society, 1929), p. 367.

82 Williamson, *The Wet Flanders Plain*, p. 70.

83 Christopher Isherwood, *Kathleen and Frank* (Methuen, 1971), p. 358.

84 Gibbons, *Roll On, Next War!*, p. 134.

85 R. H. Mottram, *Journey to the Western Front* (G. Bell & Sons, 1936), p. 1.

86 Stanton Hope, *Gallipoli Revisited* (1934), Chapter VI.

87 Vera Brittain, *Testament of a Generation: the Journalism of Vera Brittain and Winifred Holtby*, ed. Paul Berry and Alan Bishop (Virago, 1985), pp. 209–10.

302

NOTES

88 Frank Fox, *The King's Pilgrimage* (Hodder & Stoughton, 1922), Ch. 1.

89 Fox, *King's Pilgrimage*, Ch. 4.

90 Fox, *King's Pilgrimage*.

91 Ian Hay, *The Ship of Remembrance* (Hodder & Stoughton, 1926), p. 9.

92 Trevor Allen, *The Tracks They Trod* (Herbert Joseph, 1932), p. 54.

93 *Gallipoli. Salonika. St Barnabas Pilgrimages, 1926* (St Barnabas, 1927), p. 17.

94 Hay, *The Ship*, pp. 25–6.

95 *St Barnabas Pilgrimages, 1926*, p. 2.

96 Allen, *The Tracks They Trod*, Chapters VI and VII.

97 Hay, *The Ship*, p. 39.

98 Private Papers of H. Harris, 'The Gallipoli Pilgrimage' [IWM Docs.9355].

99 *Menin Gate Pilgrimage* (St Barnabas Society, 1927), p. 1.

100 *Menin Gate Pilgrimage*, pp. 34–8.

101 *Souvenir of the Battlefields Pilgrimage*, p. 6.

102 *Souvenir of the Battlefields Pilgrimage*, p. 109.

103 *Souvenir of the Battlefields Pilgrimage*, p. 45.

104 *Souvenir of the Battlefields Pilgrimage*, p. 135.

105 *Souvenir of the Battlefields Pilgrimage*, also quoted in Walter, 'War Grave Pilgrimage', p. 71.

106 *New York Times*, 18 November 1918, p. 11, quoted by John W. Graham, *The Gold Star Mother Pilgrimages of the 1930s* (McFarland, 2005), Ch. 4.

107 *Chicago Tribune, Paris Edition*, 25 May 1930, p. 3, quoted by Graham, *Gold Star Mother Pilgrimages*, Ch. 8.

108 Henrietta Haug (ed.), *Gold Star Mothers of Illinois* (Brussels, 1941), p. 150, quoted in Graham, *Gold Star Mother Pilgrimages*, Ch. 9.

109 Quoted in Bart Ziino, *A Distant Grief: Australians, War Graves and the Great War* (University of Western Australia Press, 2007), p. 172.

110 W. W. Murray, *The Epic of Vimy* (The Legionary, 1936), p. 29.

111 Murray, *Epic of Vimy*, p. 119.

7 SYSTEMATIC SEARCHING

1 John Masefield, quoted in Geoff Dyer, *The Missing of the Somme* (Hamish Hamilton, 1994), p. 120.

2 Private papers of Lady Londonderry, IWM Docs.15569.

3 'The Record of a Journey to Photograph the British Women's Service Overseas in March 1919', Private papers of Miss O. Edis, IWM Docs.140.

4   *The Ypres Times*, Special Pilgrimage Number, Vol. 1, August 1922, p. 19.

5   Stephen Graham, *The Challenge of the Dead* (Cassell, 1921).

6   Edwin Lutyens to his wife, Lady Emily, dated 12 July 1917, in Percy and Ridley (eds), *Letters of Edwin Luytens*, p. 350.

7   Lt. Col. Neil Fraser-Tytler, *With Lancashire Lads and Field Guns in France* (John Heywood, 1922), p. 226.

8   William Frampton McBeath, Diaries of Graves Detachment Digger, AWM PRO0675.

9   Report by IWGC, December 1918, CWGC/1/1/7/B/42 (WG 1294/3 PT.1).

10   Graham, *The Challenge of the Dead*.

11   Graham, *The Challenge of the Dead*, p. 124.

12   J. O. Coop, *A Short Guide to the Battlefields* (*Daily Post*, Liverpool, 1921), p. 150.

13   CWGC/1/1/7/B/42.

14   'Instructions as to concentration of isolated graves and groups of graves into cemeteries', CWGC/1/1/7/B/48 (DGRE 46).

15   CWGC/1/1/7/B/48 (DGRE 46).

16   CWGC/1/1/7/B/48 (DGRE 46).

17   CWGC/1/1/7/B/48 (DGRE 46).

18   Papers relating to Death in Action and Burial, First World War, of 2nd Lt. P. Farquharson, IWM. Docs.8782.

19   Private papers of Mrs L. K. Briggs, IWM Docs.21795.

20   IWM Docs.21795.

21   W. N. Collins, quoted in 'Clearing the Dead' by Peter E. Hodgkinson and in 'Human Remains on the Great War Battlefields: Coping with Death in the Trenches', dissertation by Peter E. Hodgkinson, University of Birmingham.

22   Private papers of Reverend David Railton, IWM Docs.4760.

23   Bickersteth (ed.), *Diaries, 1914–1918*, p. 101.

24   Bickersteth (ed.), *Diaries, 1914–1918*, p. 274.

25   Private Papers of J. McCauley, A Manx Soldier's War Diary, IWM Docs. 6434.

26   Private Papers of J. McCauley, A Manx Soldier's War Diary, IWM Docs. 6434

27   Captain J. C. Dunn, *The War the Infantry Knew 1914–1919* (Jane's, 1987), p. 582.

28 William Frampton McBeath, AWM PRO0675.

29 AWM PRO0675

30 Papers relating to the Labour Corps on the Western Front, Autumn 1919, IWM Docs. 5336.

31 NAA: MP367/1, 446/10/1840.

32 NAA: MP367/1, 446/10/1840.

33 NAA: MP367/1, 446/10/1840.

34 Report of Committee of Enquiry into Hooge Crater Exhumations, CWGC/1/1/7/B/48.

35 CWGC/1/1/7/B/48.

36 CWGC/1/1/7/B/47; WG 1294/3/2.

37 Percy Buckley, 2 March 1921, NAA: MP367/1, 446/10/2216, quoted in Ziino, *A Distant Grief*, p. 97.

38 Revised Instructions (Records Branch), 1921, CWGC/1/1/7/B/47.

39 Report from *Evening News*, August 1921, CWGC/1/1/7/B/45, WG 1294/3 PT.4).

40 CWGC/1/1/7/B/47.

41 CWGC/1/1/5/26 (WG 1294 PT.1).

42 CWGC/1/1/7/B/47.

43 CWGC/1/1/7/B/47.

44 CWGC/1/1/7/B/47.

45 Minutes of IWGC meeting of 18 October 192, CWGC/1/1/7/B/37 (WG 909/7).

46 Richard van Emden, *Missing: The Need for Closure After the Great War*, <<p?>>; I am indebted to Richard van Emden for the story of Francis Mond.

47 CWGC/8/1/4/1/1/27–1 and CWGC/8/1/4/1/1/27–2 (AA13233 PT.1).

48 CWGC/8/1/4/1/1/27–1 and CWGC/8/1/4/1/1/27–2 (AA13233 PT.1).

49 CWGC/8/1/4/1/1/27–1 and CWGC/8/1/4/1/1/27–2 (AA13233 PT.1), *Dundee Advertiser*, October 1924.

50 Edward Hempenstall, CWGC/1/1/7/B/45.

51 *Daily Mail*, 15 September 1921, CWGC/1/1/7/B/47.

52 *Herald*, 1 November 1920, quoted in Ziino, *A Distant Grief*, p. 85.

53 Lt. Col. E. A. S. Gell, CWGC/1/1/5/26.

54 *Daily News*, 3 April 1923, CWGC/1/1/7/B/45.

55 Gell, CWGC/1/1/5/26.

56 Gell, CWGC/1/1/7/B/45.

8 FROMELLES AND BEYOND: THE SEARCH GOES ON

1 'Souvenirs', *The Golden Horseshoe* (Cassell, 1919), quoted in Nicholas J. Saunders, *Killing Time: Archaeology and the First World War* (Sutton, 2007), Ch. 2.

2 Saunders, *Killing Time*, Ch. 5.

3 Saunders, *Killing Time*, Ch. 5.

4 Yves Desfossés, 'Arras, "Actiparc", les oubliés du Point du Jour', *Sucellus*, 54, pp. 84–100.

5 Martin Brown and Richard Osgood, *Digging Up Plugstreet* (Haynes, 2009), pp. 53–6.

6 *Sydney Morning Herald*, 2 July 2010.

7 Major Phillips, dated 21 December 1920, NAA: MP367/1, 446/10/1840.

8 *Daily Mail*, 15 September 1921, CWGC/1/1/7/B/4 (WG 546/2).

9 NAA: MP367/1, 446/10/1840.

10 Australian Red Cross Society Wounded and Missing Enquiry Bureau files, 1914–18 (AWM 1DRL/0428), quoted in Patrick Lindsay, *Fromelles: Australia's Darkest Day and the Dramatic Discovery of Our Fallen World War One Diggers* (Hardie Grant Books, 2008).

11 William Barry (AWM PRO0814), quoted in Robin Corfield, *Don't Forget Me, Cobber: The Battle of Fromelles* (Miegunyah Press, 2009), p. 324.

12 IWM photos.

13 History of 21st BRIR (published in 1923), quoted in Corfield, *Don't Forget Me*, p. 434.

14 Order No. 5220, quoted in Lindsay, *Fromelles*, Appendix VI.

15 Lindsay, *Fromelles*, Appendix VI.

16 Rudyard Kipling, *The Irish Guards in the Great War* (Doubleday, 1923), Vol. 2, p. 13.

17 R. Hugh Knyvett, *'Over There' with the Australians* (Hodder & Stoughton, 1918).

18 Walter H. Downing, *To the Last Ridge* (Grub Street, 2002), pp. 8–10.

19 Charles E. W. Bean, quoted in Tim Lycett and Sandra Playle, *Fromelles: The Final Chapters* (Viking, 2013), Ch. 3.

20 Knyvett, *'Over There'*.

21 General Haking, quoted in Julie Summers, *Remembering Fromelles* (Commonwealth War Graves Commission, 2010), p. 20.

22 British communiqué, quoted in Lycett and Playle, *Fromelles*, Ch. 3.

23 German communiqué, quoted in Corfield, *Don't Forget Me, Cobber*, p. 5.

24 Diary of C. E. W. Bean, 11 November 1918, AWM 38 3DRL 606/117/1.

25 Australian Red Cross Society Wounded and Missing Enquiry Bureau files, AWM 1DRL/0428.

26 GUARD report, 2008, quoted in Lycett and Playle, *Fromelles*, Ch. 7.

27 Major G. L. Phillips, Imperial War Graves Commission Australian Representative in France, 1927, quoted in Summers, *Remembering Fromelles*, p. 21.

28 Louise Loe et al., *Remember Me to All* (Oxford Archaeology, 2014), Ch. 5.

29 Loe et al., *Remember Me*, Ch. 5.

30 Loe et al., *Remember Me*, Ch. 5.

31 Loe et al., *Remember Me*, Ch. 5.

32 Loe et al., *Remember Me*, Ch. 3.

33 Loe et al., *Remember Me*, Ch. 4.

34 Loe et al., *Remember Me*, Ch. 7.

35 Kenyon Report (*War Graves. How the Cemeteries Abroad will be Designed. Report by Lieut.-Colonel Sir Frederic Kenyon*), pp. 13–14, quoted in Summers, Julie, *Remembering Fromelles*, pp. 12–13.

36 Loe, *Remember Me to All*, Ch. 7.

37 CWGC news, 12 June 2019.

38 CWGC news, 19 June 2019.

EPILOGUE

1 Stamp, *Memorial to the Missing*, p. 42.

2 King's proclamation, quoted in Dan Todman, *The Great War: Myth and Memory* (Hambledon and London, 2005), Ch. 2.

3 John McCrae, 'In Flanders Fields'.

4 *The Times*, 12 November 1920, *Supplement*, p. 27.

5 Newman Flower, 'My War Garden', *Through My Garden Gate* (Cassell & Co., 1945).

6 Flower, 'My War Garden'.

Bibliography

Allen, Trevor, *The Tracks They Trod* (Herbert Joseph, 1932)

Anderson, Ross, *The Forgotten Front: The East African Campaign, 1914–1918* (Tempus, 2004)

Bagnold, Enid, *The Happy Foreigner* (William Heinemann, 1920)

Baker, Herbert, *Architecture and Personalities* (Country Life, 1944)

Barrett, Michèle, 'Subalterns at War: First World War Colonial Forces and the Politics of the IWGC', *Interventions*, 9:3, pp. 451–74

———'White Graves and Natives', in *Bodies in Conflict*, ed. Paul Cornish and Nicholas J. Saunders (Routledge, 2014)

Barton, Peter, *The Lost Legions of Fromelles* (Constable, 2014)

Beauman, Nicola, *Morgan: A Biography of E. M. Forster* (Hodder and Stoughton, 1993)

Bickersteth, John (ed.), *The Bickersteth Diaries, 1914–1918* (Leo Cooper, 1995)

Bickersteth, Samuel, *Morris Bickersteth, 1891–1916, by his father* (CUP, 1931).

Birkenhead, Frederick, Earl of, *Rudyard Kipling* (Weidenfeld and Nicolson, 1978)

Blomfield, Sir Reginald, *Memoirs of an Architect* (Macmillan, 1932)

Blunden, Edmund, *We'll Shift Our Ground or Two on a Tour* (Cobden-Sanderson, 1933)

Blythe, Ronald, *The Age of Illusion: England in the Twenties and Thirties* (Hamish Hamilton, 1963)

Boss, Pauline, 'Ambiguous loss in families of the missing', *Lancet Supplement*, Vol. 360, December 2002

Bowler, Peter J., *Reconciling Science and Religion* (University of Chicago Press, 2001)

Brittain, Vera, *Testament of Youth* (Gollancz, 1933)

——— *Testament of a Generation: The Journalism of Vera Brittain and Winifred Holtby*, ed. Paul Berry and Alan Bishop (Virago, 1985)

Brown, Callum G., *Religion and Society in Twentieth-Century Britain* (Pearson Longman, 2006)

Brown, Martin, and Osgood, Richard, *Digging Up Plugstreet* (Haynes, 2009)

Buck, Claire, *Conceiving Strangeness in British First World War Writing* (Palgrave Macmillan, 2015)

Byrne, Georgina, *Modern Spiritualism and the Church of England, 1850–1939* (Boydell Press, 2010)

Cannadine, David, 'War and Death, Grief and Mourning in Modern Britain', in Joachim Whaley (ed.), *Mirrors of Mortality: Studies in the Social History of Death* (Europa, 1981)

Carrington, Charles, *Rudyard Kipling: His Life and Work* (Macmillan 1978)

Christie, N. M., *For King and Empire: The Canadians at the Somme, September–November 1916* (CEF Books, 1998)<<??>> Or Futility and Sacrifice

Clayton, P. B., *Plain Tales from Flanders* (Longmans, Green, 1929)

———*Tales of Talbot House* (Toc H, 1934)

Clout, Hugh, *After the Ruins* (University of Exeter Press, 1996), Commonwealth War Graves Commission, Report of the Special Committee to Review Historical Inequalities in Commemoration (2021), www.cwgc.org

Conan Doyle, Arthur, *The New Revelation* (Hodder and Stoughton, 1918)

——— *Memories and Adventures* (Hodder and Stoughton, 1924)

——— *Arthur Conan Doyle: A Life in Letters*, ed. Jon Lellenberg et al. (HarperPress, 2007)

Connelly, Mark, 'The Ypres League and the Commemoration of the Ypres Salient', *War in History*, Vol. 16, No. 1, January 2009

Connelly, Mark, and Goebel, Stefan, *Ypres* (OUP, 2018)

Contested Objects: Material Memories of the Great War, ed. Nicholas J. Saunders and Paul Cornish (Routledge, 2009)

Coop, James O., *A Short Guide to the Battlefields* (Daily Post, 1921)

Coren, Michael, *Conan Doyle* (Bloomsbury, 1995)

Corfield, Robin, *Don't Forget Me, Cobber: The Battle of Fromelles* (Miegunyah Press, 2009)

Crane, David, *Empires of the Dead* (William Collins, 2013)

Craster, J. M., *Fifteen Rounds a Minute* (Macmillan, 1976)

Dafoe, John W., *Over the Canadian Battlefields* (Thomas Allen, 1919)

Damousi, Joy, *The Labour of Loss: Mourning, Memory and Wartime Bereavement in Australia* (Cambridge University Press, 1999)

—— *Living with the Aftermath* (CUP, 2001)

Das, Santanu, *India, Empire and First World War Culture* (Cambridge University Press, 2018)

Downing, Walter H., *To the Last Ridge* (Grub Street, 2002)

Dunn, Captain J. C., *The War the Infantry Knew 1914–1919* (Jane's, 1987)

Dyer, Geoff, *The Missing of the Somme* (Penguin, 1995)

Earle, Lionel, *Turn Over the Page* (Hutchinson & Co., 1935)

Ewart, Wilfrid, *Scots Guard* (Rich & Cowan, 1934)

Farson, Daniel, *Henry: An Appreciation of Henry Williamson* (Michael Joseph, 1982)

Feilding, Rowland, *War Letters to a Wife* (Medici Society, 1929)

Fleming, Atherton, *How to See the Battlefields* (Cassell & Co, 1919).

Forster, E. M., *Selected Letters of E. M. Forster*, Vol. 1 (1879–1920), ed. Mary Lago and P. N. Furbank (Collins, 1983–85)

—— *Alexandria: A History and a Guide; and Pharos and Pharillon*, ed. Miriam Allott (Deutsch, 2004)

—— *The Journals and Diaries of E. M. Forster*, Vol. 2, 'The Locked Diaries', ed. Philip Gardner (Pickering & Chatto, 2011)

——'Incidents of War' Memoir, in *The Journals and Diaries of E. M. Forster*, ed. Philip Gardner (Pickering and Chatto, 2011)

Fox, Frank, *The King's Pilgrimage* (Hodder & Stoughton, 1922)

Fraser-Tytler, Lt. Col. Neil, *With Lancashire Lads and Field Guns in France* (John Heywood, 1922)

Freud, Sigmund, *Civilisation, War and Death*, ed. John Rickman (Hogarth Press, 1939)

Furbank, P. N., *E. M. Forster: A Life* (Secker & Warburg, 1977–8)

Galgut, Damon, *Arctic Summer* (Atlantic Books, 2014)

Gallipoli, Salonika, St Barnabas Pilgrimages, 1926 (St Barnabas, 1927)

Gavaghan, Michael, *The Story of the British Unknown Warrior* (M&L Publications, 1995)

Gibbons, John, *Roll On, Next War!* (Frederick Muller, 1935)

Gilmour, David, *The Long Recessional: The Imperial Life of Rudyard Kipling* (John Murray, 2002)

Graham, John W., *The Gold Star Mother Pilgrimages of the 1930s* (McFarland, 2005)

Graham, Stephen, *The Challenge of the Dead* (London, 1930)

Granville-Barker, Harley, *The Red Cross in France* (Hodder and Stoughton, 1916)

Graves, Robert, *Goodbye to All That* (Cape, 1929)

Greenberg, Allan, 'Lutyens's Cenotaph', in *Journal of the Society of Architectural Historians*, Vol. 28, No. 1 (March 1989)

Gregory, Adrian, *The Silence of Memory: Armistice Day, 1919–1946* (Bloomsbury, 2014)

Hanson, Neil, *The Unknown Soldier: The Story of the Missing of the Great War* (Doubleday, 2005)

Harrison, Ted, *Remembrance Today* (Reaktion Books, 2012)

Hay, Ian, *The Ship of Remembrance* (Hodder & Stoughton, 1926)

Hazelgrove, Jenny, *Spiritualism and British Society Between the Wars* (Manchester University Press, 2000)

Hodgkinson, Peter, 'Identifying the Dead of Tyne Cot', the Western Front Association *Stand To!*, No. 11

Holt, Tonie and Valmai, *My Boy Jack?: The Search for Kipling's Only Son* (Leo Cooper, 2001)

Hope, Stanton, *Gallipoli Revisited* (1934)

Howell, Georgina, *Daughter of the Desert: The Remarkable Life of Gertrude Bell* (Pan, 2012)

Hurst, Sidney, *The Silent Cities* (Methuen, 1929)

Hussey, Christopher, *The Life of Sir Edwin Lutyens* (Antique Collectors' Club Ltd, 1984)

Hynes, Samuel, *The Edwardian Turn of Mind* (Oxford University Press, 1968)

Isherwood, Christopher, *Kathleen and Frank* (Methuen, 1971)

Jalland, Patricia, *Australian Ways of Death. A Social and Cultural History. 1840–1918* (OUP, 2002)

Jolly, W. P., *Sir Oliver Lodge* (Constable, 1974)

Jones, Kelvin I., *Conan Doyle and the Spirits: The Spiritualist Career of Sir Arthur Conan Doyle* (Aquarian, 1989)

Kenyon, Frederick, *War Graves: How the Cemeteries Abroad Will Be Designed* (HMSO, 1918)

Kilmer, Annie Kilburn, *Leaves from My Life* (Frye Publishing Co, 1925)

Kipling, Rudyard, *The Graves of the Fallen* (HMSO, 1919)

———— *The Irish Guards in the Great War* (Doubleday, Page & Company, 1923)

———— 'The Gardener', in *Debits and Credits* (Macmillan, 1926)

———— 'The Silent World', in *The War Graves of the Empire* (The Times Publishing Company Ltd, 1928)

———— *Rudyard Kipling to Rider Haggard: The Record of a Friendship* (Hutchinson, 1965)

———— *The Letters of Rudyard Kipling*, Vol. 4: 1911–1919, ed. Thomas Pinney (Macmillan, 1990–2004)

Knyvett, R. Hugh, *'Over There' with the Australians* (Hodder & Stoughton, 1918)

Kollar, Rene, *Searching for Raymond: Anglicanism, Spiritualism, and Bereavement Between the Two World Wars* (Lexington Books, 2000)

Laqueur, Thomas W., *The Work of the Dead: A Cultural History of Mortal Remains* (Princeton University Press, 2015)

Lamond, Rev. John, *Arthur Conan Doyle: A Memoir* (John Murray, 1931)

Lamplugh, Lois, *A Shadowed Man: Henry Williamson* (Exmoor Press, 1991)

Leonard, Gladys Osborne, *My Life in Two Worlds* (Cassell & Co, 1931)

Lever, Tresham, *Clayton of Toc H* (John Murray, 1971)

Lindsay, Patrick, *Fromelles: Australia's Darkest Day and the Dramatic Discovery of Our Fallen World War One Diggers* (Hardie Grant Books, 2008)

Lloyd, David W., *Battlefield Tourism: Pilgrimage and the Commemoration of the Great War in Britain, Australia, and Canada, 1919–1939* (Berg, 1998 or Bloomsbury 2014?<<>>)

Lodge, Sir Oliver, *Raymond, or Life and Death* (Methuen, 1916)

———— *Past Years: An Autobiography* (Hodder and Stoughton, 1931)

———— *Letters from Sir Oliver Lodge, Psychical, Religious, Scientific and Personal, Compiled and Annotated by J. Arthur Hill* (Cassell and Co., 1932)

Loe, Louise et al., *Remember Me to All* (Oxford Archaeology, 2014)

Longworth, Philip, *The Unending Vigil* (Pen & Sword Books, 2010)

Lowe, Thomas A., *The Western Battlefields* (Gale & Polden, 1921

Lutyens, Edwin, *The Letters of Edwin Luytens to His Wife Emily*, ed. Clayre Percy and Jane Ridley (William Collins, Sons & Co, 1985)

Lycett, Andrew, *Rudyard Kipling* (Weidenfeld & Nicolson, 1999)
——— *Conan Doyle: The Man Who Created Sherlock Holmes*
    (Weidenfeld & Nicolson, 2007)
Lycett, Tim, and Playle, Sandra, *Fromelles: The Final Chapters*
    (Viking, 2013)
Macdonald, Lyn, *1914* (Michael Joseph, 1987)
Macnaghten, Angus, *Missing* (Dragon Books, 1970)
Mallett, Phillip, *Rudyard Kipling: A Literary Life* (Palgrave
    Macmillan, 2003)
The Marne Battle-fields: 1914 (Michelin et Cie, 1917)
Masefield, John, *The Old Front Line* (W. Heinemann, 1917)
McKenzie, J. Hewat, *If a soldier die, shall he live again?* (London, 1915)
Menin Gate Pilgrimage (St Barnabas Society, 1927)
Mercier, Charles Arthur, *Spiritualism and Sir Oliver Lodge* (Mental
    Culture Enterprise, 1917)
Miller, Russell, *The Adventures of Arthur Conan Doyle* (Harvill
    Secker, 2008)
Moffat, Wendy, *E. M. Forster: A New Life* (Bloomsbury, 2010)
Moore, Mary Macleod, *The Maple Leaf's Red Cross: The War Story of the
    Canadian Red Cross Overseas* (Skeffington & Son, 1919)
Morton, Desmond and Wright, Glenn, *Winning the Second Battle:
    Canadian Veterans and the Return to Civilian Life, 1915–1930*
    (University of Toronto Press, 1987)
Mosse, George, *Fallen Soldiers: Reshaping the Memory of the World Wars*
    (OUP, 1990)
Mottram, R. H., *Through the Menin Gate* (Chatto & Windus, 1932)
——— *Journey to the Western Front* (G. Bell & Sons, 1936)
Muirhead, Findlay, *Belgium and the Western Front* (Macmillan, 1920)
Murray, W. W., *The Epic of Vimy* (The Legionary, 1936)
Nelson, Geoffrey K., *Spiritualism and Society* (Routledge & Kegan
    Paul, 1969)
Nicolson, Juliet, *The Great Silence* (John Murray, 2009)
Northcliffe, Lord, *At the War* (Hodder and Stoughton, 1916)
Oliver, Beryl, *The British Red Cross in Action* (Faber, 1966)
Oppenheim, Janet, *The Other World: Spiritualism and Psychical Research
    in England, 1850–1914* (Cambridge University Press, 1985)
Osgood, Richard, *The Unknown Warrior: An Archaeology of the Common
    Soldier* (Sutton, 2005)

Over There: A Little Guide for Pilgrims to Ypres, the Salient, and Talbot House, Poperinghe (Toc H, 1935)

Paice, Edward, *Tip and Run: The Untold Tragedy of the Great War in Africa* (Weidenfeld & Nicolson, 2007)

Parker, Graham and Legg, Joanna, 'The Unidentified Irish Guards Lieutenant at Loos: Laid to Rest', The Western Front Assocation *Stand To!*, No. 105 (January 2016)

The Pilgrim's Guide to the Ypres Salient (Talbot House, 1920)

Ponton, Dorothy, *Rudyard Kipling at Home and at Work* (1953)

Pulteney, Sir William, and Brice, Beatrix, *The Immortal Salient* (Ypres League, 1925)

Reports by the Joint War Committee and the Joint War Finance Committee of the British Red Cross Society and the Order of St John of Jerusalem in England (HMSO, 1921)

Richards, Andrew, *The Flag: The Story of Revd David Railton MC and the Tomb of the Unknown Warrior* (Casemate, 2017)

Ricketts, Harry, *The Unforgiving Minute: A Life of Rudyard Kipling* (Chatto & Windus, 1999)

Robertshaw, Andrew and Kenyon, David, *Digging the Trenches: The Archaeology of the Western Front* (Pen & Sword Military, 2008)

St Barnabas Pilgrimages (Ypres–The Somme) 1923 (St Barnabas, 1924)

Saunders, Nicholas, *Trench Art: A Brief History and a Guide, 1914–1939* (Leo Cooper, 2001)

Saunders, Nicholas J., *Killing Time: Archaeology and the First World War* (Sutton, 2007)

——— *The Poppy* (Oneworld, 2013)

Seymour-Smith, Martin, *Rudyard Kipling* (Queen Anne Press, 1989)

Sheftall, Mark David, *Altered Memories of the Great War: Divergent Narratives of Britain, Australia, New Zealand and Canada* (I. B. Tauris, 2009)

Skelton, Tim, and Gliddon, Gerald, *Lutyens and the Great War* (Frances Lincoln, 2008)

Smith, Susy, *The Mediumship of Mrs Leonard* (University Books, 1964)

A Souvenir of the Battlefields Pilgrimage (August 1928) (British Legion, 1929)

Stamp, Gavin, *Silent Cities* (RIBA Publications, 1977)

——— *The Memorial to the Missing of the Somme* (Profile, 2006)

Stape, J. H., *An E. M. Forster Chronology* (Macmillan, 1993)

Stoneham, Martin W., *West Kingsdown Remembers*, <<?2019>>
——— *Captain Cecil Thomas Tuff and his Brothers*, 2019 <<?>>.
Summers, Julie, *Remembering Fromelles* (Commonwealth War Graves Commission, 2010)
Swinton, E., *Twenty Years After: The Battlefields of 1914–18*, ed. E. Swinton (Newnes, 1936–8)
Thomson, Denise, 'National Sorrow, National Pride: Commemoration of War in Canada, 1918–45', *Journal of Canadian Studies*, Vol. 30, No. 4 (Winter 1995/6)
The Times History of the War: 1914–1919 (The Times, 1921), Vol. 21.
Todman, Dan, *The Great War: Myth and Memory* (Hambledon and London, 2005)
Tomlinson, H. M., *All Our Yesterdays* (William Heinemann, 1930)
Tudor Pole, Wellesley, *Private Dowding: The Personal Story of a Soldier Killed in Battle* (Spearman, 1966)
Turner, E. S., *Dear Old Blighty* (Michael Joseph, 1980)
Vance, Jonathan F., *Death So Noble: Memory, Meaning, and the First World War* (UBC Press, 1997)
van Emden, Richard, *The Quick and the Dead* (Bloomsbury, 2011)
——— *Missing: The Need for Closure After the Great War* (Pen & Sword Military, 2019)
Walbrook, Lilian, *The Case of Lester Coltman* (Hutchinson & Co., 1924)
Walter, Tony, 'War Grave Pilgrimage', *Pilgrimage in Popular Culture*, ed. Ian Reader and Tony Walter (Macmillan, 1992)
War and Remembrance in the Twentieth Century, ed. Jay Winter and Emmanual Sivan <<?>>
Ware, Fabian, *The Immortal Heritage* (The University Press, 1937)
War Graves of the Empire (Times Publishing Company, 1928)
Webb, James, *The Occult Establishment* (Open Court, 1976)
Williamson, Henry, *The Wet Flanders Plain* (Faber & Faber, 1929)
——— *Contributions to the Weekly Dispatch* (J. Gregory, 1969)
Winter, Jay, *Sites of Memory, Sites of Mourning: The Great War in European Cultural History* (Cambridge University Press, 2014)
Winter, J. M., 'Spiritualism and the First World War', in R. W. Davis and R. J. Helmstadter (eds) *Religion and Irreligion in Victorian Society* (Routledge, 1992)
Woolf, Virginia, *The Letters of Virginia Woolf*, ed. Nigel Nicolson, Vol. 2 (1912–22) (Hogarth Press, 1976)

———— *The Diary of Virginia Woolf*, Vol. 2 (1920–24), ed. Anne Olivier Bell (Hogarth Press, 1978)

Wootton, Graham, *The Official History of the British Legion* (Macdonald & Evans, 1956)

Ypres and the Battles of Ypres (Michelin et Cie, 1919)

Ziino, Bart, *A Distant Grief: Australians, War Graves and the Great War* (University of Western Australia Press, 2007)

Acknowledgements

It would not have been possible to write this book without the extensive historical archives of the United Kingdom and Commonwealth. I am grateful to the staff at the Australian War Memorial Research Centre; the Bodleian Library; the Churchill Archives Centre at Churchill College, Cambridge; the Durham University Library Special Collections; the Hatfield House Archive; the Imperial War Museum; the Archives at King's College, Cambridge; the National Archives at Kew; the National Archives of Australia; Newcastle University Library; the Special Collections belonging to the University of Sussex at the Keep; and to the Keeper of Muniments at Westminster Abbey. Above all, I thank the archivists at the Commonwealth War Graves Commission (CWGC) for help at their headquarters in Maidenhead and for their great achievement in digitising most of their records. I have also spent many productive days in both the British Library and the London Library, and have been so impressed by the way in which both institutions have coped with the restrictions and temporary closures caused by the pandemic, and relieved by the speed with which they reopened as soon as they were able to do so.

I was lucky enough to hear Victoria Wallace, the former Director General of the CWGC, talk inspirationally about the Commission's work, and then benefitted from her introductions. Dr George Hay, the Commission's brilliant historian, kindly read the manuscript, pointed me towards several different avenues of research, and suggested important amendments. He has saved me from some glaring errors and omissions; I, of course, take full responsibility for the others. Gareth Hardware and the CWGC team at Beaurains in France introduced me to the Commission's continuing work in identifying and honouring the dead, and I am immensely grateful for their time and hospitality.

It will be obvious from the bibliography how indebted I am to the scholarship and publications of others. In particular, I would like to thank a number of people who have provided help at first hand: notably Fergus Fleming, for introducing me to the works of Newman Flower; Dr Peter Hodgkinson, for his generosity in sharing research on battlefield clearance after the war; Martin Stoneham, for his quest for Captain Cecil Tuff; and to Prunella Scarlett, Tuff's great-niece, for describing her delight at his discovery.

Various knowledgeable friends have read and suggested improvements to individual chapters: specifically psychologist Dr Belinda Giles, Dr Samir Shah, Ian Doherty, Dr Matt Edwards and Yousuf Mohamed Ahmed. I am extraordinarily grateful to my dear friend Dr Chris Greenhalgh, writer and educator, who read every word and, with the greatest grace, helped me spot and iron out infelicities of style, substance and sentiment.

Thanks, as ever, to literary agent Caroline Michel for encouraging me to write this book in the first place, and finding for it the perfect publisher. Michael Fishwick at Bloomsbury is an exceptional editor, combining an eye for both the broad sweep of a story and for the tiny, telling detail. Once again, I cannot think of a single suggestion he has made with which I have disagreed. His colleagues at Bloomsbury, notably managing editor Sarah Ruddick, have nurtured the book through all stages of its development with great charm and efficiency.

I was especially lucky (for the third book in succession) to have Kate Johnson as the copy-editor: not only does she have a deep knowledge of the subject but also an eagle eye and an elegant turn of phrase.

And finally, my family. I thank my children: Freya, for helping me access some of the more elusive academic sources during the pandemic; Arthur for accompanying me on a trip to the Ypres salient; and Edie for her IT support and general good humour. My wife, Jane, is my favourite editor. She, too, read every word – twice – and as, always, improved the book in so many ways. I thank her, with all my heart, for that and for her love and support.

TEXT PERMISSIONS

I am grateful to the following for granting me permission to quote:

The family of C. E. W. Bean
Mark Bostridge and T. J. Brittain-Catlin, Literary Executors for the Estate of Vera Brittain 1970
The Provost and Scholars of King's College, Cambridge and The Society of Authors as the E. M. Forster Estate
Julian Hardinge, Baron Hardinge of Penshurst
The Estate of Christopher Isherwood
David Railton QC
The Estate of Siegfried Sassoon
The Dean and Chapter of Westminster Abbey
The Henry Williamson Literary Estate

Picture Credits

p. 5 © Davis/Topical Press Agency/Getty Images
p. 6 top: © CWGC; © TopFoto
p. 7 top and bottom: © CWGC
p. 8 top left and right: © CWGC; bottom: © Australian War Memorial

Index

A Note on the Type

The text of this book is set in Adobe Garamond. It is one of several versions of Garamond based on the designs of Claude Garamond. It is thought that Garamond based his font on Bembo, cut in 1495 by Francesco Griffo in collaboration with the Italian printer Aldus Manutius. Garamond types were first used in books printed in Paris around 1532. Many of the present-day versions of this type are based on the *Typi Academiae* of Jean Jannon cut in Sedan in 1615.

Claude Garamond was born in Paris in 1480. He learned how to cut type from his father and by the age of fifteen he was able to fashion steel punches the size of a pica with great precision. At the age of sixty he was commissioned by King Francis I to design a Greek alphabet, and for this he was given the honourable title of royal type founder. He died in 1561.